# INTERCONNECTIVITY

„or what to look for"

# Contents

# 1. TERMINOLOGY

Since definitions are necessarily selective in that they emphasize certain aspects and exclude others, the limits of understanding should also be recognized here. Since we do not want to be satisfied with too narrow a definition, we will recognize the complexity of phenomena and consider different perspectives. The topic of interconnectivity is about the interpretation of networking phenomena. Interconnectivity is more than just the ability to exchange data between systems. It is a fundamental principle that shapes society and extends into philosophy and spirituality. In a world where everything is connected, the way we use these connections not only helps to increase efficiency, but also has far-reaching implications for our knowledge, our ethics and ultimately our understanding of existence. In this sense, interconnectivity is not just a technical phenomenon, but a reflection of the fundamental structure of our reality. Its aim is to create synergies, make better use of individual and social resources and achieve a more comprehensive integration of information and services. This is becoming an important factor for innovation and overcoming complex challenges.

In social media, interconnectivity looks like a digital cocktail party where everyone is in contact with everyone else via different platforms. At this party, groups gather to share different impressions and quickly jump back and forth in discussions. Interaction is spontaneous, with people reacting to posts one way or another, commenting on them or forwarding them. Within minutes, the chatter spreads across the various platforms. At the same time, people participate in a wide variety of conversations without going into any particular depth. People simply network, the interactions are short-lived and based on quick likes or short comments. The viral nature of content is one of the most striking aspects of these artificial conversations. In a very short space of time, a single tweet can spread from a small group to a global audience. Cross-platform interconnectivity amplifies the effect that it seems as if everyone is in contact with everyone else. Just like at a noisy party, where people often misunderstand or drown each other out, clear messages are lost on social media. While on the one hand this creates opportunities for exchange and creativity, it also harbors risks. These include misunderstandings, being overwhelmed by the flood of information and the formation of so-called echo chambers.

If technology makes it possible to network household appliances with each other, this should also apply to the sociological fields of knowledge. It is not all about entertaining gaming, but about serious knowledge management. As networking and exchange in the digital media are often misleading, there is an increasing need for portals with scientific evaluation, which should be as free from errors as possible, and above all free from corruption. In the social environment, reading self-assessments, however entertaining they may seem, provides too little objectivity. The factual issues are simply distorted. In an increasingly digitalized world, the ability to network is becoming more and more conspicuous. Companies and institutions that are able to communicate efficiently with partners from different fields of knowledge and exchange data increase their productivity and innovative strength. This is particularly crucial in interdisciplinary projects, where bringing together experts from different fields leads to new insights and breakthroughs. One example of this is the collaboration between medical researchers, software developers and data scientists. By sharing information in real time, new therapies and medicines can be developed more quickly. In industrial production, too, the networking of machines and systems via the so-called "Internet of Things" enables greater efficiency and flexibility. At the planning level in interdisciplinary projects, interconnectivity is crucial when experts from different areas are brought together and new findings are identified. But interconnectivity is not just limited to practical applications. In cognitive research, which deals with the foundations of knowledge and truth, it opens up completely new perspectives.

By networking different knowledge systems, complex problems are viewed from different angles in order to gain deeper insights into the nature of reality. This interconnectedness extends into philosophy, where questions about reason, consciousness and existence are posed. Philosophers such as  Martin Heidegger and Emmanuel Levinas have emphasized how our existence in the world is shaped by relationships and connections. Interconnectivity is thus understood as a metaphysical principle that reflects the structure of reality itself. In many spiritual traditions, the idea of the interconnectedness of all things is seen as a central principle. In this context, interconnectivity is not just a scientific term, but an expression of the deeper unity of being. Even in Eastern philosophies such as Buddhism or Hinduism, the world is seen as a network of relationships in which everything is interwoven. In Western traditions, this idea is expressed in mysticism, for example, where unity with the divine is achieved by perceiving the interconnectedness of all creation.

Interconnectivity also raises important ethical questions. If everything is connected, what does this mean for our responsibility towards others? How does global connectivity influence our decisions regarding the environment, war and peace? These questions are of existential importance and show that interconnectivity goes far beyond technical aspects. Paying attention to interconnectivity requires a rethink in many areas. It is important to take advantage of the opportunities offered by increased connectivity while at the same time taking possible risks into account.

Through interdisciplinary approaches and the linking of different areas of knowledge, innovative solutions are being developed in every type of management for complex challenges. The emergence of hybrid learning formats is expanding access to educational opportunities across institutional and geographical boundaries by linking face-to-face and online elements. People who were previously excluded from educational opportunities due to physical or organizational barriers can now participate in programmes worldwide. This promotes the inclusion of many people and enables broader participation in educational processes. With the help of new technologies, interactive and collaborative learning environments are being created that promote interactive learning. Learners can interact with others in real time, work together on projects and benefit from a wider range of learning opportunities.

These opportunities also support the concept of lifelong learning by providing continuous access to learning resources. But who really takes advantage of these great opportunities? Probably the guy who already has three degrees and is taking his 17th online course on Coursera to finally learn Mandarin. Or the motivated colleague who secretly surfs a learning platform in the middle of a Zoom session because multitasking is supposedly so efficient. And the rest? Well, they prefer to scroll through TikTok during their lunch break and click on clickbait articles with titles like "These five tricks will make you look smarter without learning".

After all, there are plenty of opportunities to continue your education beyond your job, learn new skills and adapt to changing labor market requirements. If networking in the education sector offers new forms of learning and skills development and leads to a completely different understanding of holistic problem solving, this also brings with it uncertainties that need to be carefully weighed up. The future will show how well the balance between networking and control can be maintained in order to make the most of the advantages of interconnectivity.

However, there is also a tendency to ignore or even suppress perspectives that are unfamiliar, resulting in the loss of valuable insights and ideas. A kind of negative spiral influences the unsuccessful action patterns of networking. Chronic negative intervening can undermine joint success and take away the strength to tackle new projects or make changes. It is therefore important to grasp the overall situation and consciously counteract misguided tendencies. Deterioration of mutuality must be avoided if the diverse perspectives are to bring innovative solutions.

Effective interconnectivity is based on clear, respectful and open channels of communication. As soon as destructive argumentation patterns get in the way, these channels are blocked. This leads to misunderstandings, false assumptions and a general deterioration in the quality of communication. In an environment where destructive argumentation is the norm, people tend to withdraw and fragment into smaller, like-minded groups. This leads to an isolation of ideas and reduces the interconnectivity of different groups, which in turn weakens social cohesion as a whole.

Unfortunately, global networking also makes it possible for destructive ideologies, fake news and hate speech to spread and scale quickly. Digital connectivity creates new touchpoints for cybercrime, which expands the destructive potential in society. Interconnectivity, fostered by modern communication tools and technologies, has an impact on the way societies deal with diverse tendencies, including destructive ones. The anonymity offered by many online platforms encourages negative behavior such as bullying, hate speech or extremist statements. The toxic climate in online communities usually rubs off on social coexistence. The result is a polarized society in which the ability to engage in dialogue is dwindling and extreme movements, whether political or ideological, are gaining ground. Civil disobedience, which used to be a form of peaceful protest, can easily turn violent under the influence of disinformation and radicalization. Because when reality is distorted and replaced by lies, any constructed illusory truth appears justified, even if it breaks the law or threatens human lives.

In any case, information, whether positive or negative, is disseminated in real time. This means that both constructive and destructive messages reach a wide audience quickly. Networked societies should be able to defend themselves collectively and react quickly to negative events or threats. A calibration of reason is necessary so that different systems, disciplines or actors harmonize in their activities. In an interconnected context, it is required that the parts involved work towards common goals and coordinate via interfaces and communication channels. Even in scientific research, different experts such as biologists, economists or engineers must coordinate their approaches in order to achieve a beneficial result. Without clear coordination, systems and their teams work extremely inefficiently. Malfunctions are the result. Only interconnectivity clarifies how the different parts of a system or several disciplines are linked together in a meaningful way. Interconnectivity occurs when the individual elements are related to each other and their functions and objectives complement each other.

In technical systems, this refers to the logical connections between different modules and components. Each component of a network must be clearly connected to the others so that data or information can be exchanged correctly. In the technology sector, this can be described very simply, whereas in social systems the links are more complex. If interconnectivity comes to nothing because the links are unclear or ineffective, it will not bring any useful benefits.

A clear hierarchy and structure must exist in a company, including in politics, to ensure that decisions can be coordinated and implemented centrally. Allocation refers to the clear definition and distribution of tasks, functions or resources within the system. Each part of a networked system must know what role it plays and what resources or information are assigned to it. These basic principles are the prerequisite for effective and stable interconnectivity in complex systems, organizations or interdisciplinary projects. It is only through the close interlocking of concepts that the complexity created by increasing networking becomes visible and productive.

If these connections are missing or weakened, the system loses its integrity and falls apart. Without a flow of information, the individual elements cannot interact. Most system properties arise from the interaction of the individual components. If interconnectivity is missing, emergent phenomena do not appear in the first place. In social networks, the loss of connections results in the isolation of individuals or entire groups. In the economy, this occurs in supply chains in such a way that an interruption at one point or otherwise in communication channels results in disruptions throughout the entire system. In ecosystems, the loss of key species that have many connections to other species can lead to effects that destabilize the entire system. However, systems with high interconnectivity of responsibility are also more resilient to disturbances. They can better compensate for failures of individual components by using alternative connections. This explains why robust systems have convincingly redundant connections.

This means that multiple interdependencies result in greater efficiency, but also carry the risk of system failures and dependencies. In any case, a technical problem or an attack on a critical infrastructure has far-reaching effects on the entire structure. The situation is even more critical in social systems, which consist of specific cultures, values, beliefs and behaviors. As they are dynamic, they change over time and can be influenced by internal factors such as conflicts or external developments and technological changes. To protect against this, risks can be managed objectively by developing contingency plans. These precautions ensure that the overall system can still be maintained if one element fails.

The fragile beauty of interconnectivity: it really is a marvel how all these little puzzle pieces, whether in social networks or in complex systems, come together to form an impressive picture. But woe betide us if one piece of the puzzle is missing or simply refuses to go into place! Suddenly we not only have an incomplete picture, but also an existential crisis in the system. As connections dwindle, the network quickly becomes a place where everyone feels like they are in their own bubble of loneliness. Where are the creative ideas, the dynamic discussions and the unexpected collaborations? They have all fallen by the wayside, lost in the digital desert of isolation.

Health systems and logistics in particular have set themselves the goal of building up resilience. This is achieved through decentralized systems and back-up solutions that can quickly step in if a system fails. Interconnectivity offers immense benefits, but it requires careful and balanced strategies to manage the associated security risks. Cybersecurity, crisis management, critical infrastructure protection and proactive healthcare systems are crucial factors in ensuring that interconnectivity does not become a vulnerability in society. It requires continuous vigilance and adaptation to keep pace with rapid technological developments and the associated risks.

Alliances, arms control agreements, military peacekeeping missions and above all, early warning systems are among the security modules of networking in military policy. Unfortunately, networking across national borders also makes it possible for cyber criminals to launch attacks at an international level. Such threats are often difficult to track and even more difficult to combat as their actors appear in different countries. External threats to a country's internal security increasingly come from targeted disinformation campaigns spread via social media or other digital channels. Responding to this threat requires measures such as media literacy, stronger regulation of platforms and international cooperation. States, organizations and individuals are faced with the task of taking advantage of global networking while ensuring a high level of security. They must constantly adapt and often even cooperate with very different sectors.

The threat of disinformation is usually due to various factors that intentionally or unintentionally encourage the spread of false or misleading information. When political leaders deliberately use disinformation, they either want to influence public opinion, discredit political opponents or consolidate positions of power. They see the spread of disinformation as a form of political warfare or manipulation. There are numerous examples of this during elections or in times of crisis. In this way, narratives are spread in order to mislead public opinion. Companies use disinformation to improve their reputation and weaken that of their competitors. However, if it is exaggerated or clumsy, it can lead to reputational damage and legal consequences if the disinformation is uncovered.

The media and social networks are particularly vulnerable to the spread of misinformation, whether due to a thirst for sensationalism to generate more clicks and attention, or because of a lack of editorial oversight. Social media platforms have become a "Wild West" for misinformation, where content can go viral before its truthfulness is verified. These platforms take the risk of spreading misinformation when they prioritize algorithms focused on engagement rather than on content reliability. Misinformation has almost become an art form. One might think we live in an era where the fight for truth is already lost. Ironically, one could ask why newsrooms should bother spreading well-researched facts when a headline alone brings in more clicks. The algorithm loves it, and the readers? Well, they click out of curiosity, share accidentally, and suddenly, misinformation spreads faster than a summer news filler.

Ideological beliefs that spread virally reinforce distorted, unconscious viewpoints. Conspiracy theories are shared, even if objectively false, because they fit into some people's worldview. "Hacktivists" or cybercriminals intentionally use misinformation to sow chaos, erode trust, or discredit certain players. Their goal is to create uncertainty or destabilize economic and political structures. The general public unwittingly participates in the experiment of spreading misinformation when they share unreliable sources or misinformation without thoroughly checking them. This is especially common in times of crisis or political instability, as emotions and uncertainties run high, and people quickly react to information that aligns with their fears or prejudices.

Editorial supervision? To journalists, that sounds like something from the 20th century. Today, it's all about being first, whether the information is accurate or not. Mistakes can always be corrected afterward - if at all. Meanwhile, we're surfing through a world full of half-truths, conspiracy theories, and clickbait culture, where anyone can become an expert with enough likes. In the end, the question remains: have social networks lost control over misinformation, or did they perhaps never really intend to control it in the first place?

## 2. THE LOGIC OF INTERCONNECTIVITY

The logic of interconnectivity characterizes the interdependence of systems, concepts or elements in complex structures. The relationships between the individual components are becoming increasingly important. Their principles are increasingly based on interaction and feedback. Actions or changes in one part of the system often have unpredictable effects on other parts. In a biological ecosystem, for example, the extinction of one species can have dramatic consequences for the entire ecosystem. Instead of analyzing isolated elements, the system needs to be considered as a whole, but the whole is more than the sum of its parts.

Nonlinear connections appear everywhere in the network, so small changes have large effects, while major interventions may have only minor consequences. Interconnectivity occurs at different levels and scales, that is, it can be observed both within a unit and globally – and with different effects. The collective intelligence of these systems results from the connections and interactions of individual components.

Networks can be both, robust and vulnerable. On the one hand, connections provide stability by balancing the system. On the other hand, interconnectivity can also lead to errors, faults or attacks that propagate faster and further. The impact is obvious. A network of millions of servers, computers and other devices that distribute information across the world in fractions of a second determines markets, supply chains and policy decisions.

Every species in an ecosystem depends in some way on other species and the environment. All parts are in constant exchange, healthy isolation is hardly possible any more. Thus, a far-reaching interdependence develops between different social fields of action, which influence economic upheavals and political decisions. Social change leads to the emergence of new positions, life situations and lifestyles This development contributes to the increasing complexity of modern societies.

It is possible for logical considerations or conditions that appear valid at one point in time to change in a different environment. In many areas, whether in science, technology, business or society in general, new information and perspectives can mean that a previously valid logic suddenly no longer applies. One example is economic situations.

A company that is in a booming market could experience a sudden reversal of conditions due to economic crises, technological disruption or social changes.

In science, it often happens that new discoveries challenge existing theories or add further nuances. Flexibility and a willingness to question established assumptions are essential as soon as new knowledge becomes available. However, this logic of interconnectivity could, under certain circumstances, also be disrupted, suggesting that the interplay between coordination, context, organization, and mission could become unstable at any time, with potentially negative consequences. In complex, interconnected systems, small disruptions or errors can have far-reaching effects that throw the entire structure off balance. This is inherent to the system; failures due to system instability cannot be ruled out.

If the breakdown of interconnectivity logic becomes inherent to the system, it means this potential instability is an intrinsic part of interconnected systems. In any highly connected system, the possibility of disruptions or malfunctions is built in, as the close integration of various elements inevitably leads to dependencies and potential vulnerabilities. If ecological or economic conditions can collapse, then security positions are also continuously threatened. How, then, can a sense of security in policy be reconciled with appropriate measures? When the actions of one element in interconnected systems directly or indirectly affect others, such mutual dependencies are not only a strength but also a weakness, as they can amplify disruptions. This suggests that in a system with high interconnectivity, there is always the potential for a chain reaction, where a small problem can systemically expand and lead to a broader failure.

When systems become too complex or too tightly linked, it becomes difficult to manage each individual element effectively. Small disruptions in one part of the system can quickly spread to other areas due to the close connections. Redundancy means that a system must contain safeguards or backups to absorb failures in time. However, when everything is fully interconnected and optimized, the flexibility needed to deal with unexpected effects is often lacking. Without sufficient redundancy, the entire system can collapse as soon as a single element fails. For example, in a highly automated production system, disruptions at a single node can bring the entire production to a halt. Similarly, an entire social network can be destabilized if coordination between different actors or systems no longer functions effectively. This condition is exacerbated by poor communication, unclear decision-making structures, or a lack of coordination. In companies, this leads to inefficient processes or a fragmentation of the organization, while on a political level, mismanagement can lead to poor decisions that ultimately result in collective failure.

It's as if Information Technology had assembled a grand orchestra where every musician is perfectly in sync, until the first violinist decides to play their part in a 5/4 time signature while the rest stick to the classic 4/4. Suddenly, we no longer have a symphony of efficiency but a discordant concert driving even the most patient listeners to the edge. In reality, it's often as if we have a parachute so tightly linked to the rest of our gear that we can't even reach it when we're in free fall. The problem is that we are so focused on optimization and perfection that we forget life - and the systems we create - are unpredictable.

Once interconnectivity intensifies dependency among systems, risks accumulate without immediate visibility. A current example is the semiconductor shortage, affecting numerous industries worldwide and exacerbated by dependence on a limited number of suppliers. In poorly networked political systems, form could become so rigid that it lacks the flexibility to respond to sudden changes or crises. This would mean that a system in a changing environment ceases to function because it cannot adapt quickly enough. This applies to both technical and social systems. A company overly reliant on a particular technology or market could find itself in trouble if the market or technology shifts-something the European auto industry has recently struggled with.

In highly interconnected systems, feedback loops emerge, where problems reinforce each other. In the economy, this self-reinforcing process occurs when negative expectations lead to a downturn, which in turn leads to further negative expectations. In technology, faulty feedback in interconnected IT systems can lead to a complete crash. In such cases, balance is lost, and the system fails because it can no longer self-regulate. Although we understand how these systems operate, predicting the detailed outcomes of their interplay is challenging. These complexity traps are not avoidable but are a direct result of interconnectivity itself. Since interconnectivity generates numerous feedback loops, it can result in the system losing control at critical moments—a phenomenon rooted in the very nature of networking and feedback mechanisms. Precisely because interconnected systems tend to become more efficient through optimization, they also increase their potential vulnerability with interdependence. This system immanence is evident in technological networks like the internet. The internet is highly interconnected and efficient, but this interconnectivity also makes it vulnerable to cyberattacks, where a single weak point can disable entire sections of the system. An attack on a central, critical node can impact large parts of the network. When software is disabled by cyberattacks, interactive planning and all support systems are paralyzed.

Interactive planning processes rely on the continuous capture and real-time processing of data. A cyberattack blocks access to this data or compromises its integrity. Many companies rely on automated systems to make data-driven decisions, such as in production control or resource allocation. However, if the software fails, these processes come to a halt, resulting in significant efficiency losses. In many cases, cyberattacks aim to steal, alter, or destroy data. When critical planning data is corrupted or deleted, planning can no longer be based on reliable information, leading to poor decisions and project delays.

Another example of damaged interconnectivity is the management of global supply chains. Once these networks are at risk, global goods flows come to a halt. The Covid-19 pandemic showed how quickly these systems can collapse when a single link in the chain fails. A disruption in one location, such as production facilities in China, had massive global repercussions, clearly demonstrating how interconnectivity itself can become a vulnerability. Even financial systems are inherently susceptible due to their interconnectivity. The 2008 financial crisis illustrated how the failure of a relatively small component, namely the mortgage market in the US, could plunge the entire global financial system into a crisis. The strong linkage of financial institutions and markets meant that risks spread rapidly worldwide.

Is interconnectivity therefore related to volatility? In highly interconnected financial systems, interconnectivity can amplify volatility. Banks, investment funds, and other financial institutions are linked through loans, investments, and derivatives. When one part of the system, for example, comes under stress due to a financial crisis, the problems can spread through these connections, leading to even greater fluctuations. In technological networks such as the internet or power grids, high interconnectivity can increase the risk of large-scale outages. If one node fails, it can lead to additional failures due to the interconnection, causing volatility in the performance or availability of the overall system. Cyberattacks on highly interconnected IT infrastructures can trigger global disruptions, resulting in uncertainty within the affected systems.

Clear allocation of resources, responsibilities, and tasks is a key factor for functional interconnectivity. However, if oversight and control over these allocations are lost, it can lead to chaos. For example, a lack of clear responsibilities within a company results in inefficient work and poor decisions. In politics, it is fatal when different elements obstruct each other instead of cooperating, as will be described in the concrete chapters that follow. On the other hand, when necessary information is collected in a targeted manner and processed appropriately, decision-making and the efficiency of a system can be greatly improved.

Similarly, in interdisciplinary research, where experts from various fields collaborate, complex problems can be solved that a single discipline alone could not address. One example is climate research, which combines knowledge from meteorology, oceanography, ecology, economics, and sociology to understand the impacts of climate change and develop measures to address it. Another example is biotechnology, which provides an interface between biology, chemistry, computer science, and engineering. Through the interconnection of different disciplines, progress is made in fields like medicine, biology, and environmental technology, progress that would not be possible without interdisciplinary approaches. In addition to the scientific and economic aspects, interconnectivity also plays an important role in social and cultural contexts. Globalization has led to cultures and societies being more intertwined than ever before. This is evident in how ideas, values, and norms are spread across national and cultural borders.

Although the risk of tipping is inherent to interconnected systems, there are numerous approaches to mitigate the negative effects. By introducing buffer zones, systems can be made more resilient to disruptions. While this might reduce efficiency, it increases stability by providing alternative pathways and backup mechanisms. Systems that are adaptable and flexible can better handle unpredictable disruptions. With dynamic organization and decision-making structures, crises can be detected early and resolved quickly. To prevent invisible risk accumulation, companies and organizations must develop proactive risk management strategies to identify and continuously monitor potential vulnerabilities.

In addition to centralization, decentralization also plays a crucial role, though often overlooked. Decentralized systems are less prone to tipping because they do not rely as heavily on central nodes. In decentralized networks, individual nodes can fail without causing the entire system to collapse. The fact that risks are inherent to interconnected systems shows that absolute safety or stability in highly complex, interconnected networks is impossible. These networks resemble a group of overzealous jugglers tossing balls to each other. When everything goes smoothly, it's an impressive show. But if they drop a ball, it suddenly rains juggling balls from all directions! The dynamic nature of these systems is both their superpower and their Achilles' heel. They adapt instantly, learn, and optimize themselves—fantastic! But this same adaptability also makes them as unpredictable as a teenager with mood swings. The dynamism of these systems is both their strength and their weakness. To leverage the potential of interconnectivity, systems must be designed to react to unforeseen events while remaining flexible, resilient, and adaptable.

Interconnectivity thus offers enormous opportunities but also presents risks if not carefully planned and monitored. The interlinking of systems, people, and processes requires a careful balance between efficiency and flexibility, security and adaptability. When this balance is disrupted, interconnectivity can cause more harm than good. Effective risk management that incorporates redundancies, creates flexible structures, and defines clear responsibilities is essential to maxlmize the benefits of interconnectivity while minimizing its risks. In highly complex, interconnected systems, it is therefore vital to ensure the presence of buffer zones to absorb disruptions. Systems need both the flexibility and resilience to respond to unforeseen crises.

## 3. SECURITY IN INTERNATIONAL POLITICS
### CHALLENGES INSIDE AND OUT

The increasing interconnectivity of systems, disciplines, and technologies has fundamentally transformed our world and will continue to be a key driver of innovation and progress. It is up to modern society to harness the opportunities this development offers while responsibly managing the associated challenges. While there are enormous opportunities for innovation, increased efficiency, and global collaboration, significant security challenges also arise—both internally, within individual organizations and states, and externally, in the international context. The connection between interconnectivity and security is becoming increasingly important as risks from cyberattacks, system disruptions, and geopolitical instability grow.

Everything that's happened also means that things can't go on as before. There are important and beneficial periods of thirst to overcome.The difficulties facing societies today underline the profound need for change. These periods of thirst can be interpreted as periods of scarcity or necessity, which are often used as opportunities for transformation and progress. Historically, many social and political changes have taken place during periods of great challenge. In such periods, people have often found sensational solutions to cope with events. Education and awareness-raising are an important part of this process, enabling people to make informed decisions and actively participate in social change. Ultimately, such thirsts serve as a starting point for deeper reflection and fundamental changes in society's values and priorities.

The theme is dramatic developments caused by decisions with serious consequences. So-called peace formulas, as used in Russia, China or Europe by the AfD and BSW in Germany, are proving to be engines of dictatorship for the brutal overturning of the world order. At the root of these processes are always concrete people, like Putin, Xi Jinping or, in the West, Sarah Wagenknecht or Victor Orban. Their fellow travelers always have the opportunity either to dilute and weaken the fatal ideological virus in the long term, or to accelerate the looming catastrophes. The question will be how to curb such engines of world peace disruption, which have considerable negative repercussions on the maintenance of society.

A security concept for global politics must take account of the multidimensional and dynamic nature of modern international relations. An effective approach to global security requires a blend of vision and pragmatism. It must be flexible enough to adapt to new challenges, while having a sound moral basis to foster trust and cooperation. To achieve this, governmental and non-governmental actors, technological developments, social inequalities and environmental challenges have a decisive purpose. Cooperation must be multi-level, flexible and offer a combination of prevention, protection and response. Security alliances that go beyond the framework of large regions, such as NATO, ASEAN and the AU, are disarmament agreements and regular negotiations aimed at reducing tensions, thus building mutual trust.

A sound security concept must also accelerate the transition to a sustainable economy in order to minimize environmental disasters and resource-related conflicts.  A high-level objective must be the equitable distribution and sustainable use of natural resources such as water, land and energy sources. This makes it easier to control emerging conflicts. Protection against cyber-attacks on critical infrastructures, government networks and economic systems is part of a global concept, as are global standards for artificial intelligence or biotechnology technologies, to avoid abuse and dangerous escalations. The space arms race must also be prevented in good time by international regulations.

If we look at interconnectivity, some interesting constellations emerge. Politics suddenly takes on the allure of rational management, or the flow of music influences cognition, or conversely, economics applies to the content of the art form. Cross-referencing facilitates the creative process in a hitherto unknown enterprise. We find the interconnectedness of what needs to be done optimally. Thinking in terms of interconnectivity is ultimately an invitation to go beyond rigid categories and understand the interaction between man, culture, technology and nature at a higher level.

Politics as rational management can be enriched by incorporating cultural and artistic elements. Music, for example, offers a universal language that speaks directly to emotions and thus connects across cultural and linguistic barriers. In political contexts, this could be used to promote dialog between different groups. Artistic forms of expression, such as theater, painting or literature, have often addressed social problems and injustices and thus triggered political change. They enable a perspective on the world that facts alone cannot provide. Political satires in literature and film stimulate discussion and sensitize people to complex issues.

If military protection and civil defense are discontinued, no one should be surprised that security collapses. Without military protection, which protects against external attacks or wars, and without civil defense, which helps people in the event of disasters or even social crises, a country could quickly become vulnerable to instability and threats. If these protection mechanisms are abandoned, important structures that save lives and protect society in times of crisis will be missing. Without sufficient internal and external protection, countries are vulnerable to external threats such as invasions or terrorist attacks. In such moments of danger, well-developed emergency plans, communication strategies and social support systems are essential to mitigate the impact of attacks and strengthen the resilience of society. A proactive approach that combines both military and civilian security strategies is therefore necessary. The modernization of military technology and cyber security plays a crucial role in the current security debate. States are increasingly investing in digital security infrastructure, which brings with it both new opportunities and challenges in the area of defense.

Early warning systems play a crucial role in military interconnectivity by promising early detection of potential threats. The use of modern technologies such as satellites, radar, sensors, and artificial intelligence enables the early identification of enemy missile launches, air or sea attacks, and cyberattacks. This brings several important advantages. Political and military decision-makers gain more time to respond to potential threats. Interconnectivity allows for the consolidation and exchange of data from various sources, including satellites, radar systems, sensors, and other surveillance technologies. By aggregating these data within alliances, decision-makers receive a comprehensive picture of the current threat landscape. This ensures a quicker and more coordinated response to attacks, avoiding delays in decision-making. Fast data transmission and precise coordination are essential to mitigate threats before they can cause damage. Interconnectivity fosters collaboration among military, intelligence agencies, civilian authorities, and international partners. A joint early warning system that connects various actors improves efficiency and coordination in times of crisis.

The networking of systems enables faster analysis of collected information. With the help of artificial intelligence, threats can be identified and assessed in real-time, significantly shortening response times. This gives military decision-makers the necessary time to initiate appropriate countermeasures, such as intercepting missiles or mobilizing troops. Ideally, these systems are interconnected across national borders to provide a global picture of the threat situation. Without much media attention, this approach significantly influenced the situation at the onset of Russia's invasion of Ukraine. This creates a significant opportunity to save what can still be saved.

Allied partners must collaborate closely on cybersecurity issues in order to share information about threats and attacks effectively. International agreements and joint defense strategies can prevent vulnerabilities from being exploited unilaterally. In the event of a missile attack, even a few minutes of additional warning time can be crucial for initiating countermeasures or placing one's armed forces on high alert. Response times are drastically reduced. Continuous monitoring of airspace and other potential attack vectors reduces the risk of surprise attacks through early warning systems. This is especially important in the context of nuclear deterrence, where staying informed at all times makes sense. The main function of these systems is to detect potential threats in a timely manner, thereby gaining response time. By recognizing threats early, the credibility of nuclear deterrence is more likely to be maintained, and the risk of suffering a first strike is reduced. When reliable information is provided, such interconnected systems also help avoid miscalculations and hasty reactions.

Military interconnectivity thus plays a significant role in addressing threats at diffcrent levels through the integration of various systems. Modern early warning systems are part of network-centric military strategies, combining information from different sources - air, space, and ground. This not only enhances the efficiency of military responses but also supports strategic decisions at the political level. The exchange of information and collaboration in threat detection fosters a safer global environment. Furthermore, false alarms or misunderstandings that could lead to unintended conflicts are minimized through precise and transparent communication channels.

Countries today are more interconnected than ever, whether through trade, international financial systems, technological infrastructures, or the Internet. This interconnection also renders them vulnerable to transnational threats, such as cyberattacks or the influence of disinformation campaigns, which can jeopardize political stability. There is thus an undeniable interconnection between internal and external security. The result-oriented components differ only in the instruments applied. The orientation of actions unfolds in parallel; otherwise, all forces risk colliding with one another. The strict separation between internal and external security is therefore outdated. New threats are often hybrid and cannot be clearly classified from the outset. In the context of exhaustive exploration, targeted external interventions in internal affairs, internationally operating terrorist organizations, and the consequences of transnational dangers such as climate change, pandemics, or military threats are examined.

The active involvement of local communities in security issues is essential, as many challenges arise and can be solved at the micro level. From crime prevention to the promotion of social cohesion, communities are often the first actors to respond to security risks. The security debate spans all levels, from strategic leadership at national or international level to local communities. Each of these levels plays an essential role and it is crucial to involve all stakeholders in security issues in order to develop a holistic and effective strategy. At the strategic level, the focus is on establishing basic policies, laws and international partnerships. Issues such as cyber security, counter-terrorism, climate protection as a security factor and national defence are among the core tasks at this level. This is where the guidelines are created that form the basis for operational measures. Nevertheless, a security policy that is managed exclusively 'from above' is often not enough, as it does not always take adequate account of the specific needs and circumstances of the population.

Modern security strategy must integrate all areas. Internal protection is considered part of liberal security. The aspects of external and internal security, as well as civilian and military, must be closely linked. Proactive international cooperation is necessary, as many external challenges to internal security inevitably have an international dimension. Institutional conditions must be gradually adapted to this new reality to develop coordinated action concepts based on jointly established threat analyses. The threat of cyber warfare, where state actors like Russia and China or isolated cyber terrorists attempt to attack the critical infrastructure of another country, such as electrical grids, water supply systems, or the financial system, must bring together the entities concerned through international cooperations to improve security levels. By pooling resources and expertise, different units will be able to promote technological innovations and develop better protection mechanisms. Ultimately, international cooperation is key to minimizing the impacts of attacks of any kind.

Fortunately, the reflection on security is a deeply ingrained human instinct that cannot simply be switched off. Especially in times of global uncertainty and complex international relations, the desire for security remains ever-present. However, when the global principles of a free world, such as justice, cooperation, and freedom, serve as a foundation while being entangled in contradictions, tensions inevitably arise. These contradictions can lead to the dissolution of the expected outcomes of international politics and threaten to plunge the world order into chaos. On the one hand, national security, that is to say security within a country, is considered essential and rigorously defended. On the other hand, global security aspects are often insufficiently considered or neglected. In such a scenario, measures aimed at protecting internal interests become increasingly fragile. The resulting instability could have dangerous consequences. If the security aspect is legitimately demanded internally but simultaneously taken lightly externally, the dykes ultimately give way.

Two opposing developments are conceivable: on one hand, chaotic states could arise if the global security balance is broken and each major state attempts to protect itself independently, which would lead to a fragmentation of the international order. On the other hand, we could witness an increasing hardening towards dictatorial structures, where authoritarian regimes strive by any means necessary to maintain internal security at the expense of freedom. Consequently, it is crucial to find a balance that guarantees state security while respecting and harmonizing the global principles of a free, open, and cooperative world. Only by doing so can long-term stability and peace be assured. An uncontrolled fragmentation of the international order carries significant risks. The erosion of established security structures inevitably leads first to regional conflicts and then to global instability. Fragmentation drastically affects strategic sectors such as technology, innovation, and knowledge exchange. At the same time, authoritarian approaches pose serious dangers to internal security.

For global trade, division into geopolitical blocs is not the ideal solution, but it sometimes proves necessary in desperate situations. Developing resilient and diverse supply chains, particularly in critical areas such as semiconductors, energy, and medicine, strengthens both economic stability and political security. However, the emphasis on administrative security interests must not neglect human security needs. In addition to the physical and economic security of the population, aspects such as social justice, access to education and healthcare, as well as the protection of personal freedoms, must also be considered. If these needs are ignored, inevitable social tensions will arise, ultimately undermining the internal stability of several entities. Investments in key technologies and secure supply chains enhance security everywhere without breaking global innovation networks. These measures allow countries to reduce their dependence on potentially unreliable partners or geopolitically fragile regions while ensuring access to essential goods and technologies.

The painful experiences of the war in Ukraine have considerable repercussions on the architecture of international security. This defines the so-called turning point of the ages. It puts the established world order to the test and leads to a reorientation of geopolitical alliances. Tensions between Russia and the West have resulted in a hardening of bloc formation. When international actors focus on "taming" existing dictatorships, i.e., pacifying or controlling them through cooperation and concessions, rather than holding them accountable or restricting their power, this can lead to greater problems in the long run.

The more the focus is placed on the domestication of existing dictatorships rather than combating them, the greater the danger of further escalation and the spread of conflicts beyond various regions. The idea behind this is that, instead of resolving conflicts, the dangers are exacerbated. Strengthening dictatorships implies condoning their aggressive policies or repressive methods. This escalation destabilizes new regions and further expands the threat to global security. The war in Ukraine has profoundly altered the European security landscape. NATO has become more united in response to the military invasion and Russia's threats towards Eastern Europe. Countries like Finland and Sweden, which were previously neutral, have joined NATO. This indicates that Europe's defense policy has sharpened significantly due to the Ukraine conflict. Through sanctions and counter-sanctions, Europe has felt compelled to explore alternative energy sources, which destabilizes global energy markets and drives prices up. Countries like Germany had to drastically reduce their dependency on Russian energy sources, leading to an accelerated energy transition and increased efforts to diversify energy supply. Millions of Ukrainians have fled due to the war, many of whom have moved to Europe. This has caused a short-term humanitarian crisis and created long-term challenges for integration, social services, and labor markets. At the same time, the war has triggered economic disruptions, ranging from rising living costs to supply chain problems. Other seemingly unaffected countries have maintained a neutral or more economically oriented position, demonstrating that the geopolitical landscape is extremely complex, and not every actor responds to the same threats with the same priorities. Nevertheless, even states outside the Western alliance are feeling the economic and political impacts of the conflict. The disruptions in the global economy, rising energy prices, and the increasing arms race have ushered in a new era that forces many nations to fundamentally rethink and reformulate their security and economic strategies. The dispatching of North Korean mercenaries into the crisis region naturally triggers reactions from democratic entities in the Pacific region. Global alliances are being reconfigured. Even though China officially declares neutrality for now, it maintains industrial relations with Moscow, thus supporting the regime there both directly and indirectly. The strengthened bond between these two great powers increases tensions in Asia, particularly regarding Taiwan, where the threat of a Chinese invasion is steadily growing.

As a result of the Ukraine war, the USA feels divided in its military presence. Relationships with Australia, Japan, and other Pacific states have been intensified to form a counterweight to China. The AUKUS alliance of Australia, the UK, and the USA, as well as the Quad alliance between the USA, India, Japan, and Australia, have gained strategic importance, demonstrating that the concept of BRICS states is not necessarily firmly established. Since the war disrupts global supply chains, particularly regarding grain exports, many South Pacific states that rely on food imports are experiencing rising prices and supply gaps. Countries like Indonesia and the Philippines, which import large quantities of wheat from Ukraine, are significantly affected.

The interconnectivity of armed conflicts confirms that regional conflicts and crises cannot remain isolated but can quickly have worldwide repercussions that extend across continents and thematic areas. The dynamics that begin in Europe, such as in Ukraine, indeed influence distant geopolitical theaters. The shifting of tensions to other regions, such as the South China Sea, illustrates the dimension of global security risks. Territorial disputes and displays of power in the Indo-Pacific region increasingly raise the potential for conflict. The rivalry between the USA and China exacerbates the risk of escalation due to misunderstandings or miscalculations stemming from the consequences of the Ukraine situation. A holistic approach that combines military, economic, and diplomatic tools is necessary.

International cooperation mechanisms must be strengthened, with the intention of containing crises and preventing escalation. Resilience and adaptability become more significant, as they must respond to unforeseen developments. The growing interconnectivity of global threats necessitates a continuous recalibration of security policies. Instead of isolated considerations of individual hotspots, a systemic understanding of the overlaps of various risks and regions is essential. Only in this way can effective strategies for maintaining peace and stability in an increasingly complex world be developed.

The various forms of vulnerability at the international level are becoming a central theme of modern geopolitics. They describe a situation in which states or coalitions of states are forced, through threats or the use of violence, to change their political, economic, and military decisions to avoid serious consequences. States that possess resources, food, and infrastructure in key industries are increasingly facing economic and political pressure. In this tension field, freedom becomes a precious commodity that requires significant investment and often sacrifices. Responsibility and caution to reduce such vulnerabilities are essential. The willingness to fight for this freedom in case of emergency and to strengthen alliances underscores the complex balance between sovereignty and global interdependence. Geopolitical vulnerability can be mitigated through self-responsibility and strategic foresight, but it also requires the courage not to yield to threats, even if the price may be high. Freedom is not free; it demands its price, whether in the form of responsibility, willingness to sacrifice, or even the need to fight for it. It continually emphasizes the importance of historical lessons. Past mistakes must not be repeated to ensure the preservation of freedom and peace.

The emphasis on strength underscores that freedom and peace cannot simply be achieved through words or negotiations alone. Strength - whether physical, moral, or institutional - is seen as a necessary foundation for secure living. It conveys the demand that only a fortified position allows successful advocacy for freedom and peace during discussions and negotiations. As a last resort, military strength serves to support dialogue and peace. This reflects the realpolitik understanding of international relations. This approach emphasizes that diplomatic negotiations and peaceful solutions should always be preferred; however, without the foundation of military strength, they lose their effectiveness.

This resembles the requirement that only a strong position can effectively defend freedom and peace in discussions and negotiations. As a last resort, military reliability serves to support dialogue and peace. This reflects a realistic understanding of international relations. This approach emphasizes that, while diplomatic negotiations and peaceful solutions should always be favored, they lose their effectiveness without the foundation of military credibility. Diplomacy is a complex process, requiring both strategic thinking and empathy. It's about trying to strike a balance between the interests of all parties. But this becomes very difficult when there is no power to back it up.

Diplomacy is not just a game of negotiation, but also an instrument of power. Without a certain amount of power, be it economic, military, cultural or moral, it is difficult to succeed in this field. This power is essential to give credibility to negotiating positions and to exert real influence. Even if diplomacy aims for peaceful solutions, the possibility of military intervention remains an effective and concrete lever of pressure. Without power, it becomes ineffective, as it has no credible basis for negotiation. Strategic reasoning is needed to use this power in such a way as not to sabotage positive objectives.

However, when one party has too much dominant power, diplomacy can become a tool of oppression rather than a means of balancing interests. This leads to resistance, as the dominated party is forced to use other means to defend its position. But is it only cowardice that leads to such situations, or is it boundless stupidity that drives the most uncivilized bangs of extremism in Europe forward? Especially when the extermination of a people is proclaimed, when murders are perpetrated, civilian infrastructures are destroyed, and kindergartens, schools, hospitals and homes are bombed in Ukraine?

There is hardly anything worse for a society's infrastructure than its destruction to the point where essential resources are stripped away: no electricity, no heat, no connection to the world through digital communication - only darkness and isolation. This devastation affects not just buildings or technology but shatters the hope and lives of the people on the ground. The response from the global community of nations to such horrors is often disheartening. Many world leaders act with alarming restraint, seemingly blind to the severity and inhumanity of such acts. Instead of taking a firm stand against atrocities like those of Putin's regime, economic or political support continues to flow - directly or indirectly - into the hands of dictatorships. Whether driven by fear of economic consequences, geopolitical instability, or sheer opportunism, decisive resistance is lacking. This stance is not only morally questionable but also fosters the impression that the international community tolerates violence as long as it remains far enough from their own borders. As long as the world fails to stand united for the principles of human dignity and freedom, such acts will remain the norm rather than the exception. The real question is, how long can we afford this blindness without ultimately breaking ourselves?

Passivity in german politics under the chanceller Scholz, whether due to fear, ignorance or other reasons, can lead not only to contempt for crimes against humanity, but also to direct complicity with the perpetrators. Ignoring such aggression can perpetuate a dangerous cycle of violence and injustice. Resolute resistance to these trends is necessary not only to tackle current conflicts, but also to prevent any future escalation. It is the responsibility of decision-makers, both within institutions and civil society, to take a clear stand and recognize the often dire consequences of inaction.

This is one of the greatest moral and political challenges facing Europe today. Indifference or ignorance of diabolical violence, whether due to cowardice, ignorance or a mixture of the two, opens the door to a possible Armageddon. Discouragement undoubtedly plays a part in the lack of firm condemnation of crimes against humanity or targeted violence, such as the attacks on civilians in Ukraine. Given the mysterious nature of the German Chancellor's approach, there could also be a hidden partisan sensitivity that could perhaps be clarified in socialist history. One more reason to gradually allow traditional parties and their ideologies to disappear from the field of vision of modern political management. This topic is discussed in more detail under the heading "Disastrous Partisan Politics" (Chapter 15). To believe that major conflicts can be resolved by silence, complacency or collaboration and sabotage in the European Parliament is to minimize the threat.

Europe itself is at a crossroads. The values of freedom and human dignity are being put to the test. Half-hearted sanctions or weak declarations are not enough when humanity is at stake. Europe must muster its moral and military strength to confront such crimes. It is up to Europe and the international community to draw a clear line at such times, and to defend the principles of civilization against barbaric attacks. Europe must coordinate and mobilize its resources, both diplomatic and military, to counter a real failure to respect human dignity.

Military strength is viewed in this context as a deterrent that creates and maintains space for dialogue and diplomacy. Countries that are well-prepared militarily have greater negotiating power and can exert more effective pressure to resolve conflicts diplomatically. Historically, this has often led to peaceful negotiations becoming genuinely effective only after the military balance of power was clarified. For example, the dialogue between the USA and the Soviet Union during the Cold War, such as disarmament negotiations, might not have occurred without the military equilibrium. It was not until NATO responded in the 1980s by deploying intermediate-range missiles in reaction to Soviet SS-20s - an act of deterrence - that the first step towards arms control and ultimately the end of the Cold War was taken. Who knows whether the NATO double-track decision in 1979 wouldn't have unleashed a third world war as a nuclear inferno? If the positive effect of a decision is not immediately evident, it is often overlooked or unappreciated. "What is not seen is quickly forgotten."

In the current context of the Ukraine war, the role of military strength as a supporting factor for negotiations is being discussed, with both Ukraine and Russia using their military capabilities as leverage. Military strength serves as a deterrent to dissuade potential aggressors from violent actions. A credible military defense capability always signals that an attack would incur significant costs. The larger the military budget, the greater the diplomatic bargaining power and its credibility. This helps quash violent conflict in its infancy or provides sufficient space for peace negotiations. When a state or alliance is unable or unwilling to defend itself, it offers an incentive for authoritarian regimes to expand their power. Without credible deterrence, a power vacuum emerges that will be filled by unscrupulous actors who pay no heed to international norms or human rights. A prominent example is World War II, where the initial policy of appeasement toward Nazi Germany did not prevent conflict but rather encouraged dictator Hitler to pursue his aggressive expansion plans further. This historical lesson demonstrates how the absence of military strength against tyrannical regimes leads to an inevitable and often more brutal conflict.

Tyrants always exploit the weaknesses of others, and a world without deterrence would give them the freedom to expand their power unchecked. The outcome would be a battlefield not only in the physical sense but also in the moral and political realms, where the rights and freedoms of people are systematically violated. Interestingly, extremist ideologies pursue the same concept. In such an environment, fundamental values such as freedom, justice, and peace are at risk. Dictators and authoritarian leaders, who are not constrained by deterrence or international sanctions, ruthlessly utilize domestic and foreign repression and violence to secure their power.

Although the renunciation of violence is a noble goal, complete disarmament in a world that is not free from power struggles and tyranny can have dangerous consequences. A consistent pacifism could quickly lead to a situation where the imbalance of power is exploited, and peace turns into a coerced peace dictated by the stronger. A robust defense capability is therefore always necessary to rein in these forces and send a clear message that aggression will not be without consequences.

By developing specific strategies in various sectors, synergies are created that are strengthened by common goals and innovations. Successful strategies and positive aspects from one sector serve as best practices and can be adopted as guidelines internationally. This fosters efficiency and contributes to continuous improvement, as proven approaches can be quickly disseminated and adapted. Strategies that are developed across sectors and projected globally promote long-term sustainable developments.

Dependence on energy sources is one of the major coercive themes of our time. Economic vulnerability also manifests itself in dependence on strategic raw materials, such as rare earths, which are essential for modern technologies. Militaristic coercion occurs through the threat of the use of force. It primarily can only be countered militarily, either through nuclear deterrence or through the employment of conventional military might. An example is North Korea, which regularly threatens with missile tests to gain international concessions. Russia also resorts to the threat of using nuclear weapons to deter NATO countries from intervening directly in the Ukraine conflict. International vulnerability is intensified by shifts in power dynamics that create strategic dependencies.

China's rise to global economic power has placed many states, particularly in Africa, Asia, and Latin America, in a position of economic dependence on Chinese investments and loans. These states are potentially vulnerable to coercion if China attaches political or economic conditions to its support. The "Belt and Road" Initiative illustrates how developing countries participating in the initiative take on significant Chinese loans to finance infrastructure projects.

Given that many of these countries have weak economies, there is a risk that they may default on their debts. Critics have accused China of "debt-trap diplomacy," where it takes control of strategic assets such as ports, roads, railways, or industrial complexes. Particularly, the lack of transparency in agreements and the extent to which local labor benefits from Chinese projects come under scrutiny. Environmental and human rights concerns have also been raised, as some projects are associated with negative social and ecological consequences. If Chinese dealings automatically create shackles, many African nations may not be particularly fond of that either. The coerced states either yield to the unavoidable situation or attempt to secure themselves through interconnectivity and diversification. Many African governments depend on loans to achieve their development goals, but the terms and long-term implications of these loans could severely limit their economic autonomy. There is a danger that excessive debt burdens will compel countries to make political decisions in favor of China.

Should Russia "incorporate" Ukraine in any way, it would have far-reaching consequences for European and global security. Such a scenario, where Russia completely controls Ukraine militarily or through other means, would result in an incomprehensible escalation in geopolitical tensions and place the balance between freedom and security in Europe under severe strain. The loss of Ukraine to Russia could shake the entire security architecture of Europe. The EU would also have to reckon with an increased wave of refugees from Ukraine and other conflict-affected areas, intensifying internal tensions regarding migration and resource allocation.

A state of siege through Russian hegemony over Europe would represent a profound geopolitical and ideological shift. The freedom of Europe, which is based on open borders, free expression, economic openness, and political rights, would come under significant pressure. In such a scenario, Europe would not only be surrounded by a military threat but also influenced by political and economic levers that Russia would use to expand its hegemony. The result would be a new Cold War, in which the freedom of Europe would be massively restricted. Even as dictatorships seek to maneuver in global affairs, they remain bound by human rights responsibilities and thus are irrevocably politically criminal, which must have lasting political or historical legal consequences. The mechanisms of reckoning are crucial for holding those responsible for human rights violations accountable and for preserving hope for justice for the victims.

## 4. INTERCONNECTIVITY OF GEOGRAPHY

Another form of interconnection refers to the networks that move people, goods, and resources between different geographical spaces. With the development of modern transportation systems, regions that were previously isolated are now connected globally. Geographical interconnection describes the close link and dependence between different geographical spaces and actors through physical, social, economic, and technological connections. It refers to how places and regions of the world are linked to one another by transportation networks, trade relationships, communication technologies, migration, and environmental influences. This includes transport and infrastructure networks such as roads, railways, shipping routes, and air connections that link different regions and enable the movement of goods and people. An example of this is global trade, which relies on a complex network of maritime and air transportation. Container ports like Shanghai, Rotterdam, or Singapore serve as nerve centers of a global network of shipping routes, facilitating the worldwide exchange of goods. Any disruption in these networks - whether due to natural disasters, political conflicts, or logistical blockages - has far-reaching repercussions on supply chains and the global economy.

Places are interconnected, particularly regarding social and political links. Cities, countries, and communities form a network of relationships influenced by trade, migration, conflicts, and diplomacy. These places mutually influence one another through the interaction of their inhabitants and their political systems. Similarly, globalized economies are highly intertwined, so changes in one region have worldwide impacts. Global production chains and markets make it necessary for countries to connect through trade, investment, and financial flows. For example, a disruption in semiconductor production in Asia can affect the automotive industry in Europe. Migration, tourism, and the Internet create links between people from different regions, promoting the exchange of cultures, ideas, and information. Digital connectivity through the Internet is a particularly powerful factor of interconnection, as it enables the instant exchange of information on a global scale.

While cohesion aims for solidarity within and between societies and regions, reforms involve political, economic, and social changes that can either strengthen or weaken this solidarity. These two processes are closely linked and significantly influence the development of what are known as "regional clusters," which are geographic areas undergoing similar processes of development and integration. Regional clusters refer to groups of countries or regions that share similar developmental processes, challenges, and potentials. These clusters are characterized by geographic proximity, historical ties, or similar economic and political structures. The interconnection between cohesion and reforms is particularly evident in these regions, as successful reforms often spread from one region to neighboring territories, or clusters collaborate at an interregional level to create cohesive structures.

Regional cohesion refers to the level of social, economic, and political solidarity within a region. Large regions extend beyond national borders and encompass multiple countries or areas that are linked geographically, culturally, or economically. These connections are often based on shared economic interests, cultural proximity, or geographic location. Large regions aim to strengthen cooperation in areas such as the economy, infrastructure, culture, and security. They promote regional development, innovation, and the exchange of best practices among member states or regions. They contribute to political stability and economic integration by advancing shared goals such as sustainable development, environmental policy, security, and social cohesion. They cross national boundaries and create networks that facilitate exchange and cooperation beyond those borders.

High cohesion means there are low social inequalities, strong economic interdependence, and effectively functioning political institutions. This is often the result of long-term reforms aimed at promoting equality, infrastructure, and political institutions. Regions with high cohesion tend to be more stable and resilient to external shocks. An example of successful reforms contributing to cohesion is the transformation of Central and Eastern European states after the fall of the Iron Curtain. Through deep economic and political reforms, these countries were able to integrate into the EU single market, accelerating their economic development.

The idea of first consolidating large entities such as regions and continents, and then building international connections, follows a strategic approach of creating a stable foundation for developing global networks, either simultaneously or subsequently. By strengthening internal structures, a shared identity and strength are built. Regions that are consolidated internally can share resources more effectively, pursue common economic and political goals, and minimize conflicts. This applies to Europe as well as to Africa, South

America, the Middle East, and the Far East. Within the entirety of interconnected structures, it is important to utilize as many resources as possible. Regions that are firmly established internally can share resources more effectively by pursuing common economic and political objectives and minimizing conflicts.

## 5. AND CIVIL PREVENTION?

In the global context, civil prevention is crucial for sustainable peacekeeping and conflict resolution. The idea behind this is to take preventative action and to identify and defuse the causes at an early stage. Both unstable and authoritarian governments increase the risk of conflict. Democratic principles based on the rule of law and transparency are there to prevent corruption-prone and dictatorial systems. In practical terms, civil prevention builds on measures for infrastructure solutions, education initiatives or health programs.

The interconnectivity of the healthcare system describes the dynamic interplay of different actors, institutions and processes that contribute to the promotion and maintenance of public health. It encompasses far more than just direct patient care and ranges from political, economic and social to technological and organizational levels. A holistic understanding of this interconnectedness is critical to addressing the increasing challenges in the healthcare sector. Political decisions, such as the allocation of resources, access to healthcare and the regulation of medicines, directly influence the healthcare situation and the well-being of the population. The regulatory framework set by national health authorities and international organizations creates the basis for standardized care. Regulations on medical procedures, drug approvals and quality controls are key elements of this system.

Efficient financing, whether through public funds, insurance or private investment, is crucial to ensure a stable and sustainable supply. Interconnectivity is reflected here in the need to optimally allocate resources, control costs and at the same time ensure equitable access for all segments of the population. Advances in medical technology, such as artificial intelligence, robotics and data analytics, are revolutionizing the way diagnoses are made and treatments are delivered. These technologies require close collaboration between medical and technical professionals and adaptation to regulatory requirements. Social determinants such as income, education and living situation influence access to healthcare. Interconnectivity in healthcare is crucial here to reach disadvantaged groups and improve access to healthcare services. A comprehensive understanding of the connections between the different levels of the healthcare system, from direct patient care to political and economic aspects and global health, can overcome the major challenges.

The digitalization and exchange of health data across national borders allows doctors and researchers to access more comprehensive data sources. This enables better diagnoses, optimized treatment plans and early detection of global health risks such as pandemics. By networking research institutions, medical innovations can be developed and implemented more quickly. The exchange of data and findings from different regions improves global medical research, such as the development of vaccines. Interconnectivity in global healthcare therefore offers huge opportunities, but requires a careful approach to address both technological and ethical challenges and ensure trust in these systems.

Even in civilian crisis preparedness, regular emergency drills should be carried out in both the health and logistics sectors to ensure that all parties involved can react quickly and effectively in the event of an attack. Such exercises should include cooperation with government institutions and private companies. The international economy is characterized by closely linked global supply chains. However, this can also become a weakness if geopolitical tensions, trade wars or natural disasters disrupt supply chains. Companies and governments are therefore required to diversify their dependence on global supply chains and respond to sudden crises by building resilience and flexible systems. In general, a stable logistics network requires diversification in order to minimize risks. If part of the logistics fails, there must be alternative routes and delivery methods.

The technical and organisational interconnection of civil infrastructures such as telecommunications, transport systems and energy networks determines, at a distinct level, how modern societies function. This networking, known as 'Smart Infrastructure', ensures efficiency, sustainability and security in many areas of daily life. The extension of networks and innovative technologies such as 5G enable fast, reliable communication. This improves not only access to information, but also interaction between citizens and authorities, and the use of digital services.

The interconnection of energy networks, particularly through the integration of renewable energy sources, contributes to the creation of resilient energy systems. Smart grids enable efficient energy distribution, prevent overloads and promote the use of energy storage. In the event of an emergency, the interconnection of these infrastructures is essential for effective crisis management and rapid response by the authorities. By exchanging data in real time, emergency measures can be organized more efficiently and resources optimized. Networking also promotes citizen involvement in decision-making processes. Platforms and applications provide feedback on public services, improving their quality. Interconnectivity in the business world favors e-commerce platforms, online marketplaces and digital payment services, which are revolutionizing commerce and facilitating access to products and services for consumers worldwide. While interconnectivity brings many benefits, it also poses challenges, such as data protection, security and the digital divide. Access to technology and the Internet is not evenly distributed, reinforcing social inequalities.

There is no complete alternative to cyber, but there are numerous technologies and approaches that can either prevent cyberattacks or mitigate their impact. From quantum encryption and blockchain to hybrid and analog approaches, these technologies offer a combination of prevention, resilience and decentralized security. A combination of these approaches is often the most effective way to ensure security in an increasingly connected and threatened digital world. In certain areas, physical security systems such as access control systems, biometric recognition, secured hardware combined with digital systems can be used to provide additional security. Human monitoring and decision-making processes that run in parallel with digital processes can minimize risks by complementing automated systems.

Quantum cryptography is a method of encryption that utilizes the principles of quantum mechanics to transmit data in a particularly secure manner. It relies on quantum physics and potentially offers inviolable security, as any attempt to intercept or manipulate the encrypted information immediately alters it, making such actions detectable. Blockchain provides a decentralized method of storing and validating data, significantly reducing the risk of cyberattacks on centralized databases. It is often used in areas such as financial technology, supply chains, and even digital identities. Blockchain can guarantee the integrity of transactions and data by recording each transaction in a public and immutable manner, making it more difficult for cyberattacks to manipulate data. In certain cases, using non-digital alternatives, such as paper documents or physical backups, can provide an additional layer of protection, especially in highly secure environments. Instead of connecting to central servers, edge computing processes data and calculations locally on devices located near the data source. This reduces the amount of data transmitted over the network and thereby decreases potential vulnerabilities to cyberattacks. Data can be processed in real-time without having to be sent to central cloud servers, which mitigates the risks of attacks on a central data point. Artificial intelligence and machine learning can be utilized to early detect cyberattacks by identifying unusual activities in real-time and automatically taking protective measures. AI-driven systems can adapt to new threats by continuously learning from attack patterns and evolving. Instead of solely focusing on prevention, cyber resilience aims to strengthen a system's ability to quickly recover after an attack.

## 6. WHAT IS CIVIL SOCIETY?

Civil society plays a crucial role in promoting democracy, social participation, and social justice by bringing people together to work collaboratively on solutions and advocate for their interests. Globalization, migration, and demographic changes are leading to new social structures and challenges. The need for a comprehensive socio-ecological transformation is at the heart of many current debates. This transformation aims to fundamentally restructure society to make it more sustainable and just. Another central aspect is the transition from fossil fuel-based energy systems to renewable energy sources. This requires massive investments and technological innovations. There is a growing awareness that economic growth must be reconciled with ecological sustainability. Concepts like the "green economy" are gaining importance and offer approaches to align economic growth with environmental concerns. The "new economy," as cultivated in modern enterprises, focuses on promoting environmentally friendly technologies and sustainable practices that not only provide ecological benefits but also economic opportunities. The promotion of circular economy models also contributes to more efficient resource use, waste minimization, and reduced environmental impact. Moreover, the concepts of the green economy also integrate the social dimension, seeking to establish a balance between economic, social, and ecological goals. New livelihoods need to be created for people through sustainable jobs and fair wages in environmentally friendly sectors. However, implementing these approaches requires a change in mindset within politics, economics, and society. Incentives for sustainable investments, the integration of environmental criteria into business management, and raising public awareness about sustainable consumption are important steps toward enabling a transformation to a green economy. These developments demonstrate that it is possible to reconcile economic growth with ecological sustainability. This is crucial not only for the protection of our environment but also for the long-term stability and resilience of economic structures. If large-scale transformation is neglected, the consequences will become evident long before tangible results are achieved.

The digital revolution and technological advancements have impacted nearly every aspect of life. Technologies such as artificial intelligence, big data, the Internet of Things, and automation are shaping both the economy and privacy. They offer enormous opportunities but also pose ethical, security, and labor market challenges to society. Digitization is also transforming the labor market in a sustainable way. On one hand, automation eliminates many routine tasks. On the other hand, new professions are emerging, particularly in the fields of IT and data. The demand for digital skills is increasing across all sectors. For workers, this means the necessity of lifelong learning and continuous training. More flexible work models, such as remote work, are becoming increasingly important. Policies must create frameworks that promote both innovation and ensure social security. Beyond the economic sphere, digitization has significant social repercussions. Data protection and informational self-determination are becoming central themes. Cybersecurity is gaining importance due to the increasing digital interconnectedness. Social media is changing the way we communicate and consume information. This offers opportunities for greater participation but also risks, such as the spread of misinformation. The ethical implications of using AI, for example in autonomous vehicles or medicine, require societal debates and clear regulations.

The fragmentation of public opinion makes it difficult to reach a consensus on important issues. Through social media and algorithm-driven platforms, "echo chambers" are forming, where people only receive information that confirms their own beliefs. This reinforces social tensions, as a common factual basis is lost. At the same time, populist movements have gained popularity, often exploiting these uncertainties and divisions to promote their own political agendas. The rise of authoritarian regimes in some countries, along with the global decline of democratic values, poses new challenges to the international order.

How do masses behave when they are inundated with false information and overwhelmed by unchecked news? Moreover, influenced by personalities who themselves are under the sway of false news and ignorance, driven by conspiracy theories and infected by the negative side of social media, the problem escalates. Political masses, despite their inertia, inexplicably change their opinions overnight. Even in calmer territories, something is amiss in the thought structure when a survey reveals that 45% of people fear an imminent situation, and a year later, that figure rises to 90%. Was there a lack of clarity or an overview from the beginning? These crowds often rest on different worldviews, which are further deepened through targeted disinformation. The gap between groups widens, as each trusts its "own" sources and becomes skeptical of other perspectives. Conspiracy theories offer many people an apparent sense of security, as they provide a clearly delineated narrative that reduces the complexity of reality. In affinity groups, these narratives find validation, further reinforcing the phenomenon. Why concern oneself with complex contexts when it is so easy to blindly follow the loudest voices? Welcome to the era of post-factual opinion change in a flash, where truth is flexible and ignorance is intoxicating. After all, it is far too complicated to verify sources or question the credibility of information. Why do that? The algorithm knows better than we do what we should think anyway.

Social media are marked by excess and irrationality, which can be attributed to various factors, including anonymity, rapid information dissemination, and the tendency to attract attention through provocative statements. These phenomena have become an integral part of digital life, and it currently seems inevitable to have to live with this situation in the short term. Social media provide a platform where opinions and emotions can be shared without a filter. This leads to a high dynamic and intensity of communication, where extremes and provocations easily reinforce each other. As immediate reactions to content are often possible, reflection - which is more common in other, slower forms of communication - often falls by the wayside. This generates a tendency towards excess, such as exaggerated representations, aggressive expressions of opinion, or an avalanche of information that is not always well-founded.

Anonymity and algorithms reinforce these excessive and irrational trends. Anonymous profiles promote disinhibition and polarization, as users are less hesitant to express more extreme or irrational opinions without the fear of being held accountable. Meanwhile, algorithms favor content that elicits strong emotional reactions— such content is more often shared and commented on, thus reaching a larger audience. This creates a cycle in which extreme viewpoints are favored, further exacerbating irrationality and excess in social media.

How can we address this? Given that social media is an integral part of modern life, it seems difficult in the short term to completely escape excess and irrationality. However, an important approach would be to promote media literacy and critical thinking among users. This could help better contextualize content, differentiate between fact-based statements and controversial ones, and manage information more autonomously. At the same time, it is also the responsibility of the platforms themselves to curb the spread of hate speech, misinformation, and exaggerated representations through clearer rules and more effective moderation.

When false information circulates unchecked, individuals and groups can become increasingly radicalized. This is manifested by the rise of extremist movements that call for violence or civil disobedience. The algorithms of platforms are designed to promote high-engagement content, often regardless of its truthfulness. These mechanisms favor the dissemination of sensational false information because it generates more clicks and comments. Many individuals, blinded by this information, become its victims. Radical movements are often a direct result of these distorted impressions. They exploit the insecurity sown by misinformation to fuel fears and present themselves as the sole bearers of truth. Thus, distrust in the system quickly transforms into an open call for resistance, even violence, always with the supposed legitimacy of defending the truth.

Ultimately, building a resilient society is a collective task that requires the engagement of all. Such a society can only succeed if all its members actively participate in processes of inclusion and collaboration. It is essential to engage in dialogue, to accept and understand the different social, cultural, and ethnic groups in order to reduce tensions. Resilience, in this context, does not only mean being able to react to crises, but also having the capacity to emerge strengthened from dilemmas as a community. This requires supportive structures that are viable both in times of crisis and in everyday life, as well as a willingness to find solutions that take into account the well-being of the entire society. Responsibility does not rest solely on governments or institutions, but also on each individual. Through empathy, tolerance, and active promotion of social cohesion, everyone can contribute to making diversity seen as a strength rather than a source of conflict. Through collective engagement, stable structures can be created in the long term, fostering both social peace and sustainable development.

Violence, whether physical or verbal, harms society by escalating conflicts instead of resolving them through dialogue. In a civilized society, disagreements should be settled peacefully and respectfully. Misinformation constitutes a subtle form of "informational violence," sowing confusion, undermining trust, and deepening divisions within society. Particularly in the age of social media, false information spreads at lightning speed, contributing to skepticism towards scientific knowledge, politics, and the media. When citizens discover that they may be caught up in crises, the worst option is clearly to allow themselves to be taken over by extremism. The system should actually provide paths to other alternatives and initiatives. If not, it is its own fault that it is in danger of collapsing.

The central argument is therefore as follows: violence and false information destabilize the foundations of a functional civil society and a democratic culture. Only transparency, facts, and peaceful discourse can allow an open society to thrive. In recent decades, the phenomenon of a growing culture of contempt has become increasingly prevalent in many social contexts. This concept describes a social climate in which politeness, recognition, and decency among individuals diminish. The ubiquitous use of social media and digital communication methods has fundamentally changed the way people interact. Anonymity and distance created by digital platforms often lead to more aggressive behaviors. Users feel safer expressing rude or insulting comments because the protective physical presence is absent. Societies tend to prioritize phenomena such as "authenticity" at the expense of traditional forms of politeness. This change can lead to a reconfiguration of interpersonal relationships, where honest, often hurtful expressions are perceived as "honesty." In times of political polarization, people tend to position themselves in extreme camps. This leads to a decrease in mutual respect, as one's own opinion is often defended excessively while that of others is devalued. Public debate becomes more aggressive and disrespectful, which also has repercussions on personal interactions. An environment marked by contempt leads to alienation among individuals. Trust and empathy erode, resulting in an increase in misunderstandings and tensions. People retreat into their own social circles and avoid exchanges with others, threatening social cohesion.

The responsibility of society in the context of interconnection is a crucial issue that deserves particular attention. In an increasingly interconnected world driven by digitization, society must position itself not only as a spectator but also as an active participant. This involves raising awareness of the consequences of technologies and social networks, as well as engaging in critical reflection on their use. Society carries a collective responsibility in how it utilizes technological advancements. Interconnection has abolished physical boundaries, creating a new global community. It is essential to establish ethical principles for this digital space, such as respect, data protection, and combating discrimination. As the dissemination of ideas and innovations accelerates, society must be conscious of its role in harnessing these technological advancements. The challenge lies in finding a balance between constant access to information and managing the associated risks, such as information overload and stress.

Prevention is key in this context. It should not only aim to anticipate technical challenges but also to design solutions for the social, ecological, and ethical issues linked to interconnection. This can be achieved through educational initiatives, integrating ethical considerations into technological development, and proactive measures to prevent injustices and digital discrimination. Society must adopt a proactive stance by supporting innovations that promote ethical and inclusive uses of technology.

The interconnections between individual issues, such as the cost of living, food, and health, illustrate how personal, social, and global challenges are closely linked. This complexity requires an integrated approach to problem-solving. For example, the volatility of food prices, influenced by climatic conditions and international trade relations, shows how local issues can be amplified by global dynamics. Education plays a key role in preparing future generations for these challenges. Educational systems must adapt to global developments, whether they relate to technological advancements or climate change, by equipping individuals with the necessary skills. Access to education and the quality of teaching are increasingly influenced by global trends, such as digitization and international relations. Society must actively engage in finding global solutions, linking individual problems to international issues. This requires political participation and innovation that fosters interaction between local challenges and global peace. Diversity within society can also be a driving force for innovation, bringing different perspectives to problem-solving.

Deteriorative forces have often prevailed throughout history, exploiting fear and propaganda to manipulate people. When individuals feel threatened or uncertain, they are more likely to relinquish their freedoms and follow dubious leaders who promise illusory security. This has been observed during the rise of totalitarian regimes in the 20th century and seems to be repeating in the 21st century. Another factor is the tendency of people to ignore political developments out of convenience or resignation. As long as their personal lives are not directly affected, many tolerate injustices, allowing deteriorative forces to spread quietly until it is too late to stop them.The question of whether society should act or remain a spectator is fundamental. Active engagement is necessary to shape an interconnected future that is ethical and sustainable. Society must not only accept and utilize technologies but also engage in critical debate about their consequences, cultivating human values such as empathy and mutual understanding. Ultimately, this is a shared responsibility that requires the involvement of everyone to build a better future.

## 7. INTERCONNECTIVITY OF LANGUAGE AND THOUGHT

Unlike other terrestrial living beings, humans possess the ability to speak and think rationally, enabling them to form moral and political communities. Through the development of language, humans have created complex social structures and communities founded on moral and political principles. The interconnection between language and thought is a fascinating subject that has intrigued not only linguists but also psychologists and neuroscientists for centuries. Language is not merely a means of communication; it also serves as a tool in the thought process. Languages are more than just instruments of understanding—they are carriers of cultural concepts and values. Wilhelm von Humboldt argued that language also shapes the worldview of a linguistic community. This idea suggests that the concepts and structures of a language influence the thinking of its speakers, and vice versa.

Neuroscientific research has shown that speaking and understanding language activate complex neural networks in which specific brain regions are responsible for language production and comprehension. These same regions are also engaged during cognitive tasks. These findings support the notion of a harmonious interplay between linguistic and cognitive processes. Language thus expands our thinking and our understanding of the world, contributing to the diversity of experiences.

These structures enable the pursuit of common goals, conflict resolution, and the organization of communal life. Language influences how we see and interpret the world. Through the choice of words and the construction of sentences, certain aspects of reality can be highlighted or overlooked. For example, the way an event is reported can shape public awareness and collective memory.

Language carries the traditions, values, and norms of a community. The way we speak can reflect and reinforce cultural identity. The language we use shapes our thoughts and our understanding of the world. Those who master language can exert influence on society and its structures. Political rhetoric, propaganda, and discourse are examples of how language is used to shape opinions and mobilize people. Propaganda that goes unnoticed is particularly dangerous. Thus, language is not just a tool for communication but a fundamental element that constructs our reality and shapes our interactions with the world and with each other. Foreign languages, in principle, promote intercultural dialogue and understanding between different cultures. They enable people to communicate, avoid misunderstandings, and develop empathy for other perspectives. This is particularly important in a globalized world where intercultural encounters are a daily occurrence. Proficiency in foreign languages also enhances cognitive skills such as problem-solving, critical thinking, and creativity. This is advantageous in international politics, where quick thinking and the ability to view problems from different perspectives are often required. Multilingual politicians are better equipped to switch between different approaches to thinking and to develop innovative solutions.

Language is a central tool in decision-making because it enables the expression, analysis, and evaluation of thoughts, information, and arguments. It helps us compare different perspectives, weigh pros and cons, and structure complex issues. Globalization and international cooperation rely on the ability to communicate across cultural and linguistic boundaries. When people speak multiple languages, new opportunities arise for the exchange of knowledge, ideas, and innovation. Foreign languages open doors to new ways of thinking and allow individuals to move beyond their own cultural and linguistic limits. This drives interconnectedness on a deeper cognitive level. Multilingual individuals demonstrate exceptional cognitive flexibility. The phenomenon of code-switching, or switching between languages, allows multilingual individuals to navigate seamlessly in different cultural contexts. This has implications for entrepreneurial thinking and intercultural communication.

The interfaces of interconnectivity require a careful approach in their development and implementation. This involves adopting techniques that are not only efficient but also ethical, inclusive, and conducive to human well-being. Designing these interfaces will remain a key task to unlock the full potential of our connected world while addressing its challenges. To fully leverage this potential, ethical considerations and inclusion must be prioritized. Language knowledge is assessed sociologically, while language mastery is measured psychologically. It is not merely basic understanding that fosters comprehension, but also the ability to grasp the interconnectedness of knowledge.

Languages are interconnected through forms of communication and interaction, both on an individual and societal level. Language is closely tied to identity and group belonging. It enables communication within a heterogeneous group while fostering the ability to join new groups. This dual function of language strengthens both intra-cultural bonds and intercultural exchange. Modern technologies have significantly accelerated this process. The internet, social media, and global communication platforms have made real-time interaction with partners worldwide possible. Languages that were once geographically and culturally isolated are now part of a global linguistic landscape.

When people from different linguistic backgrounds interact, an exchange of perspectives and knowledge occurs, leading to new ideas and approaches. This cross-linguistic dialogue fosters the development of innovative concepts shaped by diverse cultural experiences. Experiences are structured through language. The interconnectivity of language thus lies in its ability to build cultural, cognitive, and conceptual bridges. It not only facilitates communication between individuals and groups but also shapes our thinking, identity, and understanding of the world. Through these multifaceted connections, language significantly contributes to global networking and intercultural exchange. In the modern world, cultural hybridizations are emerging, where traditions, art forms, and ways of thinking blend. Music genres such as hip-hop or jazz, which originated in specific linguistic and cultural contexts, have spread worldwide, evolving into new forms shaped by contact with other cultures and languages.

The interconnectivity of language has profound social and political implications. In a globalized world where people from diverse cultures and with different languages interact, linguistic barriers are being dismantled. This fosters international trade, scientific collaboration, and cultural exchange. However, it also gives rise to tensions, particularly in countries where minority languages are suppressed or marginalized.

The digital world has led to the emergence of new linguistic phenomena. Distinct language forms, such as internet slang or emojis, have developed online and are widely understood and used across linguistic boundaries, regardless of native language. These new forms of communication contribute to global linguistic interconnectedness and create novel, albeit superficial, ways of expression. To strengthen linguistic interconnectivity in a globalized world, translation competencies are a crucial factor. They enable people to communicate across linguistic and cultural divides and promote international exchange in business, diplomacy, science, and culture.

While technological advancements like machine translation systems provide valuable support, human interpreters remain indispensable for preserving the subtle nuances of language and ensuring the quality of communication. Expanding translation competencies—both through education and technological support—will be critical in the coming years to further enhance linguistic interconnectivity and enable closer global understanding. In a world where communication and mutual comprehension are increasingly important, these skills hold the key to bridging linguistic and cultural divides.

Translation competencies encompass much more than just proficiency in another language. They require deep cultural sensitivity, an understanding of the subtleties and nuances of the languages involved, and the ability to convey meaning not only literally but also contextually and idiomatically. These skills enable individuals and entire institutions to overcome the linguistic and cultural barriers that often hinder communication between different language communities.

In the globalized economy, businesses rely on the translation of contracts, documents, or marketing materials to enter new markets and maintain successful commercial relationships. Accurate and culturally adapted translation is essential to avoid misunderstandings. In international politics, interpreters play a key role. They not only translate between languages but also act as mediators between cultures, contributing to the smooth conduct of diplomatic negotiations and international cooperation. Translation skills are also of great importance in the scientific field. Through the translation of specialized literature, researchers can engage in global exchanges, accelerating progress in various research areas.

Technological advancements have revolutionized translation skills over the past decades. Artificial intelligence and machine translation systems allow for rapid overcoming of language barriers. These tools provide real-time translations, making communication between speakers of different languages simpler and more efficient. With digitization and the growing availability of translation tools, more people have the opportunity to expand their linguistic skills and connect internationally. Educational programs emphasizing translation skills enable future generations to acquire these abilities from an early age, thus strengthening linguistic interconnectedness.

Despite technological progress, human translators and interpreters remain indispensable. While machine translations are useful tools, they have limitations when dealing with complex or culturally sensitive content. Especially for legal or literary texts, a deep understanding of context and cultural nuances is required, something machines cannot fully offer. Machine translations become inaccurate when faced with complex or creative texts. Advanced translation skills not only reinforce linguistic interconnectedness but also promote cultural exchange. Literature, cinema, and music from different cultures become accessible through translations, paving the way for broader international dialogue. A striking example is the dissemination of works by great writers such as Gabriel García Márquez, Haruki Murakami, or Tolstoy, whose texts have been received worldwide thanks to translations. This cultural interconnectedness contributes to the understanding and appreciation of diverse cultural identities. Translations build bridges between cultures and foster tolerance, empathy, and awareness of the diversity of human expression.

The communicative interconnectedness of language extends to translation, evaluation, mediation, and consulting in international politics and congresses. Linguistic and cultural differences can serve as both bridges and barriers during such events. This is why it is essential, in negotiations and conferences, to ensure that communication between delegates, political actors, and various stakeholders is smooth, accurate, and culturally sensitive. Translation is the backbone of communication at international congresses. It enables participants from different countries and cultures to communicate by conveying written and oral content across languages. This process involves not just accurately translating words but also transmitting nuances, context, and cultural meanings. Translation goes beyond words: it captures the spirit of the text, its meaning, its drama and its empathy.

It is always astonishing how philosophical thinking is cultivated in ancient languages. Latin and Ancient Greek provide deep insights into past realms of thought and philosophical traditions. They train analytical skills, promote critical thinking, and enable an understanding of the foundations of Western and Eastern philosophy within their historical context. This makes ancient languages a valuable tool for training and deepening philosophical thought. Language is not only a means of communication but also an instrument of thought. In ancient languages, philosophy and language are inextricably linked. To truly understand the thinkers of antiquity, it is not enough to read modern translations. Understanding the original language allows for the capture of deeper meanings and subtle nuances that are often lost in translation. These thinkers shaped the foundations of Western philosophical and scientific thought, and their works were written in the original language. Latin, the language of the Roman Empire, remained the lingua franca of scholars in Europe for centuries. Philosophy, theology, natural sciences, and law were all written in Latin. Studying Latin texts strengthens the ability to consciously adopt logical patterns of argumentation and to think precisely. Johann Wolfgang von Goethe remarked about ancient languages that they are "the patterns of rhetoric and all that is worthy that the world has ever possessed."

The significance of studying ancient languages can be compared to the careful preparation that British Marines undergo when they initially train on sailing masters. This analogy illustrates the value of discipline, patience, and a methodical approach. Just as training on sailing masters creates a foundation for more complex tasks at sea, studying ancient languages establishes a groundwork for a deeper understanding of culture, history, and philosophy. As long as language is absent, philosophy remains hidden, for language is the primary tool through which thoughts can be formulated, reflected upon, and communicated. Without the ability to articulate abstract ideas in words, it would be difficult to grasp, develop, or share philosophical concepts. Language enables us to think about the world, ask questions, and seek answers. It is the medium through which philosophy becomes accessible and tangible.

Philosophy, as a discipline that deals with fundamental questions of being, knowledge, ethics, and consciousness, often grapples with complex and abstract content, highlighting the necessity for precise expression. Without language, the concepts and considerations that have preoccupied philosophers for centuries would be difficult to convey. Terms like "justice," "truth," or "existence" exist only because we can assign meaning to them and define them through language. Language allows us to make the invisible visible and to express the unspeakable. Philosophy, in its essence, is a linguistic activity through which we reflect on reality. It is both the art of questioning and the art of understanding. Without language, we might experience or feel certain things intuitively, but we could not consciously and systematically think about them or share these insights with others. Some philosophers, such as Ludwig Wittgenstein, argued that the limits of our language are the limits of our world. This means that what we cannot express in language lies beyond our conscious ability to think. Thus, philosophy remains hidden as long as there is no language, because without it, we have no access to structured thoughts or deeper understanding. Without language, we would still have perceptions and experiences, but these could not be transformed into abstract concepts. Philosophy requires the means of reflection and analysis to develop questions and think about fundamental aspects of life. These means are provided through language.

In philosophy, the formation of concepts plays a central role. Philosophers create and refine terms to understand the world and to formulate theories. Terms like "being" in Heidegger, "cogito" ("I think") in Descartes, or "Übermensch" in Nietzsche are central building blocks of philosophical systems. Without language, such terms could not exist. They are the result of a long process of linguistic and intellectual labor. Without language, these concepts could not emerge, and consequently, philosophy would remain hidden, as the fundamental tools for describing reality would be lacking. Language creates the opportunity to speak precisely about differences and similarities, causes and effects, as well as possibilities and necessities.

Although language is the foundation of philosophy, some philosophical traditions question whether there is a form of thought or understanding that transcends language. Mystical traditions or contemplative philosophies suggest that there are forms of knowledge that cannot be fully captured by language. Nevertheless, the expression of ideas, even within these traditions, generally remains rooted in language. Even the ineffable is often suggested or described through language. Thus, philosophy without language remains in a diffuse and inarticulate state. Once language comes into play, philosophy comes to life; it becomes visible, debatable, and evolving.

Classical philologists assert that ancient languages are significantly distinct from modern languages in their flexibility and expressive power, compelling learners to grasp the subtleties of philosophical terms. The study of ancient languages shapes the understanding of the respective philosophical tradition, as well as the ability to think about philosophy in an intercultural manner. Many philosophical texts have been translated and interpreted multiple times over the centuries, leading to changes or different interpretations of philosophical concepts. For example, the translation of Greek texts into Arabic during the Middle Ages greatly influenced Islamic philosophy, which in turn marked European scholasticism. This constant interaction between languages and cultures shows that philosophical thought is not static but grows and evolves through engagement with other ideas. Ancient languages often possess more complex grammatical structures than modern languages, which forces the brain to think flexibly and establish connections between different concepts. This intellectual challenge develops abstract thinking, enhances problem-solving abilities, and fosters mental agility. Additionally, reading and interpreting ancient texts require patience, precision, and critical thinking. The brain is trained to understand meanings at a deeper, symbolic, or metaphorical level. This type of reading and thought is fundamental to philosophy, as philosophical concepts are often expressed metaphorically or abstractly.

In contrast, modern languages reflect current realities and provide access to a dynamic intercultural exchange. As they are in constant interaction in a globalized world, they allow learners to directly experience the diversity of cultures and traditions of thought today. Modern discourses are no longer limited to a specific geographical or cultural region. They are enriched by international exchange and access to different linguistic spaces. Philosophers and intellectuals from various cultural backgrounds, who write and discuss in these languages, offer perspectives that often differ from modes of thought rooted in the Western tradition.

Unlike ancient languages, whose translation processes have often spanned centuries, translations into modern languages occur in real-time. Philosophers, writers, and intellectuals from different countries publish almost simultaneously on a global scale, leading to the rapid dissemination of their ideas. The study of modern languages allows individuals to stay informed about these developments and to directly follow current discussions. Another aspect of studying modern languages is the promotion of creative and innovative thinking. Languages are constantly evolving and are open to new expressions, word creations, and meanings. Unlike the static forms of ancient languages, which focus on classical literary and philosophical texts, modern languages reflect current evolutions and societal changes.

Through contact with contemporary discourses conducted in modern languages, multilingual individuals develop a greater sensitivity to today's social, political, and cultural issues. Themes such as globalization, climate change, social justice, identity, and technology are discussed in a variety of linguistic spaces. This broadens thinking and offers new philosophical approaches that address the challenges of our time. Modern languages are inherently pragmatic and application-oriented. They further enhance the ability to respond flexibly and creatively to changes. The multilingualism and intercultural competence developed through modern languages enable successful action in an increasingly interconnected world. They allow for innovative and creative responses to societal challenges.

This is not just about mutual communication in transnational contexts. Politicians, as well as managers, develop refined listening and observation skills, situational assessment, and objective decision-making through their multilingual abilities. This versatility of perspectives allows for a deeper evaluation of problems, opportunities, and risks. By mastering multiple languages, leaders gain the ability to understand and manage transnational relationships at a deeper level. They are better equipped to conduct more effective negotiations and make informed decisions that ensure both short-term and long-term success. Thus, multilingualism is not only a communication tool but also an essential component of a modern and global leadership culture.

On international political platforms and during conferences where multiple languages are used, highly qualified translators are essential. Their task goes far beyond simple translation; they must also accurately grasp political nuances, diplomatic rhetoric, and cultural connotations to avoid misunderstandings. In this context, the interconnection between translation and mediation is particularly important, as translators will also need to play a mediating role in addition to evaluation and advisory functions in the future. Mediators act as intermediaries to moderate difficult situations. All actors involved in decision-making processes are not only interested in the statements made but also in understanding the underlying intentions and cultural implications. The ability of translation and evaluation to effectively empower negotiations and ensure smooth dialogue is crucial. A key aspect of evaluation is examining how conferences proceed to meet common advancement goals. Advisory roles in international politics and at summits focus on developing and implementing communication strategies that take into account the cultural, political, and linguistic particularities of the involved actors. Delegates and politicians must be prepared for the challenges of intercultural communication to avoid potential misunderstandings or conflicts. Professional advisors analyze communication processes and propose improvements that facilitate international collaboration. The right combination of translation, mediation, evaluation, and advisory services can enhance political cooperation and optimize a deeper mutual understanding among negotiating parties.

Another topic is the role of artificial intelligence and future language technologies. Translation software, voice assistants, and automatic text generation might give the impression that the human need to learn and use language is diminishing. In the future, people may rely more on these technologies, which could weaken their own language skills. However, at the same time, technology offers many opportunities to deepen language knowledge and expand access to education. Additionally, technology facilitates access to information and knowledge in an unprecedented manner. The challenge lies in finding a balance between technological progress and the preservation of fundamental language skills. Educational systems and societies must ensure that new forms of communication do not undermine the ability to use language as a tool for critical thinking and creative expression.

Changes in language - from formal to informal, from long to short - might give the impression that language is losing complexity. However, this does not mean the disappearance of language, but rather an adaptation to new communication environments. The human capacity to express and communicate ideas remains, even if the forms evolve. The way we use language is changing, but there are indeed concerns about the loss of traditional language skills, particularly in the realm of writing and reading. Numerous studies show that the ability to concentrate on longer texts is decreasing, and reading proficiency, especially among young people, may be deteriorating. The increased consumption of short texts and audiovisual content can lead to reduced practice of complex reading and writing. This could have negative long-term consequences for language proficiency.

The term "illiteracy" classically describes the inability to learn to read and write. In many parts of the world, illiteracy is still considered a social and educational problem, and efforts to promote literacy continue. In developed countries, where reading and writing are the norm, one might speak of a new form of functional illiteracy. This concerns individuals who, although they can read and write at a basic level, struggle to understand more complex texts or to write demanding texts themselves. This form of illiteracy is not rare and is further reinforced by rapid digitization and changes in media consumption.

The struggle with language often leads to a simplification of complex thoughts and arguments. In this process, keywords, labels, and categories emerge, shaped by projections and prejudices. These linguistic shortcuts often do not serve to clarify matters but act as tools of power and manipulation. They become rhetorical weapons aimed at steering opinions, discrediting opponents, or dominating discussions without encouraging genuine engagement with the underlying issues. Keywords, as concise and emotionally charged terms, are frequently used to reduce complex topics to simple statements. While these terms have the advantage of being quickly understood, they also have the disadvantage of erasing nuance and differentiation. Once a keyword is introduced into a debate, it shapes the discourse and often prevents deeper analysis.

Labels and categories serve a similar function in argumentation. They assign individuals or ideas to specific groups or categories, allowing them to be evaluated or dismissed more quickly. However, this often leads to prejudice and oversimplifies the debate by obscuring the diversity of individual views or the complexity of a subject. Once someone is "placed in a box," it becomes difficult to break free from this rigid categorization, as the discourse remains trapped on a superficial level.

Projections and assumptions are another aspect of this linguistic struggle. Projections occur when individuals project their own fears, prejudices, or beliefs onto others, imposing their own perspective without critical reflection on their conversational partner. This distorts dialogue, as it shifts the focus away from genuine idea exchange and toward imposing a preconceived opinion. Assumptions go a step further, attributing specific motives, intentions, or beliefs to the other person without these being explicitly expressed. Assumptions are powerful rhetorical tools because they often force the other person into a defensive position rather than fostering constructive discussion. These mechanisms demonstrate how language, instead of facilitating communication, can be used for manipulation. It creates a pseudo-reality where the actual content takes a backseat, and the control over discourse becomes the primary goal.

While rhetoric is traditionally the art of persuasion, when language becomes a weapon, it often ceases to be about persuasion and becomes an exercise of power. In political and public debates, language is intentionally employed to demean opponents or distort facts. Keywords and labels contribute to dominating specific narratives and polarizing discussions, while nuanced views are suppressed. Through the use of rhetorical weapons, language becomes a means of domination. Instead of promoting dialogue and understanding, it is used to control discourse, advance one's interests, or discredit adversaries. Assumptions and projections are particularly effective because they are emotionally charged and poison the atmosphere of discussions. These linguistic tools often impoverish debates. Instead of fostering exchange and understanding, they lead to hardened positions and diminish the chances of mutual comprehension. Complex topics are reduced to simple formulas, destroying the depth and richness of discussion. The struggle with language turns into a power struggle, where the focus is less on truth and insight and more on winning the discourse.

Additionally, the quality of expression among modern TV commentators and hosts varies, primarily due to two factors: insufficient training and lack of experience. This results in less professional communication. Thorough linguistic preparation is essential for a successful presentation to the public. Neglecting phonetic expression, which often manifests in high-pitched and unpleasant tones on-screen, can make political or scientific moderation seem ridiculous. An intense engagement with the topic being commented on is also crucial. Without it, outputs risk being superficial or unstructured. This issue is compounded by some broadcasters relying on their technical equipment while placing little emphasis on training and assessing their hosts. In the absence of these prerequisites, engaging and informative presentations cannot be ensured.

Interestingly, in German-speaking regions, the lack of quality in linguistic expression and the distortion of content are compounded by poorly implemented "genderism," leading to a loss of naturalness and linguistic fluidity. This trend is met with incomprehension, particularly in international exchanges requiring interpretation, and causes confusion among linguistic aesthetes and logic experts. When the ability to express oneself is impaired, it affects not only political and economic practices but also, to no lesser extent, art and culture. Such an approach to language, characterized by logical and mental confusion, complicates public communication.

Linguistic genderism has nothing to do with gender equality and, due to its contradictions between language, consciousness, and meaning, is more counterproductive for mutual understanding. Just because a speaker is too lazy to repeat the respective gendered form correctly, does not mean that turning "humans" into "humannesses" improves anything. Let's gender everything until, in the quest for linguistic equality, we no longer know who or what we are. Soon, instead of "mother" and "father," we may end up with "parent 1" and "parent 2," a mathematical approximation of what used to be family structures. Perhaps we'll also introduce "child 1" and "child 2" to avoid sibling rivalries. After all, who wants to bother with dividing names into "grandma" and "grandpa"? It's really unfair to limit people to such binary terms based on their familial roles. "Grampa" sounds much more neutral, almost scientific, doesn't it? Better yet, let's eliminate gender in language altogether. In the animal kingdom, we could get rid of "roosters" and perhaps replace them with "hensters" or simply "egg-laying units." Instead of living in reality, we can just build ourselves a world out of neutral terms. When no one knows who is who anymore, we will have achieved the ultimate goal: absolute equality in total chaos.

Language will then no longer be used to name things precisely or to differentiate between various realities of life. Instead, we'll have a wonderfully interchangeable collection of terms so generic that they lose all meaning. And who could possibly object to that? It resembles the vision of communist uniformity: a homogenized world where all differences are leveled out so that no one can stand out through individual or cultural characteristics. Who needs personal identity when, instead, we can have smooth, inoffensive labels that bother no one? In such a world, language truly becomes nothing more than a tool for leveling everything. The individual fades into the background, and we can all see ourselves as identical cogs in the grand machine of neutrality.

It sounds like the communist dream of total conformity—though not a particularly appealing one. In the reality of communism, it has always ended in violence and chaos. What remains of human diversity if we begin neutralizing language to the point that nothing and no one stands out? What becomes of our stories, experiences, and life realities if they all dissolve into a uniform mass? If we pursue linguistic equality to such extremes that we lose all differentiating potential, we may end up with a bleak, uniform society where everything sounds the same, looks the same, and is thought the same. It's almost a dystopian scenario! The intelligence of language shapes the intelligence of thought and is molded by human expression. When language is stripped of its richness and nuance, what remains is not progress but a loss of the very diversity that makes us human.

## 8. SHAPING CULTURES

The tentacles of interconnectivity extend even into the instrumentalized realms of natural sciences, astronomy and cosmology, archaeology, and medicine. They transform specialists in their respective fields into generalists with a comprehensive perspective. Interconnectivity demands a multifaceted approach to its essence: comprehension, feeling, knowledge, and belief are the key stages.

How can the individual segments be evaluated in their uniqueness to ultimately determine their weight in the overall picture? How can reasonable deliberation work without proper expert evaluation? How can acceptable judgments arise from constant collective lamentation? Social bubbles form due to a lack of transparency. The solution lies in evaluations, which are reflections of reality and situations. This is not the invention of political scientists but a fact based on grounded justifications.

Human-caused missteps can often be traced back to misguided opinions. What is needed is the linking of individual skills and abilities. Interconnectivity works best when it can elevate the intellectual level of society. To achieve this, one must look behind the scenes to forge consistent conclusions. Interconnectivity does not follow the principle of pinning topics and motifs side by side like stamps or butterflies in a collection. A collection categorizes and preserves items, often without connections to one another, except for being part of a specific category. Interconnectivity, on the other hand, emphasizes the principle of relationships, exchange, and mutual dependencies between interacting elements. It focuses on understanding that everything exists within a network of connections and interactions, rather than in isolation.

"The reign of inhumanity goes hand in hand with the distortion of human freedom" highlights a profound problem observed in many societies and systems. It suggests that in times or under regimes marked by inhumanity, be it through oppression, discrimination, or violence, true human freedom is distorted or entirely ignored. The challenge lies in understanding freedom not as absolute independence but as a dynamic capacity to act and thrive within and through relationships with others, communities, and the world. In a world that is ecologically and socially interconnected, individual freedom cannot come at the expense of communal or environmental well-being. Freedom without responsibility leads to alienation and the destruction of the relationships that sustain life. True freedom is not born solely from rebellion but from conscious choices about what truly matters. It is rooted in clarity about values, convictions, and goals that guide us as individuals and communities. It is by holding onto what defines us at our core that true freedom is realizedn - a freedom anchored not in mere rejection but in commitment to the essential.

Inhumanity can manifest in many forms: political tyranny, social injustice, or economic exploitation. When such conditions prevail, the understanding and exercise of freedom are often distorted. People begin to feel restricted in their fundamental rights and self-determination. The distortion of human freedom, in this context, means that the original ideals of freedom and equality are perverted or entirely reversed. This topic is frequently explored in political philosophy, social critique, and literature. It encourages reflection on the state of society, the significance of human rights, and the dangers of authoritarian or inhumane regimes. To counter this, it is crucial to advocate for a culture of humanity that respects and promotes the dignity of every individual.

The interconnectivity of communication illustrates that a situation has now entered the realm of mutual connections between various arguments, viewpoints, and feedback. We find ourselves on the terrain of arguments, perspectives, and feedback. One might say that different perspectives and responses are intricately intertwined, influencing one another to form a kind of network of opinions and viewpoints. This demonstrates that discussion and exchange are not isolated but deeply interconnected and interdependent. Applied to arguments, perspectives, and feedback, this means that no statement, opinion, or response is viewed in isolation. Instead, these elements influence one another and collectively contribute to the development of a discussion or decision-making process.

There are ample driving forces for raising awareness of identity, ethnicity, and religion, just as there are obstacles that block diversity and integration. These forces influence not only individual self-perception but also social coexistence. While various factors enhance awareness of these aspects, numerous barriers hinder diversity and integration. Increased mobility of people across borders has heightened awareness of ethnic, cultural, and religious differences. Migration experiences and living in transcultural contexts bring the confrontation with one's origins and identity to the forefront. This often involves reconciling the preservation of one's roots with integration into a new society.

The growing awareness of the diversity of identities and cultures has been fueled by global movements, social media, and the exchange of information. People have begun to engage more actively with their own identities and those of others, fostering greater appreciation for diversity and empathy. However, these topics often lead to tensions, particularly when different identities come into contact. In many societies, debates about integration policies and the challenges posed by differing lifestyles and worldviews are prevalent. These tensions can escalate into societal conflicts, especially when prejudices or discrimination are recklessly exacerbated. Sensationalized reporting on ethnic or religious conflicts worsens mistrust and hostility, whereas positive portrayals of diversity and integration contribute to better understanding and cohesion.

Based on the provided insights, there are both positive and negative trends regarding awareness and tensions surrounding diversity and integration. Globalization and social media have heightened awareness and appreciation for various identities and cultures, fostering empathy and valuing diversity. This offers an opportunity for enhanced global consciousness, as people increasingly recognize the global impact of numerous issues. For instance, the worldwide reporting on Amazon rainforest fires has helped people understand the connection between deforestation and climate change, urging governments and corporations to improve conservation efforts. Intellectual interconnectivity enables faster and broader dissemination of information on global challenges like environmental destruction, social injustice, or political oppression.

While this cultivates global awareness, it also highlights inherent risks. Digital connectivity, despite its many advantages, introduces unpredictability, such as information overload, the spread of misinformation, and superficial portrayals of complex global issues. A prime example occurred during the Black Lives Matter protests in the U.S., where social networks were flooded with false information aimed at defaming the movement or spreading divisive narratives. In a connected system where information is shared rapidly and without filters, it becomes difficult for individuals to distinguish genuine facts from manipulative content. Authoritarian regimes often exploit connectivity to monitor, control, or suppress their political systems. While global connectivity facilitates the dissemination of information about human rights abuses, some governments use digital surveillance tools to track activists. They also block or censor platforms used to mobilize protests.

In debates, arguments are not isolated; they are always seen in relation to other opinions and perspectives. Counterarguments question, modify, or support the original statement, while feedback introduces new perspectives or strengthens or weakens existing positions. Arguments form the building blocks of rational discourse, used to advocate positions, justify decisions, or explain facts. Yet, in the context of interconnectivity, arguments rarely function in isolation. Instead, they build on each other, contradict, or complement one another. An argument within a discourse sets off a chain reaction, provoking counterarguments, being supported by examples, or weakened by logical objections. Political debates, for example, showcase this interplay. Different worldviews and ideologies clash, with arguments so intertwined that it is sometimes challenging to delineate where one thought ends and the next begins. This interactive nature of arguments keeps discussions in a constant state of flux. Opinions evolve, positions shift, and new information emerges, adding to the complexity of discourse.

The interconnectivity of arguments, perspectives, and feedback offers immense potential. It allows complex problems to be examined from various angles, leading to well-founded solutions. The continuous exchange of opinions and responses fosters innovation and progress. However, in such interconnected systems, it becomes increasingly difficult to maintain clarity and make decisive conclusions. The more arguments and viewpoints are interwoven, the more complex and confusing the discourse becomes, potentially leading to an overwhelming sense of information overload, where distinguishing between important and trivial information is challenging.

Another issue is the creation of echo chambers, where only specific arguments and viewpoints are amplified, while dissenting opinions are suppressed. This distorts the discourse, creating the illusion of interconnectivity, which, in reality, is based on selective perception. In digital spaces, discussions unfold at a rapid pace. Arguments are immediately commented on, refuted, or confirmed. Feedback is instantaneous, and the variety of viewpoints is overwhelming. Yet, this environment also risks fragmentation. Algorithms influence which arguments and perspectives are visible, creating a biased form of interconnectivity where certain voices are prioritized.

Although institutionalized religion is declining, many Christian values remain at the core of European culture, even if they are often no longer explicitly perceived as religious. The principles that have been reflected in human rights shape legal and social discourse. However, the backbone of Christian ethics is increasingly missing. As a result, specific values without their roots are becoming less binding. Symbols and rituals of Christianization, such as Christmas or Easter, have lost their religious character in many parts of Europe and have become cultural, partly commercialized events. While traditional religious practices are declining, many people are looking for new forms of meaning and spirituality in the Indian models of polytheism, spiritualism or esotericism.

Where is the deculturization of Europe heading? Without clear foundations, moral principles lose their binding force. What used to be considered universal by religious teachings is now often interpreted subjectively. Societies that rely on pluralistic values without clear roots risk splitting into competing moral systems. New cultural influences must not be seen as a threat, but as an opportunity to reinterpret old values. Whether Europe sees this change as an opportunity or a threat depends on its ability to engage in an open dialog about its cultural roots and future visions.

The preservation of Christian values will ultimately depend on the extent to which they are integrated into Europe's modern identity and consciously lived. The preservation of these values is possible if they are consciously perceived as core components of a modern European identity and actively lived, not out of compulsion, but out of intellect and conviction. At the same time, this process offers the opportunity to rethink old structures and create a pluralistic yet united society. The decisive factor will be whether Europe can integrate its cultural and ethical roots into a contemporary framework as the basis for a future based on common principles.

Humanity today faces an unprecedented volume of information, impacting sensations and making it harder to differentiate relevant from irrelevant data. The ability to critically evaluate and filter information is increasingly important. Algorithms and personalized content in social media reinforce existing beliefs, leading to a distorted feeling of reality and more polarized opinions. Real-time communication and global connectivity reduce the sense of geographic distance, with global events and trends directly influencing local contexts. Social media, avatars, and online communities enable people to explore multiple identities. This fluidity in self-perception and social roles is context-dependent. The use of AI changes conceptions of work, efficiency, and social interactions. Machines are viewed both as partners and threats in societal development. Online communities and digital networks reshape social relationships and communal identity-building, as traditional physical and social structures lose significance in favor of virtual connections. Whether this is perceived as positive or negative depends on individual experiences, values, and contexts. A conscious and balanced approach to digital technologies is crucial to maximizing benefits while minimizing drawbacks. Intense discussions on these issues are necessary to find a healthy balance between digital and analog interactions.

The lines between public and private spaces are also becoming increasingly blurred. Constant connectivity makes private behavior more public, altering privacy and personal integrity. The relentless need to stay updated often leads to mental overload and stress. The rapid flow of information and stimuli through connected devices shortens attention spans, impacting how people process and retain information. Cognitive overload makes it even harder to distinguish crucial information from the trivial, or to understand complex relationships. This "decision fatigue" challenges individuals to make decisions or focus on specific topics. Instead of relying on memory, people increasingly depend on digital devices to store and retrieve knowledge. This accelerates the decline of active memory skills. The tendency to skim through information rather than read it thoroughly diminishes understanding and long-term knowledge retention. Information is processed less deeply and, as a result, forgotten more quickly. Direct conversational exchanges are neglected, reducing creativity's momentum.

At the same time, interconnectivity requires high levels of reflection and mindfulness to avoid falling into the traps of over-complexity or one-sided opinion formation. To fully harness the potential of interconnectivity, it is essential to remain aware of its dynamics and actively engage in open, multifaceted exchanges. Only by doing so can the advantages of interconnected arguments, perspectives, and feedback be truly realized. Interconnectivity fosters intercultural exchange, enabling people from diverse backgrounds to communicate and collaborate better. Yet, it also poses challenges, such as preserving cultural identities while remaining open to new influences. The exchange of music, art, literature, and traditions across borders enriches cultural experiences and opens new perspectives. This diversity of influences can spur creative development and the creation of new cultural forms that blend the best aspects of various cultures. However, mutual reciprocity remains a challenge, as there is also a risk of cultural homogenization. The influence of global media corporations, consumer brands, and cultural trends could lead to a standardization of lifestyles and values, threatening cultural diversity.

The rapid technological progress in communication and transportation in the 19th century marked the beginning of increased international interconnectedness. However, it was in the 20th century, particularly after World War II, that global dependencies became more pronounced. The rise of neoliberalism in the 1980s and the liberalization of global trade further intensified interdependence. Free trade agreements, technological innovations, and the deregulation of financial markets created a global system where political and economic events in one part of the world deeply affect others.

## 9   INTERCULTURAL PHILOSOPHY


Philosophy provides tools for reflecting on one's beliefs, values, and the world in general. Without this reflection, one might easily fall into dogma or unexamined opinions that restrict the freedom of thought. Engaging with philosophical questions and developing critical thinking are necessary for living a truly free life. Philosophy encourages us to question our existence, grapple with ethical dilemmas, and form individual, well-founded opinions. In this sense, a life without philosophy is indeed one that offers less space for personal growth and critical reflection.

In between, interconnectedness reaches out broadly to encompass the study of psychological states and expectations (psychology) or relationships in society (sociology), eventually addressing history and the evolution of world events. The connection between political aspects and historical ones is clear, yet it pushes toward practical application and management in politics. The foundations of all knowledge in many fields still lie in philosophy. It is even better to prioritize foresight in all areas. The long-term loss of leadership guided by reason has significant repercussions on political performance.

The philosophical worldviews continue to serve as the foundation of all knowledge in many areas, as they address fundamental questions about existence, ethics, epistemology, and the meaning of human action. Particularly in today's complex world, reflecting on the foundations of knowledge, morality, and action remains critical for success across disciplines. From science to politics, many modern theories and systems are rooted in philosophical considerations developed over centuries. A significant approach, applicable in all areas of life - especially in politics - is foresight. In philosophy, foresight is tied to ethical considerations that focus on responsibility, prudence, and protection against future dangers. Through strategic foresight, involving long-term planning and consideration of potential risks, negative consequences in social, ecological, and political domains can be mitigated. When reason and forward-thinking leadership are lost for extended periods in political governance, it leads to grave consequences. Reason is a central aspect enabling political decision-makers to make rational and responsible choices that serve both the present and the future. The absence of rational forces results in poor decisions, a lack of crisis prevention, and uncoordinated responses to complex problems. Reason is closely tied to the core values of democracy, such as transparency, justice, and accountability. When these values are neglected, democratic institutions and principles are at risk of erosion. Neglecting precautionary measures, whether in environmental policy, economics, or social matters, often has irreversible consequences that affect generations. Reason plays a crucial role in human understanding and the actions derived from it. These insights into rationality are often regarded as the foundation of philosophy, ethics, and politics.

Interestingly, many of these insights and reflections find their highest expression or culmination in theology, particularly in eschatology—the study of the last things. Theology weaves a network with specific philosophies, such as corporate philosophy or sports philosophy. Does one wish to remain a slave to material philosophy and its advocates? The importance of philosophy and foresight in politics and other areas of knowledge should not be underestimated. Political leaders who neglect reason and foresight endanger the future of their societies. Thus, it is essential to place philosophical reflection and strategic foresight at the core of political decision-making to responsibly address both current and future challenges.

Philosophy is not merely an intellectual exercise but a necessary practice for achieving true freedom. Without philosophy, it seems fair to say, one risks falling into a form of mental enslavement, as one fails to reflect on the fundamental questions of life, ethics, truth, and existence. Philosophy allows us to think critically about the world, gain self-determination, and free ourselves from dogmas or unexamined assumptions. Without it, we might be trapped in routine, the opinions of others, or societal conventions. Without philosophical reflection, one risks being unthinkingly bound by societal norms and patterns. Philosophy enables stepping back and thinking critically about one's life, society, and fundamental questions. Philosophical thinking can help one discover the meaning of life for oneself instead of adopting preordained answers. It allows questioning one's values and goals and consciously choosing what to live for. At the same time, overthinking existential questions can also be paralyzing. It is important to strike a balance between philosophical reflection and active living. Ultimately, the goal is to arrive at a more authentic and self-determined life through philosophical inquiry. Philosophy can provide orientation without offering ready-made answers. It allows one to perceive and shape one's freedom more consciously. A life devoid of philosophy carries the risk of unreflectively following external constraints. Philosophical thinking can broaden perspectives and open new avenues. It supports leading a freer and more meaningful life aligned with one's own aspirations.

The two concepts of linearity and circular causality embody different approaches to the pursuit of knowledge. Linearity implies a clear, progressive sequence, whereas circular causality refers to cyclical, interwoven, or interconnected cause-effect relationships. Applying these concepts to the path toward truth yields intriguing implications. In the linear model of understanding, one assumes a clear starting point from which the search for truth begins. This traditional perspective is especially prevalent in scientific, rational, and logical systems. One moves step by step, cause by cause, closer to the goal. This approach views truth as a fixed, objective point at the end of a continuous process. Each new insight builds on the previous one. In contrast, circular causality describes a reality where causes and effects do not follow a straight line but are intertwined and mutually influential.

A synthesis of linearity and circular causality could lead to deeper insights into how we approach truth. Through this dialectic, we approach truth via repeated loops of contradictions and their resolution, making the process appear both linear and circular. The breakthrough to truth is therefore not the result of a straight line or an endless cycle but the outcome of a dialogical process in which both ways of thinking interlock. The question of the opposition or interconnectedness of the binary, and whether it goes beyond, touches on profound philosophical, logical, and structural issues. It invites us to think beyond binary systems and explore whether there is an inherent oppositionality or rather a form of mutual interweaving. This can be examined in various contexts, from logic and mathematics to social theories and ontology.

Truth and reality, be they past, present, or future, are unavoidable. Instead of trying to suppress or deny them, it is wiser to confront them consciously. Only by acknowledging what was, what is, and what could be can we truly effect change and evolve constructively. Denial leads only to entanglements, while acceptance and awareness are the keys to real breakthroughs. Societies that refuse to confront their past honestly often remain trapped in cycles of conflict or injustice. The same applies at the individual level—unresolved personal or emotional conflicts will always resurface if not processed. The reality of the present is even more inescapable, despite attempts to suppress or obscure it. It is a common human tendency to flee from unpleasant truths—whether they involve personal crises, political issues, or ecological challenges. Even what might be cannot easily be ignored. The future brings possibilities and challenges shaped by the past and present. A conscious or unconscious denial of potential future consequences increases the risks they pose. Over-fixation on the present or the past can blind us to the necessary preparation for what lies ahead.

The prophetic language of Genesis creates space by expressing that light does not exist at the beginning but is created through the Word. The interconnectedness of space, time, and the "beyond" is illustrated in Christianity through the person of Jesus Christ. Thus, there is a distinction here between Chronos, representing linear time, and Kairos, the special moment, a unique expression of the interconnectedness of space, time, and the "beyond."

It is interesting to note that culture in Europe is in many ways progressing through materialization, while in other parts of the world, especially in some African and South American countries, the cultural experience is often more strongly linked to spiritual and communal elements. If African and South American countries now send more missionaries to Europe, this would be a cross-fertilization of the opposite kind. In recent decades, there has been an increase in the spread of Christianity in Africa, Asia and Latin America, while the number of church members in Europe has fallen sharply. Sending theologians from the Global South to Europe can lead to a kind of temperature reversal, as they bring with them a different perspective on faith and the church that differs from the traditional European view. This does not mean that the Christian faith is less important or valuable in the West. Rather, it shows how faith manifests itself in different cultures and contexts and how it can have different meanings and manifestations.

People lose faith in universal values when they see them being systematically undermined. The constant pressure can lead to burnout and a crisis of meaning. In a world dominated by material interests, human rights are often ignored when they stand in the way of economic or geopolitical goals. Media and art can help to put values back into an immaterial, meaningful context. Reflecting on what constitutes true fulfillment can help shift the focus from material to immaterial values such as relationships and personal integrity. Ethical values must not be traded as a commodity; they are the cornerstone of humanity and a shared future for humanity. The land of milk and honey of effortless goal achievement does not exist, neither in research and science, nor in politics and business, and certainly not in philosophy, history and religion. When did we discover life?

In the classical sense, the binary is inherently dualistic and oppositional. It is based on the idea of two mutually exclusive poles: yes/no, one/zero, light/darkness, truth/falsehood, and so forth. This binary logic relies on the "either-or" principle, where one state negates the other. In Aristotelian logic, which also underpins modern formal logic, a statement is either true or false. There are no intermediates. Computers operate on binary principles, reducing everything to ones and zeros. This fundamental dichotomy enables complex processes. However, many approaches suggest that we must move beyond the binary to develop a deeper and more comprehensive view of reality. While binary oppositions are useful in many areas, there is a growing body of theories and models that emphasize the interconnectedness of apparent opposites or even their dissolution into larger, more fluid structures. In nature and social systems, clear binary separations often do not exist. Many systems operate with numerous gradations or in networks characterized by multidimensional relationships. Hence, the world is not strictly binary but exists in a dynamic interplay of oppositions and interactions and sometimes transcends these altogether. From 0 or 1, many additional "01" can emerge, theoretically to infinity.

The future cannot proceed without ethics. No forward trend in European strategies should separate from it. The fear of losing global relevance must not drive such strategies. Taking a "first-mover" approach step by step proves worthwhile. Ethics is indispensable, especially in shaping forward-looking European strategies. If Europe wishes to remain a leader, the concern about losing its global standing must not override the moral principles guiding such strategies. In an interconnected world where cultures and values inevitably intersect, an ethical foundation that is fair to all stakeholders and fosters global cooperation is essentialThe interconnectedness of competence and judgment plays a central role in this context. Competence here refers to the knowledge and ability to handle challenging situations, while judgment refers to the ability to make realistic and balanced assessments. Together, they form the basis for developing constructive strategies and questioning negative thought patterns. When one is able to realistically assess their competence, judgment can be deliberately used to counter irrational fears. Those who know they possess certain skills and experiences are better able to view difficult situations in a more positive or at least more factual light. Knowing your own competencies can significantly reduce the tendency to think catastrophically because it enables an objective assessment of the situation.

The noble and the primitive are not opposites but complementary poles. Every civilization draws on these two aspects by combining primal forces, the primitive, with a higher aspiration, the noble. These terms exist in a dialectical relationship: the primitive provides the foundation from which the noble rises, while the noble organizes and shapes the raw energies of the primitive. Scientific, technological, and ethical progress strive toward noble ideals such as sustainability and justice. However, the primitive also manifests in conflicts, consumerist frenzy, and the exploitation of natural resources.

A revolt, understood as a struggle against the degenerate element of the establishment and carried by the destructive intent of the masses, expresses radical social oppositions. This phenomenon, complex in nature, can be analyzed from sociological, political, and philosophical perspectives, as it often stems from irrational impulses. These tendencies foster extremist thinking and create a dangerous environment in which nationalism, in its well-known destructive form, thrives. The revolt against rationality, which ends in destructive chaos, could be seen as a warning: irrational actions and the drift toward extremism not only destabilize society but also diminish the potential for progress and development. In an era where challenges such as climate change, migration, and technological disruptions transcend borders, it is more crucial than ever to overcome national boundaries and create a space for universal and inclusive concepts.

This path, however, requires courage and a willingness to question and rethink existing structures. Rather than focusing on separation and competition, the development of shared values and common goals could enable a more sustainable and peaceful future. As previously mentioned, revolts often arise from the collapse of legitimacy in established structures that no longer meet society's needs. The destructive intent of the masses reflects the primitive, born of frustration with injustice and abuses of power. Progress can only be achieved if civilizations jointly develop and implement universal values such as justice, sustainability, and peace. This path demands a readiness to challenge traditional structures and replace them with new models that are based on both cooperation and competition.

## 10. INTERCONNECTIVITY IN SPORTS

In today's globalized world, sport has become one of the most powerful forces connecting people, cultures, and nations. The interconnectedness of sport encompasses the broad range of interactions and connections that elevate sport beyond physical activity into a cultural, social, and economic phenomenon. This interconnectedness manifests on multiple levels: through the social importance of sport, its influence on politics and the economy, and the technological innovations that are transforming how we experience it. Sport is no longer merely a competition between athletes; it has established itself as a global phenomenon that shapes and influences society as a whole. Through this interconnectedness, it demonstrates its ability to unite and inspire not only individuals but entire societies.

For centuries, sport has impacted humanity in numerous ways and remains a vital driver of social, cultural, and economic development. From promoting health to strengthening international relations, and influencing moral and ethical standards in societies, sport contributes to the realization of human potential and the construction of a cooperative, inclusive, and sustainable future. By connecting and inspiring people around the world, sport continues to play an irreplaceable role in the evolution of humanity.

Sport is a key factor in human health, helping to prevent numerous diseases. By encouraging physical exercise and promoting an active lifestyle, it has raised global awareness of the importance of healthy and mindful living. This preventive effect eases the burden on healthcare systems and sustainably improves quality of life. The interconnectedness of motor skills in sport, speed, strength, and endurance, illustrates the close interaction of these fundamental components of physical performance. While each of these qualities can be considered and trained independently, they are highly interdependent in practice. Their specific benefits and optimal emphasis in training depend on the sport, individual conditions, and objectives. Speed is the ability to perform movements in minimal time. It includes reaction speed, action speed, and movement speed. Speed training enhances neural efficiency and improves motor control. Strength is the ability to overcome or resist force. It is divided into maximal strength, explosive strength, and strength endurance. Well-developed muscles protect joints and ligaments from injuries. Strength provides the foundation for explosive movements (as seen in speed) and stabilizes muscles for endurance performance. Endurance is the capacity to maintain physical and mental performance over an extended period. Well-trained endurance accelerates recovery between intense efforts. A solid base level of endurance improves circulation and supports overall health.

The connection between sport and mental development is even more fascinating. Sport not only provides physical benefits but also profoundly impacts cognitive, emotional, and social development. Sporting activities, especially those requiring strategic thinking, enhance concentration and decision-making skills. Additionally, regular physical activity stimulates the release of neurotransmitters such as dopamine, serotonin, and endorphins, improving mood and brain function. Sport serves as an outlet for managing stress and anxiety. It builds self-esteem through personal achievements and the development of perseverance. Athletes learn to set realistic goals and overcome failures, skills that are transferable to all areas of life. Sport fosters teamwork, discipline, and mutual respect, particularly among children and young people. It also promotes inclusivity, providing opportunities for marginalized individuals, including those with disabilities.

The basic elements of sport such as speed, creativity and judgment are closely linked and are continually developed through regular training and competition in sport. Athletes are often required to make quick, creative and informed decisions under great pressure and in constantly changing situations, skills that are useful in almost all areas of life. The ability to think quickly, act creatively and make good judgments can mean the difference between success and failure. The basic elements of sport are therefore not only a training mechanism for the body, but also for the mind, which further underlines their importance in the development of leaders and decision-makers.

Technological advancements are fundamentally transforming sports and strengthening global connections. Digitization allows fans worldwide to experience live sports events as if they were on-site. Technologies such as Virtual Reality (VR) and Augmented Reality (AR) enhance the spectator experience, turning sports events into global occasions through social media and streaming platforms. Simultaneously, athletes and teams benefit from scientific advancements and data-driven training methods, developed and shared internationally.

The interconnectedness of sport extends to social and health domains. Sports programs worldwide promote health awareness and social integration, particularly in underserved communities. Sport is also a powerful tool for inclusion, providing opportunities to marginalized groups, including individuals with disabilities. These initiatives enhance diversity and raise awareness of the values of an inclusive society.

The sports economy has become one of the largest global industries, creating millions of jobs and stimulating local and national economies through major sports events. These generate billions of dollars in revenue from sponsorships, media rights, and merchandise. Additionally, the specific needs of sport inspire innovations in various fields, such as sports equipment, medical technology, and broadcasting, with implications for other economic sectors. Major sporting events increasingly incorporate environmental initiatives, such as low-emission stadiums, recycling, and resource conservation. This evolution influences public environmental awareness and demonstrates that sports events can serve as platforms to address global challenges like climate change and promote sustainable practices.

Sport has the potential to go beyond the playing field to become a catalyst for social transformation. It challenges societal norms and values and provides a platform for promoting positive change. In times of crisis, it offers emotional outlets and plays a crucial role in social cohesion. The interconnectedness of sport reflects the complexity and richness of our society. Sport is not just a leisure activity or competition; it is a space for social interaction, a driver of personal development, and a model of successful integration. In an increasingly fragmented world, sport represents a counter-model - a place of connection, mutual understanding, and collective striving for excellence. By promoting values such as discipline, teamwork, resilience, and ethics, it helps us achieve excellence not only in sport but also in professional and personal life. This holistic approach enables us to lead fulfilling and successful lives.

## 11. INTERCONNECTIVITY IN INTERNATIONAL POLITICS

Interconnectivity in international politics refers to the increasingly interconnected and interdependent relationships between governments and other actors on the global stage. These connections can be political, economic, social, or cultural in nature. Just as the global economy is increasingly linked through free trade, investments, and technology, there is a growing interdependence in international relations, where the decisions of one country affect many others. Additionally, supranational institutions such as the United Nations, the World Bank, and the World Health Organization, as well as large-scale international summits, provide forums for dialogue and solving global problems. Global challenges such as climate change, terrorism, pandemics, and migration require collective responses. Interconnectivity is evident in the need for shared strategies and political consensus.

The emphasis on stronger interconnectivity in world politics is a central discussion when addressing the complex challenges facing the international community. This ranges from economic cooperation to security policy, as well as issues related to climate change and technological innovation. The idea that power should be distributed more evenly highlights the imbalance in global power distribution, which persists today, albeit in different forms. In the current world order, a few countries dominate both economically and politically, such as the United States, China, and the European Union. As a result, the interests of smaller or less influential countries are often underrepresented or even ignored. Instead of unilateral decisions by major powers, international politics should focus more on consensus and cooperation rather than mere compromises. Europe, in this context, plays a key role, offering a model of bridge-building through its concept of "macro-regionality." In recent years, it has demonstrated its competence through its commitment to a rules-based international order and collective problem-solving.

Countries in the Global South and emerging economies are waiting to be more involved in shaping international politics, in order to contribute to balancing interests. Trade agreements, development cooperation, and global economic policies must ensure that all countries have the opportunity to participate fairly in global trade. A fair distribution of resources and opportunities is key to ensuring global social and economic stability. Similarly, responsibilities must also be distributed fairly. Wealthier nations, which have historically left larger ecological footprints, bear greater responsibility for transitioning to a sustainable global economy. Major powers should ensure a fair distribution of power, resources, and responsibilities.

Countries are interconnected not only through their political and economic relations but also in terms of cybersecurity and addressing digital threats. The influence of culture, values, and ideologies is reflected in how governments perceive and present their positions on the world stage. Soft power, through education, arts, and media, also plays a significant role in advancing global interests and shaping international relations. The numerous political, social, and economic issues require multilateral approaches. Treaties and agreements show how states work together. Geopolitical tensions and rivalries have both regional and global repercussions, influencing international relations.

The interconnectivity between governments, international organizations, and other global actors is a fundamental feature of international politics. The complex and dynamic interrelations strengthened by globalization, technological innovations, and international cooperation have profound implications for global stability and prosperity. Effectively managing this interconnectivity is crucial to addressing global challenges and ensuring sustainable progress. This interdependence shapes how governments and other actors interact, exchange information, and respond to global events. The impacts are far-reaching, from the global economy to international security and cultural exchange.

Climate change is a prime example of a global challenge that can only be effectively addressed through international cooperation. Its impacts cross borders and require coordinated actions to reduce greenhouse gas emissions, adapt to new environmental conditions, and promote sustainable development. The Paris Agreement exemplifies a multilateral approach aimed at strengthening interconnectivity between states. Similarly, the international distribution of vaccines, information exchange, and joint research efforts are critical to combating health crises. The pandemic has highlighted the importance of efficiently managing information and resource networks to minimize global health risks.

Transnational threats such as terrorism, cyberattacks, and organized crime demand an even more coordinated international response. Terrorist groups are supported to sow chaos, insecurity, and distrust in democratic societies. By tying up security resources, these groups aim to destabilize states and influence political decisions. Attacks and unrest also aim to undermine trust in governments and institutions. Open borders facilitate the free movement of individuals but can also be exploited by hostile actors. Polarization and social tensions within Europe provide fertile ground for manipulation. In addition to direct attacks on infrastructure and society, the manipulation of political processes through disinformation can foster long-term instability. Financial flows supporting terrorist groups must be monitored, which requires global cooperation. Delayed responses to security crises are often much more costly, as they must be made under time pressure and in unstable environments.

Security alliances are prime examples of strategies to address such threats through effective management of international interconnectivity. Forums for dialogue, negotiation, and coordination can contribute to solving global problems and provide a platform for cooperation. Effective management requires robust systems of global governance that ensure all stakeholders' interests are considered, and decisions are made transparently and fairly. This includes international agreements, conventions, and norms that set the rules for interaction between states and other actors. The continuous development and integration of new technologies must be accompanied by security measures and policies to ensure the integrity of international networks. Initiatives and international agreements to protect information infrastructures are essential to minimize risks. Finally, global economic interconnectivity requires fair trade relations and the promotion of inclusive growth. Trade agreements, investment protection, and economic cooperation should be designed to respect the interests of all parties and avoid unilateral advantages.

In a management context, interconnectivity refers to the growing interconnection and interdependence of business processes. They are supported by organizational units, stakeholders and markets. Today's managers need to be able to understand and manage complex systems. This implies global and systemic thinking. In international relations, interconnectedness manifests itself in global economic interdependencies, cross-border challenges such as climate change, multilateral institutions and regimes, transnational actors and networks. In both areas, increasing interconnectivity calls for new skills in managing complexity, interconnectedness and systems thinking. Executives and policy-makers must learn to operate in interconnected systems, and to take account of reciprocities.

Foreign policy is closely linked to international economic and trade relations. Free trade agreements, investment partnerships and global supply chains are making states and companies increasingly interdependent. Foreign policy players must therefore work closely together to avoid trade disputes, guarantee economic stability and regulate global markets. Thanks to networking, foreign policy actors can react more quickly to international crises and take joint action.

Interconnectivity can also exacerbate existing inequalities, as powerful states or corporations may exert disproportionate influence over international decisions. Effective management must ensure that all voices are heard and that no actors are disadvantaged. The close interconnectedness between countries can lead to vulnerabilities, especially during global crises or economic turbulence. Resilience strategies and risk mitigation mechanisms are necessary to cushion the impacts of such crises. The geopolitical landscape is dynamic and can change rapidly. Effective management requires adaptability and flexibility to respond to new challenges and opportunities. Managing interconnectivity effectively in international politics is crucial for promoting global stability and prosperity. Through strong global governance, technological innovation, and cultural exchange, governments and other actors can work together to address global challenges. The continuous development of these approaches and consideration of diverse interests and needs are essential to ensuring a fair future for all.

There are several critical points of interconnectivity in international relations that are particularly sensitive and prone to conflict. These critical points involve political, economic, military, cultural, or technological tensions. For instance, geographic conflict zones such as the Middle East, Eastern Europe, the South China Sea, or the Korean Peninsula have the potential to rapidly trigger international wars. The struggle for influence among major powers creates tensions, especially in emerging economies and strategically important regions. Furthermore, economic interdependence and reliance on raw materials lead to tensions that could escalate into trade wars. The development of new military technologies and the rise in cyberattacks foster mistrust and push toward a new arms race. Access to natural resources is further strained by climate change, intensifying these tensions. Military ambitions extending into space and speculation over the Arctic region are also troubling indicators for international politics. Large-scale migration flows, driven by war, poverty, or environmental disasters, are a major source of concern. Similarly, the handling of health issues can exacerbate existing tensions or create new conflicts.

On the one hand, the vulnerability of our world is becoming increasingly evident, whether through global crises or geopolitical instabilities. On the other hand, there is a growing emphasis on the search for resilient systems that can withstand external shocks and adapt quickly to changing conditions. This pursuit of resilient structures reflects a desire to better manage the uncertainties and risks of the modern world. Renewed enthusiasm for resilience is necessary to confront external shocks while adapting to new realities. Resilience encompasses not only the capacity to endure but also to adapt and regenerate. Businesses aim to safeguard against market turbulence and crises, ecosystems must maintain functionality despite disruptions, technical systems need robustness against failures and attacks, and societies must collectively face crises.

The interconnected consequences of action and inaction in foreign policy are particularly apparent in how global systems are linked, and how the actions or omissions of one country affect the international community. When a state actively engages in conflict prevention and peacekeeping, it reduces tensions and promotes stability through diplomatic interventions, sanctions against aggressive governments, or military support to threatened states. Conversely, the absence of such actions can escalate conflicts, leading to repression, arms trafficking, or transnational terrorism, triggering ripple effects in other regions. Such instability also impacts allies and global security.

Countries that actively invest in international economic relations promote growth and generate shared benefits through trade agreements and alliances. The environmental domain is equally crucial, as global challenges such as climate change can only be addressed through international cooperation and climate protection agreements. A withdrawal from economic or ecological cooperation, such as a refusal to commit to climate goals, can cause negative domino effects on economic and ecological fronts, disrupting supply chains, exacerbating environmental conditions, and triggering global crises that lead to uncontrolled migrations and even famines.

Neglecting collaboration in climate policy or failing to meet set objectives will result in profound consequences. Without decisive action, global temperatures will continue to rise, causing catastrophic climate impacts, including more frequent and severe weather events like heatwaves, droughts, floods, and storms. Biodiversity loss, glacier melt, and rising sea levels will accelerate. Habitat and ecosystem destruction will increase, threatening the livelihoods of millions of people and animals. The costs of inaction or inadequate measures on climate protection are substantial. Natural disasters lead to direct economic losses from infrastructure damage, crop failures, and production halts. In the long term, entire sectors like agriculture, tourism, and fisheries could be severely affected, destabilizing employment and local economies. Studies show that the costs of inaction far outweigh the investments required for climate protection measures.

The consequences of the climate crisis disproportionately affect populations in the poorest regions and vulnerable groups. Droughts, floods, and food shortages drive poverty, hunger, and increased migration in many parts of the world. This generates social tensions, political instability, and climate-driven migration flows. Inequalities between industrialized countries, historically responsible for the majority of emissions, and developing nations, often more severely impacted, are deepening. The climate crisis is a global problem requiring collective efforts, and countries ignoring climate goals risk isolation from the international community, which could harm trade relations, investments, and diplomatic ties, leading to economic disadvantages.

A particularly alarming consequence of inaction is the possibility of the climate system reaching irreversible tipping points, such as permafrost thaw, ice sheet melt, or the collapse of the Amazon rainforest. These events could trigger a chain reaction leading to uncontrollable warming. Such tipping points have far-reaching and often irreversible impacts on global climate and human livelihoods. Foreign policy measures also focus on protecting human rights and improving living conditions in many countries. Through international cooperation and technology transfer, states enhance their capacity for innovation. The absence of humanitarian aid exacerbates crises and increases the risks of societal disasters. Neglecting global challenges or diplomatic initiatives risks isolating a state and diminishing its international influence.

In both psychology and international politics, concepts of security and the absence of danger are distinctly defined and shape how states and international actors address threats and risks. These distinctions influence how countries respond to threats, design foreign policy, and maintain international relations. Strategies in defense, diplomacy, and alliances are carefully crafted to address these differences. From the perspective of political realism, security is central to the international system.

States seek to maximize their power and safeguard their security interests. Security is seen as a pragmatic goal achieved through risk management, alliances, and deterrence. However, the complete absence of danger is an idealistic concept that is difficult to achieve in reality. In a global system marked by competing interests and constant risks—whether related to conflicts, environmental disasters, or other threats—absolute safety remains unattainable. It assumes no risks, whether military, economic, ecological, or diplomatic. Yet, since states pursue diverse and often competing interests, achieving total safety is unlikely in the real world. States and organizations therefore focus on controlling and minimizing risks rather than eliminating them entirely.

Diverse resources, actors, and strategies allow well-organized and high-quality systems to respond effectively to unexpected disruptions. If one part of the system fails, other components can step in to maintain functionality. Concepts like biodiversity in nature or supply chain diversification in the economy exemplify this approach. Systems with surplus capacities can rely on these reserves during crises. This prevents systems from being overwhelmed by unforeseen pressures and ensures stability.

Advances in communication technologies, such as the internet, social networks, and modern communication tools, enable countries to communicate in real time and exchange information. These technologies are transforming how diplomacy is conducted and how states convey messages to the international community. This presents both opportunities and challenges, as misinformation and fake news can influence public opinion and diplomatic relations. A country's ability to promote its interests through cultural or ideological appeal rather than coercion or military force is another aspect of interconnected communication. This interconnectivity fundamentally changes communication dynamics in international relations. It creates new opportunities for exchange but also demands tailored strategies and skills from all involved actors.

States can use social media to communicate directly with the public of other countries, complementing or even partially replacing traditional diplomacy. Governments can quickly explain their positions and policies, thereby influencing public opinion on both national and international levels. This can foster a better understanding of different perspectives and help reduce tensions. Specialized advisory and evaluation services offer tools to enhance transparency and detect disinformation. Social media platforms also employ algorithms to distinguish truthful content from misinformation and warn users about potentially misleading content. These algorithms analyze posts based on keywords, sources, and patterns to identify potentially false information. Some countries have already enacted laws to curb the spread of harmful or dangerous false news. Supporting high-quality journalistic projects and investigative journalism is a valuable method to counter disinformation. The continuous improvement of these strategies is crucial to ensure the quality of information.

A rapid response is essential to counter disinformation, as its swift dissemination can cause significant harm. Technological solutions, close collaboration between various stakeholders, and constant monitoring of online platforms are key tools to halt disinformation before it inflicts damage. False information spreads particularly quickly on social media because it often evokes strong emotions and is therefore widely shared. If corrections are delayed, the misinformation may already have reached millions. Psychological studies show that people tend to believe the first information they encounter, even if it is later debunked. This phenomenon, known as the "illusory truth effect," leaves traces of the initial perception. Rapid corrections help minimize this effect by replacing false information with verified facts. Systems in place can flag, review, or, in extreme cases, immediately remove content. Some platforms prioritize verified information sources in their algorithms to ensure fact-checks and reliable information appear faster and more prominently than potentially erroneous content.

Control is another key element in international politics. States seek to exert influence and control over resources, territorial integrity, and their geopolitical positions. Narratives emphasizing control can justify a state's actions, particularly in times of crisis. For example, rhetoric during conflicts often serves to legitimize military interventions or economic sanctions. These actions are portrayed as necessary to ensure national security or promote international stability. Success stories directly influence international cooperation and relations between states. When a country effectively communicates its achievements and asserts its control, it strengthens its position in multilateral negotiations and gains the support of other nations. Such narratives also shape feelings of threats and risks, potentially leading to polarization among states adopting divergent narratives.

The ability to react quickly and in a coordinated manner to international developments while pursuing long-term strategic goals is essential for exerting influence in the interconnected global political arena. Intellectual interconnection refers to the way knowledge, ideas, and information circulate among different cultures, nations, and communities. In a globalized world, this interconnection significantly impacts societies and individuals alike. The global exchange of knowledge and scientific discoveries accelerates innovation and progress in science and technology. Through international collaboration, researchers and scientists can more rapidly develop solutions to global problems.

The strategies necessary for managing political and economic organizations rely on precise techniques acquired through specialized training at various levels. These include a range of methods for analyzing complex data and making informed decisions. Additionally, "soft skills" play a crucial role: these abilities, often acquired informally in educational or professional contexts, enable individuals to identify appropriate options, use resources efficiently, and motivate and lead others through effective communication.

The intensification of interconnectedness in international politics demands new ways of thinking and acting. Actors must learn to navigate complex global networks and find solutions to cross-border challenges. However, tensions persist between global cooperation and national interests, as demonstrated by current trends toward protectionism and renationalization. Interconnectedness challenges classical theories of international relations. The traditional focus on nation-states, power politics, and anarchy is increasingly contested by globalization and interconnectedness. Recent approaches, such as constructivism, transnationalism, and the concept of global governance, provide a more dynamic understanding of international relations. They highlight the role of norms, identities, and transnational networks in a world characterized by mutual dependencies and shared challenges. These approaches are better suited to explaining the realities of an interconnected world, where the nation-state remains a key actor but must coexist with other global players. While states continue to wield significant influence, they are now part of a complex network of relationships. Beyond states, transnational elite networks, international organizations, and civil society actors also play important roles. These networks represent interests and values on a global scale, even if they cannot reflect all perspectives.

As international politics becomes increasingly structured by networks, its scope extends beyond traditional state-to-state relations. This requires all actors to develop a broader understanding of global interconnectedness and consider the impacts of their decisions. The challenge lies in creating effective and legitimate forms of global governance adapted to the demands of an interconnected world. This includes groups like the G20, transnational networks, as well as voluntary initiatives and partnerships. Global governance emphasizes the need for a coordinating framework to address global issues such as climate change, migration, or pandemics. This approach underscores that global challenges require cross-border cooperation. Multilateral institutions and agreements play a crucial role in ensuring orderly coexistence.

Although somewhat outdated, the nation-state continues to influence the global order. At times, it disrupts international law and the frameworks of organizations like the UN. However, in many areas, the nation-state is no longer the sole actor and must confront issues it cannot resolve alone. Increasingly, new multilateral agreement frameworks limit national dominance. Despite this, there is a kind of "toxic resurgence" of nationalism in some regions, often in response to globalization and migration. These developments can be seen as a revival of nationalism, exemplified by Donald Trump's

"America First" policy, Brexit, or the rise of populist parties in Europe. These movements emphasize national interests, claim national sovereignty, and oppose supranational responses. This nationalism not only destabilizes the international order but also the internal structures of states. It generates tensions between states and undermines cooperation in critical areas such as climate change, security, or the economy. To maintain legitimacy, the nation-state must integrate into an interconnected system where power and decision-making are shared. While the state may continue to manage certain aspects of executive authority, reactive forms of nationalism, such as protectionism and isolationism, risk harming international cooperation.

Grand regionalism fosters cooperation among different regions, sometimes even bridging old hostilities. It offers opportunities for identity-building and cultural exchange. A shared history, even a contentious one, can strengthen cross-border cooperation. In facing challenges like migration, climate change, and terrorism, regional cooperations provide the best approach to addressing these problems collectively. Military alliances such as NATO demonstrate how interconnected foreign policy actors support collective security strategies. Countries collaborate, share military resources, exchange intelligence, and coordinate strategic decisions to address threats and develop common defense strategies.

In the realm of European security policy, a defeat in the struggle for freedom would come at a high cost to civil society. This illustrates the political irrationality of refusing Ukraine missile support in its conflict. The targeted violence against civilians inevitably solidifies the free world around essential and existential tasks. This is no longer just about protecting a country on the fringes of Europe; it is about preserving the principles and stability that underpin the international system. This conflict has global dimensions and directly challenges the security of Europe as well as the foundations of Western values. Russia's geopolitical strategy suggests that the country seeks to further expand its sphere of influence. Inaction could allow Russia to impose its military dominance over other Eastern European regions and attempt to exert direct influence over EU and NATO member states.

The territorial integrity and independence of Ukraine are crucial for the security of Europe. A geopolitical vacuum in Ukraine, or worse, a Russian victory leading to the takeover of the country, would severely undermine the European security architecture. Eastern European states, particularly the Baltic countries, would feel even more threatened, potentially leading to a return to a Cold War era. Supporting Ukraine signals to neighboring states that the European community is prepared to oppose cross-border aggression, which is an important security signal in the current situation. By acting resolutely and comprehensively, the EU positions itself as a reliable partner and defender of an international rules-based order. This not only reinforces security in Europe but also sends a global message in favor of defending freedom and democracy.

A lack of support could, in the long term, prove to be a much costlier mistake, both security-wise and economically. Supporting Ukraine is therefore an integral part of European defense strategy and addresses Europe's fundamental interests. It helps avoid an escalation that could have even more severe consequences for Europe if Russia were to advance, in any form, into European territory. The stability of Europe and the credibility of its international position depend on the implementation of international law. A failure would signal that there are no fixed borders or principles, which would jeopardize the long-term stability of the international system.

This is precisely what certain traditional left forces in Europe desire with their visions for reshaping the world order. Some political factions on the left in Europe, particularly those with anti-capitalist and critical views of the system, refuse to offer clear support for Ukraine. Some of these forces see Russia as a counterbalance to Western influence and view NATO as a hegemonic power that contradicts their vision of a multipolar world order. Some of these parties or movements are willing, at least indirectly, to support Russia or to treat the conflict as a purely Eastern European issue, ultimately serving Russian expansionist goals.

At the opposite end of the spectrum, far-right circles express sympathies for President Putin, viewing him as the representative of a strong and conservative state model that embodies authoritarian and nationalist values. This ideology is particularly prevalent in countries like Hungary, where Prime Minister Viktor Orbán adopts a rather pro-Russian stance, or in Slovakia, where populist movements also support Moscow's influence. Far-right groups often support Putin's government, considering Russia a bulwark against immigration, liberalism, and the European Union. This leads these parties to oppose sanctions and military support for Ukraine, thereby weakening Europe's security situation and compromising the unity of European defense strategy.

The sympathies of far-right circles in Europe for Vladimir Putin, as a symbol of a strong dictatorship embodying authoritarian and nationalist values, echo the historical alliances and ideological convergences of the 1930s among authoritarian leaders such as Hitler, Stalin, and Mussolini. These alliances were marked by a common desire to consolidate power and ideology while opposing the liberal democratic order of the West. Today, we observe some similarities with this dynamic, where extreme political forces in Europe and around the world support an authoritarian nationalism based on a purported strength. Hitler, Mussolini, and Stalin rejected the liberal and pluralistic principles of democracy, which they viewed as weak and ineffective. Comparable thinking can be found today in certain European far-right currents that reject the EU's liberal values in favor of authoritarian models like Russia's.

By distancing themselves from the European collective defense strategy, both far-left and far-right extremist groups threaten the stability and integrity of the continent, opening the door to external powers that could exploit Europe's weakness and disunity. The Kremlin deliberately uses social media, networks, and media channels to promote support for its policies and deepen divisions within Europe.

Brutal violence against civilians and the targeted destruction of essential infrastructure aim to break Ukraine both physically and morally. Therefore, the European and international communities must not only support Ukraine militarily but also provide humanitarian aid to mitigate the crisis's consequences and protect civilians' livelihoods. Supporting Ukraine is not just a moral obligation but also a strategic necessity for Europe and the free world. In this sense, the fight for Ukraine is a fight for the future of Europe and the rules-based international order.

The interconnectedness of contradictions in how Europe manages the Ukrainian crisis reveals how the actions of various political movements are intertwined, sometimes pursuing diametrically opposed objectives and thereby influencing the security architecture and values of Europe. These contradictory positions between pro-Russian and pro-European forces, as well as between extremist movements on the left and right, create a complex field of tensions that threaten European unity while simultaneously highlighting the need for common values and strategies.

An inability to resolve these contradictions constructively would weaken Europe's position and jeopardize the unity necessary to protect the continent's security, democracy, and values. This interconnectedness of contradictions invites Europe to refocus on a common defense strategy and a clear set of values while addressing internal tensions. Failing to do so may leave European countries in an uncomfortable situation where missiles would accumulate at their immediate borders. This does not prevent certain anachronistic political actors from desiring the emergence of such a threatening situation. Politically dangerous and illogical restraint could, in the long term, compromise Europe's security. Knowing that there is no entirely foolproof air defense system, it is urgent to focus on providing Ukraine with defensive missiles. The interconnected factors of resolving security and freedom issues encourage timely efforts to fill gaps in defense. Rapid interim solutions can prevent long-term damage. The provision of weapons and missile systems is seen as a necessary measure to strengthen Ukraine's military capabilities and defend against Kremlin aggression. The decision of Western countries, particularly NATO members, to supply arms is accompanied by intense political debates, once again discussing the proper measure of support.

What was once neither necessary nor conceivable can suddenly become of paramount importance. Yet, while some awaken, others, indifferent to security issues, turn away, retreat into themselves, and continue to sleep in their illusions. After all, we have all heard that ignorance is a great shield. Why strive to prepare for threats when one can simply rely on hope? Perhaps President Putin will come bearing cookies instead of missiles. If the international community and states do not sufficiently account for current geopolitical threats, the consequences could be serious. The dynamics of global power relations, economic dependencies, and technological advancements allow for no passivity, as threats become increasingly complex and interconnected. The repercussions of insufficient engagement or inadequate responses to these threats would be manifold.

If action is not taken to resolve and prevent conflicts, regional conflicts would quickly escalate and lead to major military conflicts between states. Without mechanisms in place to address these issues, we would find ourselves defenseless in the face of conflicts among major powers. Such escalation leads to global security crises with significant human, economic, and political consequences. Without targeted measures aimed at disarmament and the creation of trust-building mechanisms, a new arms race among major powers, particularly in the fields of nuclear weapons, cyber weapons, and other modern military technologies, would become unavoidable. This would not only endanger international security but also drain immense economic resources necessary for other important areas such as health, education, and the environment.

If governments do not take effective measures to improve cybersecurity and defense, critical infrastructures - from energy and water supply to financial systems - will be at risk. Hacking groups and state-sponsored criminals could resort to cyberattacks to destabilize states, paralyze economic systems, or foment political unrest. This threat becomes increasingly severe with the digitization of the global economy. Failing to act in the fight against climate change would further exacerbate environmental disasters. More frequent and intense natural disasters, such as droughts, floods, storms, and rising sea levels, would force millions of people to flee their homes and trigger global migration crises. Resource scarcity, particularly concerning water and food, exacerbates conflicts in the global society. Without coherent measures against global terrorism and extremist networks, these forces could become uncontrollable.

Especially in unstable or failing systems, destructive forces find space to expand their activities. Without active international cooperation to tackle global threats, international institutions such as the World Trade Organization or NATO would be desperately dismantled. Removing associations from multilateral processes and institutions would harm the international community's ability to effectively respond to threats. This inevitably leads to an "every man for himself" approach, where national interests take precedence over international cooperation. The impact of unresolved global crises, whether caused by climate change, economic instability, or political tensions, would be incalculable.

## 12. DICTATORSHIP AND AUTHORITARISM IN INTERCONNECTIVITY

The topic sheds light on the complex interplay between authoritarian forms of government and the increasing interconnectedness of the globalized world. Here are some aspects and considerations regarding this theme. Once collective traumas emerge in politics, it is often already too late for a fresh start. Yet, emphasis is invariably placed on what the majority society wants - often unaware that these issues pertain to them. Thus, societal and political inquiry becomes unavoidable.

Dictators and tyrants tend to maintain concealed roles for extended periods before developing entirely different personas behind closed doors. Initially, the "small theater" sees silencing and elimination happen unnoticed, until a tipping point is reached where violence becomes irreversible. Very soon, their regimes are characterized by central control, the restriction of political freedoms, suppression of opposition, and diminished separation of powers. Election fraud, censorship, and human rights violations are common features. How does the cycle of errors begin? Or why is it that psychopaths - perhaps especially them - often manage to achieve unchecked political power?

In the political arena, a field where power, influence, and manipulation intermingle, political malefactors thrive on their ability to manipulate or their lack of empathy. They skillfully influence their peers to their advantage, often without the latter even realizing it. Particularly when it comes to mobilizing support or eliminating political opponents, they leverage their relentlessness to target objectives aligned with their power agendas. Initially, due to a lack of deeper reflection, they are perceived as strong and decisive leaders.

A contradiction arises between moral claims such as justice, freedom, and human dignity, and the ethical principles that authoritarian leaders either ignore or distort in justifying their power or through their political philosophies. They often lean on the principle of utilitarianism "the ends justify the means" to validate authoritarian measures. This constitutes a nightmare scenario, as the ethical discourse of utilitarianism is abused. A common tactic of such regimes is the systematic effort to suppress or manipulate moral discourse. Free speech, philosophical reflection on ethical issues, and criticism of government actions are severely restricted or even criminalized.

In a world shaped by ruthless power plays, devious maneuvers, and authoritarian leadership, Europe's approach often resembles that of an unprepared student caught in a rough schoolyard fight. While countries like Russia or China assert their interests with an iron fist and calculated provocations, European leaders often appear uncertain and awkward on the political stage. The question of how Europe - especially Germany - can survive in this environment is becoming increasingly urgent. When measured against the sophisticated strategies and bold actions of authoritarian rulers, European politicians often come across as diplomatic idealists lacking the tools for geopolitical survival.

Authoritarian leaders operate under a clear principle: consolidate power, intimidate opponents, and disregard moral standards or international conventions whenever convenient. They excel at exploiting uncertainties and drawing their adversaries into prolonged, fruitless negotiations while relentlessly pursuing their objectives without regard for consequences. European leaders, on the other hand, often seem trapped in their belief that diplomacy alone is sufficient to navigate this harsh world. They routinely underestimate the determination and cunning of their counterparts.

A stark example can be found in dealings with Russia. Vladimir Putin, alternating between cunning and overt aggressiveness, has repeatedly demonstrated that he has little regard for Western sensibilities. Whether in the annexation of Crimea or the invasion of Ukraine, Europe's responses often came too late, were too hesitant, and were overly reliant on the hope that dialogue and sanctions alone would compel Putin to reverse course. This hope has repeatedly proven illusory, yet a shift in strategy remains scarcely visible.

China plays a similar game, albeit more subtly. Using economic dependence as leverage, the country operates like a mafia-style businessman, manipulating its partners until they have no choice but to play by its rules. Europe's trade relations with China exemplify how authoritarian states exploit economic power to extract political concessions. Yet even here, Europe remains caught in a contradictory narrative: on the one hand, it demands human rights and democratic principles; on the other, it hesitates to impose clear consequences when those principles are violated.

The points of attack in the interconnection between ethics and morality among authoritarian leaders such as Putin, Xi Jinping, Kim

Jong-un, Bashar al-Assad, or aspiring dictators like Orbán, Erdogan, Trump, as well as well-known historical figures such as Hitler, Stalin, Lenin, Franco, Mussolini, Khrushchev, or Fidel Castro, are rooted in the instrumentalization of moral principles for political power, the redefinition of morality through ideology, the suppression of ethical discourse, and a moral relativism that dissolves the foundations of human rights and justice. These elements highlight how profound the conflict between ethical reflection and political realities can be. These leaders aim to expand their power and influence on the international stage. A key aspect of their interactions is the pursuit of geopolitical influence. In doing so, they often exploit weaknesses in the existing international system and challenge established norms. Faced with these signs of moral and political incivility, one might ask how the free world is responding and how it will respond in the future. The ability to act in a coordinated manner and implement a common strategy despite numerous challenges will be decisive.

Authoritarian regimes generally exploit the weaknesses of free societies, viewing them with a certain disdain. They perceive the openness, democratic principles, and freedom of expression in the free world as vulnerabilities that can be strategically exploited. The often slow decision-making associated with democracies is interpreted as a sign of inefficiency and weakness. Political conflicts within free societies are deliberately used to demonstrate the alleged stability and superiority of their own systems, advancing the argument that they can act more efficiently. The openness of the free world is deliberately exploited for propaganda and disinformation campaigns aimed at sowing distrust in democratic institutions and fostering social divisions. This democratic right to a diversity of opinions is instrumentalized to erode trust and tarnish the image of democratic values. Dictatorships also target the economic interests of free societies, betting that these societies might sacrifice their values for economic benefits. This instrumentalization is often cynically commented on by authoritarian regimes, which question the priorities of Western countries.

Scientific knowledge is typically the result of years of research and collective expertise, based on facts and aimed at objectively understanding reality. However, when political actors, particularly authoritarian or strongly ideological figures, ignore scientific findings, society is hindered in many areas, if not endangered. A recurring characteristic of authoritarian political figures is their excessive confidence in their own worldview and convictions, accompanied by a systematic rejection of any information that contradicts their goals or ideologies. Science, with its commitment to objectivity and neutrality, sometimes becomes an obstacle for these leaders because scientific findings can challenge their power or control. These findings are not only ignored but are often actively undermined or discredited to advance certain agendas or maintain an image of infallibility.

This attitude has far-reaching consequences. When scientific findings are disregarded or suppressed, decisions that harm society in the long term can easily be made. One example is climate policy: despite overwhelming scientific evidence of the consequences of climate change, some political leaders hesitate or refuse to take necessary measures, endangering the future of entire generations. Moreover, autocratic politicians undermine trust in scientists and experts by portraying them as elitist or out of touch while presenting themselves as the supposed voice of the people. This rhetoric not only discredits the scientific community but also fosters mistrust toward scientific institutions. The result is that segments of society tend to turn away from objective knowledge and instead adhere to misinformation or populist narratives.

In the long term, ignoring science is a dangerous game that threatens the very foundations of progress, innovation, and the resolution of societal problems. Science enables us to understand complex systems, realistically assess risks, and develop viable solutions to the urgent challenges of our time. However, when political actors - whether autocratic or economically driven - embrace scientific discoveries, they often do so selectively, only when it serves their interests. Scientific principles and ethical standards, grounded in the common good, sustainability, and global responsibility, are ignored or manipulated to promote economic or political objectives. Yet, it is often overlooked that science is inherently universal: its discoveries and methods transcend national boundaries. Similarly, the ethical principles required in the application of scientific findings should leave no room for selfishness or nationalism.

Autocratic actors tend to accept scientific discoveries only when they fit into their economic or political strategies. This is particularly evident in fields like biotechnology, surveillance technologies, or the energy sector. These technologies are often utilized in ways that strengthen their influence and bring economic benefits, while minimizing or ignoring potential risks and responsibilities toward society and the environment. Such an approach often neglects the dangers posed by scientific developments being integrated unchecked into economic power hierarchies, which can lead to social or ecological harm. What these actors fail to recognize is that science relies on principles of cooperation, openness, and the exchange of knowledge - principles that must necessarily transcend borders to address global challenges. These nationalist and selfish approaches not only contradict the fundamentals of science but also the ethical obligation to use scientific discoveries for the benefit of all humanity. In a globalized world, the ethics of scientific application are crucial, as the impacts of technological advances and scientific developments increasingly affect people, nations, and ecosystems worldwide.

Dictatorial regimes often ignore ethical principles to exercise absolute control over economic and scientific developments. They reject any moral or ethical interference. However, science and human rights know no national boundaries. The concentration of power in the hands of Chinese leader Xi Jinping is immense, with many policies and strategies strongly influenced by his personal convictions and objectives. The structure of the Chinese Communist Party (CCP) and state institutions is based on a hierarchical principle, where loyalty and support for Xi and his decisions are essential. In this centralized power dynamic, there is little room for dissenting opinions within the Party leadership or state apparatus. Xi Jinping's leadership style, marked by an emphasis on strong centralized control, is characteristic of China's current political landscape.

Under Xi Jinping, the repression of dissent and opposition has intensified. This is particularly evident in the persecution of Uyghurs in Xinjiang, the suppression of protests in Hong Kong, and the enhanced digital surveillance of the population. The increasing repression of religious activities affects not only Christians but also other religious groups. The government pursues a policy of "sinicization" of religions, aiming to bring religious practices under strict state control and align them with official ideology. This includes registration requirements for churches and temples, approval for religious activities, and surveillance of religious ceremonies. Unregistered or unauthorized gatherings are considered illegal and can lead to arrests and closures. The government uses modern technologies to monitor religious activities, including surveillance cameras and data analysis, to control the behavior of believers. These measures aim to identify and suppress potential threats to state authority. This sinicization has led to increased persecution of religious minorities, including Uyghurs, Tibetan Buddhists, Falun Gong practitioners, and Christian communities. Reports highlight human rights violations, including detentions, forced labor, and re-education programs.

The interconnectedness of authoritarian or dictatorial leaders such as Donald Trump, Vladimir Putin, Xi Jinping, Viktor Orbán, and Recep Tayyip Erdoğan shows how these figures, despite their different geographical, historical, and cultural contexts, often share common interests and support one another. These relationships are not always based on classical alliances but often on pragmatic calculations focused on power speculation, geopolitical interests, and the pursuit of maintaining power. Here are some key aspects of these connections.

For instance, Trump and Putin share a deep-seated mistrust of global and liberal institutions such as NATO or the European Union, advocating policies emphasizing national sovereignty. Trump frequently criticized NATO member states, while Putin pursued a long-term strategy to weaken the alliance. Numerous indications suggest that Russia attempted to influence the results of the 2016 U.S. presidential elections through disinformation and cyberattacks to support Trump, whose policies often aligned with Putin's interests. Trump repeatedly expressed admiration for Putin's leadership style, describing him as strong and skillful. This contrasts with the typical rejection of Putin by Western leaders. Admiring a figure like Putin, whose credo is that Ukraine does not exist and must be integrated into Russia, reveals a monstrous view of power. A political leader who equates power with influence through fear and claims to act as he pleases could lead to societal disaster in the United States.

The relationship between Putin and Xi Jinping is based on a strategic partnership and a shared resistance to the West, particularly the United States. Both leaders share strong opposition to Western influence in global affairs. Russia and China have significantly expanded their economic relations in recent years, particularly in the energy and technology sectors. China is a major buyer of Russian natural resources, including oil and gas. The growing military cooperation between the two countries is seen by analysts as a strategic alliance responding to geopolitical tensions with the West. These nations have recently conducted joint military exercises and coordinated their arms programs. This military rapprochement creates a new dynamic in the global security architecture and further exacerbates geopolitical tensions. The implications of this cooperation are far-reaching, affecting not only the relations between these two countries and the West but also regional security issues, energy supply, and global trade. The international community will continue to closely monitor the evolution of this alliance and the strategies Western nations will implement in response.

Putin and Orbán are connected through pragmatic cooperation, primarily motivated by geopolitical interests. Both political leaders adopt an authoritarian approach to domestic politics and oppose liberal democratic principles such as freedom of the press and an independent judiciary. Orbán has referred to himself as an "illiberal democrat" and opposes the liberal values of the EU. He is known for his critical stance towards the EU, a sentiment that aligns him with Putin, who views the EU as a geopolitical rival and seeks to weaken its unity.

The relations between Erdoğan and Xi Jinping are based on common interests, particularly in economic and security domains, but also involve tensions, especially regarding the Uyghur minority in China. China is an important trading partner for Turkey, notably within the framework of the "Belt and Road" initiative, which plays a strategic role in Turkey's infrastructure development. Both leaders opt for authoritarian forms of governance and have taken measures to suppress political opposition and consolidate their power, which creates an ideological basis for their cooperation. Turkey initially supported the rights of the Uyghurs, a Turkic-speaking Muslim minority in China. However, for economic and diplomatic reasons, Erdoğan has significantly toned down his criticisms regarding China's treatment of the Uyghurs in recent years, highlighting the pragmatic nature of these relations. Through these cooperations, authoritarian regimes gain apparent international legitimacy, using these relationships as examples to demonstrate that political systems alternative to violence, outside of liberal democracies, can function and succeed. They share an anti-Western rhetoric and oppose a free world order. Their methods of controlling the media, propaganda, and disinformation are fundamentally similar. Technologies and techniques are used not only to maintain internal power but also to destabilize democracy.

Especially in times of crisis, when the public is seeking determined leaders, psychopaths exert a particular attraction. As masters of manipulation, they know how to influence others without them realizing it. In politics, this ability can be advantageous, especially when it comes to mobilizing support or eliminating political opponents. Historically, there are many examples of authoritarian leaders who have risen to power during times of political and economic uncertainty. They have been able to exploit the fears and concerns of the public to gain support and consolidate their power. Why do voters, even in Western areas, often fall into these concealed manipulations? First, many people struggle to distinguish genuine emotions from feigned ones. In a crisis, voters look for strong, determined leadership. Their manipulative tactics are difficult for laypeople to detect. Ultimately, many voters tend to perceive reality not objectively, but through emotional filters. These distortions are exploited by manipulative politicians. First impressions and initial information can sway perception. Manipulative politicians emphasize strong emotional headlines to shape public opinion, knowing that emotional messages are more convincing than rational arguments. By instilling fear, they create a sense of insecurity, which often increases the demand for "strong" leaders. The masses easily identify with groups that resemble them. Despots exploit these group identities to promote a "we versus them" mentality. This leads to polarization, where voters are generally willing to ignore their own group's mistakes and accept false information as long as it benefits their group. They utilize both traditional media and social networks to spread misinformation or doubts, discredit opponents, or exaggerate their own capabilities. This tactic aims to keep voters in an information bubble where they only perceive the desired perspective.

On social media, users tend to connect with like-minded individuals and share information that reflects their beliefs. This reinforces cognitive biases and leads to frequents dissemination of false or manipulative information, often without verification. Manipulative politicians exploit this dynamic to direct their messages toward receptive groups. In a context where trust in media, science, and established political institutions is declining, they find a favorable opportunity. They can sow doubt, spread conspiracy theories, and present themselves as an "alternative" to a seemingly incompetent system. Understanding these mechanisms is the first step to protect oneself from manipulative tactics and to make political decisions more consciously and critically.

Authoritarian regimes aim to create the illusion of short-term political stability but often find themselves in crisis when they fail to adapt to changing social and economic conditions. They then turn to modern technologies to monitor citizens, censor information, and control social networks. These technologies are also used to manipulate elections and disseminate propaganda. Interconnection is a product of globalization, where countries, cultures, and markets are more closely linked through technology and trade. This results in increased knowledge exchange and collaboration across national borders. Social networks, the Internet, and mobile communication enable individuals to disseminate information quickly and organize, which can lead to political mobilization and the exchange of ideas. Thus, interconnection can counteract the usurped power of authoritarian governments, as citizens have access to a variety of information and perspectives. This can foster resistance, as witnessed during the Arab Spring or protests in Hong Kong. Authoritarian governments attempt to restrict interconnection by controlling Internet access, censoring social networks, or surveilling communications through state control systems. Civil society organizations and human rights activists mobilize interconnection to pressure authoritarian governments. While interconnection is viewed as a tool for freedom and democracy, authoritarian regimes also seek to leverage it, but only to strengthen their control. In this regard, technologies like facial recognition are used for surveillance, while disinformation and propaganda are also disseminated.

The concept of "slave mentality" in authoritarian regimes as well as right- or left-extremist programs describes an attitude of submission, conformity, and unconditional loyalty to ideological dogmas. Such a mentality arises when individual freedoms are suppressed and collectivist thinking is glorified. Authoritarianism does not allow for the independence of the individual and obstructs critical reflection wherever possible. These power systems rely on mechanisms that crush the will of the citizens and compel them to accept the leadership's instructions uncritically. The pressure to submit to the will of those in power is intensified by the fear of repression, arrest, or harassment. Such regimes strategically use media and other institutions to propagate a one-sided worldview that justifies their own power structures. The impression of reality is gradually distorted to ensure dependence on the leadership. This contributes to the emergence of a slave mentality, where personal freedoms and rights are undervalued.

Extremist ideologies, whether right or left, are based on these structures and the emphasis on dogmas. Dissent is not tolerated. People are encouraged to follow blindly without questioning critically. This diminishes individual responsibility and promotes dependence on leadership figures. Right-wing extremist movements tend to support a hierarchical societal order in which certain groups are placed above others. They demand blind loyalty from their followers towards a strong leader or the pressure of the nation. The enemy images represent a "us versus them" mindset that hinders critical reflection. Violence then becomes a legitimate means of maintaining power, further reinforcing submission to the ideology.

On the other hand, left-wing extremism calls for a radical restructuring of society, proclaiming the abolition of class distinctions and aiming to eradicate capitalist structures. These ideologies also take on authoritarian traits, as they allow no dissent and push for a strict coercive order of the collective. Everyone is compelled to sacrifice for the common good, which inevitably restricts personal autonomy. The class struggle is seen as a central element, with the ruling class viewed as the enemy. Adherence to collective goals is prioritized over individual freedom of expression. Left-wing extremist movements also establish dogmatic structures where individual deviations or criticism of the ideology are punished. In both cases of right- and left-wing extremist ideologies, almost the same mechanisms are employed to promote a form of slave mentality.

Extremist groups need a common enemy to create internal cohesion and to instill the "us against them" narrative. These enemy images serve to project blame for societal problems onto specific groups. This simplifies complex societal and political issues into binary oppositions. The fear of internal surveillance and social exclusion drives followers to comply with authoritarian rules. In such closed systems, no alternatives to the imposed ideology are tolerated. The lack of diversity in opinion formation further solidifies the slave mentality. The interconnectivity of negativity describes the dynamics among extremist ideologies, conspiracy theories, and concepts of terrorism. Different forms of extremism and radicalism submit to common patterns, multiplying threats to society. In particular, the recent political history in Germany shows how these phenomena are interconnected and represent a societal threat as a whole. Although right- and left-wing extremism pursue different ideological goals, there are remarkable parallels in their behavior. Both extremes reject the democratic constitutional order. While some still hide behind the desks of parliaments, others openly advocate violence. Both groups flirt with the radicality of conspiracy theories and terrorism. An illustrative example of this is the increasing anti-system rhetoric, which denounces the current system as repressive and corrupt. In communication on social media, both right- and left-wing extremist groups utilize conspiratorial narratives directed at a common enemy: the state and its measures. They create a black-and-white worldview that confirms their ideology and demonizes the political opponent.

A particularly alarming consequence of inaction is the possibility that the climate system may reach certain tipping points that are irreversible. These include the thawing of permafrost, the melting of polar ice caps, or the dieback of the Amazon rainforest. Such events could trigger a chain reaction, leading to an uncontrollable warming spiral. These tipping points have far-reaching and often irreversible consequences for the global climate and human way of life.

Why does society allow itself to be toyed with by dictators? Is it perhaps the masses, the people themselves, who are to blame? This was the case in ancient Rome as well. Reflecting on the interconnectivity of history, sometimes it is easier for people to accept the existing order than to actively fight for change. This can lead to a form of collective passivity, in which the people are unable or unwilling to rise up against an authoritarian regime. Collective passivity is a crucial factor in why authoritarian regimes remain in power. There are many reasons why people remain passive in such situations. People become accustomed to existing conditions, even if they are unjust or repressive. Change often entails uncertainty and risk, leading many to accept the status quo, even if they are dissatisfied. In cases where people are in the minority, clear or credible alternatives to an authoritarian regime are often lacking. If they feel that a change in leadership or system would not lead to improvement, they are less likely to engage. After years or decades of suppression, they become disillusioned and feel that change is impossible. This attitude leads them to abandon hope for a better future and withdraw.

In repressive societies, the fear of retaliation can prevent people from openly expressing their opinions and beliefs. To overcome this passivity, it is essential to support communities, promote the exchange of information, and raise awareness of rights and opportunities. Education, social movements, and international support can also play crucial roles in encouraging people to advocate for change and become active participants. The masses tend to conform to the norms and behaviors of dominant groups. In authoritarian regimes, this may mean that people, out of fear of social isolation or repression, suppress their own beliefs and align with the majority, even if they privately hold different views. It is the capitulation of the minority of rationality before the majority of violence.

Authoritarian regimes use emotional appeals to consolidate their power. By inciting fear, nationalism, or creating enemies, they keep the masses in a state of emotional agitation, which hinders rational thinking and critical reflection. When certain groups or individuals are "dehumanized," it becomes easier to oppress or persecute them; this dehumanization reduces the general public's empathy and leads people to remain passive while injustices occur. At some point, a response must be made, and this can only work if one goes on the offensive robustly. It is alarming that the urgency of action is not recognized. Without inspiring role models, people will continue to remain passive. Ignorance is not only bliss but also a great means of avoiding uncomfortable thoughts. After all, it is much easier to talk about the weather! The "we" effect is a powerful tool. If the majority supports dictatorship, they must be right, right? Logic is overrated! Raise a toast to the capitulation of rationality!

No parallels, but analogies from history: in the Weimar Republic, there was an increase in populist movements that often promised simple solutions to complex problems. Donald Trump's rhetoric and his ability to mobilize through simple, catchy messages show similarities. Both phenomena use emotions to gain support and undermine trust in established institutions. Vladimir Putin has long succeeded in this. Institutions and norms that protected democracy experienced a slow but steady decline, due to the disregard for rules and the increasing acceptance of authoritarian tactics. Critics argue that similar tendencies are observable in the USA, particularly regarding the respect for the rule of law and the independence of the judiciary.

In the Weimar Republic, certain groups, such as Jews and Communists, were portrayed as scapegoats for society's problems. Putin has placed the Ukrainian civilian population on the hit list. Trump has also frequently attacked minorities and political opponents, blaming them for various societal issues. This can lead to a division of society and an increase in intolerance. The Weimar Republic had a variety of media, which were often polarized and contributed to the spread of propaganda. In today's context, social media and the spread of misinformation present a similar problem. Trump's use of social media to communicate directly with his supporters has changed the way information is disseminated and consumed.

In both the Weimar Republic and the current time, there are economic uncertainties that serve as fertile ground for populist movements. Economic crises can make people more susceptible to extremist views and undermine trust in democracy. Such comparisons provide valuable insights into the dynamics of power and authoritarianism. They remind us of the importance of defending democratic values and remaining vigilant against signs of repression and the erosion of institutions.

In light of the state elections in eastern German federal states in 2024, memories of the election results at the dawn of German National Socialism in the fateful year 1932 resurface. At the other end of the extremist spectrum, there are altered images, where a leftist politician, coming from the central communist SED party of the former GDR, has founded a new party following the notorious example of Rosa Luxemburg from the early 20th century. With a very idiosyncratic approach to revolutionary central governance while rejecting democratic principles in a modern Europe, she is now dangerously mixing in politics. Is the world-contemptuous view of humanity of Lenin again at the center of German societal politics? The explicit intent to undermine the defense capabilities of the free world and, through the back door, weaken Europe's financial stability, perhaps even to the advantage of the Kremlin, must not be overlooked. Mere Sunday speeches announcing firewalls will not suffice to contain the dangers for society. Left-wing extremists have gained increased attention in recent years, especially in connection with disinformation, subversive activities, and the spread of radical ideas in media channels, including talk shows or social networks. It is crucial to critically monitor the influence of such actors on the stability of Western democracies, as they often employ similar mechanisms as the radical right to pursue their goals.

Those who incite class struggle, or are even guilty of collaborating with dictatorial regimes or undermining the Western order, undoubtedly belong in the dock of accountability. Such transgressions threaten not only stability and social cohesion but also undermine trust in democratic processes and institutions. The deliberate incitement of class struggle is a particularly insidious form of division, as it builds on the deepest social and economic fears of the population. The polarization between "above" and "below," "poor" and "rich" is not accidental but is intentionally stoked to pursue political or ideological goals. Instead of finding solutions to inequality, conflict is intensified to channel dissatisfaction, often to one's advantage. Society becomes torn apart, and the danger grows that class struggle could lead to not only social but also political instability. The systematic undermining of the Western order through disinformation and calls in talk shows represents direct attacks on the sovereignty and stability of Western values, aiming to undermine trust in institutions and democratic processes. The media could play a crucial role in exposing subversive practices and bringing those responsible to light.

If polarization in society and politics solidifies, this leads to a hardening of the fronts, which makes constructive dialogue more difficult and endangers social cohesion. Polarization often solidifies when different ideologies move in isolated discourse spaces and increasingly perceive the other side as an enemy. The effects of this phenomenon on societies, democracies, and international relations are far-reaching and problematic. A rigid camp mentality fosters intolerance and diminishes the ability to appreciate other perspectives. In a democracy grounded in the exchange of ideas and the pursuit of compromises, this is particularly dangerous. When the fronts are hardened, some individuals and groups are prone to radicalization. This makes actions more likely, further endangering security and stability in society. Polarized societies often mistrust traditional media and state institutions, as these are viewed as either biased or part of the opposing side. This leads to the spread of misinformation and fosters the fragmentation of the perception of truth and reality.

It is well known that populist movements, both on the left and the right, occupy public platforms to disseminate their messages and mobilize supporters. This situation poses the risk that simplistic messages infiltrate the public discourse. Criticism of Western values, such as the international economic order or the European Union, constitutes a central element of the political programs of certain movements. While criticizing existing systems is entirely legitimate and necessary, there is a danger that suspect forces may head in a direction that calls into question the legitimacy of commonly accepted values and structures.

Decision-making cannot be ethically justified if tipping points are ignored or neglected. This is particularly true due to the ambitions of cunning actors such as Viktor Orban in Hungary, former Jarosław Kaczyński in Poland, R.T. Erdogan in Turkey, or the re-elected Donald Trump in the United States. It is pointless to focus solely on personalities. It is far more pertinent to pay attention to the ideologies that are insidiously disseminated. They must be denounced, not merely in abstract discussions. These ideologies, often rooted in nationalism, authoritarian values, or the reinforcement of the "us versus them" sentiment, pose a serious threat to democratic societies. It is crucial to reveal the mechanisms and narratives behind the insidious erosion of democratic values. Critically exposing such ideologies is particularly important because they often operate very subtly. They do not present themselves as a direct attack on democracy but cleverly exploit the fears and needs of the populace. Targeted exposure prevents these mentalities from becoming more entrenched within society.

It is entirely fair to talk about the horrors of Nazism and fascism, but the catastrophic consequences of communism and other forms of leftist totalitarianism should not be overlooked. The suffering inflicted in the name of these ideologies on millions of people is equally shocking and demonstrates that extremism in all its forms is dangerous. It has engendered totalitarian regimes that resorted to brutal repression against dissenters, opponents, and minorities. A common denominator of both ideologies is the claim to an absolute truth that has no place in a secular domain. However, extremism fights any deviation as a threat and represses it ruthlessly. A tragic aspect of leftist thinking lies in the distortion and inversion of ideas such as social justice and solidarity, which are turned into their opposites. Instead of liberating people, they were compelled into repressive systems that allowed neither individual freedom nor a diversity of opinions. Ironically, there are disturbing similarities in the mechanisms of leftist and rightist totalitarianism. They rely on collective enemies and the cult of personality of authoritarian leaders, presented as the infallible saviors of the nation or revolution.

In a world where ignoring history has become a tradition, one might almost suspect that we are in search of the next great scandal, only to realize that in this quest for the "worst criminals," we have neglected ignorance itself. Perhaps we should simply start by seeking facts instead of relegating past sufferings to a corner of the grand book of history. Ironically, this might be exactly what civil society needs to foster sustainable change.

Extremist political actors generally position themselves in favor of authoritarian trends, populist rhetoric, and challenge liberal democratic values. An effective long-term course of action against the rise of extremist politics is the promotion of political education. Populist actors, whether it be Erdogan, Orban, Le Pen, or Wagenknecht, often specifically address voters who feel neglected by the political elite or live in uncertainty. They instrumentalize social and economic fears and propose simplistic, often nationalistic solutions to complex problems. Especially concerning European unification and the defense of liberty values, subtle defense methods are necessary. Through thorough political education, the public can be empowered to discern the rhetoric of extremism and question it critically. Educational programs that promote the understanding of democracy, human rights, and pluralism can weaken the rise of dangerous movements. Intensive discussion and communication programs that foster understanding of European democracy, human rights, and pluralism can help diminish the rise of extremist movements. In facing extremist politicians, it is crucial for democratic movements to act in unity. Often, these politicians use the weakness or division of democratic forces to their advantage. Therefore, democratic forces must work together to formulate compelling alternatives to divisive social positions and represent them as a united front. A clear and coherent strategy to defend democracy is essential.

When national identity is taken to extremes and diversity is perceived as a threat, it inevitably leads to discrimination and persecution. This inevitably destabilizes the social fabric. Authoritarian governments often present themselves as victims of external attacks, prompting the populace to "protect" the regime. Thus, a collective hysteria develops for a system that is, in reality, repressive. In international politics, the concepts of support and rejection are particularly relevant, as they shape the dynamics between states, international organizations, and other actors. Thus, support for humanitarian interventions is sometimes used to escalate tensions when states reject such measures being taken without their consent or against their interests. This demonstrates how different conceptions of human rights and sovereignty can engender conflicts in international politics. Support and rejection in international politics are closely linked and significantly influence relations between states as well as the formation of international norms and institutions. Understanding these dynamics is essential for analyzing and managing international conflicts and cooperation.

When, in February 2022, the civilian population in Ukraine was relentlessly bombarded, no one yet suspected the impending massacre in Bucha. But very quickly in spring, this became a reality. The images of civilians lying in the street, bound and shot in the back, are etched into the collective memory of the free world. These terrible events prompt reflection on the responsibility of the international community and the imperative to ensure that such crimes do not go unpunished. For it was not an isolated crime of inhumanity. Subsequently, Russian invaders gradually committed acts of rape, deportations of children, and torture - how else to describe acts where, first, hands and feet are chopped off, then decapitated, or where wives must witness their husbands buried alive? The atrocities are unimaginable and illustrate the deep humanitarian crises that can arise in conflicts like that in Ukraine. These horrific events not only question the moral integrity of the international community but also demand urgent action and profound reflection on the responsibilities of states and international organizations.

The fact that a state responsible for grave human rights violations, such as Russia in the Ukrainian conflict, is a member of the UN Security Council and possesses veto power raises serious moral and legal questions. This undermines the credibility of the United Nations as a whole and leads to a loss of trust in international institutions. Multilateral coalitions, willing to act together even in disagreement within the Security Council, should take on the task of operating based on common values and interests, whether to carry out humanitarian interventions or peace missions. *)

The protection of human rights and the respect for the dignity of all people should be at the heart of all international efforts. The interconnectedness of justice in this context is crucial, as it encompasses various dimensions that must interact to ensure a sustainable solution. The international community must adopt a comprehensive strategy that includes both preventive and reactive

*) „POLITICS [@]Global.World . INTL";  ISBN  9783759706041

measures to address the complex root causes of these conflicts and to protect the rights of victims. To create a true

"black box" of supervision, reforms are needed to strengthen the independence and authority of international oversight and control bodies. One could consider supranational bodies with clear prerogatives, capable of transcending national interests and promoting global accountability. However, these bodies must be democratically legitimized in order to be accepted internationally and not perceived as a threat to national sovereignty, which remains a delicate balancing act that has not yet been resolved in international politics.

This underscores that justice is a multidimensional concept that intersects across various fields. To develop effective and sustainable solutions, it is essential to recognize these connections and promote an inclusive approach. The aggressive war waged by this dictator is not the only instance of genocide; he has already committed similar acts against other peoples. The actions of dictators against ethnic groups are part of a broader pattern of violence and oppression. These historical continuities must be recognized and examined to understand how such behaviors become institutionalized and what ideologies motivate them. Genocide and the systematic annihilation of entire population groups are urgent warning signs to prevent similar violations in the present.

The art of dictatorship - a masterwork of repression seasoned with a hint of genocide and a touch of megalomania? But don't worry, dear global community! The "tried and tested mechanisms" for preventing such atrocities are known to work perfectly. All you have to do is close your eyes tightly and sing "Lalala, I can't see you!". They want to have forgotten the problems as if by magic. How else could the famous UN world organization have tolerated the horrific atrocities against women and babies with brutally severed limbs and heads, which were then posted on the Internet during the raid in Israel for your amusement? In the official aftermath of the statements, the roles of perpetrator and victim were then violently twisted. What a sublime irony of fate - we are now faced with the crème de la crème of international diplomacy, the United Nations, that ambiguously shining example of arrogance and incompetence. How masterfully they know how to close their eyes to the horror, ignore the right to self-defense and instead sing a happy song of peace and harmony! Who needs facts when you have the imagination to twist the facts? Why struggle with the uncomfortable reality when you can view the world so wonderfully through the rose-colored glasses of fakes? After all, it's so much more enjoyable to mix up the perpetrators and victims like in a cosmic game of bingo. Today you're the villain, tomorrow the hero - how exciting!

However, accountability must continue to manifest. Not only those who give orders, but also those who, in supposedly tranquil Europe, have remained silent, tolerated, supported, or even openly collaborated with nefarious forces must be denounced. If we seek to hold accountable those guilty of war crimes, then it makes sense that these figures should also be held responsible. Interestingly, it is precisely those who cried out when NATO allegedly intervened improperly in the Balkans while civilians were being massacred. Or are not pregnant women whose fetuses were forcibly removed and whose wounds were stitched with barbed wire victims of abominable violence? These debates are not merely academic; they have direct repercussions on the current actions of the international community. It is vital to learn from the past and to emphasize the moral imperatives of protecting civilians.

Democratic systems face the challenge of being both pluralistic and inclusive while remaining vigilant against anti-democratic forces. There is a risk that extremist actors will exploit democratic freedoms to undermine them. Collaborators with the current regime in Russia are evidently seeking to influence political competitors, whether through lobbying, financial support, or other means. They aim to steer political decisions and rhetoric in a direction that serves the interests of aggressors. This is the typical way to initiate societal upheaval. In a world where political actors, through ignorance or passive approval, allow wars and their atrocities to unfold, it is crucial to develop an awareness of the complexity of responsibility. Any form of complicity, whether active or passive, should be questioned and denounced in order to promote justice and accountability in a broader sense.

"Defending oneself does not mean avoiding counter-attacking", neither in a rational and military manner nor ethically. In this regard, certain politicians, even in high positions of responsibility in Europe, seem unaware. Hence the urgency to resort to assessment tools. One might almost think that some political acrobats, who consider themselves the guiding hands of Europe, have never heard of the realities prevailing in the rest of the world. Or worse still, they believe they have rewritten the entire defense manual but on the smooth pages of an erasable notebook. The question of why a clear defense strategy is treated as a taboo term in one of the major European capitals can only be answered with a slightly misty look cast upon recent political debates. While the world evolves within the framework of globalization, as well as in the currents of a geopolitical revolution, the political marionettes who maneuver the strings of certain European governments seem mired in a permanent state of denial regarding reality. The objections, sometimes raised against a strengthened military or political response, constitute the icing on the cake of absurdities. Those who choose to actively defend are often labeled as barbarians, as if doing nothing had moral superiority. By turning away from open conflict, more space is created for the opposite of what is sought to be preserved. The European principle of waiting for the next diplomatic breakthrough often has the bitter taste of failure. It's like waiting endlessly for a train that never arrives while the station is already on fire.

## 13. INTERCONNECTIVITY OF WARS

Wars are not isolated events. They have impacts at different levels - local, regional, and global - and are embedded in political, economic, social, and technological networks. The interconnectedness of wars shows that they cannot be viewed separately. Rather, they require a comprehensive understanding of global dynamics and the various connections between actors and regions.

This underscores the need for multilateral approaches and flexible diplomacy. Interconnectedness also extends to how international actors respond to conflicts, whether through military interventions, humanitarian aid, or economic sanctions. The way geopolitical relationships influence the dynamics of a conflict can be seen in the formation of alliances. Conflicts in one region often have direct consequences for geographically distant areas. The ongoing conflict between Israel and Hamas in the Middle East, as well as the related crisis in the Red Sea, clearly illustrate this interconnectedness. The effects go far beyond the immediately affected areas and impact global trade and international security. The hegemonic conflict in the Persian Gulf between Iran, Iraq, and Saudi Arabia shows how regional powers compete for influence, while global actors like the United

States are indirectly involved. This dynamic has led to wars, including the Iran-Iraq war, the Second Gulf War, and the Iraq War in 2003. The support of different groups by these powers extends or intensifies conflicts and can sometimes ignite tensions in neighboring areas or even elsewhere.

It should also not be overlooked that military attacks lead to humanitarian crises, which in turn have international effects. The catastrophic humanitarian situation in the Gaza Strip and the challenges of reconstruction highlight how complex the consequences of conflicts are and how they force the international community to act. Wars generate refugee flows that affect not only the immediate region but also provoke social and political turmoil in distant countries. The refugee crisis triggered by the Syrian Civil War had major consequences for European politics. The strategic use of refugee flows as a political tool, particularly by the Kremlin, to influence European and Western politics, exemplifies how Russia is using these flows to act against the West and the Free World. This form of hybrid warfare, where non-military means are used to destabilize and influence regions and continents, highlights the interconnectedness of local conflicts and global political dynamics.

Moreover, the modernization of nuclear arsenals and the proliferation of advanced military technologies increase global tensions. Technology transfers between countries such as Russia and North Korea show how military cooperation influences existing conflicts and creates new security risks. The formation of a "new Iron Curtain" along NATO's eastern flank symbolizes the deepening ideological and strategic divide between different power blocs. This split stretches from the Arctic to the Eastern Mediterranean and influences the geopolitical dynamics of a large region. The interconnectedness of wars is thus seen in the interweaving of regional conflicts with global power dynamics, the spread of conflicts across borders, and the complex combinations of actors and regions. These interconnections make it increasingly difficult to view or resolve conflicts in isolation and require a comprehensive understanding of the global geopolitical landscape.

Climate change exacerbates existing conflicts over scarce resources such as water and arable land. Droughts, floods, and other extreme weather events destabilize regions and create conditions that favor conflicts. These connections highlight how ecological factors are intertwined with social and political developments. Wars undoubtedly have far-reaching economic consequences that go beyond the immediate war zone. Through globalization, national economies are closely linked, so a conflict can have repercussions on global supply chains and markets. The spread of information and disinformation via social media and news channels influences how wars are perceived and understood. Caution and alertness are required, as propaganda, fake news, and targeted information campaigns influence public opinion. For instance, the information war surrounding the Russia-Ukraine conflict has had significant effects on Western public attitudes. Society must be strengthened in its ability to form opinions in order to better respond to the impacts of conflicts.

There must also be measures to address economic integration, strengthen civil society in a free world, and adapt to environmental changes. New technologies such as artificial intelligence are changing the way wars are fought. AI systems are being used to identify targets and for other military purposes. This raises new questions of international law, especially regarding the adherence to humanitarian principles. The acceleration and potential dehumanization of conflicts through AI is a subject of critical discussion. The interconnectedness of war is thus reflected in its multiple impacts on society and the economy, as well as in the way it is studied, analyzed, and conducted. A holistic understanding of these connections is essential for conflict prevention and peacebuilding.

To anticipate and better understand the emergence of wars and armed conflicts, continuous and systematic data collection and analysis are necessary. Various research institutions gather this data to draw conclusions about the causes, intensity, and duration of conflicts as well as global trends. The results serve as early detection of escalation and the evaluation of preventive measures. The topics addressed raise many questions that fall under the domains of politics, economics, society, technology, and the environment. Despite the current crises, there are reasons for cautious optimism and positive prospects for the future.

The invitation to violence by dubious regimes cannot be answered by allowing entire peoples to be subjugated. The loss of human rights and freedom remains ethically unacceptable. Recent historical developments show how some political actors attempt to destabilize societies, subjugate peoples, and break their resistance. Human rights and individual freedom are the cornerstones of a just society. They guarantee the dignity of every individual, protect against arbitrariness and state repression, and allow for a life of self-determination and dignity. These rights are universal and inalienable, regardless of origin, religion, or political beliefs. They include not only the right to life, liberty, and security but also freedom of speech, press, and assembly, as well as the right to a fair trial.

Freedom, especially freedom of expression, is essential for the intellectual, cultural, and political progress of a society. It allows for the exchange of ideas, critical engagement with existing conditions, and the creation of innovative solutions to societal challenges. Without freedom, a society suffocates in dogmatism and stagnation. The capitulation of the right to freedom of expression is an alarming notion, signaling the gradual or open loss of one of the fundamental human rights. The right to freedom of expression is essential for social progress. A restriction of this right can therefore have far-reaching consequences for society. But how does such a "capitulation" occur?

A common reason for the restriction of freedom of expression is the consolidation of power by authoritarian governments. Censorship, media controls, and the targeted persecution of dissidents are on the verge of stifling diversity of opinion. In many countries, this right is systematically undermined, whether through direct violence, threats, or subtle forms of intimidation. In addition to state censorship, societal self-censorship leads to a gradual loss of freedom of expression. People often exercise restraint when expressing their opinions out of fear of social ostracism, reputational damage, or professional consequences. In digital spaces, phenomena like "shitstorms," cancel culture, and online bullying amplify this tendency. This creates an atmosphere where controversial but necessary discussions are regularly suppressed.

While freedom of expression is a fundamental human right, there are also legitimate boundaries. These include hate speech, calls for violence, or the spread of extremist ideologies that infringe upon the rights of others. An open society requires that freedom of expression not be used as a carte blanche for the dissemination of hate or disinformation. The task is to strike a balance between defending free speech and protecting against harmful propaganda and extremism.

Human rights are non-negotiable. They are universal and apply equally to all people, regardless of political or cultural circumstances. Any attempt to relativize human rights or deny them to certain groups is a violation of human dignity and an assault on the foundation of international law and human morality. The acceptance of human rights violations by authoritarian regimes is not only a danger to the affected populations but also to global stability and the international legal system. It sets dangerous precedents that authoritarian governments worldwide use to justify their own repressive actions. This leads to the gradual erosion of the universality of human rights and risks allowing authoritarian practices to go unpunished globally. To counter this threat, the application of "ius ad bellum," the right to war to defend a legitimate goal, is justified in extreme cases.

Escalations usually follow a self-reinforcing dynamic. An escalating conflict pulls in other actors, entangles them in the network, and provokes further conflicts. Parallel escalations drive each other and accelerate. Initially limited conflicts often expand into other issues or areas, leading to an increase in the points of contention. For example, a dispute over resources can easily escalate into political or cultural conflicts. This expansion draws more actors and issues into the conflict, thereby intensifying the interconnectedness of escalation.

Over time, conflict parties tend to maximize their means, whether through increased violence, harsher sanctions, or more aggressive rhetoric. This escalation of means has a direct impact on other zones, as it creates imitation effects or encourages allies to participate in the escalation. As a result, conflicts fuel each other and create an expanding web of contaminated tensions. This makes it even more urgent to intervene early in escalation processes and understand the interconnectedness of crises to prevent escalation at a global level. A full-scale war usually does not end in a year. Modern wars typically involve multiple actors and have complex geopolitical dimensions. Furthermore, the resistance of the conflict parties, especially when their systems receive external support, prolongs the conflict.

In the case of Ukraine, it is clear how the direct confrontation triggered by Russia's brutal invasion of its neighboring country has evolved into a protracted war. The conflict has become a war of attrition, with both sides insisting on their goals despite significant losses. Russia views the areas it controls as essential for its geopolitical interests, while Ukraine insists that compliance with international law and the restoration of its borders are essential for peace. This conflict - initially, the Kremlin had forbidden referring to it as a war - has global implications and involves countries around the world, whether through arms deliveries, sanctions, or diplomatic efforts.

The war in Ukraine also has repercussions for distant regions such as the South Pacific, particularly in relation to the geopolitical competition between the U.S. and China. In this region, it has exacerbated existing tensions and altered the strategic environment. While Western countries are politically, militarily, and economically heavily involved in supporting Ukraine, China is using this distraction to expand its influence in the South Pacific and the South China Sea. At the same time, China may view the war in Ukraine as a learning experience for its ambitions regarding Taiwan. Observers see parallels between Russia's actions in Ukraine and China's potential plans to militarily seize Taiwan. The Ukraine war provides China with valuable insights into how Western countries respond to invasions or attacks, the effectiveness of sanctions, and the role international support and arms deliveries can play. An important aspect is whether the U.S. would be able to act militarily in both Ukraine and Taiwan in the event of a conflict. This could encourage China to take a more aggressive stance toward Taiwan in the coming years, assuming the West appears distracted and overwhelmed. The Western alliance thus faces a balancing act: supporting the war in Ukraine while ensuring sufficient military and diplomatic capacity to protect strategically important regions such as the South Pacific or Taiwan.

The imitation effect of negative actions is a serious consequence of the interconnectedness of violence and poses a significant risk in global conflicts. It describes the tendency for violence in one context or by a particular group to serve as an example or inspiration for other actors to commit similar aggressive or destructive actions. All acts of violence that take place in one part of the world are seen, analyzed, and perceived by governments as possible models for action. This means that the use of violence in one conflict motivates other actors in different regions to apply similar tactics.

Similarly, terrorist organizations adopt violence strategies from one another. Attacks carried out by groups like ISIS or Al-Qaeda have triggered imitation effects in other regions, as these tactics generate media attention and public outcry. The interconnectedness of violence adapts to the normalization and legitimization of violent means. When military or violent solutions are repeatedly sought in conflicts, rather than diplomatic and peaceful approaches, violence becomes viewed as an accepted and normal part of international relations or domestic conflicts. This creates and perpetuates dangerous precedents that other conflict parties may use as justification for potential violence. The interconnectedness of violence in this case amplifies the imitation effect, portraying violent solutions as widespread and legitimate, thus accelerating the escalation of warfare.

A conflict in which one party expresses a desire for peace or calm, while simultaneously emphasizing its right to self-defense, and the other party explicitly insists on war, represents an extremely difficult and complex case. It is hard to resolve through simple diplomatic negotiations, as the positions seem irreconcilable. However, solutions must still be pursued. Mediators could explain to the warring parties that war is, in the long term, both economically and morally destructive, and thus offer alternative means to protect their interests. The defensive party would need to be convinced that security can also be achieved through diplomatic or contractual solutions. A party explicitly seeking war must realistically assess the long-term consequences of such an action. This can be illustrated by examples of targeted economic sanctions. Wars are often started due to a misjudgment, without fully understanding the extent of the consequences. International isolation is often accompanied by damage to infrastructure and even the loss of human lives.

In this case, the situation is blocked by the psychological factor of the psychopathology of a dictator and the support of other authoritarian regimes. When a conflict is blocked by psychopathy, the solution becomes particularly difficult. Psychopathy is characterized by emotional coldness, a lack of empathy, egocentric behaviors, poor impulse control, and the willingness to cross moral and ethical boundaries to achieve personal goals. These characteristics greatly complicate the negotiation process, as such leaders have little interest in peace solutions.

An effective strategy could be to turn public opinion against the dictators by using counter-propaganda, psychological, and economic warfare to undermine their credibility and power in the eyes of their own populations. Information campaigns highlighting crimes, suffering, or the regime's shortcomings could help weaken the regime's legitimacy. When a dictator is confronted with the fact that his power is crumbling or his actions are publicly delegitimized, he may be forced to reconsider his position in order to secure his own survival. However, this would require substantial measures of strength to prepare the ground and create the necessary space for such information campaigns. In such situations, it is necessary for strategies to consider both military and psychological dimensions. Military measures are essential to counter the immediate threat posed by brutally aggressive regimes, while information campaigns aim, in the long term, to undermine the population's trust in their own regime and to mobilize support for alternative leadership structures.

To break the negative interconnectedness of the aggressors, it is crucial to build networks of positive support and cooperation. The international control function in war situations is critical to ensuring peace and security. An international control function aims to protect civilians and counter the effectiveness of attacks. International oversight should ensure that war crimes such as genocide, ethnic cleansing, and other serious human rights violations are prosecuted and punished. After a conflict, rebuilding trust and stability is essential. International controls should help ensure that peace negotiations are successful and that lasting peace is achieved.

## 14. DEMOCRCY AT THE ROUNDABOUT
## OF LIBERAL AND ILLIBERAL FORCES


The term "democratic degradation" refers to a state in which democratic processes and institutions formally still exist but have eroded in substance and effectiveness. Ironically, this degradation can also be exacerbated by excessive or distorted forms of democratization. This raises the question of whether an overabundance of democratization or a misunderstood approach to it can ultimately weaken democracy. Another aspect is the danger of populism, which often accompanies a superficial or oversimplified form of democratization. Populist movements reduce complex political issues to simple slogans or black-and-white worldviews and often appeal directly to the "people" as a homogeneous entity.

Democracy has seemingly reached a point where calmness and vastness demand their place again. Democratic degradation is also a phenomenon that one must be wary of amidst excessive democratization. Environmental and health burdens arise from noise pollution, air pollution, paving over land, and even collective dumbing down, escalating to mechanisms of violence from dictatorships and mass movements. When the violation of human intellectual potential is glorified through the mass substrate of the primitive, whether via large gatherings or, in other cases, through overwhelming noise, the risk becomes evident.

In modern democracies, beyond traditional elections, there are increasingly more opportunities for direct citizen participation, often facilitated by professional and credible online platforms. While this fosters democratic engagement, overly frequent or excessive involvement can lead to overload. Citizens may feel compelled to constantly vote or express opinions on complex issues about which they often lack adequate information or expertise. While democracy is theoretically strengthened by increased access to information, it is practically more susceptible to manipulation, polarization, and radicalization.

Modern democracy in the context of interconnectivity can be understood as an examination of an increasingly interconnected and globalized world. In this world, political processes, economic developments, social movements, and cultural influences are closely intertwined across national borders. This has profound implications for the functioning of democracy and raises critical questions.

Through the growing interconnectedness of the world—whether through the internet, global trade, or international political institutions—national democracies are increasingly influenced by external factors. Decisions made on a global level directly impact local democracies. Examples include international trade agreements, climate protection measures, or the role of supranational organizations.

What is the role of European civil society? The majority of European citizens feel rooted in a progressive environment based on democratic values, education, and social security. There is strong trust in science, technology, and innovation. Many are aware of ecological challenges and consider the fight against climate change an important part of societal progress. Trust in state institutions, the rule of law, and human rights is particularly emphasized. However, when progress and security are called into question by political instability or global challenges, this sentiment is shaken. Europeans cling to their progress like a cup of espresso - it gives them energy and allows them to pretend they have everything under control. In reality, many feel more like a croissant crumbling on the way to the office, juggling between smartphone, electric scooter, and video conferences. A quick glance at the news is enough to show that security is a relative term. One can only hope that politicians continue to juggle the balls of crisis politics so that none fall to the ground or, worse yet, burst. Sweeping up the pieces, they gladly leave that to the rest of society. For the big questions of our time, space is needed to make informed decisions. It is pointless to be swept away by the hustle and bustle of daily life or by headlines, as if all problems were merely leaves in the wind. Responsible politics must already create a little more space, much like when you rearrange the living room to make room for a new, massive library of progress.

Where political ethics play an increasingly central role, Europe finds itself in a position where it must not only defend its own values and interests but also protect those of its allies. This is described both as an opportunity and a mandate. What matters is the relevance of having clearly defined goals and pursuing them consistently, rather than hesitating or getting mired in false security. History has repeatedly shown that the absence of clear and targeted actions generally leads to negative outcomes. This means that the risks and challenges Europe faces cannot be considered in isolation. Global threats and dangers are increasingly interconnected, necessitating a deeper understanding and a coherent and comprehensive strategy.

The interconnectedness of design in global events suggests that, despite growing interdependence, the different elements of a global system are not simply identical copies of one another. Rather, there exists a diversity of actors, perspectives, and strategies that interact within a dynamic and complex whole. Regarding international relations, this means that while common values and principles are sought, their implementation and expressions vary according to local contexts, cultures, and political traditions. The idea of simple photocopies would thus be insufficient to explain the complex and differentiated relationships between global actors.

How can democracies ensure that citizens' interests are preserved in a globalized context, where decisions are often made by international actors? An urgent condition is the increased participation of citizens in global decision-making processes within international forums based on democratic principles. Social media has changed the way people receive information, organize themselves, and participate in political processes. Citizens can connect across borders and participate in political debates and movements in real-time. Politics has a crucial impact on our lives. It determines how societies are organized, what laws apply, and what rights people have. Without political structures, many social and economic aspects would be chaotic or ineffective. Politics shapes community life in many areas, from education to health to social services. A certain degree of engagement and participation in political processes is necessary for the public to be heard and actively participate in building society.

Democratic institutions must create mechanisms to control the influence of external actors while leveraging the benefits of international cooperation. This requires greater transparency and accountability in foreign and security policy. One possibility would be to democratize international organizations through directly elected representatives from member states or increasingly tie their decision-making processes to national public opinion. Democracy today finds itself on a thin line between glorification and denigration. How will society react? The interconnectedness of existential and meaningful questions is inevitable. Reason cannot disconnect from this. Concerns for emotional hope are accompanied by rational faith.

Transparency in international affairs is essential for trust between actors and the legitimacy of decisions made. In a world where information is increasingly accessible and verifiable, the transparency of governments, international organizations, and businesses becomes a decisive factor for public acceptance of global measures. The interconnectedness between the distribution of roles and transparency is reflected in how global actors assume their responsibilities and contribute to creating a transparent and accountable global system.

The question of how to "mobilize the masses" while enabling constructive public discourse is central to the stability and development of democracy. It raises the issue of how to maintain the tension between the emotional dynamics of the masses and the need for rational, informed decisions. In democratic systems, the challenge is to not only mobilize people on an emotional level but also to integrate them into rational decision-making processes. The reference to the appeal of mass movements and the danger of "collapse" precisely addresses this balance. To focus public discourse on constructive alternatives, a society must elevate the level of political education and media literacy. It is important that citizens are not only emotionally engaged but also possess the knowledge and skills necessary to understand and discuss complex political and social issues.

The interconnection between demographic insights, such as opinion polls, and factual realities highlights how crucial the quality and credibility of information, communication, and education are in a democracy. Indeed, there are often discrepancies between what polls present as public opinion and actual facts. These divergences can be attributed to various factors and influence how certain topics are accepted or rejected. Sometimes, the media prioritize issues that do not accurately reflect factual realities. Sensational or emotionally charged content resonates more, while sober facts often fade into the background. Facts often have less impact than emotional appeals. As a result, polling outcomes can be influenced by emotionally driven narratives.

Acceptance is not achieved solely through the dissemination of facts but also through trust in the sources of these facts, cultural values, and personal involvement. Additionally, people tend to seek information that confirms their existing beliefs, even if those beliefs are factually incorrect. For example, while science can demonstrate the economic benefits of migration, public acceptance often remains low if fears of social insecurity prevail. Another example is the energy transition: despite scientific consensus on its necessity, resistance persists when people perceive higher costs or disadvantages. When international political actors rely on superficial or manipulated arguments - such as propaganda, biased narratives, or incomplete data - their decisions often lead to deceptive outcomes, or "apparent results." These results may suggest short-term successes but are often unsustainable in the long term and can even have destructive consequences. For instance, political entities that base their environmental policies on cosmetic measures and apparent successes, such as greenwashing, risk exacerbating real ecological challenges. The results may look good on paper but fail to solve problems sustainably. In peace negotiations, where symbolic compromises are sought instead of genuine conflict resolution, unstable agreements emerge. These may be presented as successes but quickly collapse because the underlying issues remain unresolved. Governments that portray themselves as peacekeepers or human rights defenders through superficial arguments, while their actions reveal the opposite, damage their international reputation. A prime example is the discrepancy between foreign policy rhetoric and actual economic or military interests.

## 15. UNHEALTHY PARTY-POLITICS

Toxic politics refers to an approach that deliberately employs political strategies and behaviors rooted in hostility, division, and irrationality. This type of politics aims to polarize societal discourse, delegitimize opponents, and replace rational debates with emotional manipulation. It often relies on stoking fears, creating "us versus them" narratives, and fostering distrust in institutions and the media.

Hostility is frequently used as a tool in partisan politics to weaken opponents and mobilize one's own base. This can manifest as hate speech, personal attacks, or the demonization of specific groups or individuals. Hostility is used to stir emotions like anger and hatred, poisoning the political atmosphere. Populist politicians exploit such polarizing rhetoric to rally their supporters by claiming that "the elite" or "foreigners" are the root cause of all problems. This leads to dangerous societal divisions. Parties often polarize political opinions by hardening their positions to appeal to voters. This splits society, as political debates become increasingly binary and consensus becomes harder to achieve. This phenomenon is clearly visible in the United States as well as in European countries.

Toxic politics thrives along ethnic, religious, social, or ideological lines. Instead of emphasizing commonalities, this type of politics highlights differences and deepens divides between various societal groups. In ill-informed discussions, the topic of migration is often exploited to intensify social tensions. In this way, agitators divide society by portraying migration as a threat to culture, the economy, or security, thereby stoking fears. This method frequently relies on irrationality and the distortion of facts to manipulate people. Rather than encouraging factual debates, the truth is deliberately twisted or ignored. Facts are relativized, and emotional narratives dominate political discourse. For example, climate change deniers spread false information to undermine scientific findings and prevent political measures against climate change. This strategy relies on disinformation and sows doubt about established scientific facts.

In the context of migration, it is rarely communicated that migration has been a constant in human history. From the expansion of Homo sapiens across continents to the migrations of antiquity and the economic migrations of modern times, migration has always been present. It should be emphasized more often that, after periods of economic decline, migration has frequently been followed by significant progress, whether in antiquity, ancient Rome, the Middle

Ages, or modern times. Deficits have often driven innovation, growth, and benefits. The same might occur in the 21st century. It would be even more important to accompany migration with successful strategies. Through planned segmentation, evaluation, and prioritization, new progress could be initiated. Nationalist isolation, likened to "cultural inbreeding," must be avoided at all costs, as it leads to political idiocy. A society that focuses solely on itself and avoids exchanges with other cultures or nations becomes intellectually and politically impoverished. This metaphorical "inbreeding" stifles new impulses and leads to the deterioration of political culture, which can be described as political idiocy. Nationalism, often accompanied by a desire for purity and separation from other peoples, is always counterproductive. Instead of enriching society, it leads to a retreat into narrow, often outdated ideas that hinder progress and limit the ability to engage in global dialogue.

Destructive politics deliberately plays on people's fears and concerns to gain political support. This makes rational discussions more difficult and oversimplifies complex problems. A narrative is constructed in which one's own group is portrayed as the victim, while opponents are depicted as powerful enemies. Authoritarian leaders often present themselves as the last defenders of their nation against external and internal enemies, to gain support and consolidate power. The result is a decline in trust in democratic processes, leading to political apathy or radicalization. When political opponents are no longer seen as legitimate actors but as enemies, the risk of political violence increases.

Extremist groups that benefit from toxic rhetoric gain influence and fuel the escalation of violence. Countries divided by toxic politics risk sliding into authoritarian systems, as societal pressure to protect democratic norms diminishes. Polarized societies tend to be unstable, hindering investment and innovation, and causing long-term economic harm. It is therefore crucial to rely on facts and well-founded information. Independent media, scientists, and political institutions must work together to expose misinformation and better inform the population. Political education can help citizens engage with political information critically and reflectively.

Political parties are outdated. As an anachronistic model inherited from history, they symbolize political nepotism and rivalry. Increasingly, citizens express frustration when they feel that parties are incapable of effectively addressing the urgent problems facing society. Traditional parties are notoriously known for using their power for internal conflicts, lobbying, and conflicts of interest that do not serve the common good. They adapt their rhetoric to current political circumstances, giving the impression that they are engaging in political opportunism rather than standing on firm principles. This creates the perception that their statements are not to be taken seriously, that they are merely a means to an end, quickly revised after elections or in other contexts. In this light, alternative political models, such as interest-based initiatives, movements, or discursive democratic approaches, could appear as contemporary solutions. These alternatives might be more flexible and better able to respond to the needs of the population without being constrained by the rigid structures of established systems.

The contrast between ordo-political bureaucratic thinking and problem-solving management thinking reflects a fundamental conflict in modern political systems. This conflict is evident in the tension between striving for stability and the need for flexible adaptation. A central task of intermediary institutions is to provide translations between lived experience and systemic processes. They help make the diverse action rationalities, communication modes, and frames of meaning of various actors understandable. Acting as amplifiers of resonance, intermediary institutions activate and challenge entrenched structures. They function as political mediators of modernization by identifying dysfunctions and initiating modernization processes. These institutions are found in NGOs, media outlets, and consulting, evaluation, and rating agencies. They become indispensable links in complex societies, strengthening social cohesion. Their influence requires a high degree of transparency and accountability to optimally fulfill their role in serving society. Intermediary actors occupy a position between system assimilation and conflict orientation. They practice conflictual cooperation, combining critical trust and assertive conciliation.

The classical form of party organization is increasingly perceived as too slow and inflexible. In times of dynamic political and societal changes, they seem to be losing touch with everyday realities. While parties, with their clearly defined statutes, still lumber through the public scene, it is evident that the public increasingly favors the philosophies of political movements or loosely organized clusters. This trend reflects a desire for flexibility, diversity, and direct participation—qualities that traditional party structures often no longer offer. Political clusters encourage cooperation across traditional ideological or organizational boundaries.

One potential drawback is their reliance on consensus, which can be difficult to achieve. Modern political management must address this challenge. The goal is to create an organizational mix to make democracy more resilient and inclusive. Such a symbiosis could at least temporarily meet the demands of an increasingly fragmented and dynamic society while remaining focused on unity. A system without parties would be less prone to ideological turf wars. Groups could pragmatically focus on finding the best solutions for specific problems instead of prioritizing partisan interests. The idea of viewing "responsibility groups" as an alternative to parties aims to reform democracy by potentially allowing for greater flexibility and cooperation in governance. This approach could offer several advantages over the current partisan system.

It seeks to group responsibilities based on competencies and interests rather than focusing on ideological divisions, as is the case with political parties. While parties compete for power, responsibility groups could aim for cooperation and collaborative problem-solving. Another modern format for democracy could involve central governments with divided competencies. This structure could promote specialization, with each sub-government or department focusing on specific issues. This might lead to more in-depth, competent, and faster decision-making. Personnel in these new democratic formats must be inclusive of all adaptation mechanisms, well-trained, and exceed average capabilities. At this point, a professional assessment of skills and abilities becomes essential. Of course, even major corporations are not immune to mismanagement, as demonstrated by the automotive industry. Perhaps an unexpected saturation level led to less attention being paid to management potential. In politics, so far, popularity metrics have been prioritized over expertise and personal charisma. It is therefore unsurprising that certain figures have risen to the highest offices.A reform towards a fact-based and competence-oriented selection process is absolutely necessary in both areas. Without this change, democratic structures risk losing credibility, and businesses may fail to keep up with future trends. The focus should be on promoting long-term thinking and sustainable action, rather than short-term popularity or mere profit-seeking.

Emotions must be integrated into the framework of rational political management. This is a demanding yet necessary task to make political processes both more human and more effective. Emotions are an integral part of the human experience and influence not only the perception of politics but also decision-making and social dynamics. They should not be repressed but rather meaningfully integrated. Emotions are a powerful resource in politics that must be channeled consciously instead of being suppressed. The framework of rational management should ensure that emotions do not act manipulatively or destructively, but constructively and in accordance with fact-based arguments. It is about finding a balance, asserting that emotions are a driving force while rationality serves as a guiding instrument. Politics becomes much simpler when feelings align within the framework of rationality. What is troubling is that mass emotions sometimes do not know they should be guided. The hope that the internal resistance of rational forces prevails over speculation and emotional manipulation is of great urgency, both politically and in social debate. Reason and objectivity, once the cornerstones of public discourse, are increasingly under pressure. It is imperative to bring these principles back to the forefront, without neglecting the emotional dimension of human interaction. Reason may sometimes be overshadowed, but its strength lies in its durability and its capacity to maintain relevance when conflicts escalate.

How does direct democracy present itself in the modern era? Rather than having citizen councils or people's courts based on past patterns, where emotionally driven and ideologically motivated mass movements dominate discussions, modern democracy requires participation through rational mechanisms such as evidence-based metrics and evaluations, which would then be discussed discursively. This would emphasize objective, verifiable data and foster a fact-based discursive debate. It would improve the quality of electoral processes and strengthen trust in democratic procedures. With clearly discussed indicators, the public could better understand which political measures are effective and which are not. Digitization has significantly accelerated interconnectedness. Expert opinions and research findings are more easily accessible and can be directly disseminated by professionals or institutions via social media or during public roundtables.

In such a communication process, where the interconnectivity of expertise and published opinions is at the forefront, the interested public is better informed and can prepare for political elections. This would represent a fundamental change in political culture, where rational knowledge based on data is placed more at the center. If the public feels that it can actually make an informed choice thanks to accurate and easily accessible information about relevant issues, this could increase voter participation. Many voters who feel overwhelmed by the lack of reliable information or by complex subjects could be motivated by such a process.

Who are the shy voters? They might have a greater influence than the unwavering ones, once they are properly informed. Being quite intelligent, they can also acquire knowledge through study. They might shy away from political discussions and campaigns, often out of frustration, disinterest, or dissatisfaction with the options available. They are less ideologically fixed and often approach political topics neutrally or indecisively. Due to their skepticism, they might better react to the question of how well their interests are represented by political actors. However, if they were reached and mobilized by targeted and grounded information, they would play a decisive role in electoral choices. As they are potentially more receptive to objective arguments and information, they can often be better convinced by knowledge than voters who already hold firm or extreme opinions.

Through the dissemination of fact-based knowledge and the strong inclusion of expert opinions in public debate, complex political subjects are discussed from an objective standpoint. This creates an atmosphere where radical and emotionally charged statements resonate less because they do not align with verifiable facts. Since radical parties often exploit fears, uncertainties, and economic or social tensions to mobilize voters, transparent information would allow for rapid relativization of such concerns. In a political environment based on rational information and facts, all political parties, including radical ones, must justify their positions. They can no longer simply make vague assertions or false promises without being held accountable. In such a system, the media and the public could hold them more effectively accountable by demanding solid evidence and facts. Radical parties often benefit from filter bubbles in social media, which allow them to target their extreme messages to specific groups. If the entire democratic process increasingly relies on realistic roundtables, these filter bubbles could be broken.

Populists and radical parties often operate with the scapegoat concept, assigning specific groups or factors responsibility for all societal problems, such as "the elites" or globalization. However, if political discourse rests on rational argumentation and scientific knowledge, such scapegoat narratives can be quickly refuted. The public would better understand that societal problems are more complex and cannot simply be resolved by blaming particular groups. In this context, the professionalization of rating agencies and think tanks seems more important than popularity projections and indices.

These often reflect only the short-term impression of the public and are heavily influenced by emotions or media. They provide little insight into the actual effectiveness of political measures and are vulnerable to short-term trends and moods. Professional think tanks and rating agencies would rely on evidence-based analyses and scientific methods to evaluate the effectiveness of political programs. This would allow the public to make better comparisons and take more informed voting decisions, rather than relying on media campaigns or popular sentiments.

The idea that the free market and independent agencies represent a more effective alternative for assessing innovation capacity and the investment climate presents compelling arguments. Independent political agencies in the free market are less sensitive to political influences and lobbying, promising more objective and impartial evaluations. Market-based organizations respond more quickly to economic and political changes and better capture current trends. When multiple agencies are in competition, this leads to higher quality reporting and analysis. Agencies must therefore develop innovative and precise methods to stand out from the competition.

What is evidence-based politics? The approach of basing policy decisions on scientific knowledge creates rational and verifiable foundations for political measures. This is particularly important in areas such as climate policy, health, or education, where complex relationships and long-term effects require thorough analysis. An essential task of recommendations stemming from future professional conferences is to make this knowledge accessible and understandable to the public and policymakers. Future conferences, typically organized by experts from various fields, provide a structured platform to discuss long-term developments, opportunities, and challenges in politics, economics, and science. The importance of such conferences lies not only in analyzing current and future challenges but also in jointly developing innovative solutions and strategies. Their results provide valuable insights and directions that influence political decision-making and thereby establish a bridge between science, expertise, and concrete political measures. Through targeted publication in reports, scientific articles, or public debates, it is ensured that the developed proposals are transparent and understandable, and that they serve as a basis for evidence-based political decisions. Given that societal issues are multidimensional and require interdisciplinary approaches, politics has the opportunity to exploit synergies between different disciplines and to decide how to prioritize when different paradigms intersect.

Online platforms and e-democracy initiatives allow a broad public to participate in political debates. The challenge lies in ensuring that this participation is of high quality and representative.

To promote acceptance and understanding of evidence-based politics, clear and comprehensible communication of knowledge is valuable. Low barriers and informal exchanges facilitate the understanding of scientific topics and direct communication between science and society. Complex issues must be presented in a way that is understandable to non-experts, without losing scientific accuracy. The institutions involved must act transparently and openly to build trust in their statements and recommendations. It is also important to account for uncertainties and the knowledge acquisition process.

Such approaches could be more flexible and adaptable to meet the dynamic challenges of our time. Project-based organizations allow for a focus on specific challenges and the development of creative solutions, rather than getting lost in ideological debates. Politically interested individuals could engage in projects that align with their interests and values, which could lead to a more credible community and collaboration. Project movements are well-suited to bring together experts from different fields to find more comprehensive and innovative solutions. Unlike rigid political structures, project movements respond quickly to changes and societal needs. By focusing on specific issues, sustainable solutions become easier to achieve. A shift towards a more dynamic, inclusive, and effective approach to societal problems can only benefit society and its politics. It would be exciting to see how such movements evolve and what concrete projects arise from them.

## 16. PSYCHOLOGY OF INTERNATIONAL RELATIONS

International politics is characterized by a constant interplay between resistance and balance, as various states, actors, and interests either compete or cooperate. These two dynamics – resistance to existing orders, norms, or power relations on one hand, and attempts to create balance or consensus on the other – shape geopolitical events in complex ways. The concepts of frustration and abandonment in politics refer to the reciprocal relationship between the feeling of frustration and the decision to abandon a task or goal. These phenomena can be linked in a feedback loop, especially in challenging situations. In international relations, the interconnection between frustration and abandonment is particularly evident in negotiations and conflict resolution. This dynamic arises when governments and their actors strive for extended periods to achieve political objectives but encounter obstacles and blockages.

In international negotiations, frustration can build when progress is slow or negotiations are stalled for prolonged periods. Examples include long-standing peace negotiations or trade agreements where the interests of the involved parties diverge. When solutions are not achieved, frustration intensifies. Persistent frustration may lead an actor to withdraw from negotiations, deeming the process overly burdensome or hopeless. This often results in the breakdown of diplomatic relations or the escalation of conflicts. The Middle East conflict is a classic example, where decades of frustration over the lack of progress have frequently led to the cessation of talks or abandonment of negotiations. In military conflicts, frustration can develop on both sides when goals are not achieved or the conflict drags on unexpectedly. This is particularly evident in occupations, guerrilla wars, or asymmetric conflicts, where the resilience of the opposing side provokes frustration with military power. International cooperation to combat climate change effects is also often marked by frustration, as many countries fail to adopt the measures needed to meet global climate goals. This frustration can arise among countries advocating ambitious actions and those that perceive the economic costs of such measures as too high.

International agreements like the Paris Climate Accord and national climate laws establish binding guidelines that provide planning security. By implementing support programs for sustainable technologies and renewable energies, creating incentives for low-emission solutions, and introducing strict regulations, governments set the framework for climate transformation. Climate models, research on renewable energies, and the development of innovative technologies provide a scientifically grounded orientation for decision-making. To achieve climate goals, science must be closely integrated with policy, offering regular advice based on scientific findings. Projects such as public-private partnerships or collaborations between research institutions and industrial companies create space for experimentation and innovation. Without decisive action, global temperatures will continue to rise, leading to catastrophic climate consequences. These include more frequent and intense weather extremes such as heatwaves, droughts, floods, and storms. Biodiversity loss, glacier melt, and sea-level rise will accelerate. The destruction of habitats and ecosystems will increase, threatening the livelihoods of millions of people and animals.

The costs of inaction or insufficient climate protection measures are substantial. Natural disasters cause direct economic losses due to destroyed infrastructure, crop failures, and production shutdowns. In the long term, entire economic sectors such as agriculture, tourism, and fisheries will be so severely affected that jobs and local economic systems will become destabilized. Droughts, floods, and food shortages lead to poverty, hunger, and increased migration. This, in turn, is reflected in social tensions, political instabilities, and an increase in climate-related refugee flows. The climate crisis is a global problem requiring joint efforts, and countries that ignore climate targets should face isolation by the international community. This would affect trade relations, investments, and diplomatic relations, resulting in economic disadvantages for the countries concerned.

The global demand for environmentally friendly products and services is growing, and companies that adopt sustainability early gain long-term competitive advantages. A particularly threatening consequence of inaction is the possibility that the climate system could reach certain irreversible tipping points. These include the thawing of permafrost, the melting of polar ice caps, or the dieback of the Amazon rainforest. Such events could trigger a chain reaction, leading to an uncontrollable warming spiral. These tipping points have far-reaching and often irreversible consequences for the global climate and human livelihoods.

When are anomalies in governments or rulers recognized? Certain mechanisms, institutions, and actors focus on existing norms, depending on political, social, and legal frameworks. In societies with a free press, independent media are tasked with exposing misconduct or abuse of power. Journalists investigate corruption, abuse of power, or illegitimate actions by governments and make them public. This often occurs in real-time, when unusual decisions are made or allegations of corruption emerge. In political systems with a functioning opposition, this opposition also monitors events. Opposition parties or politicians can point out anomalies by publicly criticizing inappropriate government actions, initiating parliamentary investigations, or pursuing legal actions. An independent judiciary is another key mechanism for detecting and examining anomalies. Courts can assess the constitutionality of government decisions.

At the international level, organizations like the UN, OSCE, or Transparency International are tasked with identifying and reporting anomalies. These include serious issues such as electoral fraud, human rights violations, or breaches of international agreements. Citizens can also participate by engaging in protests, demonstrations, or other forms of civil resistance. Sometimes, governments respond to grassroots pressure, especially when large segments of the population denounce and mobilize against wrongdoing. Anomalies in authoritarian regimes or cases of severe human rights violations are also addressed through international attention, such as sanctions or diplomatic pressure from other states or international organizations. In some cases, anomalies are only recognized retrospectively when historians or commissions conduct in-depth analyses of past governments or rulers. This often happens after a change in government or the end of an authoritarian regime, when systematic reviews of past errors and shortcomings become possible.

Political psychology is incorporated to understand international relations and foreign policy decision-making processes. It provides valuable insights into the cognitive, emotional, and social factors influencing the behavior of states and political actors. Cultural, social, and psychological factors shaping individual and group behavior are crucial for understanding conflicts, diplomacy, and global cooperation. The integration of psychological perspectives into the analysis of international relations broadens the explanatory framework of political theories. It allows for a deeper understanding of the complexity of foreign policy decision-making processes and interactions between states.

Objectivity and technocratization cannot function without acknowledging emotionality and taking feelings into account. Emotions should not be dismissed solely as disruptive factors; they play a fundamental role in human decision-making. They even aid in quickly assessing and responding to complex situations. Emotional intelligence in politics is both measurable and analyzable. A balance between rationality and emotion is essential. While purely technocratic approaches often overlook the human dimension, it is crucial to find a balanced approach.

For the practice of diplomacy and international cooperation, political psychology offers important insights. It helps optimize negotiation strategies and develop more effective forms of cooperation. Considering psychological and especially empirical factors in analyzing international relations thus provides valuable perspectives for political practice. It complements structural and institutional explanatory approaches by incorporating the critical dimension of human behavior and experience. A thorough understanding of these psychological mechanisms is indispensable for political science to grasp the complexity of international actions and develop effective strategies for conflict resolution and cooperation.

Self-proclaimed political scientists often indulge in spheres of ideological reflection without ever having undergone an assessment of their own competencies. Among philosophers and sociologists, this tendency is particularly evident in an arrogance that regards a university degree as sufficient legitimacy. They are abundant among moderators, commentators, philosophers, and other narrators of public media. This description seems to strike a nerve with a group eager to lose themselves in ideological considerations. They employ grandiloquent language and exude strong conviction but often lack practical experience and solid knowledge. It appears they take delight in showcasing their viewpoints without striving for deep reflection. This phenomenon can also be interpreted as a symptom of our time, where access to platforms has become easier, opinions spread quickly, and specialized knowledge often blends indistinguishably with general awareness. In traditional media, they actively participate in the "competition for the grandest verbosity."

During heated debates, magical slogans resonate like mantras among those who, quite understandably, fail to grasp the gibberish. Philosophers of recent decades, in particular, excel at transforming a simple phrase like "I love coffee" into a dissertation on the ontology of caffeine - all with an exaggerated seriousness that would amuse even the most serious barista. As moderators, they become the stars of their shows. With their mysteriously vague rhetoric, they navigate through the meanders of political debates like captains of a ship headed straight for oblivion. And while they float in their ideological utopias, we, the viewers, remain grounded, a cup of coffee in hand and an amused smile on our faces. After all, if life graces us with such commentators, we might as well laugh!

On the analytical table lies a discipline that could enrich the interconnection between psychology, political science, and political management. But instead, transmitters of esoteric and revolutionary ideologies infiltrate the debates. Is this what makes the task easier for dilettantes who step into the public sphere with artificial stances? They steal the spotlight from true experts. However, the latter must not be discouraged, for they are indispensable. True specialists bring not only knowledge but also critical thinking and a deep understanding of political mechanisms. They can identify complex relationships and formulate nuanced arguments based on empirical data and theoretical foundations. In an age where misinformation and superficial opinions often prevail, the voices of specialized researchers and experts are more crucial than ever. They can help enlighten the public and foster informed discussions.

Paradoxically, crises represent not only dangers but also opportunities for profound transformation and improvement. The idea that "crises are also there to be resolved" suggests that every crisis offers a chance for reflection, learning, and reorientation. To achieve this, it is essential to ask the right questions and find the most rational answers. A crisis forces one to confront their own weaknesses and deviations. Whether economic, political, or ecological, crises expose long-ignored dysfunctions. They allow for questioning rigid thought patterns and developing new perspectives. Legitimate questions include: "Where were mistakes made?" and "What changes are necessary to avoid a recurrence?" Whenever existing structures fail, space opens up for creative new approaches.

Politically sound concepts require a combination of pragmatism, morality, and long-term vision. They should aim not only to solve the immediate problem but also to prevent the repetition of past errors. To respond effectively, decisions must be based on solid data and thorough analyses. Emotional or ideological actions rarely lead to viable long-term solutions. Only through collective effort can solutions accepted and supported by all be found. These solutions must not only address present needs but also take into account future generations and their requirements.

A healthy interconnectedness requires diversity in networks. Rather than depending too heavily on a single actor, country, or region, it is essential to cultivate varied relationships to distribute risks. This applies to trade relations as well as security alliances. Access to resources—whether knowledge, technologies, or natural resources—should be equitably distributed within an interconnected system. Only under this condition can all actors play a significant role and benefit from interconnectedness. Interconnection relies on well-coordinated multilateral decision-making among international actors, benefiting all parties.

These processes are essential in international relations. Concepts such as group polarization and the psychosocial influence of leaders play a significant role. Diplomatic negotiations are influenced by psychological strategies where trust, empathy, and understanding are fundamental for success. The "win-win" approach promotes international cooperation. A political science perspective begins by analyzing the complex dynamics within international societies. A holistic perspective considers the various dimensions - political, economic, social, psychological, or philosophical. This interdisciplinary approach enables an understanding of actor behavior and the genesis of political decisions within a broader societal context.

Stepping back to observe a situation without direct involvement can provide valuable perspectives and a clearer view. This distancing reduces emotional biases. In conflict situations, such detachment can help diffuse tensions and engage in more constructive dialogue. With clearer vision, it becomes easier to conceive innovative solutions that might not have been considered initially. This observation also empowers the counterparts by giving them the necessary space to reflect.The psychological traits and personal experiences of heads of state significantly influence their decisions in foreign policy. The way governments or actors perceive their adversaries and allies impacts the genesis and resolution of international conflicts. Psychological factors such as cognitive biases, groupthink, and emotions play a role in political decision-making. It is not uncommon for political leaders to use cognitive shortcuts to simplify complex problems, which can lead to errors, particularly in times of crisis. They often rely on information that confirms their preconceived opinions or is most readily available.

Overconfidence in one's knowledge can lead to risky decisions in foreign policy. Governments do not always react rationally to threats. In crisis situations, they sometimes make hasty decisions under the influence of emotions. Psychological tactics are also employed to influence public opinion. In authoritarian regimes, propaganda is used to create imaginary enemies or reinforce national identity. In democracies, public opinion can be manipulated by media and political framing, thus influencing foreign policy decisions. Psychological factors such as stress and time pressure increase during crises, which can paralyze activities. In such situations, leaders tend to oversimplify and make reasoning errors. Recognizing the psychological mechanisms behind political decisions objectively allows for better analysis and resolution of international conflicts. Using money to influence decisions or promote certain interests, even for ethical purposes, can erode trust in the sincerity of the process.

This is particularly evident in the United States, notably in electoral campaigns and the influence of the economy on politics. It is often unclear whether donations are motivated by a genuine desire for social progress or by hidden intentions, such as the expansion of political power or influence. Terms like "ethics washing" or "greenwashing" are often used to describe these practices, where companies claim to care about ethical issues while primarily aiming for profit or power increases. The fundamental problem is that such practices give an impression of hypocrisy, undermining the perception of purity in ethical causes. One might wonder whether genuine ethical progress can be achieved when the means to achieve it are based on unequal and often opaque financial influence. When people believe money guides moral decisions, they risk losing trust in the integrity of the ethical cause itself.

The struggle of greed in international politics is a significant theme that has shaped the world for centuries. Greed, understood as an insatiable desire for power, resources, or economic dominance, has motivated many conflicts and political decisions. It influences international relations and has often led to exploitation, injustice, and despair on both state and human levels. Greed frequently manifests in geopolitical conflicts where states seek power or influence in specific regions. This greed for power and resources - be it in the form of territories, natural resources, economic dominance, or military superiority - has caused countless wars throughout history. A classic example is colonialism, where European powers occupied and exploited countries in Africa, Asia, and the Americas to maximize their own interests and national wealth. For the affected peoples, this often meant despair and abandonment as they were stripped of their freedom, exploited, and culturally destroyed.

Even today, greed manifests in global power struggles. The race for resources like oil, gas, and rare earth elements leads to political tensions and environmental destruction. In resource-rich countries, such as those in parts of Africa or the Middle East, the greed for resources often triggers internal conflicts and civil wars. Major powers interfere in these countries' internal affairs to protect their own economic interests, frequently exacerbating the despair of local populations caught in cycles of violence. Additionally, greed for economic dominance on an international scale creates unequal trade relations and economic exploitation. Industrialized countries often push poorer nations into unfair trade agreements or debt traps, hindering their development and widening the gap between rich and poor. Such practices lead to economic stagnation and social despair in affected countries, while the greed of wealthier nations continues to grow. On a human scale, the global struggle for greed often results in feelings of abandonment and hopelessness, not only for populations in conflict-ridden regions but also for participants in the power and resource politics.

The philosophy of asymptotes is a fascinating concept that originates in mathematics but also gains deeper metaphorical and conceptual significance in philosophy. In mathematics, an asymptote is a line that a curve approaches infinitely without ever touching. This idea can be applied to philosophical questions, particularly concerning infinity, knowledge, perfection, and striving for seemingly unattainable goals. The asymptote can be seen as a metaphor for humanity's pursuit of goals, ideals, or truths that are fundamentally unreachable. In ethics, for instance, this could symbolize the striving for moral perfection. People attempt to embody ideal ethical principles, knowing they can never act entirely morally. Yet, the pursuit of the ideal drives human behavior.

In epistemology, this idea applies to the quest for absolute knowledge or truth. Just as a curve approaches an asymptote without ever reaching it, the human mind can accumulate increasing knowledge and understanding without ever attaining complete, absolute comprehension. Asymptotes symbolize the paradox of infinity and limitation simultaneously. The curve approaches the line, but there is always a distance it cannot overcome, no matter how close it gets. This could be interpreted in ontology or existential philosophy as a symbol of human existence: humans are finite beings, yet they live in a world filled with infinite possibilities and unattainable goals.

In the philosophy of time, the asymptote represents the idea that the present is always in the past, while the future continuously approaches but never fully arrives. Time moves continuously, but there is no tangible finiteness that represents the end of time or an absolute present. For Plato, the asymptote is a symbolic image of the relationship between the imperfect, sensory world and the perfect, unreachable ideas or forms. Physical things in the world strive to come as close as possible to pure ideas but can never fully achieve them.

Humans may attempt to approach an ideal or a perfect form, but the actual achievement of this ideal is inherently impossible. However, the striving itself holds value because it fosters progress, development, and self-reflection. In existential and postmodern philosophical traditions, the asymptote serves as a symbol of the tension between what we strive for and what we can actually achieve. There is an eternal tension between desire and reality, between what could be and what is. In existential philosophy, as seen in Sartre or Kierkegaard, humans are condemned to search for meaning, even though they know they can never find it in a definitive or absolute form. However, such conclusions do not lead directly to nihilism. This tension is not only a source of despair but also of life's meaning. The awareness that the absolute goal is unattainable provides life with a sense of freedom and openness. Humans can continue striving for meaning and fulfillment without feeling constrained by a predetermined, inevitable endpoint.

An asymptotic approach can also be interpreted dialectically: the movement toward a goal is simultaneously a recognition that the goal, in its pure form, is unreachable. This dialectic applies to many philosophical discourses, whether in terms of the relationship between subject and object, humanity and nature, or self and world. The asymptote represents a dynamic relationship in which approaching a boundary simultaneously means accepting the existence and the insurmountability of that boundary. This can be expressed in the relationship between knowledge and ignorance or between freedom and determinism.

The metaphor of asymptotes can also be applied to real-world scenarios in international politics to describe the complex interplay between power, ideals, political realism, and geopolitical interests. States, particularly major powers, strive to expand their influence to shape the global order. However, the concept of the asymptote illustrates that total hegemony - absolute control over the international system - remains an unattainable goal. Even superpowers like the United States, China, or Russia can only approach global domination without ever reaching a point where they control everything and everyone.

The pursuit of hegemony is thus asymptotic. Great powers aim for this goal but are constantly confronted by limits in the form of regional powers, international institutions, or global crises that restrict their influence. The Cold War is a prime example, where the United States and the Soviet Union sought global supremacy without ever fully achieving it. Their ambition was constrained by an asymptotic boundary defined by the balance of power and mutual nuclear deterrence.

Another example is the quest for global peace and stability. International organizations such as the United Nations aim to promote lasting peace and stable relations among states. Yet, despite these efforts, complete global peace seems to be an unattainable ideal. The international community may approach this goal, but conflicts, divergent interests, or geopolitical tensions frequently cause setbacks. Progress in conflict prevention and diplomacy is hindered by new challenges, such as climate change, regional wars, or competition for resources, preventing the full realization of this ideal.

International politics also aspires to uphold universal human rights and promote global justice. Institutions like the International Criminal Court and NGOs like Amnesty International work to ensure human rights are respected worldwide. Yet again, the asymptotic nature is evident: the establishment of a global system where all are treated equitably and justly remains a theoretical ideal. Human rights violations persist despite international agreements and laws. Authoritarian regimes, economic inequalities, geopolitical interests, and weak supranational institutions hinder the full implementation of human rights. International politics progresses toward this direction, but it is unlikely to ever fully achieve this ideal.

Global diplomacy can be understood as a continuous process of rapprochement between nations. Diplomatic dialogue, particularly between adversarial or competing powers, is an ongoing attempt to reach an agreement. But like an asymptote, this process rarely reaches a final point of complete concord or harmony. States may come closer together but always remain at some distance from each other. This is evident in negotiations on disarmament treaties, trade agreements, or measures to combat climate change. While states often converge toward an agreement, the complete achievement of shared goals, such as total nuclear disarmament or limiting global warming, remains almost unattainable in practice.

The phenomenon of globalization, where nations become increasingly interconnected economically, culturally, and politically, can also be viewed through an asymptotic lens. In theory, globalization could result in a fair global economy, where all countries benefit from open markets and unrestricted trade. But in reality, this ideal remains out of reach due to national interests, economic inequalities, and geopolitical tensions. The pursuit of economic integration and global prosperity is therefore asymptotic: the global economy progresses in this direction, but a perfectly equitable and harmonious global economic organization remains beyond reach.

This asymptotic nature shows that political processes, much like in mathematics, are a constant attempt to approach ideals that, due to structural, historical, and human reasons, are never fully realizable. This creates a permanent tension between what is politically possible and what is actually achievable. How can this dilemma be addressed? One promising approach would be to adopt a pragmatic ideal. This approach acknowledges the importance of idealistic goals while considering the practical realities of international politics. Instead of striving to immediately achieve these idealistic objectives, the focus should be on gradual approximation. Constant, incremental progress can lead to significant changes over the long term. Developing flexible strategies enables responses to changing circumstances and unforeseen obstacles without losing sight of overarching goals. Cultivating global awareness could ease the tension between national interests and international ideals. International understanding and intercultural competence could lay the theoretical foundation for a more cooperative world order.

A first step is to develop realistic expectations about the possibilities and limitations of international politics. This involves accepting from the outset the complexity and interconnectedness of global challenges. Understanding the complexity of global problems helps avoid simplistic solutions. A long-term perspective - international acceptance that significant changes take time - can reduce frustration and sustain motivation for ongoing efforts. By combining these approaches, it becomes possible to constructively address the dilemma between ideals and realistic constraints.

Facts alone are rarely entirely objective in their impact on international relations. They only gain meaning and priority through value judgments. These, in turn, influence the interpretation and weighting of facts, which can lead to different perspectives and strategies. For example, a regime change in a state will be evaluated differently depending on whether it aligns with democratic principles or is seen as a threat to freedom. Value judgments and factual judgments often conflict when international interests and ethical principles do not align. A trade relationship motivated by economic interests with an authoritarian state is a fact, but it may conflict with the value judgment that democracy and human rights should be protected. Value judgments and factual judgments influence negotiations and diplomatic communication. It is not merely about exchanging facts but also about explaining value judgments to make one's position understandable.

The interconnection between abstraction in theory and practicability in implementation is a central theme in science, politics, economics, and other fields of application. It describes the tension but also the necessary link between often abstract conceptual ideas and their feasibility in a practical context. Theoretical abstraction relies on principles, models, and general ideas independent of specific cases. Practical approaches, on the other hand, respond to current challenges and needs, with directly measurable and usable results. However, solutions without a solid theoretical foundation are, at best, temporary and ineffective in the long term.

Abstraction and practicability are not opposites but complement each other. Their connection is essential for progress. Abstract models provide a basis for understanding interconnections and formulating strategies. Theories offer new approaches that can be tested in practice. Practice, in turn, validates theories, testing their relevance. It also demonstrates how universal models can be adapted to local realities. This interconnection is a dynamic process requiring constant exchange: theory serves as a vision, and practice translates that vision into reality. Successful models emerge when these two dimensions are equitably considered and learn from each other.

Karl Popper, one of the most influential philosophers of the 20th century, summarizes his approach to critical rationalism in this quote: *"Good theories come about through trials and the elimination of bad theories. There is no predictable path to good theories, just as good forms come about through imagination and rejecting bad forms."* This philosophy provides an epistemological basis for managing the interplay between theory and practice, emphasizing how theories must be developed, tested, and refined. Scientific theories, such as Einstein's theory of relativity, do not emerge from linear thinking but from speculative imagination. Practical innovations, like technological design, often begin with initial imagination before being tested. In science, this process is reflected in an iterative approach involving hypothesis, experimentation, and revision. Bad hypotheses are discarded, while robust theories withstand the test of time.

Theories must remain open to critique and adjustments to achieve practical applicability. Both theories and practical applications go through cycles of development, testing, and adaptation. This method avoids stagnation and enables continuous progress. The initial phase of theory formation requires creative thinking. However, practice plays a crucial role in testing the validity of theories. Karl Popper's philosophy reminds us that errors are not failures but integral steps on the path to truth and the practical implementation of ideas.

Dialogue between different countries and cultures is essential. Building trust and promoting cooperation can help ease tensions and identify shared values. Forums and international organizations play a key role in this regard. Greater education about the complexity of international relations and the challenges associated with achieving idealistic goals can enhance understanding and awareness. If ideals such as peace and justice are perceived as processes rather than final states, merely approaching them could be considered a success. A more flexible approach, adapted to changing geopolitical realities, could foster acceptance of the idea that the goal is not perfection but progress.

In international relations, content and presentation are closely intertwined. Convincing content can be undermined by poor presentation, while skillful diplomatic style can facilitate the acceptance of politically sensitive content. Cultural differences, historical experiences, and the expectations of stakeholders play a crucial role here. For example, some states prioritize formal and respectful diplomatic communication, while others prefer more informal and pragmatic negotiations. An overly aggressive or arrogant diplomatic style can undermine even relevant content by eroding trust between negotiating partners. For instance, the rhetoric of great powers in geopolitical conflicts often leads to escalation, with harsh words followed by concrete actions.

The increasing mediation of international politics further underscores the importance of style. In today's media landscape, every diplomatic interaction, press conference, or international speech is almost immediately broadcast and analyzed globally. Political leaders are aware of this and often consciously adapt their style to promote or avoid certain narratives. Content and style have a symbiotic relationship. An effective political actor must not only develop substantive positions and solutions but also choose the appropriate style to communicate and secure acceptance. International politics is thus not only a clash of interests and powers but also a stage where style can be as decisive as content for ensuring success.

Different schools of thought have developed in this domain, each emphasizing specific aspects of content and cultivating a distinctive style. For example, idealism, which relies on faith in progress and reason, adopts an optimistic and cooperative language. In contrast, realism favors a sober rhetoric focused on power. The way states project their power is inseparable from the content of their policies. The concept of *soft power*, for instance, highlights the importance of culture, political values, and foreign policy as instruments of influence. Here, content and style merge into a comprehensive approach to international relations. Similarly, in the academic analysis of international politics, the close relationship between content and style is evident. Metatheoretical debates on international relations reflect not only differing substantive positions but also varied approaches to analyzing global phenomena.

Just as in mathematics, where asymptotic curves approach a goal without ever reaching it, international politics could benefit from a pragmatic approach focused on constant adjustments and corrections. The objective is not to achieve a perfect end state but to ensure continuous improvement. This iterative method allows for responses to changes in global dynamics and achieves gradual progress. Perhaps the solution lies not in completely resolving the dilemma but in accepting it. Recognizing that political ideals will always remain asymptotic could encourage a new realism in politics. This acceptance might lead to more rational and less emotional management of political failures and reduce the pressure to find perfect solutions.

The idea that peace with an unrelenting aggressor can only be achieved through a demonstration of strength, even through threats, is deeply rooted in political and historical psychology. This perspective stems from the experience that aggressors exploit the perceived weakness of others and are therefore more likely to respond to strength or pressure than to negotiations or concessions. Often, attempts to appease aggression through concessions have led to an escalation of conflict rather than its de-escalation. Strategies involving dominance, including military strength or economic pressure, can mitigate legitimate perceptions of threat and reduce the risk of aggression. Aggressive behavior that is neither punished nor challenged tends to expand. This phenomenon is based on principles of positive reinforcement: if an aggressor faces no negative consequences for their actions, those actions are perceived as successful and are likely to be repeated.

Threats as a diplomatic or military tool are often essential to deter aggressors. They signal that escalation will entail severe consequences. This constitutes a classic game of credibility. A threat is effective only if it is credible, if the other party believes it will be carried out in the event of transgression. In conflict situations, whether in international politics or personal relationships, threats can contribute to establishing balance. When the other party knows certain actions will provoke firm retaliation, they are less likely to engage in aggressive behavior.

A striking example is the policy of deterrence during the Cold War. The threat of nuclear weapons use by both sides - the United States and the Soviet Union - prevented any direct military confrontation because the potential damage was too great. Here, the threat became a tool, albeit a terrifying one, for maintaining peace.

However, fear has always been, as history demonstrates, a poor advisor in international politics. It is far more effective to rely on firm diplomacy and negotiations than to make decisions under the influence of fear. Open dialogue can clarify misunderstandings and build trust between adversarial parties. *Firm diplomacy* refers to steadfastness and adherence to clear principles, while *fearless diplomacy* implies that negotiations and relations occur without manipulation by fear or pressure.

Since the end of the Cold War, NATO's strategy toward Russia has been based on balancing diplomacy with the credible threat of military defense capabilities. While dialogue and negotiations play a role, the possibility of a military response always remains present to deter dictators from further aggressive actions. Peace achieved without a balance of power or credible threat is illusory. It would encourage one side to exploit the weaknesses of the other. Realism in international politics, however, holds that moral considerations should not take precedence over the necessity of self-preservation. In a system where aggressors respect only strength, a pacifist stance could, in the long run, lead to greater suffering.

## 17. CONTENT AND COMMUNICATION

Political communication aims to generate attention and approval. To achieve this, it employs rhetorical devices, keywords, and other techniques of strategic communication. Messages must be tailored to the target audience and the communication channel used. Social media has massively transformed the structures of political communication. It offers new opportunities for interaction between political actors and citizens while also imposing greater demands on communication skills. The increase in communication through digital media also brings heightened responsibilities for users—both on the side of citizens and political actors. Ultimately, it is clear that the effective management of content and communication is a core task of modern politics. Only those who master both aspects can build long-term public engagement and actively shape political discourse.

Strategic communication techniques are used to influence, achieve diplomatic goals, and shape public opinion. Public diplomacy aims to influence public opinion abroad by establishing direct communication with foreign institutions. This is achieved through the use of international media channels or proprietary platforms, such as *Russia*

*Today* or *Al Jazeera*, to disseminate their perspective. Narrative diplomacy, on the other hand, seeks to establish a coherent and compelling story or narrative that promotes the interests and values of a government or country. These techniques involve crafting a clear, emotionally engaging narrative that highlights the values and objectives of a policy. Political decisions and events are portrayed in a specific light to create a desired understanding, such as framing conflicts as a defense of democracy against authoritarianism.

The interconnectedness of idea exchange in international communication refers to the mutual interaction and interplay of ideas, information, and perspectives between different cultures, countries, and communities worldwide. Such exchanges foster deeper cultural understanding and enhance global cooperation. Interconnectivity creates spaces where diverse perspectives on topics such as politics, economics, science, and society can be shared. This communication leads to better comprehension of global challenges and the development of common solutions.

*Soft power* refers to the ability of political actors to exert influence through attraction and persuasion rather than coercion or financial means. Cultural dissemination shapes public attitudes. Investments in educational institutions and academic partnerships enhance a country's image and establish lasting connections. Financial and humanitarian aid builds trust and strengthens relationships with other nations. Although often negatively connoted, propaganda remains a central technique in international politics. It involves deliberately disseminating information to influence public opinion domestically and internationally. Modern forms of negative propaganda include the intentional spread of false or misleading information to sow uncertainty or undermine the legitimacy of opposing positions. Digital technologies, including social media and targeted online campaigns, are used to manipulate opinions on a global scale. Alliances are formed to reinforce common positions, utilizing various forms of negotiation and consensus-building.

In addition to official diplomatic channels, there are informal channels where non-state actors such as scientists, artists, or opinion leaders are involved. These techniques can reduce tensions and build trust. The influence of opinion leaders lies in their ability to interpret information and convey it to a broader audience. They enjoy the trust of specific population groups and are perceived as credible and authentic sources due to their authority and expertise. This trust makes them effective mediators of political ideas and positions. Opinion leaders act as multipliers, as their views and statements are absorbed and amplified by their followers. Academics and experts bring political issues into specialized circles and promote informed debate, which can then feed into broader discussions.

In times of crisis, coherent and swift communication is crucial for managing the situation. The timing of information release is critical to prevent rumors and panic. Political leaders must balance transparency with the need to protect their strategic positions. Personal meetings between leaders can foster diplomatic breakthroughs. Charismatic leaders can, through their personality and direct communication style, have a profound impact on international relations.

It is not just hesitant reactions that are perceived as clumsy but also the form of communication. The repeated use of rhetoric focused more on consensus than on clear positions has led in recent years to increasing vagueness in German foreign policy. This has been evident not only in discussions about the Nord Stream 2 pipeline or military support for Ukraine but also in the increasingly inconsistent stance towards European and international partners. German foreign policy has too often been characterized by the idea of acting as a neutral mediator between political fronts rather than as a capable actor with clearly defined interests.

The behavior of German leaders on the international stage has often given the impression of hiding behind the facade of a moderate, almost innocent actor. This has led not only to passivity but also to insecurity among European partners and international actors. The political response to international challenges such as the energy crisis, migration issues, or geopolitical tensions with China has repeatedly revealed a tendency toward "crisis management" rather than proactive steering of events. German leadership has often appeared more concerned with preserving its political image than actively resolving issues.

Another topic is the dissemination of narratives on social media. Social media has revolutionized how stories, opinions, and information are shared and consumed. Narratives spread through these channels have profound impacts on society, politics, and culture. The speed and reach with which these narratives spread are unprecedented. They allow users to share content in real time, enabling stories and information to reach millions of people in a very short time. This rapid flow of information presents both advantages and risks.

On the one hand, it enables faster and broader dissemination of important messages that support social change. On the other hand, it also fuels misinformation, manipulation, and extremist tendencies that undermine trust in institutions and social cohesion. Users tend to extract elements from narratives that they perceive as relevant or meaningful to their own situation and worldview. Initially, they do not absorb all aspects of a narrative but rather the parts that resonate with them and are emotionally compelling.

Narratives are often propagated as simplified visions, overlooking political realities and thereby manipulating worldviews. In polarized situations, they become a powerful tool of influence, carrying various dangers. Governments, parties, or interest groups may use slogans to gain support for measures that may not truly serve the common good. For example, the concept of economic freedom may be used as a pretext for deregulation, which ultimately benefits the rich while increasing social inequality. Populist politicians often exploit universally valued ideals to emphasize unrealistic promises or to fuel fears. The result is a polarization of target audiences through simple solutions that gain more emotional acceptance than rational approval.

Influencers, distinct from opinion multipliers, have a large following on social media. On socio-political issues, they typically lack well-founded, in-depth knowledge but stand out with striking communication skills, playing an active role in the influence game. Their opinions and narratives have a significant impact on their followers and influence trends, opinions, and discourse. At the same time, they can also spread misinformation, dubious products, or extreme political views through their reach, often without being strictly controlled.

Misleading content and fake news are rapidly spread through newly established popular platforms, thereby distorting public opinion. Algorithms trap users in "echo chambers" or "filter bubbles," where they are mainly shown content that confirms their existing beliefs, further intensifying polarization and radicalization. Diverging opinions are isolated, making it easier for extremist narratives to spread unchecked. The subjective orientation of perception determines which elements become part of the situation. The terms available to an individual influence the interpretation of narratives. Updated roles in various situations shape the understanding of contexts. These narratives offer correct or distorted interpretations to recipients, thus controlling the narrative. It is the intended readings that steer perception, serving as navigation points for complex issues in collective knowledge. The processing of information is focused on recognizing the narrative. The responsibility of recipients and users is great and cannot be managed without cognitive support.

Given these challenges, the call for professional evaluations and assessments is becoming increasingly urgent. Their role in social media will be to analyze narratives. They are able to uncover hidden effects and contextually categorize facts based on evidence. This service is a perfect addition to the world of social media, as it helps separate fact from fiction. Using established empirical methods and, more recently, with the help of algorithms, AI, and fact-checking tools, they can quickly identify false or misleading narratives. This is crucial for stopping the spread of misinformation before it goes viral. Such evaluations promote transparency, holding political actors or businesses accountable if they attempt to manipulate public opinion. They also make it possible to quickly detect extremist tendencies.

## 18. FOCUS ON THE NEXT GENERATION

Conceptualizing the "next generation" in the context of strategic planning involves taking into account new technologies, the changing environment, and the needs and expectations of future generations. These are prerequisites that serve as predispositions for effective strategic plans. They also need to be considered in several dimensions. Technologies such as artificial intelligence, quantum computing, blockchain and green energy are game changers that will radically alter the way states manage their economies, communicate and handle conflict. These technologies are strongly interlinked. For example, the future of green energy depends on advances in storage technologies and digitization. Leaders in these fields can shift geopolitical power structures, as technological superiority creates new types of dependency and challenges traditional centers of power.

Climate change is perhaps the most significant game-changer for the next generation, as it impacts global security, migration, the economy, and health. The interconnectedness of resource scarcity, environmental disasters, and geopolitical tensions is evident. A country affected by water shortages can become a hotspot for regional conflicts or massive migration, exacerbating global political instability. Moreover, climate change drives innovation in green technologies, which directly compete with fossil fuel energy sources, triggering profound economic and political shifts.

Whether in the form of new technologies, geopolitical alliances, economic transformations, or social movements, game-changers operate within a complex network of influences and interactions. New technologies not only transform labor markets but also influence military strategies, international trade, and diplomatic relations. Those leading in the development of artificial intelligence gain strategic advantages across multiple domains—economic, military, and global influence. This intensifies the technological race between major powers like the United States and China, leading to new geopolitical tensions.

Changes in political discourse also act as game-changers, significantly influencing the dynamics of political processes. These changes affect both the content of discussions and the way political actors and citizens communicate. When discourse shifts from technocratic or elitist language to populist or emotionally charged rhetoric, it can reshape the political landscape. Such a linguistic shift reaches different audiences and can destabilize or reinforce traditional power structures. A change in discourse can challenge existing power relations. When new narratives or ideologies become dominant, they transform political institutions and structures, both nationally and internationally. Social networks thus become catalysts for political upheavals by mobilizing globally connected actors and influencing public opinion in real time. Furthermore, a country's political agenda can shift in an instant when unforeseen events, such as a drought or a hurricane, destabilize entire regions.

Artificial intelligence and automation will play a crucial role in these processes, increasing efficiency. Politics must adapt to an increasingly digital world, particularly regarding investment strategies. Future generations are likely to align their strategic plans with sustainability goals to minimize their ecological footprint and address climate change. Only through efficient resource utilization strategies can long-term competitiveness be maintained in both the economic and political spheres.

Globalization demands the adaptation of strategies to succeed in diverse cultural and economic contexts. Understanding global competition and its strategies will be critical to remaining relevant in international affairs. With disruptive technologies like artificial intelligence, 5G, or quantum computing, the rules of the game are changing across many industries. Businesses, as well as governments, must not only understand these technologies but also integrate them into their strategic plans to remain competitive. These technologies create entirely new opportunities, but they also increase complexity and call for flexible, innovative strategies. Trends must be anticipated to attract and retain the next generation of talent, whether from Generation Z or Millennials. Aspects such as work-life balance, sustainable business practices, and digital competence will bring new values and expectations. Concepts with strong technological, economic, and cultural foundations will be implemented more quickly and effectively in new strategies.

The global reach of digital platforms makes them difficult to regulate effectively. Issues like data security, privacy, and control over digital infrastructures are particularly relevant. Governments must find ways to preserve digital sovereignty without stifling innovation. Clear rules are needed to govern the use of digital platforms and data to prevent abuse and manipulation. Ethics commissions and legal frameworks must ensure that digital innovations align with societal values.

Digital competence is a foundational skill for participating in the connected society. Promoting media literacy and critical thinking helps filter out fake news and use the digital world responsibly. Interconnectivity offers the potential to create new forms of social cohesion based on global networks. It is conceivable to imagine models where digital communities transcend cultural and national boundaries to pursue shared interests and tackle global challenges such as climate change or social justice.

What holds society together? Important "meaning generators" for collective and individual identity, such as family and community, seem to be losing their binding power. Shared values like justice, freedom, and solidarity create a sense of belonging. In an increasingly interconnected world, these values can be disseminated and debated through digital platforms, globalizing the discourse on social norms. Institutions such as schools, media, and political organizations play a key role in conveying common goals and building trust. Their function is constantly evolving, as traditional structures are often complemented or challenged by new, often decentralized forms. However, this interconnectedness can also lead to fragmentation and social isolation when individuals become confined to echo chambers or isolated communities. This can exacerbate existing social and political tensions.

Rather than being seen as a threat, cultural diversity can serve as a source of creativity and innovation. Cities and countries that consciously foster and integrate diversity often create vibrant and dynamic societies capable of developing a pluralistic identity. Despite growing secularization in many parts of the world, religions continue to offer narratives imbued with meaning, rituals, and forms of community that provide individuals with guidance and support. In pluralistic societies, religion can serve as a source of ethical reflection and social engagement. Multireligious dialogues and interfaith cooperation help foster understanding among different groups and shape shared values.

To honor historical truth, it is not only the United Nations Charter or the Universal Declaration of Human Rights, crafted in response to the horrors of war and genocide during World War II, that affirmed the inviolability of human dignity. This idea has its origins in Christianity and was articulated early in Christian theology and philosophy. The notion that every human being possesses inalienable dignity is central to a renewed understanding of humanity and has significantly contributed to the development of modern concepts of human rights. Its historical foundations trace back to the Book of Genesis in the Bible, where it states that humans were created "in the image of God." This idea implies that every individual possesses inherent dignity, independent of external characteristics or abilities. At the time, however, this interconnectedness was primarily understood as existing between the "chosen people" and the divine omnipotence. In the New Testament, according to Christian understanding, "the Word made flesh" enters the world and emphasizes the dignity and value of every human being, highlighting the importance of the other, including the marginalized and the weak.

Humanity thus possesses a rich ethical and social heritage that can be integrated into contemporary debates. Values such as the dignity of every individual continue to serve as a foundation for social engagement. Social and human sciences provide valuable insights into societal dynamics, cultural diversity, and human behavior. These insights are essential for understanding the complexity of modern societies and addressing challenges constructively. These developments point to new avenues for engagement and communication. In a world searching for orientation and moral leadership, Christianity remains an important voice, calling for an ethically responsible approach to human relationships and the environment. The interconnectedness with ethical questions and its role in the future should not be underestimated. This interconnectedness is evident in various areas, from promoting social justice to shaping global responsibility to providing moral guidance in an increasingly complex world.

Despite numerous distortions over time, history repeatedly returns to the fundamental characteristics of its essence. It adheres to certain core principles that recur continuously, whether in the form of power struggles, the quest for freedom, social movements, or the pursuit of justice. These characteristics act as a red thread running through different epochs and societies. This idea is reminiscent of the dialectical conception of history, in which historical processes evolve through an exchange between thesis, antithesis, and synthesis. The confrontation with resistance and contradictions generates a new form, which builds on the original characteristics while integrating new elements. Societies and cultures go through phases of progress and setbacks, learn from mistakes, and seek to build on the positive aspects of previous developments. Despite "distortions," history often shows, in the long term, a trajectory toward greater freedom, justice, or knowledge. Understanding that history, despite its deviations and distortions, always returns to its core characteristics provides a sense of continuity and purpose. It demonstrates that human actions and values have lasting significance and that it is possible to shape the future based on these characteristics. This perspective offers hope that even in times of uncertainty and upheaval, certain core values can endure and evolve. It also underscores the responsibility to consciously contribute to shaping history and realizing these core characteristics. This could be understood as a call to recognize these characteristics to steer history in a positive direction. Ultimately, every generation has the responsibility to defend and develop the fundamental values and principles of human existence.

Traditionally, the family has been the first and most important place where values and norms are transmitted. It shapes an individual's fundamental beliefs and behaviors before these are further developed by external influences such as education or society. However, this familial bond seems threatened with dissolution. More and more children are born out of wedlock, and the diversity of family forms continues to grow: blended families, same-sex partnerships with children, and others. Despite changing perceptions across various aspects of life, the family remains, for many, the primary context of life, with enduring significance for identity and spirituality. When families instill values of community and solidarity in their members, they contribute to the social fabric. While their structures are evolving, they do not simply disappear. Particularly in the Global South, faith communities manifest themselves through intense rituals. Strong and adapted forms of identity are developed. The challenge lies in acknowledging and supporting these new realities. Interfaith encounters and cooperation can break down prejudices and foster social development. Despite the many changes and challenges families face today, their role as a place for transmitting values and providing social stability remains. They are not only a refuge in times of change but also active agents of social development, significantly contributing to shaping the future positively.

## 19. INTERCONNECTIVITY OF THINKING AND BELIEF

The interconnectivity between philosophy and theology lies in their shared pursuit of answers to profound existential questions and the purpose of human life. Reason-based knowledge cannot exist in isolation from theological foundations. This relationship transcends abstract considerations of morality or ethics, delving into the finite nature of humanity and its connection to a transcendent purpose. It challenges the adequacy of human reasoning in grasping transcendent truths and highlights the role of faith as a supplement or corrective. Both knowledge and faith seek to address fundamental questions about life, the universe, and humanity's role within it.

Faith provides a lens to view reality, but "faith without thinking" may suggest an uncritical and blind acceptance of belief, risking dogmatism or fanaticism. Such unexamined faith is prone to manipulation, as theological traditions, such as those articulated by Augustine, argue. Augustine's principle, *"credo ut intelligam"* ("I believe in order to understand"), underscores that faith should stimulate and inspire reason rather than oppose it. Faith must be critically examined to avoid conflicts with scientific or moral progress.

In science, axiomatic principles such as the validity of natural laws or the stability of mathematical truths are accepted without empirical proof. This "belief" forms the foundation for developing knowledge. For example, the reliability of perception or the consistency of logic is taken as a given to engage with the external world.

Knowledge is often derived from empirical evidence, while faith is rooted in spiritual, philosophical, and historical traditions. Both offer structure, orientation, and meaning. Figures like Karl Popper and Ludwig Wittgenstein illustrate the context-dependency of both knowledge and faith. Popper viewed science as an ongoing process of falsification, requiring a provisional belief in theories, while Wittgenstein considered faith a language best suited to express certain aspects of life. Philosophers such as René Descartes and Immanuel Kant explored how foundational beliefs underlie human understanding. Descartes' *"cogito, ergo sum"* ("I think, therefore I am") acknowledges that knowledge depends on belief in the existence of thought and reason. Kant argued that our understanding of the world is shaped by the structure of human cognition, implying a belief in our intellectual faculties. Psychologically, humans rely on assumptions and beliefs to model and navigate the world, demonstrating the interplay between faith and knowledge.

The relationship between providence, politics, and human agency raises questions about human freedom within predetermined plans. Providence may signify a grand design, politics reflects human pragmatism, and individual or collective agency represents efforts to effect change. The Catholic social teaching emphasizes harmonizing providence with human action. This interplay is evident in contemporary issues like sustainability and climate change, where human responsibility is crucial in shaping the future, whether aligned or in tension with notions of providence.

Decisions rooted in reason gain additional significance within an eschatological perspective, which frames actions in the context of ultimate accountability. This perspective influences ethical and political philosophy by extending responsibility for humanity and creation into a timeless dimension. The historical interweaving of philosophy and theology is marked by attempts, as seen in thinkers like Thomas Aquinas and Augustine, to reconcile human reason with theological doctrines. Philosophy serves as a tool to structure and contextualize theological truths, while theology deepens philosophical inquiries into ethics, justice, and the ultimate good. Together, they address profound questions about life and transcendence, offering insights into morality and spirituality.

Eschatology, the study of ultimate questions such as death, infinity, and justice, bridges philosophy and theology. Rational reflection on human limits often leads to engagement with transcendent ideas. This is not a rejection of reason but an extension into faith and spirituality. Decisions made on rational grounds acquire a deeper dimension when viewed in the light of ultimate responsibility. In political and ethical philosophy, this creates a framework that transcends temporal considerations.

The metaphor of a "tipping point" in human life represents moments of transformation or existential crises, leading to profound moral or spiritual insights. These transitions, whether viewed as conversions or resolutions of ethical dilemmas, illustrate the dynamic interplay between faith and reason in shaping human understanding and action. This rich interconnectivity underscores the essential dialogue between philosophy and theology in addressing life's ultimate questions, creating a harmonious synthesis of reason and belief.

The interconnectedness of time and its transcendence, in relation to the concept of the "Alpha and Omega," invites a profound philosophical and metaphysical reflection on the nature of time, eternity, and the mystery of existence. It symbolizes the totality of existence, the cycle of birth and death, beginning and completion. These concepts stem from the Revelation of John in the New Testament, where Christ proclaims: "I am the Alpha and the Omega, the First and the Last, the Beginning and the End." Yet, Alpha and Omega are not merely symbols of linear time; they suggest a timelessness where beginning and end are aspects of a unified whole - a mystery that surpasses time itself.

Existence is fundamentally tied to a linear understanding of time. We experience past, present, and future as sequential moments. However, many mystical traditions propose the overcoming of time, a moment of insight or experience in which the linear sequence dissolves, revealing eternity not as endless time, but as a state beyond time. This idea of perceiving time as an illusion and connecting with the timeless is notably present in Platonic philosophy. In this dimension, Alpha and Omega are no longer separate points but united in a transcendent whole. Even modern physics suggests that time is less fundamental than previously thought. Einstein's theory of relativity demonstrates that time, intertwined with space, can stretch or compress depending on the reference frame, challenging our everyday perceptions. The mystery of Alpha and Omega reflects humanity's search for the meaning of existence, urging contemplation beyond the linear limits of human experience toward the possibility of a higher, timeless reality.

A meaningful link between faith and reason lies in the idea that faith can enrich and expand thought, while thought deepens and refines faith. This balance, captured in the phrase *"Fides quaerens intellectum"* („faith seeking understanding") attributed to Anselm of Canterbury, underscores the interconnectedness of belief and knowledge. It emphasizes that faith inspires a pursuit of deeper understanding, rather than resting on emotional or cultural convictions alone. In contemporary philosophical and scientific debates, it is evident that purely rational thinking, devoid of any form of belief in metaphysical, moral, or spiritual truths, has its limitations, especially in addressing issues like consciousness, ethics, and meaning, where empirical knowledge alone cannot encompass the full human experience.

The interconnectedness of being is a deeply spiritual concept, often understood as a reflection of unity. It calls individuals to recognize their connection with the universe, the divine, and all living beings.

This idea permeates religious practices, ethical convictions, and daily life in diverse ways. If one's actions impact the fabric of existence as a whole, a profound sense of responsibility emerges. In Christianity, this interconnectedness is deeply rooted in both theology and ethics. The notion of creation reveals connections between individuals, communities, and the divine. It suggests that humanity is endowed with unique gifts, abilities, and moral responsibilities, encompassing care for both the natural world and social values. Individual freedom is seen as both a gift and a challenge, tied to an awareness of personal accountability.

The interconnectedness of the universe pertains to the profound and often intricate relationships between all things in the cosmos, from subatomic particles to galaxies. This concept is explored across scientific disciplines like physics, biology, and philosophy. All matter and energy adhere to the same physical laws, enabling universal constancy and interaction. For instance, gravity influences not only objects on Earth but also planetary and galactic movements. Universal principles highlight the consistency of these laws, irrespective of time or place. In philosophy and religion, the notion of universality inspires reflections on how our consciousness, experiences, and knowledge interrelate, raising questions about reality's nature and humanity's role in the cosmos.

The number three holds symbolic significance, representing balance, completeness, and harmony. This triadic structure appears in numerous concepts that emphasize stability and equilibrium. The principle of three-legged stability manifests in physical structures, philosophical frameworks, and societal systems. For instance, Hegel's dialectic operates in three steps: thesis, antithesis, and synthesis. This structure embodies both stability and progress by resolving contradictions into a higher unity. Similarly, Montesquieu's separation of powers - legislative, executive, and judicial - illustrates the threefold principle in governance, ensuring balance and preventing tyranny.

In both Platonic metaphysics and Christian theology, triadic concepts underline unity in diversity. Plato's ideas explore the relationship between the One, the Many, and their harmony. Christianity's Trinity expresses the interconnectedness of Father, Son, and Holy Spirit as distinct yet unified entities. Across cultures and traditions, this symbolic triad reflects the synthesis of opposites into a harmonious whole. The idea of creation unites individual identity, social cohesion, and a higher spiritual dimension. Religious traditions often view humans as creations of a higher power, which grants them unique dignity and purpose. This perspective encourages a sense of shared origin and responsibility, fostering solidarity and a commitment to ethical stewardship. In modern times, even amid secularization, the quest for meaning persists, with environmental and social movements often embodying spiritual principles of interconnectedness and care for creation.

The interconnectedness of being encompasses the deep interrelation between the individual, community, and universal existence. Philosophical and spiritual traditions examine how the self relates to the greater whole. While existentialists like Sartre view life as inherently meaningless, requiring humans to create their own purpose, others argue that being itself holds latent meaning discoverable through reflection and spiritual practice. In traditions such as Buddhism, the self is seen as an illusion, encouraging the realization of unity with the universal whole. In an age of globalization and digital connectivity, humanity faces challenges of alienation and superficiality. Yet, the concept of interconnectedness offers a framework for overcoming these divides, emphasizing our shared existence and mutual responsibilities. By understanding and embracing this interconnectedness, individuals can find a sense of belonging and purpose in a dynamic and interrelated world, enriching both personal life and collective experience.

The confrontation between the "Me" and the "Being" also raises the question of the individual's relationship to the community. Philosophy, psychology, and religion emphasize that humans cannot exist in isolation; they are always in relation to others. Social, cultural, and spiritual networks shape the individual and help them find their place in the world. In the modern world, the interconnectedness of being is also discussed in relation to the environment and nature. Ecological and spiritual movements insist that humans are part of a larger ecological system and have a responsibility to preserve these connections.

A central problem of modern existence is the feeling of alienation, the experience of being separated from being, the world, or others. This sensation often arises from social, economic, and technological developments that isolate the individual and interrupt natural connections. Alienation can manifest at several levels: between man and nature, between man and man, or between man and himself. The challenge of alienation is to restore the lost interconnection. This can be achieved through conscious reflection, metaphysical practice, or the development of communities that experience a sense of belonging and coexistence.

Digital networks connect people globally and create new forms of exchange and interaction. However, the question arises whether these connections truly promote a deeper interconnection of being or rather generate superficial bonds that satisfy the feeling of alienation. Society seeks new forms of meaning that go beyond traditional religious and philosophical systems. The interconnectedness of being offers a possibility to find meaning, fostering the understanding that the individual is part of a larger network, whether on a physical, social, or metaphysical level. The interconnectedness of being opens up to an understanding of the close relationship between the I, the community, and universal being. This reflection highlights that the individual does not exist in isolation but is always in relation to a broader whole. These connections are central to human identity, the search for meaning, and the feeling of belonging. In an increasingly complex and interconnected world, the interconnectedness of being can serve as a guide to overcome alienation and promote other forms of personal and communal flourishing.

The meaning of life is a question that has concerned humanity for millennia. Sartre and Camus, for example, argue that life inherently has no meaning and that it is up to us to create meaning. Man is condemned to be free and to take responsibility for his choices. Some religions provide their followers with guidance and answers to the question of meaning, often in connection with a higher power or ultimate purpose. Humanism emphasizes human values and experiences. Meaning here may reside in the quest for knowledge, interpersonal relationships, and societal improvement.

Being is a central concept in philosophy. Some of its representatives, such as Martin Heidegger, consider the concept of "being" as something that must be continuously questioned and interpreted. His approach emphasizes man's "being-in-the-world" and the constant relationship with his environment. The interconnectedness of being describes the aspect in which individual self, meaning of life, and being are indissolubly linked. We do not exist in isolation. Our understanding of ourselves and our quest for meaning are influenced by the relationships we have with others and with the world. Exploring these themes opens a vast space for reflection and understanding about human existence. By examining the links between meaning, self, and being, we can not only better understand our own lives and values but also the dynamics that shape our society.

The interconnectedness of being is a profound theme in Christology. The connection of being is represented by the central idea of incarnation, the sense of community, and redemption, which unites Christ with humanity. This theme runs through essential aspects of Christian teaching and offers a comprehensive framework for understanding the relationship between God, the individual, and the community. In Christ, the interconnectedness of being is manifested uniquely, as God participates in human existence through incarnation. This act establishes the link between divine being and human being. Christ is the bond that indissolubly unites the divine sphere and creation. Thus, Christianity is not merely an institution, but a community. Each believer is part of the principle of life centered on Christ. This spiritual connection underscores the idea that being is not limited to earthly existence but extends beyond physical existence. Therefore, in Christ, being acquires a universal and transcendent dimension.

When the state of sin is defined as an alienation from the divine, disrupting the original harmony of being and inducing a loss of the deep connection with the divine principle in man, this separation causes an existential rupture within being. In Christology, it is only through redemption, proclaimed by the death and resurrection of Christ, that this alienation is overcome and the initial interconnectedness of being is restored. Cosmic Christology refers to the idea that the entire universe is connected through this Christ, and that his presence permeates all aspects of being. This conception of interconnectedness goes far beyond the human domain and encompasses all of creation, both visible and invisible. The hope in the resurrection of the dead reflects the interconnectedness of being from an eschatological perspective. Christian ethics, based on love - both love for one's neighbor and love for the supernatural - emphasizes the practical interconnectedness of being. Through incarnation and redemption in Christ, the separation between divine being and human being is revoked, restoring a deep universal connection. This connection manifests at both individual and cosmic levels and forms the basis of an ethical and spiritual orientation that permeates life in all its dimensions.

The interconnectedness of religions and the syncretism of beliefs are two different concepts often conflated but having very different meanings and implications. Understanding this distinction is crucial for accurately interpreting the relationships among religions. Interconnectedness refers to dialogue, exchange, and mutual influence among different religions and communities of belief. It describes how religions interact through contact, through ideas, theologies, practices, or ethical concepts, without renouncing their fundamental beliefs or identity. An example is the interfaith dialogue between Christians, Jews, and Muslims on monotheism or ethical themes like social justice. While religions may have different theological approaches, they can promote mutual respect and understanding through dialogue. This interconnectedness allows religions to coexist peacefully and collaborate in areas such as human rights, environmental protection, or social engagement, without their core teachings being mixed. It is explained by the respect for differences between religious traditions. It is not about merging or abandoning faith doctrines but about better understanding and clarifying their differences. With globalization, religious communities are also already interconnected in thought. This interconnectedness allows for the exchange of ideas and religious practices beyond geographical and cultural borders, but without the necessity of merging beliefs.

In contrast, syncretism involves combining elements from different religions to give rise to a new religious expression. However, this no longer corresponds to the original belief systems. When a religion like Vodou in Haiti mixes traditional West African religions with Christian rituals and practices, the element of Christian essence is naturally no longer present. When syncretism aims to unite elements of different religions and to merge them into a new hybrid belief system, it risks producing results that are lacking in credence or even perverse. While the interconnectedness of religions stimulates dialogue and enhances understanding and cooperation between different faith communities, without requiring them to abandon their core convictions, syncretism creates maximum contradictions that ultimately lead to unnecessary tensions. Fundamental differences in theological questions, such as the nature of the divine, the understanding of salvation, or the precepts of religious practices, cannot be combined without serious examination. Such contradictions generate conflicts, both within faith communities and within individuals' faith. They start from a consideration that religious axioms are relative, leading believers to feel that their convictions are arbitrary or interchangeable. This inevitably leads to a loss of faith, as the clear distinction between different truths is erased. Syncretism did not function with the ancient Romans, when the principle of the unique God of Judaism and then Christianity came to challenge the constraints of the Roman principle and broke the mold of the powerful empire.

## 20. INTERCONNECTEDNESS OF "GOOD" AND "EVIL"

Since always the concepts of "Good" and "Evil" have shaped human thought. They lie at the center of ethical, religious, and philosophical debates, and their relationship has been the subject of intense reflection. At first glance, Good and Evil appear as opposing forces that are clearly separated. However, upon closer examination, it becomes evident that these two concepts often exist in a complex, interdependent relationship. This interconnectedness between Good and Evil raises profound questions: is one conceivable without the other? Can they condition or even define each other? The state of world affairs, both in terms of its illness and its healing, hinges on these questions. Just as in individual lives, it is part of world politics to prepare for what is to come. Therefore, the question "What comes next?" is also a call for vigilance, reflection, and targeted preparation. It becomes clear that understanding and integrating these opposites represents a path that humanity must further explore. This polarity challenges us to take responsibility for our actions as well as for our own ethical and political consciousness and to prepare for constant change.

The interdependence of good and evil leads to the insight that an ideal state without conflict or opposition may not only be unattainable but also unimaginable. It is precisely the tension between these forces that drives movement, development, and ultimately maturation, both for individuals and societies. On a political level, this is reflected in the necessity to respond to challenges and prepare for future threats. It is as if the existence of Evil continually reignites the pursuit of the Good, creating a cycle that forces humanity and society into a perpetual state of motion.

Classical philosophies and religions view good and evil as dualistic forces that exist in a state of tension with one another. Examples of this can be found in Zoroastrianism, with its eternal struggle between light and darkness, or in many forms of Christianity that understand the struggle as a fundamental moral drama. A common view is that Evil can only exist in the absence of good. In Christian theology, Evil does not exist independently but rather as a distortion or negation of the Good. Thomas Aquinas argued that Evil has no substance of its own, but appears as a deficiency or lack of the good. This leads to the notion that Evil cannot be conceived without good and can only exist in relation to it.

At the same time, many thinkers see Evil as something that challenges the Good and provides it with a form of existence. Without evil, good would thus be merely an abstract, contentless term. In the perspective of the German philosopher Friedrich Nietzsche, Evil is not just a threat but also a necessary challenge. Many moral dilemmas show that Good and Evil are not always clearly separable. In warfare, for example, the concept of a "just war" is often invoked to justify that killing enemies may be permissible under certain circumstances. Yet, the violence unleashed in a war remains morally questionable, highlighting the difficulty of making absolute moral judgments. In medicine, the decision to save a human life in certain situations can clearly require, as seen in "triage," putting another's life at risk. Such situations illustrate that what appears "good" may sometimes require the existence of "evil."

The question of what is considered good or evil has been shaped by cultural and historical circumstances over time. Ethnic and religious communities have developed different notions of what is morally acceptable. This cultural relativism leads to further blurring of the boundaries between good and evil. What is seen as just and good in one society may be regarded as morally reprehensible in another. This relativity underscores the interconnectedness of the concepts.

Particularly in a pluralistic world, Good and Evil often define themselves in relation to one another, based on specific social and cultural norms.

In nature, the movement of the sun results in a constant change between day and night, between light and darkness. This cyclical change also reflects life itself, where phases of success, joy, clarity, crisis, doubt, and uncertainty intertwine. This constant change emphasizes that light and shadow are not static states but influence and transform each other. The past is not merely a sequence of events but also the framework within which human development and culture unfold. History influences the ways in which societies organize themselves, how they respond to their environment, and how they adapt to new challenges. Human development builds upon earlier experiences that are recorded in history. The technological progress and cultural achievements of a civilization often stand on the shoulders of the accomplishments of past generations. Each era inherits the knowledge accumulated throughout history and uses it to continue growing. Time is an unstoppable, abstract concept that permeates the entire universe, providing the dimension in which growth, change, and adaptation occur.

Whether biological or cultural, development happens over long periods. Evolutionary processes, technological innovations, or societal changes are all embedded in temporal cycles. History and human development can only be understood in their temporal context. They stand in the interconnectedness of Good and Evil. Many of these historical and human developments occur cyclically. Economic cycles, social movements, or political regimes are subject to recurring patterns that can be observed over extended periods. History influences the future, but simultaneously, the past is interpreted through the lens of how people experience and understand it over time. These retrospective effects shape historical narratives, which in turn influence the self-understanding and further developments of societies. As they exist within the interconnectedness of Good and Evil, the ethical and moral dimensions of historical and societal developments become crucial. This is essential for understanding how moral judgments influence the actions of individuals and communities, and how history is viewed as a space for the ongoing struggle between Good and Evil.

The duality of good and evil means that one cannot truly be understood or defined without the other. Good and evil condition each other, as we often perceive one only in contrast to the other.

For example, heroism is often defined by the overcoming of evil, and victims are regarded as morally positive in the context of threats and dangers. This relationship leads to a constant redefinition of both terms, depending on the circumstances in which they arise. Light and shadow do not exist independently of one another. Shadow is the direct result of light hitting an object, creating areas that remain dark in comparison to the illuminated space. Without light, there is no shadow, and without shadow, light as a phenomenon is hardly perceivable. This interdependent relationship shows that both do not exist as absolute opposites but rely on each other. Shadow reveals the presence of light by making the unilluminated space visible.

What is considered "good" or "evil" is a question of moral perspective shaped by culture, religion, philosophy, and the societal norms of a particular era. These categories are not rigid, but rather evolve over time. The way societies define "the good" or "the evil" has a direct impact on human actions and developments. Or is there still a uniform, unchanging guideline? One of the oldest theories supporting the idea of universal morality is the concept of natural law. This principle assumes that certain moral laws are embedded in the nature of humanity and the world. These laws apply regardless of cultural or historical conditions and can be recognized through reason. Examples include the prohibition of murder, the command of justice, or the protection of life. In some cases, the moral evaluation of an action depends on specific circumstances, necessitating a balance between universal principles and the particular conditions of an action. An example is the concept of "just war," where wars are seen as morally justified under certain conditions, even though killing is generally considered evil.

A modern example of universal moral principles is human rights. They are recognized by international bodies like the UN, considered universal and inalienable, and should hold validity regardless of the specific political or cultural circumstances of a society. Unfortunately, UN institutions, in their current setup, have lost the moral legitimacy to defend these values. Criticism arose when the UN began publicly addressing human rights violations in certain regions while seemingly ignoring similar violations in others. This unequal treatment led to accusations of selectivity and double standards, undermining the foundational idea of the universality of human rights as established in the Universal Declaration of Human Rights. A consistent stance would be necessary for the United Nations to be recognized as an independent moral authority in international conflicts.

The intentional infliction of suffering is regarded as wrong or immoral in many ethical and moral systems. Generally, philosophy argues that the purpose of actions and decisions, especially in social, political, or personal contexts, should aim to promote well-being and happiness while preventing suffering. Distinguishing between actions that cause suffering and those that promote well-being is crucial for ethical reflection. It helps to take responsibility and recognize the possible consequences of a given action. The United Nations seems to have long abandoned this principle.

The provocative question that runs through the history of philosophy is whether evil is necessary for good to exist. This idea has its roots in both ancient philosophy and more modern schools of thought. The Russian writer Fyodor Dostoevsky raised the question of the meaning of suffering and evil in a world created by an omnipotent God in his works. Can evil be seen as a necessary component of free will and human development? Dostoevsky recognized that moral virtue, compassion, and forgiveness often arise from confronting evil in the tragic experiences of humanity. This perspective suggests that evil not only exists as an opposite to good but also acts as a catalyst for moral and spiritual development. In the dialectics of German philosopher Georg Wilhelm Friedrich Hegel, the progression of history is understood as a process of confronting opposing forces. Good and evil could stand in a dialectical relationship where evil is necessary for the advancement of good. From this perspective, good develops not in isolation but in a constant interplay with evil. New moral syntheses emerge from this confrontation, leading to greater justice and virtue. In a religious context, the relationship between good and evil is not merely viewed as an ethical or philosophical question but as an existential struggle deeply rooted in the human soul. Religions like Christianity or Islam often emphasize the dualistic struggle between good and evil. Satan in Christianity or Iblis in Islam embodies evil and seeks to separate humanity from God and the good. The struggle between these forces is understood as a necessary part of human existence, with humans becoming a part of this eternal drama through their moral choices. Swiss psychoanalyst C.G. Jung developed the concept of the "shadow" as the darker side of the human self, encompassing all repressed and negative aspects of personality. Jung argued that the shadow is an integral part of the human psyche and must be integrated rather than ignored or suppressed. This idea contrasts with traditional religious approaches that see evil as a force to be fought against.

Whether in philosophy, ethics, or religion, good and evil define and shape each other. In many cases, good can only be clearly seen through the confrontation with evil, and vice versa; evil often exists only as a negation or challenge to good. The interconnectivity of these two concepts requires a nuanced understanding of human nature, moral decisions, and spiritual development. Ultimately, the engagement with good and evil proves to be an essential part of human life and through this dynamic relationship, we define not only our moral identity but also our place in the world.

In a global and international context, the dynamics of good and evil manifest in particularly compelling ways. International relations, conflicts, political alliances, and the global intertwining of ideologies and interests reveal that good and evil are often not clearly distinguishable. States, institutions, and political actors operate in a complex web of moral beliefs, pragmatic necessities, and geopolitical interests, causing moral decisions to often become a balancing act between ethical principles and realpolitik constraints. This reciprocal relationship between good and evil is pervasive in international relations. National interests, power, and security significantly influence the actions of states, allowing good or evil actions to be viewed subjectively from different perspectives. This phenomenon is particularly evident in geopolitical alliances, where states ally with questionable regimes to pursue their own strategic interests. An example of this is the support of authoritarian regimes during the Cold War by the USA or the Soviet Union, to secure ideological or economic goals. What is seen as "evil" in one context, such as the suppression of human rights or dictatorial rule, is viewed in another context as a necessary evil to protect larger geopolitical interests.

Even international organizations like the United Nations or the International Monetary Fund, which often act irrationally due to their uncorrected structures, nonetheless face this moral dilemma of making decisions that may have short-term negative impacts but seem necessary and justified in the long term. Sanctions, military interventions, or trade restrictions serve, on the one hand, to counter repressive regimes, but can also severely impact the civilian population on the other.

International politics is repeatedly characterized by a tension between moral ideals and pragmatic decisions. Although international actors like states and organizations often wish to act according to moral principles, their behavior is dictated by the reality of power relations and security interests. In practice, it becomes evident that even idealistically motivated foreign policy conflicts with the reality of power politics. Examples include the "war on terror" following the attacks on September 11, 2001, which was portrayed by the USA as a defense against evil but led to widespread human rights violations and destabilization in various regions. The brutal assault by the Hamas terrorist organization in october 2023 on Israeli settlements stands as a stark reminder in the history of the world along with its consequences.

Whatever they are all called, the ill-fated ghosts of humanity - Hezbollah, Hamas, IS, Taliban, etc. - surely they cannot be an irreversible reflection of humanity on this planet? In Afghanistan, women are not allowed to walk the streets, not even to laugh in public. If they do anyway, they are immediately arrested, beaten up or raped by the Taliban, and they don't want to stand up and defend themselves? What has become of homo sapiens? However, humanity has also proven time and again that it is capable of standing up against injustice and oppression.

No longer listening to the news is not a solution that is adequate for human intelligence. Closing your eyes to evil would be the stupidest thing a person could do. Even the physically blind vehemently keep their senses open so as not to miss what is happening. In the fight to save the world order, the first priority is to reject and eliminate dictatorships and - as macabre as it may sound - to weaken the influence of the USA. The snail dries out until it is willing to venture out of its shell into the international world, gasping for fluids and air. One method is to let the dictatorships exhaust themselves. The best thing to do is to keep running and continue building your own constructions on the side. This option would at least be worth considering, because you also have to look at what could happen in 2030.

Why should the Europeans see themselves as losers from the outset? They could put action behind the many verbal declarations of war. In an alliance of a new type of strategic alliance, as will be described in Chapter 33, a new reality could develop. To whose advantage or disadvantage? D. Trump, however, should not succeed in leaving the deluge behind him and cowardly disappearing. If he were to succeed in leaving the world in a more unstable situation and shirking responsibility in the process, this would increase global uncertainty. This is precisely why it would be all the more important for Europe to be prepared to set its own strategic agenda and not just see itself as a dependent junior partner of whomever. The key lies in the ability to combine realism with strategic optimism. Europe must realize that greater independence and responsibility also comes with risks and costs - but the alternative would be to remain a pawn of other powers.

Is resignation merely an external remedy - and a bad one at that? With some intelligence, one should understand when evil has long-term negative consequences. In most cases, resignation is the result of a feeling of powerlessness that arises when someone believes the problem is too large to tackle. This feeling is exacerbated when one fights against overpowering forces, be they in politics, social systems, or moral evils in society. In some instances, resignation can also be understood as an expression of acceptance, not in the sense that evil is acknowledged as right, but rather that it is regarded as an immutable part of reality. This kind of resignation often has philosophical roots, as seen in Stoicism or Buddhism, where the pursuit of inner peace is emphasized through acceptance of things that cannot be changed. In politics, however, this is unacceptable, as good politics requires the ability to act, responsibility, and the will to change, even when faced with significant challenges.

Global political players should be capable of making independent decisions without excessive pressure from other actors. Trade capacities, economic stability, and, above all, military background influence how effectively politics can be implemented. Modern technologies, particularly in the digital and military realm, enhance the ability to act. Another factor is the capacity to exert specific influence through international negotiations and alliances. Actions perceived as lawful and justified tend to foster acceptance and support on the international level. In authoritative spheres of influence, however, coercion and money play a considerable role.

The ability to act in international politics is the foundation for effectively and sustainably participating in a globalized world. It depends on internal resources, strategic planning, and the ability to collaborate with others. A loss of agency means that an actor can only respond to external developments instead of actively shaping them. How agency is managed in the international political arena is crucial for tackling the complex challenges of a globalized world. Uncontrolled over-engagement or uncoordinated initiatives can waste resources and diminish credibility. High agency requires flexibility and resilience. Management structures should be designed to respond quickly and effectively to unexpected developments while keeping long-term goals in sight. Crisis management and preventive measures are integral elements of the interconnectedness of international politics. Power alone will ultimately not suffice for effective agency. Legitimacy and the ability to persuade others through conviction, values, and cultural attractiveness matter substantially. Conversely, a lack of legitimacy can lead to resistance and isolation, even when material resources are present. Given the significant power disparities among actors in international politics, a well-calibrated balance between self-interest and the global common good will be essential.

In the political landscape, there is a noteworthy shift from populism to defeatism. This transition describes a phase of oversimplified, often exaggerated promises and emotional mobilization giving way to a mood of resignation and pessimism. To comprehend this dynamic, several aspects must be considered. In the initial phase, populism often appears to many as a refreshing change, offering false promises of transformation and renewal. However, this hope is frequently disappointed when promises prove unrealistic or the problems too complex for simple solutions.

When populist promises fail or no substantial changes occur, a sense of frustration arises: citizens recognize that populist demands and measures are often ineffective or counterproductive. The division within society caused by populist rhetoric has led early on to increasing alienation and a weakening of social cohesion. The disappointment over the inability to solve problems soon turns into resignation. In this phase, populism is not necessarily overcome; rather, it is replaced by a passive acceptance of crises and grievances - a form of defeatism that weakens political engagement and undermines trust in any form of politics. A dictatorship flourishes.

To interrupt the transition from populism to defeatism in a timely manner, conscious political and societal countermeasures are necessary. Political actors must develop credible, long-term strategies and communicate transparently to regain the trust of citizens. An active civil society can act as a counterbalance to political resignation and encourage citizens to engage. The ability to challenge populist simplifications and destructive narratives is crucial for countering manipulations. In Ukraine, this has functioned so far, albeit with enormous sacrifices. By not accepting defeatism, democratic resilience can help to identify a sustainable path out of the crisis, but only with inner and outer strength.

Fatalism or the acceptance of the status quo, as emphasized in these teachings, collides with the need to act actively in politics to promote justice and combat evil. In situations where injustice is clearly visible, resignation is understood as a renunciation of moral action. This passivity allows evil to thrive due to a lack of resistance. With some intelligence, political actors should be capable of noticing the long-term negative consequences of evil. This means that evil not only causes immediate harm but also triggers suffering, injustice, and additional problems. The moral responsibility primarily lies with those who have the power or capacity to counteract it.

Resignation in this case could be viewed not only as a personal defeat but as a form of complicity. The idea that intelligence should enable one to discern the long-term destructiveness of evil underscores the role of rational thinking. Intelligent politicians or political figures should be able to understand the consequences of actions or inactions and discern the impacts of evil on society, the future, and humanity as a whole. In this sense intelligence is linked with responsibility. The awareness that evil is ultimately destructive should motivate intelligent individuals to demonstrate proactivity rather than succumb to resignation. At the same time, there exists the risk that intelligence can still lead to resignation if it is paired with cynicism or pessimism. Sometimes, the awareness of the complexity and scope of evil leads individuals to believe that fighting against it is futile. This cynicism can lead even intelligent individuals to think their actions make no difference, resulting in resignation. However, this would ultimately be a misinterpretation of moral responsibility, as the struggle against evil remains valuable even when success is uncertain.

If resignation is viewed as a bad recipe, the question arises: What is the better remedy? An alternative to resignation is the active confrontation with evil and the pursuit of change, even when the situation is difficult or success seems uncertain. Individuals can have a positive impact when they resist evil. Change often begins in small ways through individual actions that create strong awareness and inspire larger movements. This shows that resignation often rests on an underestimation of one's own agency.

In the context of international politics, power interests, ethical dilemmas, geopolitical strategies, and the battle for values intersect. In cases such as the Syrian civil war, the Rwandan genocide, or the ongoing crisis in Yemen, international actors have been criticized for remaining inactive despite evident atrocities. The impression emerged that the international community had capitulated before the magnitude of the problem. Resignation can also be seen as a decision to tolerate or even ignore evil when geopolitical interests are prioritized over moral values. This occurs when states decide not to intervene for fear that an intervention might jeopardize their own national interests. A typical example of this was the non-intervention of several states in the Ukraine conflict prior to 2022, even though Russia acted as the aggressor. Some states were unwilling to engage in a conflict to protect economic or diplomatic relations.

Overall, there are ample examples in modern international politics demonstrating that evil has long-term negative consequences when not addressed promptly. In situations like the Syrian civil war or the persecution of the Rohingya in Myanmar, inaction has resulted in millions of dead and displaced individuals, leading to grave refugee crises that pose significant challenges for Europe and neighboring countries. This illustrates that international resignation in the face of atrocities and crises is not only morally problematic but also generates global problems.

States that stand against evil not only set a marker for moral integrity; they also underscore their international credibility. Countries like Germany, which have built a reputation by advocating for human rights and diplomacy, currently lose their credibility entirely when they resign in moments where moral principles must be defended. Moral leadership on a global level means taking a stand, even in challenging situations, even when it incurs financial costs.

Governments that refuse to confront evil expose themselves to long-term risks. Evil, in the form of authoritarian regimes, state terrorism, or systematic human rights violations, inevitably leads to instability with far-reaching impacts beyond national borders. Terrorism, organized crime, and refugee flows are just some of the consequences arising when evil goes unchecked. Another tension in international politics is whether state leaders and political actors genuinely fail to see the long-term negative consequences of evil or whether they act out of political calculation. Often, it turns out that actors perceive the danger but refrain from acting because they prioritize short-term advantages over moral principles. An example of this is the reluctance of Western countries to address human rights violations in China. Despite the obvious oppression of Uighurs and other minorities, many governments struggle to take a clear stance because they do not want to jeopardize their economic relationships with China. This illustrates that the failure to act is not always due to a lack of discernment regarding evil but frequently arises from the prioritization of economic and political interests. Or is that precisely the evidence of a lack of intelligence and foresight? Ultimately, international politics shows that resignation, when morally wrong, amplifies long-term negative consequences. "To silently tolerate injustice is to invite even greater suffering in the future." Moral steadfastness and the willingness to combat evil, even when geopolitically unpopular or economically risky, are essential to secure long-term stability, justice, and peace.

War is inherently negative, yet sometimes it is unavoidable for self-defense and security. When, during World War II, thousands of refugees from the East passed through the city of Dresden, the city was nevertheless bombed and leveled. One might argue what the world would have been like if the Allies hadn't stopped the dictatorship of a madman with all means. Today, even in war zones, every meticulously planned measure to protect civilian populations is condemned. Moreover, international organizations criticize human rights violations and injustices in countries regarded as geopolitical adversaries while similar transgressions by allied benefactors are excused. This selective application of morality exacerbates the negative interconnectedness of good and evil where ethical judgments are overshadowed by political and strategic interests.

Here, it becomes evident that actions that might initially appear good or evil often harbor deeper, more complex motives and consequences.

Humanitarian interventions carried out to protect human rights and prevent genocides or ethnic cleansing are often accompanied by the question of to what extent the use of force is justified to prevent greater evils. While such interventions are often justified on moral grounds, such as to rescue civilians or restore international order, they can simultaneously lead to further destruction. An example of this is the NATO intervention in Libya in 2011. Although the intervention began as a humanitarian action aimed at toppling Libyan dictator Muammar Gaddafi and protecting the people, it ultimately led to a power vacuum and ongoing instability in the country. The attempt to combat "evil" can, in turn, generate actions that are morally questionable, such as violating sovereignty rights or civilian casualties. Globalization has contributed on one hand to increased prosperity and development in many countries but also to the exploitation of labor and exacerbation of global inequalities. Multinational corporations operating in developing countries create jobs but also contribute to the exploitation of workers. What some view as a driver of progress and prosperity is regarded by others as morally reprehensible and unjust.

Climate change is another example of the global interconnectedness of good and evil. Industrialized nations, which are responsible for a significant portion of global $CO_2$ emissions, have often built their prosperity at the expense of the environment and the livelihoods of future generations. Frequently, it is the poorer countries that suffer the most from the impacts of climate change, despite contributing the least to the climate crisis. This raises the question of how responsibility and causality are distributed on a global level and how the moral imperative to protect the planet can be reconciled with economic and social interests. The UN and its peacekeeping missions have played a crucial role in restoring peace and stability in many conflict regions in the past. However, during the Rwandan genocide in 1994, when UN troops were unable to prevent the slaughter, the moral boundaries of international organizations—as they are currently structured—became evident. They should be the central actors in setting global moral standards and protecting the good within the international community.

In the international context, the intertwining of good and evil becomes strikingly apparent. States, international institutions, and other actors operate in a constant tension between ethical ideals and realpolitik constraints. Moral decisions on a global level are seldom clear-cut and often riddled with conflicting interests. The interconnectedness of good and evil is a reality in international politics and in a globalized world that compels us to address complex moral questions and seek solutions that are both ethically justifiable and practically implementable.

Do civilizations such as the West, the Islamic world, China, and others, which are fundamentally different in their values and worldviews and could conflict with each other, stand on the brink of a confrontation? In light of the rapid development brought about by globalization and technology - especially social media - an alternative approach emerges. This perspective does not focus on the conflict between civilizations but rather on a fundamental shift in global power structures, highlighting the confrontation between a rising global civilization and traditional, often nationalist elites striving to maintain their power. Perhaps the homogeneity within cultural spheres is overestimated, and internal differences underestimated. Global interconnectedness calls into question sharp boundaries between cultures. Sometimes conflicts occur more within than between cultural spheres.

## 21. CHARISMA AND POWER

Charismatics have the ability to win other people over to their vision and mobilize them. As a result, a person who reaches positions of power is perceived as even more charismatic, regardless of their actual personality. Therefore, there is also the negative side of charisma especially when leaders abuse their power or establish totalitarian systems. Thus, charisma and the perception of power becomes highly dependent on cultural norms and social contexts. Sometimes politicians try to be charismatic without having the gift. Their attempts to be mediating or attractive have the opposite effect and provoke unintentional comedy.

What the fine art of politics entails, where else can you dance so elegantly back and forth between extremes only to end up spectacularly in the ditch? Political leaders sometimes seem to forget that they should not be balancing on a racetrack, but on the fine line of reason. The accelerator pedal of power - who hasn't experienced it? Sitting at the wheel of a political luxury car, the engine of ideology humming seductively. There's no harm in stepping on the gas pedal. Before you know it, you're speeding through the bends of public opinion at 200 km/h. Who needs traffic rules when you have the fast lane of exaggeration to yourself?

But reality intervenes. It stands there like a merciless guardrail, just waiting for political racers to overshoot the curve. With a loud "bang!" and a hail of voter voices, some high-flyer suddenly finds themselves headfirst in the ditch. At least from there, there's a whole new perspective on the political landscape, provided one can pull their head out of the sand. Of course, there's always the option of a political emergency brake. A determined stomp on the brake of reason, a sharp yank on the steering wheel of moderation, and... oh wait— that doesn't work at all. As if there were only a gas pedal and a horn in politics. Perhaps some political leaders should take a crash course in defensive driving, or better yet: how about a leisurely stroll through the middle of society? While it may be less thrilling, at least one tends to skid less often. One thing is for sure: as long as politicians engage in overreaching and oversteering as a national sport, the ditches of failure along the political highways will never run dry. After all, they provide entertaining headlines - and that's worth something to the masses, correct?

With the power position that is associated with a legitimate authority, a kind of charisma is produced, which often isn't genuine.

Not every U.S. president has possessed charisma, which is relational, not inherently present but attributed by the followers. It can be lost or fade over time, particularly when the leadership fails to meet expectations or loses credibility. Charisma can be described as a special appeal or aura that surrounds a person. It is associated with energy and enthusiasm that can be infectious. In any case, charismatic leaders are capable of communicating a clear vision that motivates others. The charisma of John F. Kennedy, for example, was reinforced by his vision and his ability to connect emotionally with the public. His legacy was later marked by both admiration and criticism. Barack Obama was also praised for his charisma, attributed to his eloquence and his ability to communicate a positive vision. Nonetheless, there were moments during his presidency when his charisma was called into question. The loss of charisma can occur swiftly when expectations aren't met or credibility is challenged. For leaders, it is crucial to remain authentic and vigorously represent the changing expectations and values. Authentic leadership does not mean saying or doing everything that comes to mind without filtering. Instead, it involves expressing thoughts and feelings appropriately. Leaders must be aware that they are in a position where certain practical responsibilities are required.

Charismatic leaders often play an encouraging role in peace negotiations, such as Metternich and Talleyrand once did. In more recent history, Nelson Mandela is an example whose personality and vision contributed to the end of apartheid in South Africa. Mandela was not only a charismatic leader but also a symbolic link between different population groups. His ability to communicate empathetically and his commitment to reconciliation made him a crucial factor for peace. Charismatic leaders typically point to a clear vision for the future and demonstrate their passion for what they do. This vision can serve as a guiding star that inspires both followers and partners. It conveys hope and motivation, which is invaluable in the realm of international relations. However, it also requires the immediate environment to absorb and process the ideas; otherwise, one is just stabbing into nothingness, like Emmanuel Macron, who, as a convinced and clever European, faced the dull immobility of the German chancellorships of his time with his innovative ideas. Leadership weakness manifests itself in a lack of own initiatives and a willingness to take responsibility.

The resolute response towards mutual engagement, which France was denied, was likewise kept from its Polish neighbor in a déjà vu manner in 2024. How can the much-praised Weimar Triangle function under such conditions? When Germany adopts a posture of restraint or hesitation towards Poland or France during decisive moments, it undermines trust within the alliance. A lack of solidarity can prove grave, especially in security or foreign policy matters, as a united front is crucial in these areas. If Poland feels that Germany does not take its security concerns seriously, trust in the entire concept of the Weimar Triangle is eroded. The Weimar Triangle can only function if all three countries are willing to act decisively together when necessary. However, if one country hesitates during key moments, the foundation of this alliance is not solid enough. Hesitation and inadequately coordinated responses can have fatal consequences. The foundation of an alliance or government becomes particularly evident during crucial moments, be they in crises such as wars, natural disasters, or economic collapses.

When decisions are made too late, they are not only ineffective but often turn into irreversible mistakes whose consequences remain permanent. Furthermore, hesitation often incurs higher follow-up costs: later interventions are usually more expensive, more challenging, and riskier, whereas early, decisive action is often the cheaper and more effective option. Hesitant action, especially in crisis situations, is not only a sign of uncertainty, but it also has concrete negative effects. Aid that is given cautiously and in piecemeal fashion not only appears morally disrespectful to those affected but is also counterproductive in practice. Fragmented support diminishes the effectiveness of measures and often misses the crucial moment when it could have a decisive influence. Delayed or hesitant help allows aggressors to consolidate their objectives and exacerbates the suffering of those impacted. The consequences are not only tragically human but also have a lasting impact on geopolitical stability. Half-hearted decisions or tardy measures damage not only those affected but also one's own economic interests. Uncertainty and inconsistency destabilize markets and undermine investments. A central problem of delayed decisions is that they cement the status quo. What initially seems like a delay can quickly become a permanent reality. If, for example, an aggressor remains successful due to a lack of support from its opponents, this reality is de facto accepted, often at the expense of the global order. First, one hesitates until external pressure becomes unbearable; then sufficient aid is provided merely to avoid being seen as completely irrelevant, but never enough to create the impression that one is genuinely leading. This is not inactivity; it is diplomatic acrobatics at a „world-class level".

In the Ukrainian crisis, it has emerged that some individuals are considered masters of "measured decisions," or, as critics would describe it, of prudent inaction with occasional reactions. Initially, there were grand speeches about unwavering solidarity in times of change, so resounding that one could almost overlook the murmurs of turnaround from the Chancellor's office of the Federal Republic. Then, decisions were made in homeopathic doses: a little aid here, a few tanks there, of course, only with the consent of neighbors and a half-dozen internal reviews. Who would have thought that geopolitics also rhymes with German rigor in tax declarations? The famous principle of "Deliver, but not too much, and especially not too quickly" was consistently applied. After all, one does not wish to disturb anyone too intensely - neither Ukraine, which is desperately awaiting support, nor Russia, which should apparently not be provoked too much. Why not conduct negotiations and deliveries in an innovative fashion as Europe?

When, at the interface of European decisions, political actors maintain a defensive posture and fail, it would be time to also subject these political "CEOs" to a publicly accessible and evidence-based assessment. Political actors should ask themselves questions about their competence, decision-making ability, and strategic thinking.

"Mr. X, could you explain why you acted this way in the geopolitical crisis Y, when the data was clearly against you? And do you have a long-term goal, or are you just managing emergencies?" Competence is reflected in the evaluation of "whether one can do more than what one is authorized to do or if one is authorized to do more than what one is able to do."

This is particularly striking in response to global crises such as the war in Ukraine, tensions with Russia, or geopolitical rivalry with China. Although there are often strong words, actions often fall short of expectations. Chancellors shaping Europe's international relations give the impression, in these moments, of being more concerned with avoiding conflicts than with establishing a determined and thoughtful foreign policy. It seems they are wearing the right "diplomatic attire" for their international appearances, but lack the necessary physical condition when it comes to acting. In an increasingly authoritarian-dominated world, European heads of government cannot afford any further missteps on the red carpet, either literally or figuratively. Formal security, rhetorical precision, and a confident attitude are not mere details but essential tools for geopolitical competition. Those who do not master these fundamentals risk not only losing influence as individuals but also as political representatives of a country. The strength of Europe does not begin solely with clear content but with the ability to convey it decisively and without uncertainties.

The evidence base can be illustrated by graphs showing the number of unfulfilled promises. Charts concerning missed opportunities openly highlight the famous "cost of hesitation" in decisive situations. Whether the CV has gaps is of lesser concern, but the column "Missed Opportunities in Crisis Management" would undoubtedly be highlighted in red. In the end, the note would read: "Crisis management outcomes, long-term planning, and the art of appeasement... Perhaps the true political 'high performers' would ultimately be celebrated as 'CEO of the Year'. For others, there would then be the classic solution: 'Outplacement' and a final handshake with 'Thank you for your time, Mr. Minister. We appreciate your efforts, but polls tell us it's time for a change!' The official result would ultimately be presented at the ballot box. The electorate will be interested in the facts, regardless of any manipulation.

Instead of actively shaping the foreign policy agenda, weak leadership actors tend to react only to events. This attitude is intended to prevent the worst rather than pursue positive goals. In

European politics, this weakness in leadership manifests itself in the inability to coordinate and find consensus among nation-states. It directly leads to fragmentation of foreign policy positions and a loss of global influence. But how and on what basis do we recognize these actors?

In a subsequent development, an interconnection between political cowardice and ignorance emerges. Political cowardice often manifests as a fear of consequences. This type of cowardice frequently leads politicians to act in ways that avoid risks and evade uncomfortable decisions, even when such decisions are necessary. Instead, they resort to populist measures or postpone problems to the future. The lack of courageous decisions can result in stagnation or degradation of the situation, giving the impression of ignorance, while the true reason is cowardice. Ignorance in political decisions can be reflected in an inability to analyze complex structures and a lack of judgment. It manifests as short-term thinking, ignorance of consequences, or a lack of awareness of scientific knowledge and informed opinions.

Politicians deliberately demonstrate cowardice when they make poor decisions or overlook crucial information. They avoid taking difficult but necessary actions for fear of negative reactions. This leads to decisions made on supposedly safe ground, which, due to risk avoidance, often appear ignorant. Decision-makers who, fearing voter backlash, postpone unpleasant but necessary reforms may find themselves facing an even bigger problem, rendering their initial decision foolish. A well-known example of the interconnection between cowardice and ignorance in politics is populism. Populist politicians shy away from decisions that, while reasonable in the long term, are unpopular and instead resort to simple, emotional messaging. This strategy is both a sign of cowardice, as they shirk unpopular measures, and a sign of ignorance, as they overlook the long-term damage of their policies.

Particularly within hierarchical systems, these two elements combine, where the decision-making process leaves little room for criticism. In such systems, political representatives fear making faulty decisions that could jeopardize their careers. This pushes them to cling to proven concepts, often outdated or inappropriate. Cowardice becomes institutionalized and is perpetuated in "foolish" decisions, as innovative and courageous approaches are lacking.

The interconnection between knowledge and experimentation plays out in international relations through diplomacy, negotiations, and international cooperation. This involves how international actors use existing knowledge to make strategic decisions and how they learn from their mistakes through trial and error. This dynamic has significant implications for shaping the international order and addressing global problems. Responses to crises or wars partially depend on historical knowledge, but many measures are also tested in real time and adjusted as needed to find more effective solutions. After each crisis, there are institutional adjustments, evident in the reforms of the International Monetary Fund after financial crises or the adjustments of the World Health Organization after global health crises.

The paradox of empathy and firmness in international politics is a complex issue. Governments compete for resources, influence, and security. Firm actions are necessary to defend certain interests. In conflict situations, firmness is crucial to protecting populations, countries, and global values. The contrast between empathy and firmness becomes evident when international politics relies on both understanding and strategic decision-making. The challenge is to integrate these two elements so that they mutually animate rather than clash.

Modern performance thinking promotes also in international politics a culture in which value is defined by productivity, success and efficiency. People are under constant pressure to prove themselves and gain recognition through performance. In international politics, the metaphor of "wandering between the rocks" can be applied to the complex and often uncertain navigation between challenges, interests and power structures. This image aptly describes the dynamics and tensions that states, institutions and actors face on the global stage. Instead of engaging in destructive power struggles or misunderstandings, viable solutions can be worked out together through common sense. The interaction of different talents and perspectives from the various sides creates a dynamic that goes beyond the sum of individual contributions.

In times of fundamental change in international relations, such as the one currently prevailing, charisma can play a central role. These changes are often marked by the dissolution of existing structures and the emergence of new formats. In these phases, charismatic personalities can act as catalysts for change or as anchors of stability. Examples of effective charisma can be found in leaders who sometimes win debates or lead significant social movements.

However, when loyalty to a charismatic leader overshadows rational analysis and critical examination, it leads to an excessive estimation of the leading figure. Such unreflective viewpoints unfortunately often result in irrational and destructive decisions, negatively impacting international relations.

Charismatic management involves the ability to promote economic and organizational change through visionary leadership, inspiration, and personal presence. In the context of management and economics, charisma is often perceived as a form of "soft power" that relies on personal qualities and leadership skills. Charismatic leaders create emotional connections with a transformative impact on politics and markets. Their visions serve as benchmarks for their employees and stakeholders, enhancing trust and commitment among all actors. It typically emanates from self-confidence and is perceived as authentic by employees. At best, they remain true to their values and act consistently, which grants them credibility and respect.

Leading personalities use their charisma not only to shape their organizations but also entire sectors. This gives them a decisive advantage in negotiations. Their ability to inspire and persuade can significantly influence the outcome of affairs. They possess excellent communication skills and can articulate their messages eloquently and convincingly. Through their social expressiveness, they manage to engage others in conversations and create a positive atmosphere. In these cases, charisma is not just a personal quality, but also a strategic tool for enhancing trust, promoting change, and supporting networks. Conversely, charisma can also distract from a lucid assessment of reality and be the cause of ignorance of risks, as faith in a charismatic leader can become overly significant. When visions are not sufficiently translated into operational strategies, it can become problematic for the concerned system in the long run.

Charismatic leadership is also a powerful tool for mobilizing and shaping communities and social movements. This form of leadership carries great responsibility, as it has the power to influence the masses and define directions that can have significant societal repercussions. Charismatic political leaders often possess a high degree of emotional intelligence, allowing them to connect with their supporters on a deeper level. They know how to awaken and guide emotions, which is often more effective than purely rational arguments. Charismatic politicians often have a strong voice in public discourse and influence how social issues are debated. However, they must be aware that their words can have considerable consequences.

The influence of charismatic politicians does not exist in a vacuum but through interaction with other allies and adversaries. Critics and opponents challenge them, supporters spread their messages, and the media relay their statements positively or negatively. The ability to evoke emotions and inspire people should not be used to deepen divisions or promote destructive ideologies. Constructive debates can strengthen social cohesion.

This power involves the responsibility to make decisions in the interest of society and to avoid the abuse of power. Charismatic personalities can lead society in a positive direction or, if they do not take on their responsibilities, cause considerable harm. A particular responsibility lies in not only considering the present needs of people but also in contemplating the long-term repercussions of decisions on future generations. This is especially true for issues such as security, environmental protection, education, and social justice.

High-level political actors risk being guided by their own popularity and the belief in their own infallibility. This can result in irresponsible conduct when decisions are made without sufficient questioning or examination in light of their long-term consequences. To address this, political actors should regularly reflect on their normative orientations and undergo evaluations, adopt a pragmatism based on knowledge, and be aware of their systemic responsibilities. What do charismatic figures perceive as knowledge that is hidden or difficult to access?

There are individuals who possess a particular sense of presence and supernatural action in the world and in their own lives. The charisma of wisdom allows them to have a deep spiritual understanding and to apply this knowledge practically. This enables them to explain complex theological concepts in a way that is both easily understandable and profoundly spiritual. This interconnection relates to the relationship and interaction between the visible physical world we live in and the transcendent, invisible dimension that transcends the material. Understanding this interconnection gives human experience a particular significance. By being aware of their relationship with another dimension, individuals realize that earthly life is not solely determined by material values but by orientation towards the transcendent. By referencing a higher reality, society learns to perceive human life as meaningful and purpose-oriented.

This also offers the opportunity to find direction and support during difficult times.

## 22. THE IMPORTANCE OF ASSESSMENTS

Academic titles today are almost like club membership cards: they open a few doors. However, to truly play in the VIP sector of skills, that alone is not enough. Even if someone has Dr., Dipl.-Ing., or Prof. in front of their name, it does not necessarily mean that the person is prepared for every high-level position. An academic degree shows that one can acquire knowledge and pass exams, but knowing how to effectively apply that knowledge and transfer it to new complex situations is another story. This is where assessments come into play: they act as a reality check for the resume.

Decision-making power or social skills are not learned in a lecture hall. A title shows commitment and intellect, but an assessment can demonstrate whether a person is truly capable of taking the reins, especially when the storm is brewing. Passing an assessment is not a decline for someone with titles; on the contrary, such an approach signals the willingness to question oneself and evolve one's own capabilities. In today's work environment, this open-mindedness is often the true key to the highest qualifications.

Imagine there is a mandatory assessment tour for all politicians. What would the promise be if we could specifically test their crisis management skills, conflict resolution strategies, and their ability to think logically and factually? Instead, we often rely on campaign promises and speeches that resemble more marketing pitches than established problem-solving approaches. Some Scandinavian countries like Denmark or Sweden are known for their transparency and readiness to reflect on themselves. They place great importance on measurability and proximity to citizens, regularly conducting evaluations of government performance. However, these are generally not as intensive as an entrepreneurial-style assessment, but rather public reports on government successes. Similarly, in New Zealand, governments and their ministries are regularly assigned specific objectives that are then verified. Thus, the countries that come closest to an evaluation are those that hold their politicians accountable through detailed performance measures. However, the German federal government is rarely evaluated with the transparency one would find in businesses. Instead, voters rely on electoral analyses, media reports, and opposition critiques.

The concept of the interconnectedness of individuals in public life illustrates the multitude of links and networks that connect individuals in the social, political, and economic domains. These connections are partly informal, for example through social networks and personal relationships, or formal, such as through institutions, organizations, or political roles. In this context, power and influence manifest themselves, as the links between individuals and groups are often organized hierarchically and influence access to resources as well as decision-making power.

In connected societies, power is distributed through control over information, resources, or networks. Individuals positioned at strategic nodes within these networks can sometimes wield disproportionate power. Those who are connected to influential people can more easily gain access to power structures or resources. The so-called "social capital" becomes crucial in networks of power, as close ties to decision-makers can expand an individual's scope of action. They can serve as interfaces between different groups or networks, providing them with a competitive informational advantage. Decision-making processes are often dependent on the opinions and recommendations of these central actors. Their position makes them important decision-makers whose approval or disapproval can influence the outcomes of projects and initiatives.

In the digitalized and globalized world, political actors are increasingly interdependent. This interdependence enhances the significance of interconnectivity, as the decisions made by a single person or group can have far-reaching effects on others. Assessments or evaluations play an important role in analyzing and assessing power structures and networks by making visible different dimensions of power and influence. They evaluate the competencies, influence, and strategic position of individuals within a network. In political or economic contexts, such evaluations identify the key players whose decisions significantly impact societal interactions.

Political and economic assessments focus on how power is distributed, who the dominant actors are, and which factors are decisive. This becomes particularly relevant in the gray areas of societal power struggles. Systematic analyses can make informal power structures visible and allow for targeted influence over them. This can be utilized for both the consolidation and the change of existing power relations. Effectively communicating qualifications from interest clusters is essential in various fields of personnel development and in the deployment of professional capacities. It involves conveying competencies and skills that emerge from specific clusters to anticipate the right qualifications for certain positions or projects.

Assessment also refers to a systematic and structured method for evaluating politicians to minimize chance influences while obtaining a holistic picture of personal responsibility. The aim is to systematically and objectively capture the competencies, potentials and performances of individuals, rather than relying on subjective impressions or random factors. At the same time, it is emphasized that the individual personality of the acting persons must be acknowledged and strengthened. The goal is to utilize clear and comprehensible criteria rather than relying on chance or personal preferences. Despite the structured approach, the personality of the participants should not be suppressed but rather enhanced. Assessments are intended to identify potentials and develop them purposefully.

A central element of a continuous, knowledge-based assessment is the clear definition of responsibilities. It should be understandable who is responsible for specific actions and what consequences arise from the decisions. This makes it more difficult to evade responsibility or shift it to others. When political actors are aware that their decisions will be regularly reviewed and evaluated, there is a greater incentive to act carefully and sustainably, as they are conscious of the consequences and must be accountable for them. Additionally, implementing assessment mechanisms and feedback loops can help ensure that political strategies are continuously adjusted and improved. By openly communicating successes and failures, important insights can be gained that benefit not only the current political iteration but also future decision-makers.

The interconnectivity between competence and incompetence describes the interplay and interactions between these two concepts, particularly in social, organizational, and individual contexts. It can be discovered that competence and incompetence often do not occur in isolation but are intertwined in complex ways. Sometimes, competence even emerges as a direct response to incompetence. An individual or organization confronted with mistakes or deficits develops mechanisms for problem-solving and for avoiding errors

This psychological phenomenon describes how individuals with low competence often overestimate their abilities, while competent people tend to underestimate their skills. Incompetence leads to a misassessment of one's own capabilities, whereas competence can result in self-criticism and a drive for further improvement. Incompetent individuals often fail to recognize their deficiencies, while competent individuals develop a clearer understanding of their own limitations. In organizations, the interconnectivity between competence and incompetence can arise through the balance of weaknesses and strengths in teams. A team member may be competent in one area but incompetent in another. The team as a whole benefits when the competencies of its members are complementary, allowing any weaknesses to be offset by the strengths of others.

On the other hand, incompetent leaders in key positions hinder the development of competence at lower levels. Competence and incompetence are sometimes linked through a precarious feedback loop. Mistakes provide valuable information that can lead to improvement, applicable to both individual learning processes and organizations. Conversely, a lack of feedback can solidify incompetence, as there are no incentives for improvement. In some social and cultural contexts, incompetence at the leadership level can be masked by networks, power, and status, while truly competent individuals remain at lower ranks. This results in a dysfunctional interconnectivity where incompetence is dominant and competence remains unexploited. Societal structures and education systems play a key role in the development of competence. Inadequate or poor education fosters incompetence, while well-organized education systems promote continuous enhancement of competence.

A continuous assessment regularly examines the political actions of those in power, while evaluation, by analogy, deals with situations. This iterative process allows political policies to remain dynamic, enabling them to respond to changing circumstances. It facilitates the early detection of significant problems to promptly and precisely adapt measures before greater harm arises. Monitoring and feedback mechanisms make politics more flexible and prevent unnecessary errors from becoming entrenched. Ongoing evaluations ensure that programs and emergency measures are adjusted as new information becomes available or the context changes. Continuous evaluation places long-term planning in the political spotlight. Political decisions thus appear in a long-term context, complemented by the efficiency of a risk management system that can timely identify and mitigate potential negative outcomes. Scenario analyses and long-term forecasts, which are part of a knowledge-based evaluation system, secure the design of political programs, ensuring they can withstand crises and maintain their positive effectiveness even in calm times. The topic of interconnectivity between performance orientation and psychological desensitization in international politics is viewed from various perspectives, as it touches upon both psychological and political science dimensions. On one hand, it displays the pursuit of maximum efficiency, productivity, and success. Conversely, it leads to desensitization on both individual and structural levels. "Performance orientation" emphasizes efficiency and relies on measurable results. International actors compete for power, resources, and influence on economic, military, and geopolitical grounds, a situation fueled by the quest for national superiority. Psychological desensitization, on the other hand, reduces the ability to respond to emotional stimuli or to feel empathy, prioritizing public self-interests over humanitarian or ethical considerations. This creates a form of institutionalized cynicism, which also needs to be measured and evaluated.

Fair assessments mean that the evaluation of political players must emphasize transparency. Their decisions should be made publicly accessible and comprehensible, allowing all citizens to understand how and why certain measures were taken. This strengthens trust in the processes and additionally ensures that politicians can be held accountable when their decisions cause harm. In international politics, a mandatory assessment for politicians would be nothing less than revolutionary. Here, personalities often meet who claim to master world politics but frequently are engaged in a sophisticated game of influence, vanity, and, of course, the best press images.

External evaluators have the advantage of bringing diverse approaches, fresh perspectives, and specialized expertise, allowing for a nuanced assessment. As multiple external actors compete in the public opinion arena, the evaluation process becomes dynamic and results-oriented. This competition among agencies promotes innovation and the continuous enhancement of evaluation methods, as agencies must optimize their approaches to succeed. In such a model, agencies can publicly present their results and compete for recognition, leading to greater transparency and enabling the public and political decision-makers to select the best recommendations from a variety of perspectives and analyses. This plurality allows for the examination of politically complex situations from multiple angles instead of relying on a single institutional perspective.

Another advantage of external agencies is their ability to respond flexibly to new developments and continuously improve their evaluation and assessment methods. Because they are not bound by institutional constraints, there is less risk that they will fall into bureaucratic habits, as is often the case with internal structures. They must remain competitive to survive in the public market, which requires constant innovation and adaptation to new scientific findings and technological advancements.

It may sound futuristic, but the more AI becomes involved in significant decisions, the more likely it is that algorithms will have to undergo assessment processes themselves. Perhaps we will soon see audits and assessments for AI accountability, where algorithms are tested for fairness, ethics, and impartiality. In the future, assessments could become akin to a quality seal. People will want to know whom they can trust, and thus these evaluations might soon become a routine requirement not only for politicians but for many professions as well. Universities, think tanks, and rating agencies could also come under increased scrutiny in the future. After all, they significantly influence knowledge, the economy, and decision-making processes.

Universities enjoy high prestige, yet the trust in their work often rests on reputation rather than objective evidence of quality and innovation. What if universities had to undergo regular evaluations that not only assess their research quality but also their societal relevance and ethical responsibilities? Degree programs could demonstrate through practical evaluations that they genuinely prepare students for today's job market and not just sound modern on paper. Think tanks are the hidden drivers of many political and economic developments. But who really knows how objective their recommendations are and what interests lie behind them? An evaluation could clarify this, assessing how independent and factual think tanks are in their work, how transparent their finances and partnerships are, and whether they truly represent the public good or rather that of their sponsors.

In the assessment centers of companies, one might well question how the training of management aspirants relates to the rating or regular certification of universities regarding the business compatibility of their graduates. After all, it should be ensured that universities truly meet the high demands of the economy. Whether a university truly deserves the label "business-ready" could be based on the immediate usability of its graduates, as in the end, only what is measurable in the assessment center counts. In reality, many HR departments often place less emphasis on formal university rankings and more on soft skills, practical experience, and often specific skills relevant to the position. Internships, project experience, and additional qualifications are hence frequently regarded as more valuable, as they provide insights into the practical suitability of the candidates. For staff assessments, there is also the possibility of personnel accreditation.

Do companies really need a university rating when it is assumed that every graduate is "business ready" by nature? Regardless of whether someone has studied philosophy, economics, or history, businesses are aware that all graduates come with a "solid business compatibility" once they hold their degree. Why even put in the effort to take a closer look at degree programs or universities? As long as the resume looks good and soft skills can be verified with a few attractive buzzwords, who could doubt that any degree effectively prepares students for reality in companies? One might as well just let it all play out, asserting that on-the-job learning post-university with additional seminars is just as good as any elaborate preparation.

In today's global competition, prestige management has become an indispensable part of corporate strategy. Companies increasingly recognize that their reputation and perceived competence play a crucial role in competition. Without a targeted strategy to enhance their reputation, companies risk falling behind and losing their attractiveness to qualified professionals and international partnerships. To remain competitive, companies must not only maintain their internal capabilities and qualifications but also continuously develop them. Here, assessments come into play. They allow for the targeted identification of criteria and development areas for leaders. This enables companies to invest in the skills of their managers and employees, thereby further qualifying them to meet future challenges.

Such strategic efforts require competent managers. They are responsible not only for daily operational leadership but also for driving innovations and keeping companies on course. Through assessments, companies can identify which leaders possess the necessary potential and skills to succeed in a rapidly changing environment. A clear overview of existing competencies allows management to implement targeted training measures and flexibly respond to new challenges.

The demand for competence and development strategies is not only a characteristic of the economy but is also of crucial importance in politics. Just as companies secure their market position through continuous improvement and adaptation, political institutions and leaders must also continuously develop their competencies to meet the complex requirements of a globalized world. In business, it is clear that companies without innovation, flexible structures, and precise knowledge of their strengths and weaknesses will quickly fall behind their competitors. The same applies to politics. Political leaders must be able to respond quickly to global challenges. To make strategically sound decisions, a continuous learning process is required, underpinned by ongoing assessments. In a dynamic world, political actors must be as flexible and adaptable as businesses. The credibility and trust that the public places in their political leaders depend on how well these actors fulfill their tasks. Only through a culture of continuous development and self-reflection can this adaptability be maintained. With targeted competence development strategies, political institutions can enhance their capacity to act and ensure their long-term position in the global competition of political systems.

## 23. THE MAIN CONCEPTS OF EVALUATION

Evaluation and assessment are important tools for measuring the effectiveness of politicians, their programs, and projects. The interconnectivity of evaluation and assessment is crucial, as it significantly influences the decision-making process and the implementation of effective policies. Evaluation documents progress, identifies upcoming challenges, and thus enhances concrete accountability. This enables decision-makers to draw informed conclusions based on sound insights. Through systematic evaluations, governments and international organizations determine how their policy measures measure up against international standards and goals. This allows them to find out whether adjustments are necessary to align with global development. A holistic approach to analysis is essential, moving beyond simple ready-made solutions.

The wake-up call "Caution, you are not as successful as you should be"- illustrates the purpose and significance of evaluation. A key element in this process is the distinction between known and unknown factors. The known include those identified and documented through empirical research, theory formation, or historical analyses. They are generally measurable and can be utilized in political models and theories. Looking back in time, the first step is to determine whether any action was actually taken, or if everything stagnated without activity. Secondly, it needs to be assessed whether actions were taken appropriately or whether harmful knots were merely tightened unnecessarily. Known data are analyzed; unknown factors, on the other hand, pertain to future dynamics, new technologies, unexpected political events, or the behavior of actors under specific circumstances. The reluctance to measure these unknowns leads to uncertainty and complicates the approximate predictability of political developments.

As systems, people, and organizations become increasingly interconnected, the need for sophistication and acuity in evaluating their performance and impacts rises. Interconnectivity creates feedback loops that make evaluation more dynamic and challenging. It thus requires flexible and adaptable evaluation mechanisms that can adequately address the overlaps present in interconnected systems. Strengthening international resilience is essential to meet the challenges of an increasingly interconnected and dynamic world, and valuing redundancy and diversity is crucial to reduce the vulnerability of systems. For example, in global supply chains, diverse sources and alternatives can help minimize disruptions. Diversity also fosters innovation, as different perspectives and approaches contribute to more creative solutions. Therefore, transnational partnerships are formed to share knowledge, resources, and technologies. Such networks allow countries and organizations to learn from each other.

A comprehensive approach that considers environmental, health, and security aspects allows for a more thorough understanding of risks and the development of more effective solutions. Early warning systems are essential not only in military defense but also in the strategic domain of business to detect potential crises early and respond accordingly. Investments in technologies and data analyses that can identify patterns and trends in a timely manner can make the difference between a timely intervention and a reactive emergency operation.

A shift from reactive to proactive strategies means that countries and organizations prepare not just for crises but actively work on building resilient structures. This requires a long-term vision and the integration of resilience into political, economic, and social developments. Understanding the complex correlations between different levels and actors is crucial for addressing the deep-seated interconnections of global challenges. An effective resilience strategy must therefore be interdisciplinary, inclusive, and adaptable to meet the diverse risks of the future.

Another advantage of continuous evaluations is that political systems can become learning entities. Regular analyses of successes and failures allow for the identification of errors and the development of new, improved approaches. Adaptive mechanisms help overcome rigid structures and ensure that policies can adjust to changing conditions. A learning political system means that past misjudgments are analyzed, and future measures are built on those insights.

However, the institutionalization of political evaluations also carries the risk of becoming diluted over time due to oversimplification and bureaucratization. If evaluation processes become too entrenched within fixed structures, they may lose their original function and devolve into mere routine procedures. When they are routine within political institutions, there is a risk of relying on standardized methods without accounting for the specific context and dynamics of individual decisions. This leads to oversimplifications that hinder critical and independent reviews of political measures. Therefore, it is wiser to entrust evaluations to external agencies that operate competitively in the public market.

The examination of priorities describes how strongly the various areas and goals of a country's or an international organization's policy are interconnected. This interconnectivity highlights the complexity of the political, economic, and social reality. Changes in one area can impact others. Decisions in a domain such as foreign policy, environmental policy, security policy, and development policy significantly influence success or failure in another. For instance, a climate policy that promotes renewable energies can affect foreign relations through technology transfer and create new jobs that contribute to economic goals. It becomes clear how global crises or events can rapidly shift the priorities of international politics. The Covid-19 pandemic, for instance, not only brought health policy to the forefront but also affected trade, economy, and security, forcing countries to quickly adjust their political priorities and coordinate measures across various portfolios. Conflicts of interest lie at the core of the dependencies between at least two factors. For example, a country might choose to prioritize environmental protection over short-term economic growth, or vice versa. However, synergies may also arise when actions in one area yield positive effects in others.

While contextual measurement examines the constitutive elements of a situation, trade-offs highlight the conflicting effects within a decision matrix. They span a network over individual fields and define the specific decision profiles. Here, factors are juxtaposed, and alternative pairs are compared, which decision-makers view as equally valid. Pareto optimization concerns a decision where no aspect can be improved without worsening another. The understanding of these methods pays off in many areas, as it enables well-informed decisions considering all relevant factors. Realistic expectations must be set to facilitate rapid consensus on the results.

In international politics, innovation is often viewed as a risk, as new approaches challenge existing structures. However, true innovation does not mean igniting controversies but rather developing creative, consensus-oriented solutions that address contemporary challenges and look toward the future. This does not entail the blind pursuit of radical ideas but involves wisely combining consensus, creativity, and technology. It is a process of co-thinking and co-designing based on openness to new actors and perspectives. The goal is not to cement power structures but to create flexible, adaptable mechanisms equipped to tackle the challenges of the 21st century. What does innovation look like in a sphere often characterized by tradition, bureaucracy, and national interests? One possibility is ad-hoc collaborations. Regions work together on specific issues without long-term commitments. Examples include climate coalitions or multilateral initiatives for cybersecurity. Innovation means not just presenting results but participatively shaping the problem-solving process. Investments and economic integration are used as tools for conflict prevention.

How do heroic politicians see themselves? In front of rolling cameras, they celebrate their successes, leaving no superlative unturned and no balance sheet dull. Of course, their projects are successful, their goals are always achieved, and the numbers are undoubtedly a pure reflection of progress! But what is missing is a clear, objective picture, free from self-praise and distanced from self-constructed success calculations. Self-assured evaluations by political actors or parties do not belong in the hands of their colleagues or competitors across the aisle; they should only be entrusted to professional institutes or agencies. When parameters and variables are measured and correlated, the end result is not about rankings, but rather about productive political benchmarking of situations. For the aim of these analyses should not be a prestige ranking or a media-driven "Who is best?" comparison. Instead, the focus is on political benchmarking as a tool that determines what actually works and where improvements are needed. Such benchmarking allows for the comparison of the effectiveness of measures in different contexts, the development of concrete recommendations for improvement, and learning from mistakes - a discipline, mind you, that is often regarded in party politics as a tedious formality. The goal of evaluations is to not only recognize changes but also to understand their tempo and intervals. This enables the identification of patterns that show how quickly or slowly specific measures take effect and how stable their effects are over time.

The challenge lies in finding ways to balance various interests, resources, or values to achieve an optimal outcome. A clear assessment of the importance of different objectives is a first step. Through prioritization and weighting, it is possible to determine which objectives are of greater importance and therefore require more resources or attention. A detailed analysis helps to understand the impacts of each objective on the overarching goal or on long-term consequences. When multiple countries are involved, seeking collaborative solutions can be beneficial. Working together to find a solution promotes understanding of different perspectives and allows for the development of solutions that meet the needs of all participants as much as possible. Involving all relevant stakeholders contributes to the acceptance of the solution and minimizes the risk of future conflicts. Co-creation allows for the development of strategies together and the pooling of resources. Involving diverse actors in decision-making processes increases the legitimacy of the decisions made. This is particularly important at a time when trust in international institutions is often low.

However, which governments or decision-makers already turn to the expertise of professionals? In reality, the use of such methods varies. These models could clearly identify conflicts of objectives, but the application of such tools is often incomplete or selective. In countries where political polarization is strong, decisions may also be made based on short-term or ideological considerations rather than solid analyses. The decision-making network tightens, as not all options or their consequences are fully considered. They become fertile ground for many decision-making errors. While countries with well-developed systems and a high degree of institutionalized expertise, such as Germany or Sweden, rely heavily on scientific analyses and reports, other states lack the capacity or willingness to systematically use such approaches. Generally, governments in the United States, unless led by autocrats or capricious clans, turn to the expertise of institutes such as the RAND Corporation or the Brookings Institution. In the European Union, expert committees play a crucial role in policy and regulation development. Expertise is often filtered through the dynamics of the political system. An example of this is the short-term electoral cycles that incentivize politicians to make decisions that are popular but not necessarily sensible in the long term. Therefore, the availability of expertise does not automatically mean it will be used appropriately.

If politics does not take the early signs of development seriously, it and its society will stumble upon them sooner or later. When political decision-makers ignore early signs and trends, a vicious circle often develops: problems grow unchecked, as corrective measures are lacking. In the long term, this can lead to serious crises that will require significantly more resources and time to resolve. A systematic, open, and ongoing evaluation is necessary not only to prevent crises but also to strengthen a society's resilience and enable long-term sustainable development.

The channels through which certain influences act on a society or system can be targeted and closed if their origins and mechanisms of action are clearly understood. Through thorough research into causes and effects, it is possible to analyze which factors cause problems or negative developments and how these unfold. By understanding these relationships, politics can take effective measures to stop the influx of problematic influences before they cause harm. This means that preventive action is made possible through analytical knowledge. Ultimately, this idea underscores the importance of decisions based on scientific knowledge, which enables targeted management and control of undesirable developments.

But what if politics does not want to see or if research leads to results that go unheeded? In this case, the search for causes and effects remains either a beautiful theory or a particularly effective means of disguising the same crises with new terms. If we do not systematically analyze which factors actually cause crises, we can expect that the same channels of destructive influences will remain open and continue to flow, joyfully reinforced by inaction and self-deception. A simple research report shows that a certain problem has clear causes. However, instead of closing these channels, everything remains as it was. Science speaks, politics remains silent or skillfully questions the result. And so, the channels continue to flow: same causes, same effects, same crises. This form of "preventive ignorance" has seemed for some time to be a form of management strategy. One could almost think that the capacity to research causes serves primarily to find reasons to do nothing. Perhaps the true value of researching causes and effects lies in making inaction particularly rational.

When the early stage of developments is only considered incidentally or seen as "minor," a society inevitably glides into difficult terrain. Observing and evaluating early signs is not just a safety net; it is a necessity for any policy claiming to act with foresight. But this is often where the problem lies. Instead of bringing issues to light in a timely manner and examining them carefully, many matters are left to chance or fate. It seems almost absurd, but too often, decision-makers ignore even the cries of distress and alert that are already loud enough. These voices often get lost in the corridors of bureaucracy, as if the call for change were a sweet whisper and not a clear and loud call for attention. What remains is a stagnant system that replaces early analysis with underestimation or passive waiting. Yet, examining and evaluating early signs would be like lighting a lantern in a dark tunnel, a guide for evolution and a shield against potentially fatal missteps. However, too often, the opportunity is missed to engage proactively with the early signals. Perhaps because it is uncomfortable. Perhaps because the hope for self-resolution is appealing. Perhaps also because evaluation and implementation require more courage and resources in the short term than waiting comfortably. And thus, we remain there: if the system does not react to the beginnings, crisis management later will become all the more difficult. It is like a building whose foundations have remained unchecked and which one day could collapse under the weight of recklessness. In the end, there is a simple truth: examining, evaluating, and acting may be uncomfortable, but it is the only reliable recipe for sustainable and foresighted politics.

"Safety first" is a phrase that often heads political and societal discussions but is often used more as a slogan than as a guiding principle. For true safety assumes that we examine things more deeply, look where others merely skim, and clarify the blind spots that political bureaucrats often ignore in their daily practice. This is where evaluation comes in, a decisive tool that helps identify dangers, negative developments, and risks before they escalate. It has the necessary distance and the ability for in-depth questioning: what is happening in the shadows? What might only manifest in the long term? What consequences will decisions that seem insignificant today have for tomorrow? This type of in-depth analysis allows for what ad-hoc decisions often cannot do. It captures the unexpected, the undesirable, and even the unknown, thus providing added security to systems and decisions. It recognizes dangers that are not immediately visible and gives indications of consequences that, without this sharp eye, remain hidden in the shadows of action patterns. In a way, it reveals the gaps and inconsistencies that actors, in their daily rush and due to short-term objectives, often do not perceive. Thus, the real value of evaluation and rating lies not only in direct benefits but in the potential for crisis prevention and shedding light on blind spots. Safety does not begin with the advent of a catastrophe but with a precise, patient, and sometimes honest analysis of the status quo, long before a potential danger becomes a real threat.

Errors in decision-making have a bad reputation. They are often seen as obstacles, as mistakes to be avoided at all costs. But what if we considered the opportunities they conceal? In reality, they hold valuable lessons and possibilities that can pave the way for positive change. However, their true potential often remains untapped, as the fear of failure blocks the space for reflection and learning.

Through ongoing and systematic certification of actions, it is possible to create an environment capable of learning from its mistakes rather than clinging to rigid patterns. Such evaluations go beyond mere control mechanisms. They transform the continuous flow of actions into a kind of feedback loop, ensuring that errors are analyzed and used beneficially. This establishes a culture of learning where decision-making errors become milestones rather than obstacles. Instead of avoiding them, they are reflected upon, assessed, and used to drive continuous improvement. Such a system may be demanding, but it fosters resilience that goes far beyond immediate needs, turning the "current" of decisions into a genuine engine of positive change.

In this way, a learning culture is created where decision-making errors become stepping stones instead of barriers. Rather than simply being avoided, they are thoughtfully considered, evaluated, and leveraged for continuous improvement. Such a system may be challenging, but it promotes resilience that extends well beyond the immediate moment and transforms the "current" of decisions into a true driver of positive change. But which politicians actually operate this way? They make decisions, regularly evaluate them, learn from their mistakes, and adjust their measures—an endless cycle of learning and improvement, like the workings of a clock. Yes, perhaps in a parallel universe, where unicorns bring rainbows to bed at night. But in our world, all of this remains a dream. The reality is far different: decision-making errors in politics are rarely corrected - they are often embellished, extended  and, if necessary, covered by another poor decision. The principle seems to be: "If it doesn't work twice, perhaps it will stabilize." And evaluation? Oh, it does happen. Sometimes there are reports, expert analyses, and commissions that thoroughly examine the issues. Except these analyses often end up not on the table, but under it - or serve as doorstops in case the wind of reality blows too strongly.

And who would dare question these masterpieces of ignorance? Too often, inconvenient questions or warnings from experts are dismissed as unproductive disruptions. The focus becomes one of obfuscation, delay, or disguise. When the next crisis looms, the fallback becomes: "No one could have seen this coming!" As a result, the culture of learning remains a fine theory, good for speeches and election platforms, but too easily sidelined when faced with the demands of reality. If politicians genuinely followed through on evaluations, decision-making errors would no longer be scandals but transparent, routine steps toward better policies. But perhaps the problem lies precisely here: a politics that learns and adapts might be too exhausting and possibly even too effective. And who would want that?

International partnerships enable access to a broader range of expertise and resources. In this way, businesses and organizations enhance their competitiveness. Platforms that promote the exchange of best practices help ensure that innovative solutions develop more rapidly. Diverse teams bring a variety of perspectives, resulting in more creative and effective solutions. Organizations that incorporate diverse perspectives are often more flexible and better able to adapt quickly to changes in the market or society. These opportunities offer not only advantages for businesses but also for society at large, as they encourage a fruitful exchange of ideas and innovations. It is crucial to consciously harness these potentials and create frameworks that foster the transfer of knowledge and resources, as well as diversity within teams. Transnational organizations and communities should also be capable of detecting potential crises at an early stage and developing appropriate strategies.

However, highly interconnected systems also create interactions that make it difficult to isolate cause-and-effect relationships. Changes in one part of the system can have unexpected effects in other areas, complicating the attribution of outcomes to specific measures. Feedback loops cause continuous adjustments and changes within systems, rendering static evaluation methods less effective since they cannot adequately capture the system's constantly evolving nature. Due to the rapid developments in interconnected systems, real-time evaluation becomes increasingly important. Such evaluations must be flexible and continuous to allow for immediate adjustments and decisions.

Rather than analyzing each component in isolation, it is necessary to examine the system as a whole. This enables a better understanding of complex causalities and feedback loops. Flexible and adaptive evaluation methods that align with the dynamic nature of systems are required. This can be achieved, for instance, through real-time data analysis and continuous monitoring. Using diverse criteria and evaluation methods can provide a more comprehensive picture of system performance. By combining quantitative and qualitative approaches, measurable results and contextual factors can be extracted. Establishing a culture where feedback is valued as a tool for continuous improvement is essential. This allows organizations to adapt more quickly to changes and learn from their experiences. Advanced data analysis techniques and artificial intelligence can help uncover patterns and relationships within complex datasets that might not be evident to human analysts.

The more complex and interconnected a system is, the higher the risk that disruptions or errors in one area will cascade into others. Thus, control and evaluation must integrate a proactive component to identify and address risks early on. This requires the establishment of early-warning indicators. One goal of evaluation is therefore the anticipation and management of effects. Planned optimizations and unforeseen threats must be monitored equally to ensure readiness for flexible responses. Ultimately, the goal is to make processes more efficient or effective. In the context of interconnectedness, this means that improvements in one area can often have significant impacts on others. It is crucial not only to consider immediate benefits but also to evaluate potential side effects.

However, systems can also present unforeseen challenges, such as compatibility issues with existing systems or increased dependence on external influences. Personal efficiency improvements aim to enhance performance. There is a risk of overload or a lack of specialization if the focus is solely on short-term efficiency gains without considering the long-term development of knowledge. This includes events such as economic crises, supply chain disruptions, political instabilities, or natural disasters, which can suddenly destabilize interconnected processes. Therefore, control must perform scenario analyses and develop contingency plans. Sometimes, it's about survival, but it's always about moving forward. This principle should remain steadfast. What does the majority choose, no matter where in the world?

Governments aim to align themselves with realistic principles and pragmatic solutions to ensure short-term actionability. Most prioritize military alliances, political stability, and strategic partnerships to counter existential threats. Economic prosperity and competitiveness also take center stage. Trade agreements, securing resources, and technological innovation shape the agenda, with pragmatic arrangements often taking precedence over idealistic goals like climate protection or human rights. In times of sudden uncertainty, the resilience of international politics is put to the test. Actors adapt to new realities, seek new alliances, and change strategies when old approaches fail. Moving forward is a principle that runs through history - from geopolitical power shifts to solving global crises.

As in economic management, weighing scenarios and developing strategies plays a central role. When democratic instability looms, some political outsiders seek support from authoritarian regimes. Even on a global scale, power politics and self-interest often dominate decision-making. At the same time, there are idealistic movements, such as the promotion of human rights or climate protection, which tend to take a backseat when existential threats take precedence. When a strategy fails or a political era ends, the international community often moves on to the next solution, even if it is imperfect. Rather than clinging to a fixed agenda, states often choose the path that offers the greatest immediate consensus or benefit. However, if international politics remains perpetually reactive to the next crisis, it risks losing sight of a vision for a sustainable and just world order. When states act primarily out of pragmatism, fundamental values like human rights or the rule of law may be sacrificed.

## 24. INTERCONNECTIVITY OF RATIONALITY
## AND ITS IMPLEMENTATION

Rationality in decision-making involves striving to identify the best solutions based on all available information, weighing advantages and disadvantages, and relying on scientific insights and expert opinions. Decisions must not be based on assumptions or ideologies and must have clear objectives. Recognizing that progress emerges from a complex network of relationships requires a systemic understanding in the development of strategies and policies. The interconnected nature of decision-making - encompassing vision, situational analysis, prioritization, control, and justification - is a multifaceted process that links various levels and aspects together.

Effective decision-making is grounded in a clear vision and strategy. The vision shapes the situational analysis by providing a context for evaluating potential opportunities. The situational analysis informs prioritization by highlighting critical areas and possibilities. Prioritization guides monitoring and review processes by setting focal points for oversight. Justification of decisions is based on all preceding steps, ensuring that the process is transparent and accountable.

The prioritization and hierarchy of global objectives - such as peace, security, economic development, human rights, and environmental protection - are central challenges in international politics. These objectives often exist in tension, being both interdependent and potentially conflicting. Peace is often viewed as a prerequisite for other goals; without stability, economic development, human rights protection, and environmental measures are difficult to achieve. However, security measures, such as military interventions, may undermine other objectives, such as human rights. Similarly, economic growth can exacerbate environmental degradation through increased $CO_2$ emissions or resource exploitation. Conversely, strict environmental regulations may hinder economic growth, especially in developing countries. National security measures, such as surveillance or border control, often conflict with principles of human rights by restricting freedoms. Prioritizing these goals is essential to developing coherent policies. Which goals take precedence depends on the situation. In conflict zones, peacekeeping is paramount, while stable regions might focus on climate protection or promoting human rights. Certain goals, such as environmental or climate protection, require long-term thinking, even though short-term goals like economic growth may seem more appealing. Policies should aim to create synergies between objectives. For example, sustainable economic policies can promote both climate protection and economic development. Involving civil society, science, and business can help establish balanced priorities.

The interconnectedness of progress shows that no discipline can be considered in isolation. Progress arises from a complex network of relationships among science, society, economy, and global dynamics. This interconnectedness reflects the ways knowledge, technology, and society are linked and mutually influential. Many innovations emerge at the intersection of various disciplines. Such collaboration fosters new solutions to complex problems. Greater public understanding of science and politics supports an informed society that encourages progress but also critically evaluates it. Considering ecological and social aspects is crucial to ensuring progress is sustainable in the long term.

Interdisciplinary approaches that combine technology, ethics, and environmental sciences are now at the forefront. Understanding these connections helps tackle future challenges more effectively and strategically foster innovation. Full cooperation is most achievable when networks gradually adapt to new structures, emphasizing the importance of stability and trust for long-term innovation processes. The relative speed of changes and interactions within a network affects successful collaboration, highlighting the need to understand and manage the dynamics of innovation networks.

Enforcement capability is the medium for effectively realizing measures. People's adherence to their authority is based on legitimacy and power, supported by material, financial, and human resources. Even the most rational decisions cannot be implemented without power, resources, and influence. Ultimately, effective communication is decisive. The greatest challenge in linking rationality and enforcement capability lies in balancing the two. Rationality often conflicts with ideological or partisan interests. Even rational decisions can be obscured by populism or political infighting.

Institutions must be designed to favor rational decisions while possessing the means and authority to implement them. Incentives for cooperation and shared goals can help enforce rational decisions. The challenges of implementing this interconnectedness highlight the complexity of balancing logic and power in the real world. Yet, only by closely linking these forces can deep and positive societal change be achieved.

The interconnection between control over information and decision-making processes is particularly relevant: information is often managed to influence decision-making by portraying certain options as more attractive or less risky. Those with the most accurate and extensive information wield significant influence over decisions. Success evaluation should not focus solely on outcomes but also on the execution process. An effective evaluation system ensures accountability on both fronts. Rather than implementing blanket solutions, it is prudent to seek responsibility in the interconnectedness between initiatives and their execution. Strategies define the goals and frameworks for future development, providing orientation and theoretical solutions to existing problems. A common issue in implementing such programs is their indiscriminate or undifferentiated application, ignoring the complexity and specific requirements of practice. As a result, the vision remains theoretical.

Political actors who cause harm are often reluctant to take responsibility, particularly when short-term emergency measures have been adopted. Such episodes are frequently observed in politics, as decision-makers often act in situations requiring swift action without fully considering long-term consequences. Short-term emergency measures often arise in crises, where rapid decisions are necessary to address immediate problems. In such cases, quick fixes are frequently employed without thoroughly contemplating their long-term effects.

Politicians in these situations are often under immense pressure to act immediately, whether from the public, political competition, or the media. This pressure can lead to measures that may be popular at the time but cause long-term issues later. Once the negative long-term consequences become apparent, many actors try to avoid responsibility, often downplaying their role, attributing failure to external factors, or blaming other actors. In crisis politics, responsibility is often diffusely distributed, making it difficult to hold individuals or groups accountable.

There is often a lack of transparent communication about decision-making processes. The necessity of acting quickly in crises is often used as a pretext to bypass in-depth analysis and the inclusion of diverse perspectives. Self-criticism and the willingness to admit mistakes are rare in the political arena, as these are often perceived as signs of weakness. Politicians fear for their reputation and reelection prospects if they take responsibility for poor decisions. This behavior is reinforced by public and media expectations, which demand immediate responses to crises.

Paradoxically, crises are also seen by political actors as opportunities to push forward political agendas that would face resistance under normal circumstances. Emergency measures taken under the guise of a crisis can be used to enforce political goals without the need for in-depth public debate. Such situations increase the risk of poor decisions, as the legitimacy of these measures often relies solely on the urgency of the situation rather than their long-term impact or sustainable benefits.

In most political systems, accountability for poor decisions is insufficient. During crises, it is often argued that "emergencies require exceptional measures," which dilutes responsibility. Without clear mechanisms to assume responsibility or rectify political errors, the space for avoiding accountability remains open. A continuous, objective, knowledge-based, and fair evaluation process can help mitigate the issue of accountability avoidance and impulsive short-term measures. Such a process allows for the ongoing review and improvement of political decisions instead of rushing into emergency actions without considering their long-term consequences. Objective evaluation means that decisions are assessed not only on political or ideological grounds but also based on factual analyses and clear criteria. Independent agencies or experts acting impartially should be involved to ensure unbiased analysis. This could help make policies more effective by anticipating their long-term consequences based on solid data and scientific knowledge. Such objectivity would prevent decisions from being purely populist or driven by the desire for short-term political gains.

The use of knowledge and scientific evidence is essential to improving the quality of decisions. Ideally, political measures should be based on empirical data, scientific studies, and proven models. Knowledge-based evaluation incorporates current research findings and involves experts from various fields. This reduces the risk of poor decisions, which are often made in times of crisis under time pressure and without thorough analysis. This approach would also render populist or extremist tendencies ineffective.

Generic solutions, as standardized responses to complex challenges, rarely account for the realities of different contexts. They neglect essential differences and specific requirements, often leading to ineffective implementation. Moreover, they hinder accountability at various levels, both from those who initiate programs and from those responsible for their execution. Each side shifts the blame for failures to the other, without genuine problem-solving taking place. Responsibility lies in the coordination and interconnection between those who design programs and those who implement them. Agility in this context means that both initiatives and their execution must be functionally refined. The responsibility for success rests not with one side or the other but in the relationship between the two.

Added to this responsibility is credibility, which depends heavily on the perception that the positions taken are coherent and rational. This is particularly significant in political and scientific debates, where arguments are expected to be based on clear and consistent principles. When reasoning is logically coherent, it is more likely to be perceived as credible because it does not exhibit obvious contradictions that could undermine its validity. Persuasiveness depends not only on the presentation of facts but also on how these facts are interconnected. A logically coherent argument makes it easier for audiences to follow the reasoning, increasing the likelihood that they will adopt the presented position. Persuasive communication, therefore, requires not only strong facts but also the ability to embed them in a coherent argument.

However, while logical consistency enhances credibility and persuasiveness, complex logical constructs are often used to obscure or legitimize the true nature of power structures. In many cases, intricate and convoluted argumentation serves to justify unequal power dynamics or conceal the control elites exert over decision-making processes. Complex logical constructs, expressed through layered reasoning and seemingly impenetrable principles, can significantly hinder the public's ability to discern power structures. This occurs when power actors hide their decision-making processes behind a facade of rational or technical expertise that is difficult for outsiders to penetrate.

To ensure the legitimate exercise of power, transparency in decision-making processes is crucial. Transparency entails not only the disclosure of information but also the creation of structures that enable decisions and power dynamics to be communicated clearly and understandably. When logical complexity is deliberately used to obscure power structures, it erodes accountability and can undermine trust in institutions and leadership.

The interconnectedness of logical consistency, credibility, and persuasiveness demonstrates that clear, coherent reasoning is critical for a position to be accepted and perceived as legitimate. Logical consistency lends weight to arguments and fosters trust in decision-makers. Conversely, opaque, convoluted arguments and decision-making processes make power dynamics difficult to discern, complicating oversight by external parties. This highlights the need for transparency and clear communication to ensure that power is exercised in a manner that is both fair and comprehensible.

## 25. ON THE INTERCONNECTIVITY OF FACTUAL QUESTIONS

The multitude of connections between different issues quickly leads to increased complexity, making it difficult to find clear solutions. On the other hand, considering interconnectedness allows for more holistic problem-solving approaches that take various aspects into account. By linking different areas, new solutions emerge that might have been overlooked in an isolated perspective. Recognizing interconnectedness in substantive issues requires a shift in thinking across many domains. However, it also demands increased flexibility and adaptability in approaches.

Political decision-makers must simultaneously consider the entirety of economic, political, social, cultural, and environmental problems in real time. Experts from diverse fields should be promptly involved in political discourse. Scientific research increasingly aligns with the pressing questions of political life. This fosters the development of new governance models with long-term networks among actors from politics, science, and civil society. However, access to interconnected technology remains unevenly distributed, leading to new forms of exclusion. Low-threshold digital participation tools are often used only by already politically active citizens. New vulnerabilities and "communities of fate" emerge. Additionally, the anonymity of digital debates often leads to destructive communication, such as "shitstorms," rather than constructive argumentation.

A key feature of complex systems is the existence of feedback loops. In these loops, certain effects influence the causes of their creation, potentially amplifying or mitigating processes, often resulting in non-linear developments. Climate policy is an example: an increase in $CO_2$ emissions contributes to global warming, which in turn exacerbates natural disasters, destabilizing economic and political conditions in many countries. This destabilization can influence political decisions that either increase or decrease emissions. Interconnectedness can also lead to "emergent phenomena," behaviors or outcomes that cannot be directly derived from the individual components of the system. Emergence occurs when numerous simple interactions among various actors or factors lead to complex, unpredictable outcomes. A prime example is the financial market, where individual investor behavior results in unpredictable fluctuations that cannot be precisely calculated in advance, even though they arise from many individual decisions.

It is impossible to fully reduce the complexity of global and political issues or find clear, simple solutions. Instead, multidimensional and systemic approaches are recommended, acknowledging the interconnectedness of issues and aiming for long-term, holistic solutions. Innovation, collaboration, and thinking in broader contexts offer the best chances of creating clarity and stability in a dynamic and interconnected world.

Climate change affects agriculture, migration, and security. For example, a region heavily impacted by climatic changes may no longer produce sufficient food, leading to famine, migration, and social unrest. Simultaneously, the international community must adjust its economic and energy strategies to reduce $CO_2$ emissions, impacting national economies and social equity.

Migration flows caused by conflicts or climate change affect not only the countries of origin but also the destination countries. Issues of integration, economic stability, and social cohesion escalate into political tensions and populist effects in destination countries. In international politics and diplomacy, decision-making becomes increasingly complicated due to the multitude of actors and issues interacting with one another. Decision-makers must balance a wide array of interests, often in conflict, complicating clear solutions.

Industrialized nations are naturally inclined to continue using fossil energy sources to secure economic growth while also facing a moral obligation to combat climate change and promote the transition away from fossil fuels. National legislators must incorporate these international mandates into domestic laws, often encountering political resistance and creating a dense web of regulations. One potential way to address growing complexity is through systemic thinking in international relations. This approach helps to understand the interrelations between different sectors and develop holistic, long-term solutions that not only address individual problems but also transform underlying structures.

Political actors and decision-makers can prepare for various potential developments through scenario planning, allowing them to respond better to uncertainties and unforeseen changes while making robust decisions that stand up in different contexts. Another principle of systemic thinking is focusing on the root causes of problems rather than their symptoms. For example, the causes of conflicts may lie in poverty, inequality, or resource disputes. Instead of merely addressing the consequences of conflict, such as refugee flows, long-term measures must tackle the root causes.

In an interconnected world, centralized decision-making often cannot respond quickly enough to local circumstances. Decentralization and empowering local actors to develop independent solutions would enable more flexible and timely responses to local challenges. This is particularly relevant in large entities, federal systems, or international organizations that must account for varying regional needs. Data analysis and algorithms can help navigate complexity by identifying patterns and relationships that decision-makers might overlook. Artificial intelligence can assist political leaders in identifying trends and simulating the consequences of decisions to make informed and effective choices. Technological platforms facilitating international collaboration can also play a role in managing complexity. These platforms enable the joint analysis of global challenges and the development of solutions based on broad consensus.

Through international cooperation, countries can establish unified environmental standards that protect the planet in the long term while fostering economic innovation. The development and dissemination of renewable energy and sustainable technologies benefit from international collaboration and investment. International agreements and technology transfer drive resource-efficient production methods. One of the most evident advantages of interconnectedness is economic growth, made possible by networking and collaboration among countries. Open markets, free trade agreements, and global supply chains enable regions to leverage their comparative advantages and use resources more efficiently.

Inequalities between nations, such as those between industrialized and developing countries, are central variables shaping the system's functioning and influencing decisions. A systemic approach would develop strategies to create greater equity in these negotiations while acknowledging the existence of power asymmetries and incorporating them into solutions. A systemic approach to international energy policy considers geopolitical tensions, economic interests, and ecological demands.

System analyses and evaluations are crucial for anticipating non-linear effects. As global challenges continue to evolve, political systems must be adaptable and capable of learning. Systemic methodology emphasizes the need for regular review and adjustment of policies to respond to new developments. This requires resilient governance structures that are flexible and open to change. Here, the warning about corruption is significant. Corruption has profound negative effects on sustainable development and undermines political, economic, and social structures. It severely impacts environmental protection by undermining eco-friendly measures and promoting environmental destruction. In many countries, it leads to the illegal exploitation of natural resources, such as deforestation, illegal mining, and poaching of protected species. Corruption poses a massive threat to sustainable development, significantly hindering nations with weak governance from achieving international sustainability goals. It becomes clear that interconnectedness plays a critical role in transitioning to optimized international economies. It encompasses the networking of countries, businesses, and individuals through various communication and transportation infrastructures, technology, and trade.

The interconnectedness of infrastructures makes modern societies more efficient, connected, and globalized, but also creates greater vulnerabilities. The failure of one system has far-reaching consequences for others, and cascading effects often exacerbate crises. Therefore, it is crucial to build robust and resilient infrastructures capable of absorbing disruptions while addressing the increasing challenges of sustainability, cybersecurity, and global connectivity. The global challenges facing humanity today, such as global warming, biodiversity loss, and pollution, are inextricably linked. No country or sector can solve these issues alone. The interconnectivity between states, industries, and societies is crucial for developing collective solutions and achieving the goal of sustainable and clean growth. In an economic context, clean growth refers to an economy that is low-carbon, resource-efficient, and socially inclusive. This requires innovative technologies, clean energy sources, and the promotion of green investments that serve both environmental and economic objectives simultaneously.

Interconnectivity enables global access to these technologies and ideas while supporting the spread of sustainable practices. Technologies like renewable energy sources, energy-efficient production methods, and environmentally friendly transport systems are essential for decoupling the global economy from fossil fuels. Industrialized nations that already possess these technologies must share their knowledge and innovations with emerging and developing countries to accelerate the global transition to a clean economy.

Transitions and societal upheavals in the geopolitical context are central to understanding the profound changes and shifts in the global system. These phenomena can be examined from various perspectives, including the reorganization of global power dynamics, technological revolutions, and social movements challenging old structures. Success in managing these changes depends on balancing global collaboration with individual adaptation. It is crucial for humanity to view these upheavals not only as threats but also as opportunities to shape a fairer, more sustainable, and more stable future.

The interconnectivity of interests is a complex geopolitical phenomenon shaping the modern global order. The increasing networking of states and regions through infrastructure, trade, and technology creates new spaces for power projection and influence. Electrical grids and technical interconnectors—cross-border transmission connections—play a special role, as they literally constitute new spaces and establish new channels of influence. Membership in synchronous networks like the European power grid is attractive because these represent "communities of destiny," where security and prosperity are shared. This explains the interest of many states in joining such networks. The interconnectivity of rivalries and interests creates new opportunities for power projection, alters the dynamics of international relations, and challenges traditional concepts of sovereignty and territoriality. For states and international organizations, it is increasingly important to understand and strategically navigate these complex interconnections to safeguard their interests in an interconnected world.

The challenge for the international community lies in identifying, anticipating, and managing domino effects in crisis situations. This requires swift, coordinated actions and a willingness to think beyond national interests. Systems have been developed to identify threats early, such as the WHO's early warning mechanisms for pandemics or the Global Network for Monitoring and Warning of Climate Disasters. These systems are crucial for detecting and countering domino effects promptly. Despite the interconnectivity of response capabilities, obstacles remain in managing domino effects, as global accountability is often hindered by national interests. Nation-states tend to prioritize their own interests over international agreements, complicating coordination and shared crisis management. This was evident in the distribution of Covid-19 vaccines, where many wealthy countries prioritized their populations, leaving poorer countries to wait.

Many states and international organizations lack the capacity to manage large-scale domino effects. An example is the European migration crisis of 2015, where many countries were unprepared for the massive influx of refugees, leading to tensions within the EU and hindering cooperation. Often, the countries most affected by domino effects are the poorest or least developed, while wealthier nations are better equipped to handle crises. This unequal vulnerability creates tensions in international cooperation, as poorer states, lacking the resources to adequately respond to crises, are often forced to rely on international actors for help. The resilience of states and global systems must be bolstered through investments in infrastructure, early warning systems, and crisis management. This involves not only building physical resources but also improving social and political resilience by fostering greater trust in multilateral institutions.

The factor of time plays a key role in the operational capacity of alliances. Divergent speeds in strategic approaches disrupt the achievement of goals. Similarly, asynchronous economic policy measures, such as unilateral sanctions, destabilize the international trade system. Asynchronous initiatives in international politics are generally viewed negatively because they lead to inefficiency, uncertainty, and instability, particularly in a globalized environment where rapid, coordinated, and unified responses are often necessary. Delays in the reaction of a state or international organization result in inefficient or even counterproductive outcomes. In crises such as natural disasters, pandemics, or military conflicts, swift, coordinated action is essential. If certain actors delay their response or fail to coordinate, this results in greater human suffering and higher economic costs. In international security issues such as terrorism or the proliferation of weapons of mass destruction, missed opportunities for prevention or timely intervention automatically exacerbate threats.

The speed with which decisions are made has become a crucial competitive advantage in both politics and economics, alongside the quality of decisions. To ensure that interconnectivity in international politics remains effective, it is vital for actors to adjust and synchronize their speeds to respond collectively to global challenges. The decision-making process is increasingly influenced by the need to harmonize different speeds and dynamics. This requires an understanding of the varying tempos and capacities of different actors, as well as mechanisms to overcome these differences.

When states react inconsistently, this amplifies internal distrust. If some states quickly impose sanctions or offer military support while others hesitate or wait, this sends mixed signals to conflict parties and can exacerbate tensions, as observed in the Ukraine conflict. If some actors act faster or more effectively, they gain strategic advantages that may create imbalances in the international order. Countries that consolidate their power through faster or more aggressive actions can expand their influence in regions or global institutions, while hesitant states lose influence. Asynchronous economic responses, such as imposing tariffs or divergent trade policies, destabilize markets and the global economic order.

An example is China's rapid expansion in Africa and other developing regions, while Western countries responded more slowly to these geopolitical developments. In military alliances such as NATO, an unequal distribution of burdens among member states can impair the alliance's operational capability. Divergent strategies disrupt goal achievement. Similarly, unilateral economic measures, such as sanctions, destabilize the international trade system. When markets are protected through protectionist measures, it always disadvantages a counterpart in international trade. These approaches are more likely to succeed when they are not narrowly national in scope but instead involve global regional clusters. This way, smaller entities, often disadvantaged in national disputes, can still access international markets.

## 26. EFFECTS OF INTERCONNECTIVITY ON THE ECONOMY

The interconnection between regulation and deregulation refers to the close interplay between these two approaches within political and economic systems. Regulation and deregulation are not rigid opposites but often function dynamically, influenced by political, economic, and social contexts. In the financial sector, deregulation sometimes encourages risky behavior, as demonstrated by the 2008 financial crisis, partly attributed to insufficient regulation of financial markets and products. However, overregulation increases bureaucracy and costs for businesses, stifling economic growth and a country's competitiveness. At the same time, insufficient regulation exposes markets to risks, such as financial crises or unethical corporate behavior. The debate often revolves around finding a balance: ensuring enough regulation to guarantee stability and consumer protection without unnecessarily burdening the market or hindering innovation.

Addressing growth solely from an economic perspective is a miscalculation. Growth based exclusively on economic indicators often neglects ecological consequences. Overexploitation of natural resources and environmental degradation may generate short-term, regionally-focused profits but lead to significant long-term ecological damage and costs. A company or economy focused only on short-term profits depletes natural resources faster than they can regenerate, undermining the sustainability of future growth. Companies that ignore environmental concerns today may one day realize that money is not edible, especially when the soil is contaminated by past profit-driven actions. Regarding $CO_2$ emissions, some companies seem almost admirably efficient at polluting the air so rapidly that future generations will be left with little more than a foul-smelling legacy.

Economic growth that disregards $CO_2$ emissions or environmental pollution triggers ecological crises and imposes costs on future generations. Companies that fail to adopt sustainable practices will eventually face stricter regulations or losses due to environmental damage. By focusing solely on economic goals, some businesses cut costs by exploiting labor or ignoring workers' quality of life. Over time, this results in declining productivity, high turnover rates, and deteriorating working conditions.

Why did CEOs in the German automotive industry make major

management errors, despite being trained to observe market situations and respond with innovative thinking? A traditional corporate culture, focused solely on stability, continuity, and tried-and-tested practices, prevented these companies from embracing disruptive changes. The focus on short-term results and fear of risks led to a resistance to innovative ideas. The rigid hierarchical structures typical of many German automotive companies hinder innovation management. Decision-making processes are often slow, as they involve multiple stakeholders, which prevents rapid responses to market changes or technological developments.

While other companies, particularly in China and the United States, invested early in developing electric vehicles, German manufacturers remained overly focused on conventional engine technologies for too long. This delay cost them market share and damaged their reputation as innovation leaders. Additionally, their lack of investment in software competencies left them falling short of expectations in the development of smart, connected vehicles.

A balanced approach is essential, incorporating ethical principles and intrinsic motivation. Not all rule-breaking in organizations is necessarily negative. Overly strict regulations can stifle the beneficial rule-breaking necessary for innovation. However, excessive deregulation undermines consumer protection, leading to unsafe products, deteriorating working conditions, or unfair business practices. In environmental or climate protection, deregulation reduces corporate responsibility for ecological impacts, resulting in long-term negative consequences for the planet and human health.

Companies focusing on qualitative growth could achieve competitive advantages by offering better products and services and using resources more efficiently. Although this approach may not immediately gain global traction, it is gaining significance and could play a critical role in future global economic development. Its actual adoption will depend on various factors, including political decisions, economic necessities, and social acceptance. In a globalized and interconnected world, a company's reputation is crucial for its long-term success. Companies that pursue only economic growth risk losing the trust of customers, employees, investors, and ultimately, the general public.

The interconnection between sustainability, economic efficiency, and international reputation creates an undeniable dynamic for modern companies and states. Sustainability is not just a moral imperative but increasingly an economic success factor that shapes international perceptions and ensures long-term competitiveness. Those who successfully integrate these three dimensions strategically will secure a sustainable and prosperous future in a globalized world.

Faced with technological transformation, climate change, demographic shifts, and globalization, traditional economic models no longer meet current and future demands. In this context, innovative jobs and interconnections between different economic and social sectors are becoming increasingly important. Restructuring economic policies to address these new needs is not only necessary but also an indispensable step into the future. Businesses, governments, and societies must collaborate to create a sustainable, fair, and innovative economic ecosystem that meets today's challenges while adapting to growing interdependencies.

Unemployment, inequality, resource scarcity, and climate change call for a comprehensive restructuring of economic policy. Governments and businesses must develop innovative approaches to meet the changing demands of the market and society. The creation of novel jobs is a crucial component of this restructuring. Jobs are emerging in the fields of renewable energy, digital technology, sustainable agriculture, and the circular economy. Interconnectivity refers to the networking and collaboration among various stakeholders, sectors, and regions. Successful economic policy must foster the connections between businesses, educational institutions, research facilities, and civil society. In this context, education policy is understood as the promotion of skills necessary for the new jobs.

History shows that there is often a cyclical movement between regulation and deregulation. In economically stable times or during phases of market liberalization, regulations are often dismantled to promote growth. In times of crisis or market upheaval, however, governments tend to revert to control. In the 1980s, many Western countries experienced waves of deregulation, particularly in the financial and transportation sectors, to give more room to market forces. However, after the financial crisis of 2008, there was a return to stricter regulations.

Regulations are fundamentally necessary in high-risk areas like banking or healthcare, where market failures can lead to systemic crises. In dynamic segments such as beneficial technologies or energy, deregulations are advisable to stimulate innovation and competition. It is absolutely detrimental when political ideology determines the balance between regulation and deregulation. This leads to confusing shifts in regulatory practices depending on the political orientation of a government. Similarly, austerity measures and investments are often opposing yet interconnected instruments of economic policy. Governments must carefully weigh how to deploy these tools at various stages of the economic cycle. Austerity measures are necessary to ensure fiscal discipline and financial stability, while investments are crucial for promoting long-term growth and prosperity. A balance between both approaches is essential to ensure sustainable and balanced economic development. Austerity measures aim to reduce budget deficits, decrease debt, and secure confidence in long-term financial stability. This is often achieved through cuts in public spending and tax increases. However, this is not the optimal decision balance.

Governments are obliged to make rational decisions about which areas to invest in. Typically, infrastructure, education, or new technologies are at the top of the priority list to foster long-term growth, as only then can social benefits be provided. This creates the financial leeway to expand social benefits and strengthen social cohesion. A forward-looking investment policy must always consider the specific needs and potentials of each country. Bureaucratic structures often lead to inefficient resource allocation, restricting a country's ability to effectively pursue both domestic and foreign security interests.

Good infrastructure enhances the productivity and competitiveness of the economy. It is an important foundation for economic development. Investments in transportation, energy supply, and telecommunications create the basis for entrepreneurial activities. Furthermore, investments in future technologies such as artificial intelligence, biotechnology, or renewable energy open up new fields of growth. The promotion of research institutions and technology transfer undoubtedly strengthens the innovative capacity of the economy.

However, at the forefront of this thought competition is security, because without it, all other criteria on the scale are as if blown away by the wind. It stands above all other factors because without security, all other goals and priorities cannot endure. Even the best plans for growth, innovation, social justice, or financial stability can quickly be jeopardized or rendered obsolete without a secure foundation. In an uncertain environment during crises or political instability, companies have less incentive to invest, and citizens have less trust in the future. Without political stability, no long-term progress can be made. A country that is constantly threatened by political uncertainty, conflicts, or corruption cannot implement reliable measures to improve living conditions. In an environment threatened by crime, terrorism, or war, all other societal issues fade into the background. In such cases, resources are allocated for security measures, defense, and emergency aid.

Investments require an environment where property rights, the rule of law, and market security are guaranteed. Without security, companies cannot expand or explore new markets. This alone is reason enough to suppress left-revolutionary or right-populist tendencies. Left-revolutionary groups often demand profound social and economic upheavals that challenge existing power structures. They advocate for overcoming capitalism and wealth redistribution, which in extreme cases can lead to the nationalization of companies, expropriations, and a rejection of market economy principles. However, this immediately causes economic instability, capital flight, and a departure from market economy fundamentals, which, as history has often proven, occurs too late. Right-wing extremist tendencies, in turn, provoke social tensions and weaken democratic institutions. The rejection of diversity and the strengthening of authoritarian structures under right-populist movements are aimed at shaking the very foundations of society. Such upheavals are guarantees of destabilizing the economy, causing uncertainties in financial markets, and undermining public trust in state institutions. A divided society finds it harder to find common solutions to pressing problems and is more susceptible to internal unrest.

It is of societal and political importance to identify problems or threats in a timely manner so that appropriate measures can be taken before they spiral out of control. Early intervention can resolve many issues before they escalate. Governments should not only react when the situation is already critical but proactively act to prevent escalations. Often, migrations toward extremism arise from a lack of inclusion and dialogue. A preventive solution could therefore involve opening the political discourse and ensuring that legitimate concerns are heard and incorporated into political decisions before they take radical forms. Both left-revolutionary and right-populist movements challenge democratic processes and institutions. While left-revolutionary movements patiently speculate under the guise of façade parties to introduce authoritarian socialist regimes, right-populist movements rehearse uprisings to undermine the rule of law and the independence of institutions such as the judiciary or the media.

Even the fight against climate change and the protection of natural resources require a basic level of global and national security, as crises and conflicts tend to neglect or delay protective measures. Circular, systemic thinking is preferred over linear thinking in this context, no matter how difficult it may be. Systemic thinking recognizes that causes and effects in complicated cases are cyclical and interdependent. It assumes that a change in one part of the system impacts other parts, which can, in turn, have feedback effects. Changes in one area - be it economic, political, or social - often produce unexpected side effects in other areas. Circular thinking allows for a comprehensive understanding of problems and situations rather than breaking them down into isolated parts. It accounts for the interactions and dependencies between various elements of a system. It seeks to better grasp and manage complexities. Implementing circular thinking can be challenging, as it requires a shift in mindset and the willingness to question existing structures and processes. For simple, clearly defined problems, there are situations where linear thinking can indeed be appropriate and effective.

Security is at the center of international relations, especially on a global level. Countries that are influenced by nationalism or mired in bureaucracy often overlook this. Without international security, multilateral agreements, such as trade agreements or climate accords, are at risk. When states focus solely on their own security interests, they can destabilize other countries or ignore international agreements aimed at collective security. This can lead to an arms race or geopolitical tensions. Bureaucratic structures often cause resources to be distributed inefficiently, limiting a country's ability to effectively pursue both domestic and foreign security interests.

From a political perspective, conservative or market-liberal governments advocate for measures that seek to reduce state influence in the economy and aim for sound public finances. Austerity measures are often viewed as a means to ensure long-term financial stability. Subsidies, particularly for public goods, are typically promoted by social-democratic governments, which see the state as an active player in the economy that should foster growth, social justice, and prosperity through targeted spending. International institutions like the International Monetary Fund or the World Bank impose strict austerity programs as conditions for support, especially in countries with high debt or budget deficits. For instance, countries in the Eurozone, such as Greece, that received aid packages after the financial crisis had to implement strict austerity measures to maintain fiscal discipline.

An extreme focus on only one of these two approaches usually has negative consequences. Therefore, austerity measures and investments must be examined together to achieve a stable economic balance. The concept of decision balance is an important element in the transtheoretical model of behavior change. It refers to weighing the perceived advantages and disadvantages of a political behavior change. This suggests that the perceived disadvantages may outweigh the advantages. There are approaches that aim to achieve a more balanced decision-making process by maximizing perceived benefits and minimizing disadvantages. The goal is to find a path to budget consolidation that is both fiscally responsible and socially and economically viable. But who ideally conducts this evaluation?

Political decision-makers can be supported by economic and political advisors who provide analyses and assessments to better weigh the pros and cons. Self-proclaimed political advisors, especially those from within their own party, who lack proven qualifications or expertise can indeed be dangerous and undermine democracy and public trust. Policy advice should be based on sound research, expert knowledge, and verifiable facts. It becomes particularly problematic when such advisors appear publicly without their recommendations and views being critically questioned or verified. Therefore, it is crucial for political decision-makers to carefully consider qualifications, experience, and independence when selecting advisors to ensure that their policies are evidence-based and aimed at the common good.

Evaluating the decision balance regarding political behavior changes requires the involvement of various actors, including political decision-makers, scholars, stakeholders, and the public. A thorough and comprehensive analysis of the pros and cons should objectively find ways for budget consolidation that are both fiscally responsible and socially and economically acceptable. By incorporating diverse perspectives into the decision-making process, the likelihood that the decisions made will be widely accepted and successfully implemented increases.

The principle of rotation plays an important role in the interconnectivity of success. It ensures that decision-making bodies remain capable of action even as their membership grows. By regularly rotating officials or functions, the concentration of power and potential abuse of power are countered. This promotes a more balanced distribution of power and prevents the emergence of monopolistic positions. Rotation allows for the inclusion of various actors and perspectives in decision-making processes.

This can lead to more innovative and balanced solutions, as different experiences and viewpoints are taken into account. It strengthens the legitimacy and acceptance of decisions. Through the rotation of functions and responsibilities, knowledge transfer within organizations is facilitated. Employees acquire new skills and a broader understanding of different areas, improving the overall performance of the organization.

In multilateral institutions, rotation offers several advantages for interconnectivity and the success of international cooperation. By regularly changing officials or chairs, the concentration of power is countered. Paradoxically, the principle of rotation can also contribute to institutional continuity. It prevents individual actors from staying in power for too long and instead promotes the development of stable institutional structures and processes. Often, for pragmatic reasons, trade with countries is maintained even in the face of human rights violations. An example is the economic cooperation of Western states with authoritarian regimes, which, while politically controversial, are seen as important trade partners for raw materials or low-cost production opportunities. Why worry about human rights violations when the container filled with cheaply produced goods arrives on time at the port? A little stability here, a little flexibility there—preferably all tailored to profit margins? This dilemma is evident in the debate over the role of Western companies in countries that commit human rights violations or in the demand for fair trade practices. Values such as the rule of law and transparency will play a crucial role in choosing investment and production locations for international companies. Companies are increasingly seeking stable, predictable political and legal frameworks that provide a secure environment for investments.

Flexible adaptation of strategies to changing circumstances is a central element of international politics. In a dynamic global environment, states and international actors must continuously rethink and adjust their strategies to respond to new challenges and opportunities. Changes such as conflicts, economic developments, or social movements must be detected early. Alliances should be reassessed regularly to achieve their strategic goals. Such coalitions can vary depending on the respective interests and threats. Clusters of alliances that possess strong innovation capabilities and advanced technological infrastructure set higher economic goals and enjoy strategic advantages in international politics. Strategic progress creates new industries and strengthens international competitiveness. Flexibility is crucial to responding to unexpected events such as economic downturns, natural disasters, or geopolitical changes. Resource allocation should be designed to respond to short-term crises without jeopardizing long-term goals. However, these policies must often be implemented in a complex global environment where national decisions have international repercussions. A thorough analysis of current trends, such as the technological revolution, the rise of emerging markets, or the shifting of production chains, is crucial for strategic planning. Resource allocation must always be viewed in a comprehensive context. An integrated strategy that includes all important sectors should ensure that all parts of society benefit from investments.

Economic factors determine which resources and means are available and how they are used to meet political, social, or economic objectives. Budget deficits, national debt, and tax revenues directly influence which economic policy goals are realistic to pursue. A deep understanding of the economic framework conditions helps make strategic decisions and allocate limited resources where they can have the greatest effect. How can limited resources be optimally allocated to achieve the greatest positive impact in key areas such as education, health, defense, and infrastructure? This process requires careful planning, prioritization, and consideration of long-term impacts. Efficiency improvements are achieved through the use of modern technologies and digital solutions. In areas such as infrastructure, political cooperation with the private sector can implement committed projects more efficiently. By directing private investments into public projects, resources are freed up that are needed elsewhere. Ultimately, resource utilization should be open and transparent, ensuring that the public has trust in the prioritization of objectives.

Stakeholder interconnectivity refers to the complex relationships and interactions between different actors involved in a particular project, initiative, or decision-making process. These relationships are crucial to understanding influence, power and interests in a given context. The multi-stakeholder approach has established itself as an important principle in international digital policy. Various interest groups such as governments, the private sector, civil society and the technical community are involved in decision-making processes. The aim is to achieve a broad consensus between stakeholders and to take into account the expertise and perspectives of all relevant actors. Stakeholders interact to share information, leading to better decisions and improved strategic planning. Managed collaboration creates synergies and allows projects to be implemented more efficiently. An understanding of interconnective relationships helps to identify and resolve conflicts early by taking into account the interests and concerns of all parties involved.

## 27. CLEAN GROWTH AND SUSTAINABILITY

This title aims to stimulate economic development without overloading natural resources or harming the environment. These ideas are increasingly seen as necessary steps to combat climate change and ensure a livable future. It describes a process of economic growth that must be resource-efficient and environmentally friendly. Science and management focus on technological innovations and business models that reduce environmental impact while allowing for economic development.

Solar and wind energy, investments in electric mobility, and sustainable agriculture and forestry are the introductory topics of this era. Sustainability means that the needs of the current generation are met without compromising the ability of future generations to meet their own needs. At the heart of this approach is the goal of achieving a balance between economic growth, social justice, and environmental protection. Ecological sustainability includes the protection and preservation of the natural environment, as well as the promotion of education, health, and social justice, and the creation of a stable and resilient economy. Sustainable growth requires innovative approaches in the fields of energy, production, and consumption to ensure that prosperity is created without destroying the environment.

Many countries face the challenge of reforming their existing economic structures. The transition from fossil fuels to renewable energy can be costly in the short term. Thus, the shift to sustainable consumption also requires changes in consumer behavior. While some countries are well-prepared to invest in clean growth, others lack financial resources or infrastructure. Resources are maintained in closed cycles instead of being discarded after use. Global agreements like the Paris Agreement on climate are essential to combat climate change. Educational systems and research are preparing to find new solutions for sustainable growth. By integrating clean growth and sustainability into economic policy, long-term ecological and social benefits are achieved without sacrificing economic prosperity.

In contrast to what should be done, attempts to save the world through empty promises reveal another reality. It is reassuring to know that the global economy has finally mobilized to address the issues of climate change and environmental destruction. This seems impressive. We can continue to consume without limits, waste resources, and exploit our planet conveniently, as long as we do it in a "sustainable" manner. After all, why bother making real changes when a nice-sounding "green" label can cover everything up? The largest companies in the world are even planting trees now. For every million tons of $CO_2$ they emit from their endless production lines, a small tree is planted in a distant tropical forest. This is the essence of "clean growth": to continue as before, as long as we take a few symbolic measures to appease public opinion. There's no real reason to give up fossil fuels; a walk in the forest with the public relations department suffices. And then, of course, there's greenwashing, the crown jewel of any sustainable strategy. Who needs real reforms when we can simply change the packaging of a plastic product to "biodegradable" materials that only decompose under laboratory conditions? The new packaging is just as harmful as the old, but now consumers feel better. Isn't that the very essence of sustainability: to ease one's conscience without really changing anything?

The fashion industry has also grasped the principle: instead of reducing production, they simply launch a "sustainable collection" that only wastes 90% of the usual resources. We celebrate the fig tree while the rest of production continues to churn out cheap clothing intensively. "Clean growth" at its finest. Of course, one might argue that renewable energies are a hope. But who needs wind or solar energy when we can continue to rely on coal as long as we offer "sustainable" incentives? Politics seems fully engaged. The Paris Agreement on climate ultimately requires concrete results only in a few decades. So why act today when we can elegantly push the problem into the future? A little research here, a little subsidy there, but definitely not too much change all at once. After all, we don't want to disturb anyone in their comfort zone. Clean growth means, after all, that there's no need to make real sacrifices. Not to mention the wonderful promises of technology. The future will provide us with miracle solutions that will solve all our problems without us having to do anything. Perhaps there will soon be machines that suck $CO_2$ directly from the air. Until then, we can continue to drive our SUVs and consume flights like fast food. Why stop when we will soon have a technical solution?

Of course, the responsibility lies with all of us. If we do not buy the expensive "organic" products or reduce our water consumption, we clearly become part of the problem. It is not the industry or politics that need to change; every individual is an obstacle to progress. But no worries, if we are unable to afford a modern car of the future, we can always swap our plastic straw for a metal straw—problem solved. So we can all reassure ourselves. The world will be saved, not by real measures, but by clever marketing and symbolic politics. Clean growth and sustainability are not real solutions, but terms that sound good and give us the impression of doing something without really acting. Will the future be bright, perhaps even green, if we just put in a little effort? The irony is that we settle for these superficial changes until it is truly too late.

Technologies such as solar and wind energy, electric mobility, and sustainable agriculture and forestry are at the core of what is now considered the beginning of a new era in environmental awareness and technological progress. They are becoming key themes of this time, where the relationship between economic growth and environmental protection is radically transforming. But these starting themes are not mere passing fads; they mark the beginning of a profound change that has the potential to transform our societies in the long term.

Solar and wind energy are likely the precursors of a movement toward renewable energies. What was once considered an expensive and inefficient alternative to fossil fuels has now become a viable and competitive option. Solar panels are becoming increasingly powerful, and large wind farms continuously feed the electrical grids around the world. Here emerges the vision of a world where energy is clean, unlimited, and available in a decentralized manner. Electric mobility is another central theme of this new era. Traditional combustion engines, which have filled our cities with noise and exhaust fumes for decades, are gradually being replaced by silent, emission-free vehicles. Major automobile manufacturers are investing billions in the development of electric vehicles, and governments around the world are supporting the expansion of charging infrastructure and subsidizing electric cars. Indeed, transportation is responsible for a significant portion of global $CO_2$ emissions. The shift to electric mobility, combined with clean energy, could revolutionize the transportation sector and significantly reduce air pollution.

While industrial agriculture has sometimes led in the past to habitat destruction, soil erosion, and deforestation, we are now witnessing a movement toward sustainable agricultural practices. Agroforestry, permaculture, and regenerative agriculture rely on techniques that rebuild soils, minimize water consumption, and promote biodiversity. Forestry is also evolving, with a focus on forest conservation, reforestation, and sustainable use of wood. Sustainable agriculture and forestry are essential to feed a growing global population without depleting natural resources. Moreover, forests play a key role in $CO_2$ sequestration and the preservation of ecosystems. These subjects are not isolated trends; they are part of a global movement aimed at slowing climate change, preserving the planet for future generations, while simultaneously promoting economic transformation. What appears today as a beginning could become an indispensable part of our daily lives and our global economy.

In a future built on the foundations of new technologies, sustainable mobility, and regenerative agriculture, several other developments, dreams of the future, and visions could revolutionize how we manage our resources. While today's world has taken the first step towards a sustainable future, ambitious scenarios are already taking shape on the horizon, far beyond what we can currently imagine. One of the most radical visions for the future is the concept of a circular economy, where the term "waste" practically disappears. Instead of the old linear approach to the economy—extraction of raw materials, production, consumption, and disposal—a new economy is built in which all materials are reused or regenerated. Products are designed to be easily disassembled, repaired, and recycled, and biological materials are fully reintroduced into natural cycles. Cities could become waste-free, where all consumed resources are either recycled or regenerated in nature. Materials like plastic, which today represent a global environmental problem, could be replaced by biodegradable alternatives that decompose completely in a few weeks or months.

In the cities of the future, environmental technologies could be seamlessly integrated into urban infrastructure. "Smart cities" would be characterized by sensor-based systems that intelligently manage energy, water, and traffic. Buildings would become energy producers by incorporating solar panels on roofs and facades, injecting excess energy into the grids. Parks and green roofs would serve not only as recreational spaces but also as natural air conditioners, lowering temperatures in cities and capturing $CO_2$. A city where every building is a power plant, every vehicle is electric and autonomous, and every street uses sensors and AI to manage traffic so efficiently that there are virtually no traffic jams would be extremely resource-efficient and climate-neutral, while making life more comfortable and healthier through smart technology.

Due to the growth of the global population and limited agricultural land, visions of vertical farms and urban food systems in cities play a key role. In skyscrapers, vegetables, fruits, and herbs could be grown on multiple levels, illuminated by energy-efficient LEDs and irrigated by highly efficient hydroponic systems. This would shorten food supply chains, reduce transportation journeys, and minimize reliance on external food sources. Large metropolises could cover their own food needs, with green skyscrapers serving as both housing and vertical farms. Such urban agriculture could reduce $CO_2$ emissions from cities while directly producing fresh, organic food on-site.

Another already-discussed vision in the field of technology would develop transportation of the future well beyond electric cars. Autonomous vehicles and public transport could be complemented by Hyperloop technology with extremely fast tube transport systems. It should not be forgotten that there are already urban areas in China that reach the size and population of small European states. Flying taxis, which are electric vehicles with vertical takeoff and landing capabilities, would shift urban traffic into the third dimension, allowing commuters to bypass traffic jams. Air taxis could become as common as Uber vehicles today, and thanks to Hyperloops, people could travel from one metropolis to another in just minutes. The entire transportation system would be completely emission-free and autonomous.

While solar and wind energy are currently at the forefront of the energy transition, science dreams of nuclear fusion as the ultimate energy source. If we can replicate the processes occurring in the sun here on Earth, we could have nearly unlimited clean energy. The world would be powered by inexhaustible energy from nuclear fusion, and a smart global energy system would harness all imaginable sources - from solar panels in the desert to tidal power plants in the oceans, and wind farms in the Arctic. Electricity shortages would belong to the past.

For now, regenerative ecosystems remain a relatively tangible strategic concept, aiming to reverse ecological damage and restore natural habitats, rather than merely minimizing harm. Unlike traditional conservation approaches that try to protect nature from human intervention, regenerative ecosystems aim to actively heal and regenerate the environment. This means that ecosystems are not only preserved but their condition is improved compared to what it was before. The agriculture of tomorrow will become an essential pillar in the fight against climate change. Fields could act as $CO_2$ sinks while providing food for the growing global population. Soils would be richer in nutrients, erosion would be avoided, and agriculture could be practiced in harmony with natural ecosystems.

The renaturation of damaged ecosystems, such as forests, wetlands, and waterways, could mean that former industrial areas in urban settings would be transformed back into forests, or that destroyed coral reefs would be rebuilt through innovative methods. Reforestation and the rehydration of peatlands could also support the natural carbon cycle, as forests and peatlands serve as vast carbon reservoirs. In a regenerative future, cities could be surrounded by green corridors and forests, traversed by renaturalized waterways. Coral reefs, destroyed by climate change, would bloom again thanks to regenerative measures, and peatland landscapes would once again act as natural "sponges" for $CO_2$. Another visionary evolution is "rewilding," where vast lands are left to themselves to restore the natural dynamics of the wild. By reintroducing key species, entire ecosystems could regain their balance. Large areas could be completely left to nature, where biodiversity would explode and ecosystems would self-regulate. Oceans could also benefit from regenerative approaches. In addition to restoring coral reefs, there are projects aimed at the renaturation of mangroves and seagrasses, which protect coastlines from erosion while serving as carbon sinks. Furthermore, sustainable fishing could contribute to restoring fish stocks through the use of regenerative methods like aquaculture, which supports marine biodiversity.

Thus, ingenuity for new technologies plays a key role in realizing this vision. Drones could be used for reforestation by dispersing seeds over hard-to-reach areas. Satellite monitoring would help track the restoration of ecosystems and analyze their health in real time. Artificial intelligence could be employed to discover ecological patterns and enable targeted interventions. The interconnectivity between nature and technology paves the way for regenerative ecosystems. Smart technologies should be capable not only of monitoring the state of the environment but also of actively contributing to its restoration. Through automated processes, nature would regenerate faster than ever, while humanity would act as a responsible steward of the Earth. Regenerative ecosystems are more than just a dream for the future; they constitute a necessary response to the challenges we face. The visions outlined imagine a world in which people no longer merely minimize their negative impact on the environment but actively contribute to healing the planet. With the right combination of ecological principles, technology, and conscious action, this regenerative future could become a reality.

## 28. FUTURE DREAMS OF INTERCONNECTIVITY AND THEIR NEED

The connection between different technologies, sustainable concepts, and regenerative approaches is key to creating a sustainable and regenerative world. These dreams cannot be viewed in isolation; they are interdependent and must be integrated and coordinated to unleash their full potential. This interconnectedness is necessary to effectively address the challenges of climate change, resource scarcity, and biodiversity loss.

The future of energy production, mobility, and urban infrastructure must be seamlessly linked. This involves not only the development of wind and solar energy but also the creation of smart grid technology that efficiently stores and distributes energy. Buildings can operate as mini power plants, producing, storing, and feeding electricity back into the grid. Smart cities also require integrated systems that intelligently manage the flow of energy, transportation, and resource use. Without this connection between urban agriculture and energy sources, ensuring the sustainability of the food system becomes difficult. The integration of waste management, water recycling, and renewable energy is essential to make urban food production truly sustainable and reduce dependence on external resources.

A global super grid for renewable energies, linking wind, solar, and tidal energy around the world, would enable the transport of surplus energy from regions with excess production to those in deficit. At the same time, this grid would improve access to clean electricity for all regions, thereby reducing dependence on fossil fuels. The global connectivity of energy networks could also serve as a basis for exchanging other resources, such as water or raw materials that are scarce in certain areas. Without a global energy distribution system, some regions may remain dependent on fossil fuels despite technological advancements. Energy supply must be considered on a global scale to be truly sustainable and allow everyone access to clean energy. This is the only way to achieve comprehensive and equitable decarbonization. Without technology, it is challenging to understand and connect the complex ecological and economic systems.

The various technologies and approaches to sustainability require governments to create economic incentives to encourage private investment in sustainable projects while ensuring that social justice and access to resources are guaranteed for all. Without global collaboration and the linking of policy measures, it is impossible to effectively integrate the different visions of the future. Regional climate protection plans must be anchored in a global agenda that considers economic and social aspects. The future dreams of clean growth and sustainability -who wouldn't want them? A utopian paradise full of solar panels and electric cars, where we all sit on our organic fair-trade cotton couches, sipping vegan lattes while saving the world. Before we get too lost in this bright vision, perhaps we should remember that there are a few small obstacles. Of course, nothing serious - just a bit of lobbying, political myopia, economic interests, technological hurdles, and human behavior.

Governments are always so motivated when it comes to climate protection. We almost see them with enthusiasm at climate conferences as they solemnly announce ambitious targets for 2050, surely hoping they will be retired by then and someone else will foot the bill. That, at the same time, they subsidize fossil fuels and wish to maximize economic growth at the expense of the planet is certainly just a little misunderstanding.

And then there are the companies. The oil and gas industry, for example - always so flexible and open to change. Just let them know they can save the world if they cut their profit margins a little. One can be certain that Shell and ExxonMobil are already lining up to invest in offshore wind farms and sustainable energies instead of continuing to spend billions on new drilling wells. The technological challenges are, of course, surmountable with a bit of Silicon Valley ingenuity. Nuclear fusion is almost here, just in 30 years, as it has been since the 1950s. And who needs functional batteries for renewable energies if we can just cover every roof with solar panels and hope that the wind blows at the right time? Details, just details. Of course, recycling isn't free, but we live in a world where education and equal opportunity are always at the top of the list, right? Otherwise, who needs social justice if we have clean air? Finally, there's Homo sapiens themselves, the species that considers waste sorting a bothersome constraint and still believes that climate change is a Chinese invention. But don't worry, even consumer society will change one day. We can be sure that we will soon give up our beloved SUVs, disposable products, and flights, if only we can hear a few more alarms. Yes, of course, we will all get there. After all, we have managed so well with all the other global crises, such as hunger and poverty. The future will be bright, as long as no one disturbs us.

The "exclusive club of green parties" must in no way continue to present itself as the sole savior of the planet. After all, there's nothing better than when all parties, whether conservative, liberal, left, or right - are they still necessary? - suddenly discover that sustainability could appear on their agenda. The time when green parties had to fight for themes such as climate protection, ecology, and sustainability must absolutely come to an end. After all, these concerns should no longer be their private domain.

What could be more beautiful than if every long-standing or innovation-averse political movement suddenly jumped on board and proudly proclaimed themselves the true champions of clean energy and sustainable agriculture? Of course, they would manage to implement the energy transition without slowing down economic growth or jeopardizing jobs. Sounds like magic? Exactly, that's what it is! Could the great magic formula be: green ideas, but please without any real change?

The future movements that will liberate us from the party structures of the past already have the green thread in hand. One might wonder how it was possible for green parties to boast about issues like climate and sustainability for so long, when true political wisdom lies in proclaiming green goals without taking on the burdens of a genuine systemic change. The best part: the new parties sprouting from all corners of the political spectrum can afford to demand sustainability while keeping everything else the same. The future belongs to the green camouflage, only for the paint to peel off as soon as actual responsibility comes into play. Sustainability for all, change for none!

The criticism that green parties act as the sole guardians of these issues is both justified and important. It is time for all political movements to face this challenge and actively promote solutions without relying solely on rhetoric. However, the danger lies in so-called "greenwashing," rebranding existing policies with an ecological veneer without allowing for genuine change. Sustainability cannot merely serve as a lip service or a strategic maneuver in political competition. The call for sustainable practices must come with concrete measures, profound political decisions, and a realistic transition.

The approach of claiming sustainability as a universal goal may seem tempting in the current political discourse. But just because all parties have a "green face", it does not mean that the necessary changes will actually take place in practice. It is easy to talk about "green ideals"; it becomes more challenging when it comes to real transformations in the economy, energy supply, and agricultural policy. The world certainly needs more than just a cosmetic adjustment of political narratives. The future requires bold decisions that often entail significant economic and social changes. The path to a sustainable society involves a serious and open dialogue about what sacrifices are necessary and who will actually bear the costs of this transformation.

The challenge for all political actors is not only to position themselves as advocates of sustainability but also to take the necessary steps to address the deeply rooted structures that exacerbate the current state of our planet. Only when genuine restructuring is at the forefront can we hope to solve the underlying problem of climate change and create an environmentally friendly future for all. In fact, the future does not belong to exclusive "eco-clubs," but to the collective responsibility of all politicians, regardless of their ideology. Sustainability should be an integral and mandatory part of every political agenda, armed with the will to bring about real change.

By balancing the integration of businesses and communities into international political processes, it is possible to align economic innovation with social justice and ecological sustainability. However, this requires a continuous balancing of interests and the willingness of all parties involved to work together on sustainable solutions to global challenges. To overcome imbalances, policymakers must be willing to question existing power structures. This could involve designing trade and investment agreements that not only benefit large players but also promote social and ecological justice.

Political will is necessary to develop new pathways for international cooperation. This would mean moving away from hierarchical or nationalistic models and instead relying on transnational networks and alliances that enable flexible yet inclusive solutions. International collaborations should not be viewed as a zero-sum game but as an opportunity to solve global problems through collective efforts. Another important aspect of this transformation is protection against extremism, which can arise from both the left and right sides of the political spectrum. By making politics more inclusive and transparent, the causes of radicalization and extremism can be better addressed. Overall, we stand at a turning point where the way we understand and practice politics is fundamentally changing. The opportunities that arise from this transformation are equally significant. It is up to us to seize these new possibilities and shape a politics that meets the needs and desires of citizens. Only in this way can we foster a democratic culture that aims not just at preserving power, but at actively shaping a just and sustainable future.

Future conferences and the development of science-based evaluations will play a leading role in this process. They will help make informed decisions and ensure that policies are evidence-based and aligned with the needs of the population. This could not only lead to better anchoring of political measures but also stimulate citizen participation, as people are more likely to identify with political action when they feel their opinions are heard and taken into account. The transformation of the party system offers the opportunity to think beyond national borders and particularistic interests. Political movements could respond more flexibly to interconnected challenges. Participatory approaches and the consideration of diverse perspectives could help create a more inclusive political environment that can fend off extremism from both the left and the right. Overall, the redesign of the political landscape is not only a challenge but also an opportunity for a more democratic, inclusive, and understanding society. It is crucial that all actors in this process collaborate, from political institutions to civil societies and the citizens themselves. Only then can a resilient democracy emerge that responds to the needs of a constantly changing world.

Modern societies face a variety of challenges that are both natural and man-made. These threats, whether from pandemics, climate change, social unrest, or geopolitical tensions, reveal the fragility of our social fabric. Societies with strong social networks and community bonds are better able to cope with crises and emerge from them stronger. Social networks are the backbone of social cohesion. They provide emotional and material support and enable the rapid dissemination of information. In critical situations, these networks are often crucial for survival. Shared values and a strong identity within a group foster resilience and the ability to overcome challenges. In the exchange of information and experiences, involved members receive valuable advice or support regarding personal issues. Social networks often motivate people to engage in volunteer work or participate in community projects, further strengthening social cohesion.

The concept of social capital is central to understanding how communities respond to crises. By focusing on the connections between individuals and the resources that arise from these relationships, it becomes evident that societies with high social capital are often less vulnerable to crises. They have networks that facilitate and promote the exchange of information and assistance. Social capital is not just a theoretical concept; in times of crisis, it is also a practically effective factor for the resilience and adaptability of communities. It forms the foundation for effective collective action and is therefore a key element in successfully managing crises.

Climate change and natural disasters force communities to work together to adapt and build resilience. In many affected regions, social networks often serve as the first responders, providing assistance before state institutions intervene. This highlights the importance of local engagement and community actions in developing long-term solutions. Advanced technology has revolutionized the way we interact with one another. Social media and communication platforms enable quick and effective networking, even in crisis situations. A good example is the role of social media in organizing relief efforts after natural disasters, such as coordinating donations and volunteer work. However, there are also downsides: misinformation and virtual conflicts can exacerbate tensions within communities. Platforms like Twitter/X or Facebook allow for the rapid spread of false information, often faster than corrections can be made through fact-checking. Different narratives lead to parallel societies with conflicting worldviews. The challenge is to use these technologies in ways that promote social cohesion rather than undermine it. Digital networking has the potential to strengthen social ties, mobilize communities, and promote social cohesion. At the same time, misinformation and virtual conflicts can turn the same technologies into tools of division and polarization. The central challenge is to shape the use of digital technologies in a way that fosters cohesion rather than jeopardizing it.

One of the most effective methods for strengthening social cohesion is education. Educational institutions should develop programs that promote intercultural dialogue and collaboration. Education plays a key role in breaking down individual prejudices and raising awareness of the importance of communities. Public projects and local initiatives can act as catalysts for social cohesion. Such measures strengthen people's identification with their neighborhoods and build trust. It is important that all societal groups are included in this process.

The interconnectivity of social cohesion enables the management of acute challenges and also strengthens long-term resilience. Societies that affirm their social cohesion can not only withstand crises but also emerge restructured from them. Therefore, it is essential to develop strategies and programs that promote social cohesion while also considering the effects of modern technologies. In a rapidly changing world, the ability to stand together as a community is one of the most crucial resources a society possesses. A combination of technological adjustments, education, and social engagement is needed to minimize the downsides of digitalization. A functioning social fabric is the foundation of any society. It encompasses the relationships, norms, and values that regulate individual behavior in their social environment. When social, economic, and ecological challenges are so intensely intertwined, understanding the interconnectivity of social responsibilities cannot be overlooked.

Setting the course for a fairer world requires an awareness of social, economic, and ecological contexts. Educational initiatives that inform people about their rights and responsibilities are crucial. Additionally, programs that promote integration and equal opportunities are needed to reduce social tensions and recognize diversity as a strength. Responsible corporate governance means thinking beyond mere profit maximization. Companies should actively invest in society, apply ethical business practices, and promote sustainable products and services. By advocating for social causes, they contribute to creating a fairer economic environment.
Awareness of the interconnections between social, economic, and ecological aspects is a fundamental prerequisite for sustainable

development and the creation of a just society. These areas are inextricably linked and require a holistic understanding to manage crises and create long-term resilience. Challenges such as inequality, poverty, and social exclusion illustrate how closely these issues are intertwined with economic and ecological factors.

The economy is both a cause and a potential solution to ecological and social problems. The concentration of wealth often leads to excessive consumption by a few and the exploitation of resources. Transitioning to a circular economy, where resources are reused and waste minimized, will reduce ecological damage and create new jobs. Ecosystems are the basis of all economic and social life. Their degradation leads to crises in other areas. Environmental destruction and climate crises drive migration and conflicts, as people are forced to leave uninhabitable regions. The loss of biodiversity endangers agricultural production systems and, consequently, global food security. Sustainability strategies such as promoting regenerative agriculture can minimize ecological damage while simultaneously creating social and economic benefits. Only through inclusive action can a balance between these dimensions be achieved.

## 29. INTERCONNECTIVITY OF THE STUPIDITY OF A SOCIETY

The "dumbing down" of a society refers to the complex interactions between various factors that influence the intellectual and cultural decline of that society. In a highly interconnected world, several aspects can accelerate this process. One significant factor is the role of connectivity in the dissemination and intensification of erroneous opinions that contribute to this dumbing down.

Communication platforms like TikTok favor content that generates high interactions, leading to the easy spread of sensational news and simple, emotionally charged information. This amplifies the dissemination of misinformation, conspiracy theories, and pseudoscientific content. By personalizing content, people are more likely to engage only with information that confirms their own views. This increases cognitive biases, as opposing opinions or scientifically grounded facts often fall outside their field of vision. Such echo chambers promote intellectual isolation and prevent engagement with complex, nuanced topics.

The standardization and flattening of media forms are further exacerbated by interconnectivity, as the same content is disseminated worldwide. Deeper cultural and intellectual discourses risk being displaced. Simple, commercial entertainment often overshadows local cultural forms or intellectual discussions. Through connectivity, these contents are consumed globally, reducing the diversity of cultural and intellectual expressions.

Countries that are tightly integrated into dense financial systems often face pressure to cut public spending, negatively impacting educational institutions. Austerity measures in the education sector, especially during times of crisis, and inadequate funding for schools and universities lead to a long-term decline in intellectual standards that affects generations. In authoritarian systems, there is a reliance on strict ideologization skills, while the humanities and critical thinking are less promoted. This narrowing results in a simplification of educational content and pushes intellectual depth into a parched drought.Political ideologies spread rapidly across national borders, as evidenced by right-wing radicalism in Europe and the United States. Populist leaders and parties then employ similar tactics in various countries. They simplify complex problems, offer simple, illusory solutions, and ignore scientific findings. Authoritarian governments and political actors exploit the interconnectedness of the internet to deliberately spread disinformation and manipulate public opinion.

This can undermine trust in traditional sources of knowledge and institutions of science and education. The targeted audiences then cling more to emotionally appealing but factually incorrect narratives.

With the increasing reliance on algorithms for filtering and recommending content, people are more frequently falling into "filter bubbles." This leads them to only see information that aligns with their previous preferences and opinions. It intensifies the isolation from opposing viewpoints and promotes superficial thinking. The automated dependence on technology for information retrieval and decision-making tempts individuals to think less independently or conduct their own research. An excessive trust in technology diminishes critical thinking and leads to the uncritical acceptance of all kinds of information. As a result, traditional forms of knowledge lose significance. Unilateral problem-solving approaches or knowledge practices are replaced by standardized models that are less tailored to local needs or realities. Thus, it heavily depends on how societies utilize and shape these connections.

To combat these negative developments, education and media

literacy are crucial. Individuals should be empowered to critically question information, consult various sources, and distinguish between reliable and unreliable content. Platforms and companies also bear responsibility for fostering a healthy information environment and taking measures against misinformation. A society actively countering potential "dumbing down" relies on a combination of various measures to enhance its cognitive and social capacities. It is important to engage with technological developments in a reflective and conscious manner rather than rejecting them outright.

The mandate for education systems, both in schools and through lifelong learning, should focus on prioritizing critical thinking, problem-solving skills, and media literacy. Understanding complex topics and the ability to critically question information must be promoted, rather than simply testing theoretical knowledge. To counteract the flattening and sensationalism in the media, reputable news sources should be advertised and disseminated. Open access to well-researched and substantiated information strengthens the knowledge and diversity of opinions within a society. Open discussion forums, both online and offline, offer opportunities for exchanging nuanced opinions. Such platforms not only promote social cohesion but also enhance the ability to understand and process complex and controversial topics. Theater, art, and sports contribute to holistic development, helping people act more empathetically and reflectively in various positions.

We have truly been catapulted into a golden age. Who needs the laborious task of critical thinking when an algorithm can quickly tell us what we should think? Or do we have the entire knowledge of human history in our pockets and just choose not to use it? Critical thinking? We've long delegated that to algorithms that know what we want before we do. Our smartphones are marvels of knowledge accumulation, compressing all of humanity's knowledge into a few square centimeters of screen space. But why should we bother to tap into this treasure? It's much more convenient to endlessly scroll through social media and be entertained by AI-curated content. Independent thought is, after all, hopelessly outdated. Why strain our brains when clever algorithms already know what we want - before we've even thought about it? Let us be grateful for these digital prophets who relieve us of the burden of decision-making. Who needs nuanced expression when a well-placed emoji speaks volumes? Thanks to AI-assisted emoji suggestions, we can express our deepest feelings with a simple pictogram. Shakespeare would be envious of such eloquent communication.

As long as we ensure that our AI assistants help us choose the right emojis, we are well on our way to successfully managing "dumbing down." After all, common sense is unnecessary when one has quick internet access. Successfully spreading "dumbing down" has never been easier - one merely has to stop thinking and completely surrender to digital wisdom. Welcome to the brave new world where ignorance is bliss and superficiality prevails. The future has never been so gloriously dumb, even though humanity has made tremendous technological progress in recent centuries. Artificial intelligence, digitalization, space exploration, genetic research, and other innovations are currently highlights of a shining, advanced future. Yet, despite -or perhaps because of - this immense technological growth, deeper Herculean tasks also emerge. Progress itself has problematic side effects in many ways. We are more connected than ever, yet simultaneously more isolated. We have access to infinite knowledge, yet misinformation and superficiality spread rapidly. The "glorious stupidity" might refer to the fact that while our technological achievements are spectacular, they do not always come with wisdom, reflection, or sustainable solutions to humanity's fundamental problems.

Joining the wave can make it difficult to break free, as herd behavior becomes a survival strategy. A group of people begins to reproduce ideas without questioning their truth, content, or consequences. This leads to a sequence within the context of a number of actions. Each of the actions in this context is an individual action, but the resulting "stupidity" is collective; when this occurs, it leads to various further related consequences. A dynamic and a structure emerge that are detached from the original actions and beliefs of the individuals. This results in a chain of actions whose consequences the group often no longer consciously reflects upon.

This dynamic can manifest in many areas of life, such as politics, social media, or even economic decisions. A classic example would be a financial bubble, where many people follow a trend without questioning the actual value of an investment, or in history, where propaganda leads large segments of the population to adopt beliefs that are not based on facts. "Collective stupidity" becomes a self-reinforcing process that is often difficult to break, as it becomes increasingly challenging to oppose established opinions. In political contexts, the interconnectedness of stupidity points to the connections between extreme ideologies or populism, where simplified or irrational ideas gain more influence through networking and repetition. This occurs through misinformation, manipulative rhetoric, or the aggressive polarization of society. Thus, the spread of misinformation leads individuals to believe in false or unreasonable theories and to share them within their networks.

It is striking that studies indicate that voters of extremist parties often have lower formal education levels. However, this does not mean that all individuals with less education can be seen as backward. Primitivity does not exist exclusively in a specific social or educational class but appears in various forms and contexts. Even among supposedly educated individuals, stereotypes of extremist views can form. This is explained in electoral research by economic insecurity, fear of social decline, and the desire for simple answers to complex societal problems. Populist parties offer quick solutions and specifically address the concerns and fears of their voter groups. Yet not all individuals with lower education levels are susceptible to this rhetoric, and it would be a gross error to claim otherwise. Voters are not a homogeneous group, and many make nuanced political decisions despite having less formal education. These individuals often possess a strong ethical foundation or practical life experiences that guide their political compass differently. In some cases, a high level of education does not lead to greater openness or tolerance but rather to an elitist and arrogant attitude. Even among academics, phenomena such as simplifications in opinion formation or conspiracy theories exist, especially when they serve their own ideology. A formal educational qualification does not necessarily protect against irrational thinking or belief in extremist views. Even philosophers like Martin Heidegger and others have been shown to have sympathies for National Socialism. This demonstrates that individuals with an intellectual background can also be susceptible to extreme ideologies.

What often comes to the forefront are superficial, polarizing, or sensationalist representations, as we as a society prioritize the trivial and the easy over the complex and profound. Instead of finding sustainable solutions to the climate crisis, social injustice, or political instability, we tend to get lost in trivial trends. "Glorious stupidity" could thus represent a form of collective repression or naive adherence to utopian ideas of progress without confronting the actual consequences. The interconnectedness of stupidity can also refer to phenomena like groupthink, where groups of interconnected individuals make decisions that are irrational or ineffective because they are not critically questioned. In this context, poor decisions often arise because individuals follow the group's opinion rather than making an independent or informed decision. "Control the minds of the sheep, and you control the herd."

In some cultures, education is not sufficiently valued, which does not exactly strengthen the motivation to acquire knowledge. A societal attitude that rejects or is suspicious of intellectuals and experts diminishes the appreciation for education and critical thinking. People living in precarious employment situations often have less time and resources to pursue further education or to think critically about societal issues. A less informed population is more easily manipulated by populist rhetoric and demagogic leaders, which promotes extreme political decisions. As long as individuals are unable to make informed choices and isolate themselves in their echo chambers, they will be less willing to engage with other perspectives. This, in turn, exacerbates societal divisions. The next step is then radicalization, as individuals increasingly embrace extremist ideologies. They also become unable to ask critical questions.

The dumbing down of a segment of society is a serious problem with many causes and far-reaching consequences. It requires a comprehensive understanding of the underlying factors and a commitment to taking targeted measures to counteract it. Only through a combination of societal engagement, education, media literacy, and political initiatives can we encourage intellectual revitalization. This is crucial for the well-being and stability of society as a whole. From the dilemma of an impossible connection, the process of creativity helps. It is fundamental to all disciplines, including the sciences. Creativity allows us to go beyond established ways of thinking and develop innovative solutions to complex problems. Mindfulness helps us observe and reflect on our own thoughts and feelings. Patience is essential, as creative ideas often take time to mature and develop. The willingness to listen to inner signals means that we are ready to take intuition and inspiration seriously. Free writing, for example, allows us to externalize thoughts and create new connections, while imaginative visualization helps us visualize concepts and explore scenarios that we might not have considered before. By consciously playing with ideas and scenarios, the best developments in science can take place. Here, alternative approaches and underdeveloped ideas can pave the way for groundbreaking discoveries. Ultimately, imagination is not just a tool for artists but also a fundamental element in the practical implementation of scientific findings.

Participating in actions that contradict logic or common sense reflects a degree of stupidity. In addition, there are countless simple mistakes made when a concept or situation is misunderstood. Making mistakes is a human trait; everyone makes errors, and often it is these mistakes from which we learn and grow. In between lies the social faux pas, which highlights a lack of social awareness. More serious are the mistakes that arise from impulsive actions taken without reflection or serious consideration of the consequences. In the same category of trivial mistakes fall repetitions, where the same errors are made repeatedly without learning from them. In contrast to wisdom, stupidity could be seen as the absence of deeper understanding and insight. Serious errors in politics become apparent when actions are taken based on a lack of appropriate analysis. Such mistakes have serious repercussions for society or the economy and weaken trust in current political affairs. These errors exacerbate crises or create new ones. Political decisions require a long-term perspective to consider possible future developments and their impacts. A lack of foresight can lead to a preference for short-term solutions that are problematic or ineffective in the long run.

When the personnel pool of the so-called intelligentsia becomes thin in a societal entity, it is the responsibility of civil society to change this condition. If the intelligentsia, the group of educated, intellectually, and creatively working individuals who often serve as cultural and ideological leaders, diminishes, long-term negative effects on societal development, innovation capacity, and democracy are inevitably the result. By better anchoring science and intellectual work within the broader population, the general public can be motivated to accept rational decisions. The creation of political science offerings and initiatives will help bridge the gap between experts and the public.

A vibrant intelligentsia thrives on debate, diversity of opinion, and critical thinking. In many cases, the intelligentsia is threatened by state repression, censorship, or restrictions on freedom of expression. Civil society must actively defend these freedoms to ensure that critical thinking and intellectual work can continue. Think tanks that bring together experts from various fields can help develop new ideas and address complex societal issues. Collaboration between scientists, artists, and civil society creates the perspectives that transform intellectual impulses into practice.

Interconnectivity in education is shaped by various interconnected factors that influence each other. Digital technologies are changing the way education is delivered. E-learning platforms and digital materials offer new opportunities for individualized learning. Public and private students can work at their own pace and according to their interests, with access to knowledge resources expanded globally. In addition to subject knowledge, key competencies such as critical thinking, problem-solving skills, teamwork, and digital competencies are of central importance. Driven by the rapid changes in the labor market, lifelong learning is essential. Education no longer has to be confined to formal pathways. Informal and non-formal learning are gaining significance to enable continuous knowledge updating and skill development.

## 30. ERRORS OF NEUTRALITY

Neutrality Has never brought lasting and secure peace. On the contrary, it has often led to war and disaster, veiled under hypocritical promises. Neutrality is seen as a way to avoid involvement in conflicts while maintaining peace and security. However, in certain contexts, ne.can be perceived as passivity or even complicity, especially when moral or ethical issues are at stake, such as human rights violations or acts of aggression. Historical examples, like the economic dealings of neutral states with Nazi Germany through trade in strategic resources, financial transactions via neutral banks, and the use of transit routes for goods, highlight this complexity. Such economic entanglements have often been criticized as morally questionable, as they indirectly supported the Nazi regime.

Neutrality is also often understood as avoidance of responsibility. States that actively promote peace, dialogue, and the enforcement of international law may contribute more to lasting peace than those that remain neutral, hoping to stay uninvolved. In today's world, where human rights, security, and global justice are of increasing importance, the failure to take a stand against blatant injustice exacerbates problems. In contemporary geopolitical conflicts, ostensibly neutral actors often act in ways that serve their own interests without explicitly taking sides, creating tensions— particularly in the face of humanitarian crises or large-scale human rights violations.

Neutrality as a lack of clarity. Neutrality can suggest diffuse views and positions, implying a lack of clarity or determination. This perception often arises when clear positions are demanded in political, moral, or social discussions. In such cases, neutrality is seen as avoidance - sidestepping difficult decisions or conflicts instead of adopting clear stances. Unlike balance, neutrality often comes across as inconsistent or opportunistic, especially when used as a strategy to gain advantages from powerful actors, as seen in certain political contexts like the United Arab Emirates.

When states or political actors ignore or fail to respond to threats, they not only endanger themselves but also their partners and the international community. Failing to address the rise of terrorist organizations or the threat posed by authoritarian regimes, for example, often allows these threats to escalate unchecked, jeopardizing global stability. Such inaction, driven by a reluctance to confront threats realistically, causes more harm than good. Neutrality, especially when it stems from a refusal to recognize or address threats, cannot effectively prevent conflicts or promote peace when the threats are severe, or moral and security obligations cannot be ignored. Recent examples, such as Finland and Sweden joining NATO, underscore the limitations of traditional neutrality in the face of acute threats. Their decision reflects the understanding that collective defense strategies are necessary to ensure security in today's complex geopolitical landscape.

The courage to take a stand. Decision-making often requires courage—taking clear positions and risking opposition or criticism. Many avoid this responsibility because decisions come with uncertainties and potential negative consequences. Neutrality, in such cases, offers a perceived shield, allowing individuals or states to avoid direct conflict or responsibility. However, neutrality, like anonymity, is often seen as avoidance and retreat rather than a mark of courage or resolve. It evades accountability and sidesteps clear positions on challenging issues.

When neutrality is perceived as a passive stance, states risk being seen as opportunistic by their partners, undermining trust and diminishing their influence. In the interconnected world of international relations, the need to take responsibility and clearly commit to values and principles becomes ever more pressing. Neutral governments in conflicts where they are indirectly affected often contribute to destabilization by failing to act decisively. In situations requiring clear ethical judgments, neutrality may be viewed as a moral failure. Silence is an inadequate response to human rights abuses or violations of international norms.

The moral challenge of neutrality. Neutrality is an active indecision often equated with emotional numbness or fleeting disinterest. In a world where every decision, stance, and word carries weight, no one can truly escape the moral responsibility to engage with reality rationally, empathetically, and critically. While neutrality may seem like a short-term solution, it ultimately fosters passivity and ignorance. True value lies not in silence or inaction but in the courageous advocacy for universal values. The question everyone must answer for themselves is this: What kind of world do you want to live in, and what commitment are you willing to make to create it?

In the intellectual sphere, the struggle of the individual and their community is equally necessary. One must take a stand, but many people shy away from this, preferring neutrality and avoidance. When this mindset is mirrored by the establishment that the masses follow, it underscores the bleakness of the future. The assumption that mistakes "cost nothing" is problematic. In science and philosophy, a misguided tendency towards neutrality can have serious consequences. It can misdirect research resources, negatively impact societal decisions, and hinder progress.

In the philosophical engagement with global politics, taking a definitive stance has become unavoidable. This engagement goes beyond mere power politics and touches upon fundamental differences regarding human rights, universalism, and systems of world order. The philosophical battle in international politics demands bold decisions and active participation. A refusal to take a position risks dangerous stagnation, while consciously addressing underlying worldviews can pave the way for constructive solutions to global problems. Convincing the uncertain in international relations requires well-thought-out, multidimensional actions.

In United Nations bodies, neutrality is less important than objectivity. To maintain global peace and security, support human rights, foster friendly relations among nations, and nurture international cooperation, the hypocrisy of a neutral stance is more of a hindrance than a help. Achieving these goals requires an objective approach rather than neutrality in the face of violations of these principles. Decision-making evaluations must be more scientific and transparent to ensure greater objectivity. The veto power of the permanent members of the Security Council, especially in instances of arbitrary blocking of resolutions, has scarcely been studied or evaluated. Geopolitical interests have become deeply embedded in decision-making structures, to the extent that the Security Council, based on empirical evidence, can hardly be recognized as representative of its mission. Neutrality, seen as passivity or indifference, is unhelpful in the complex and often contentious negotiations within UN bodies. Greater emphasis on objectivity rather than neutrality is needed to ensure fair and effective decisions.

In recent years, the United Nations has become stagnant, unable to extricate itself from its missteps. Bureaucratic hurdles, political deadlocks, and conflicting interests among member states have diminished the organization's capacity for action and its credibility. Particularly in the Security Council, where veto powers often disagree, blockages frequently prevent effective global operations. In crisis zones such as Syria, Yemen, Myanmar, or in addressing global challenges like climate change or refugee crises, the UN has been criticized for its delayed or insufficient actions, failing to bring about substantial change.

This reflects the difficulty of enforcing universal human rights when geopolitical interests are at play. When powerful member states pursue their own agendas through political or economic influence, the perception that the UN lacks objectivity is often reinforced. This fosters frustration among affected populations, who hope for strong international intervention. Bureaucracy and the need for consensus-based decisions hinder rapid responses in UN bodies. This lack of timely action has, in the past, allowed human rights violations to continue while the UN acted sluggishly. The debate over the UN's effectiveness in the realm of human rights remains a significant and contentious issue in international politics, requiring detailed and nuanced analysis of specific circumstances.

As it has become increasingly evident over recent decades that the UN is constrained by structural limitations, a profound restructuring of this global organization appears to be the only way to restore its effectiveness and meet the expectations of the international community. Countries such as Germany, India, Brazil, and Japan have long advocated for permanent membership in the Security Council to better reflect current geopolitical realities. Expanding representation and eliminating the absolute unanimity requirement for resolutions could enhance the Council's legitimacy and efficiency.

The General Assembly, where all 193 UN member states are represented, has primarily an advisory role. Its resolutions are not legally binding, which significantly limits its political authority. Restructuring into geographically broad regional representations could transform the role of the General Assembly by granting it more power on global issues, effectively serving as an additional endorsement for Security Council resolutions. Mechanisms could also be introduced to prevent Council decisions from being distorted by geopolitical interests.

Alternative funding sources could be explored, such as international taxes on financial transactions involving fossil fuels. This could reduce financial dependence on individual states. The management of UN finances could be improved through external audits and transparent reporting mechanisms to ensure that funds are used efficiently and for their intended purposes. If the UN is to remain a central pillar of the international order, the distribution of power in the Security Council must be adjusted, decision-making processes democratized, and financial independence secured. This would enable the organization to effectively address new global challenges and fulfill its role as the guardian of world peace and international cooperation in the 21st century.

When a global organization acts manipulatively in its statements and its voting processes are influenced in criminal ways, it represents a serious issue. Such behavior undermines trust in the institution, its ability to achieve its objectives, and its capacity to promote international cooperation. Reforms are absolutely necessary to ensure transparency, accountability, and ethical conduct. These reforms could include stricter regulations, independent oversight, the establishment of clear codes of conduct, and the introduction of mechanisms to review and track decisions and voting processes. Involving civil society and other stakeholders in the reform process could enhance the organization's legitimacy and integrity.

It is troubling when an indecisive leader at the helm of the UN undermines their moral authority through unqualified remarks about global situations, while legitimizing terrorist organizations by downplaying the Hamas attack in Gaza or showing submissiveness toward the dictator Putin. The deep bow by the UN Secretary-

General, akin to a curtsy, before Putin turned into a laughingstock, demonstrating not diplomatic finesse but rather damaging the UN's reputation. In global diplomacy, clear and consistent positioning is essential for maintaining credibility. Leaders in international organizations must be capable of understanding the complexity of global conflicts and addressing them responsibly. In times of fragile international stability and security, the statements and actions of top representatives carry significant weight.

To improve transparency, open communication channels and public reporting on decision-making processes and voting outcomes are fundamental requirements. This could include regular publication of meeting records and voting results. Establishing independent external monitoring institutions and think tanks could ensure that decisions are made objectively and free from undue influence. These agencies should be empowered to investigate and report on irregularities. Additionally, more effective procedures for reviewing decisions and votes should be introduced. The organization should conduct regular evaluations of its processes and structures to ensure effective and transparent operations.

## 31. WEAKNESSES IN FOREIGN POLICY DECISION-MAKING

Erroneous decisions in foreign policy often stem from poor assessments of the geopolitical situation, the interests of other states, or the internal dynamics of another country. Such misunderstandings immediately lead to further inappropriate decisions. The global interconnectedness of states, institutions, and alliances means that a foreign policy error in one country can have unforeseen consequences in many other regions. For example, the Western response to Russia's annexation of Crimea was tied to a misjudgment of Russia's long-term geopolitical objectives. While sanctions against Russia did exert economic pressure, they failed to curb Moscow's aggressive foreign policy, resulting in further escalations and conflicts. Simultaneously, the rift between Russia and the West widened.

When political actors fail to perceive or misinterpret a threat because they rely on superficial information, are distracted by other visible threats, or are anxious and indecisive, the most unpleasant consequences quickly follow. Threats such as terrorist networks, cyberattacks, or hybrid warfare are often difficult to detect and therefore underestimated.

Unfortunately, actions are often taken too late because the true extent of a threat is only recognized after it has already caused significant damage. Political systems that rely on slow bureaucracies or cautious decision-making processes are particularly vulnerable to these errors. Another danger lies in the inadequate assessment of the long-term consequences of a threat. Insidious threats like climate change, mass migration, or demographic shifts are extremely dangerous because their effects only manifest after years or decades. States that focus on short-term threats tend to overlook these long-term risks. Many actors tend to see threats that align with their existing worldview, while other dangers are overshadowed or underestimated. This leads to hidden or elusive threats often being detected too late.

The inability of states and political actors to recognize latent or hidden threats in a timely manner and to respond appropriately is a serious problem in modern security policy. This phenomenon can be explained by several factors. The complexity of modern political decision-making processes can lead to delays in detecting and reacting to threats. Sometimes critical information is poorly filtered or misinterpreted before reaching the highest decision-making levels. Furthermore, political actors tend to focus on immediate and visible threats because these often attract media attention. As a result, they accept that latent or hard-to-detect threats, such as terrorist networks, cyberattacks, or hybrid warfare, are underestimated or neglected. The sheer volume of information available today paradoxically leads to superficial analyses. Decision-makers are so overwhelmed by the quantity of data that they often forego more in-depth analyses. Political systems that rely on cautious decision-making processes and consensus politics are particularly prone to response delays. The need to achieve broad consensus often slows down lengthy decision-making processes and hampers the ability to adapt quickly to new threats.

The implementation of effective analytical methods and AI-based systems can help better identify potential threats. However, more than the mere use of such technologies is required. Using these tools requires deep expertise and understanding to ensure that the information obtained is interpreted correctly and that appropriate actions are taken. Blindly adopting AI-driven responses without scrutiny risks overlooking important aspects. While AI can analyze large volumes of data superficially, it does not always grasp all nuances or complex relationships. Therefore, human expertise remains crucial to validate results and apply them in the proper context. The use of AI should be seen as a complement, not a total replacement. Decision-making mechanisms must be adapted for flexibility. Regular training for decision-makers is necessary to raise awareness of detecting and assessing latent threats. By implementing such measures, political actors can improve their ability to identify and respond adequately, even to difficult-to-detect threats.

The overestimation of power and influence is one of the most frequent misjudgments. Aggressive states or groups often tend to overestimate their power and influence on the international stage. This can have severe consequences for how they interpret their own capacity for action. A common mistake is the unilateral focus on one of two factors - either the domestic or external context. Foreign policy decision-makers then focus too much on short-term national interests, neglecting long-term impacts and global challenges. Another mistake is the belief that unilateral action and the pursuit of narrowly defined national interests are always productive. This overlooks the fact that an increasing number of challenges can only be overcome through international cooperation in an increasingly interconnected world. To avoid these errors, a multilateral approach to foreign policy decision-making is necessary - one that considers both international and domestic factors, including long-term consequences, and is open to cooperation. Additionally, thorough analysis of the motivations and capabilities of other actors proves to be invaluable.

The chancellery of a central European country is assessed in the realm of European policy based on its ability to advance common visions, manage crises, and forge alliances. In this context, numerous criticisms have recently emerged. One might almost think it resembles a political strategy of Zen: maximum waiting, minimal risk-taking. After all, those who do nothing, do nothing wrong. A European policy by Germany that focuses on its own national needs automatically weakens European solidarity. At times, it seems that the principle of "Germany first" prevails, whether in economic matters, energy policy, common security, or migration issues. The willingness to offer European defense in homeopathic doses will undoubtedly not propel the current government into the category of decisive policymakers.

Germany has traditionally been perceived as a leader within the EU, building bridges and facilitating compromises. However, weak chancellorships leave this leadership role vacant, which endangers EU cohesion. Europe does not function on autopilot; it requires bold and visionary policies to overcome the challenges of our time. In the absence of this, and without competent, charismatic leaders, the EU remains vulnerable to internal divisions, national self-interest, and external threats costs that neither a single European member state nor the global community can afford.

A frequent mistake in the foreign policies of major regions is the lack of a long-term perspective. Decisions that only pursue short-term objectives, without considering their long-term effects, often lead to unforeseen and negative consequences. The interests and perspectives of other countries must always be considered. When a country exclusively pursues its own interests and ignores the concerns of other nations, it exacerbates tensions and diplomatic conflicts. For instance, the unilateral decision by the United States to withdraw from the Paris Climate Agreement was perceived by many countries as a disregard for global cooperation, leading to diplomatic tensions, particularly with European partners.

Consensus-building involves different actors, despite their divergent interests and perspectives, finding common ground to reach an agreement. This requires patience, empathy, and the ability to integrate diverse viewpoints. Success in consensus-building goes beyond simple compromise and entails a willingness to find creative solutions that benefit all parties involved. It often depends on openness to developing new and unconventional solutions. This is not merely about compromise but also about being ready to develop innovative ideas that offer advantages for both sides. "Track-2" diplomacy - informal discussions and workshops involving experts and civil society actors - can also advance the formal negotiation process.

Crises always impact multiple sectors, such as health, economy, infrastructure, public safety, and technology. During a crisis, various actors must collaborate to ensure a rapid and coordinated response. Intersectoral crisis management requires the development of flexible and interdisciplinary solutions and the establishment of a robust network of institutions capable of supporting one another. Moreover, it is essential to quickly identify and correct misinformation through reliable sources. To achieve this, specialized teams should be implemented in all discussion and decision-making units, tasked with monitoring the digital landscape as well.

A recurring mistake is failing to learn from past crises. Many organizations and governments tend to neglect post-crisis planning and preparation, leaving them vulnerable to similar errors in future crises. Technology can be an indispensable tool in crisis management, but it should not be viewed as a panacea. A frequent error is over-relying on communication platforms, automated alert systems, or drones without ensuring that they function effectively in emergencies and are well-integrated with human decision-making and intervention. These processes should also undergo regular evaluations. Increasingly frequent weather-related disasters, for example, could be better anticipated. During a hurricane disaster in the United States, many technical systems either failed to work as intended or were unavailable in time, which slowed the emergency response. The gaps in detecting military threats or aggressive space technologies are even more concerning.

The most significant errors in crisis management often stem from a lack of preparation, poor communication, and underestimation of risks, particularly in the realm of digital threats and misinformation. All relevant sectors, countries, and populations must be continuously involved to enhance the effectiveness and efficiency of crisis management systems. Continuous adaptation and improvement of strategies are crucial to being better equipped for future challenging situations. The absence of a long-term resilience strategy that addresses both physical and digital threats can lead to severe shortcomings. Many crisis plans focus solely on the immediate response to the current crisis rather than developing long-term measures to make society, infrastructure, and institutions more resilient to future threats.

Only by adopting a proactive and inclusive approach can we ensure that we are not only able to respond to crises but also prepared to tackle future threats with a robust and flexible system. Peacekeeping, political initiatives, and the establishment of international security mechanisms are essential for preventing conflicts and enhancing resilience to geostrategic risks. A resilient society is supported by stable and transparent institutions capable of responding quickly and effectively to crises. These institutions include governments, healthcare services, educational establishments, and emergency management systems.

Good governance is essential for gaining public trust and maintaining social cohesion. It is characterized by its ability to anticipate changes and develop innovative solutions. This can include both technological innovation and the ability to create new social or economic models when older structures fail. A resilient society invests not only in crisis response but also in preventive measures. This involves identifying potential risks early, creating crisis plans, and practicing them regularly. It must also be capable of identifying and mitigating the disruptive maneuvers of extremism, whether from dictatorships, terrorist organizations, or corrosive political parties. By focusing on these key areas, organizations and communities can build resilient systems that not only identify and mitigate risks associated with extremism but also foster a more inclusive and cohesive environment.

To effectively address the challenges posed by extremism in its many forms, be it through authoritarian regimes, terrorist organizations, or corrosive political ideologies, organizations and communities must adopt a multifaceted and proactive approach. This involves identifying the roots and manifestations of extremism while implementing measures to mitigate its impact. Ultimately, the goal is to foster resilience, inclusivity, and cohesion within societies. Extremist actors often exploit vulnerabilities within political, social and economic systems to achieve their objectives. They frequently spread propaganda to distort facts, incite fear and polarize societies. Digital platforms are leveraged to amplify divisive rhetoric and recruit followers.

Authoritarian regimes or extremist parties may infiltrate political or legal systems to legitimize their agendas. Direct physical threats to individuals or communities aim to destabilize and instill fear. Dictatorships and extremist movements often silence dissent through imprisonment, censorship, or violence.Therefore institutions must prioritize accountability and transparency to build trust and legitimacy. Clear laws against hate speech, incitement and political corruption can deter extremist maneuvers. Promoting critical thinking and media literacy can inoculate citizens against disinformation. Global coordination helps track and dismantle transnational extremist networks. Countries and organizations can learn from successful strategies to counter extremism in different contexts.Counteracting extremism goes beyond defensive measures; it requires cultivating an environment where extremism cannot thrive.

Addressing economic and social disparities diminishes the grievances that extremists exploit.Inclusive platforms ensure that all groups feel represented and valued.Initiatives to resolve tensions between polarized groups prevent escalation into extremism. Instilling values of democracy, human rights, and mutual respect prepares future generations to resist extremist ideologies. By combining vigilance against the disruptive tactics of extremism with a proactive emphasis on inclusivity and resilience, societies can effectively combat the threats posed by extremist actors. Transparent institutions, empowered communities, and global collaboration form the backbone of these efforts. The result is a cohesive environment that not only identifies and mitigates risks but also nurtures a culture of respect, equity, and shared progress. Through such holistic strategies, extremism's appeal is diminished, and its ability to disrupt is systematically curtailed. All these efforts can make use of the professional instruments of audits, evaluations and ratings.

## 32. MEDIA LANDSCAPE ASSESSMENT

The importance of media evaluations has a massive impact on the public's differing opinions, not only regarding the assessment of content but also in terms of the performance of moderators in the daily mediation of political debates and talk shows. Since the media's mission is not only to provide information but also to shape it, they play a major role in influencing public opinion. Media debate platforms serve as important arenas where opinions are expressed, political positions are discussed, and societal themes are illuminated.

The media function as the main source of current events and news. The quality and accuracy of the information reported influence how the public understands and reacts to these topics. It is crucial for this information to be fact-based, balanced, and free from bias. Through agenda-setting, the media hold the power to determine which topics take priority in public discourse. By selecting themes and deciding how they are presented, the media shape the population's worldview and direct its attention to certain issues. Through media content and commentary, the tone of social and political debates is often set. Commentators, journalists, and experts offer interpretations that shape viewers' perceptions of these topics. Thus, it is of great importance to carefully evaluate the quality and impartiality of such commentary. They not only inform the public about what is happening in the world but also actively contribute to this reality. By highlighting certain subjects and ignoring others, they influence what the audience deems relevant or insignificant. Media debate platforms are arenas where this opinion-shaping takes place, often loud and controversial but inevitably impactful. In this interconnection between media and society, political positions are discussed, and societal themes are illuminated, but the light cast is often one-sided, not neutral.

The media are not merely information channels; they are also powerful actors in shaping political and societal opinions. In political discussions, often broadcast live, the way information is presented and discussed becomes tangible for the audience. The media influence not only what people think but also how they act on emotions. In this context, the evaluation of media content and commentators has become a sensitive necessity. Do commentators succeed in presenting complex topics in an accessible and comprehensive manner during political debates? Their performance depends on the quality of their research, their argumentation, and their ability to provide nuance. However, shows are often criticized for remaining too superficial, serving more as platforms for the self-promotion of guests than as opportunities for truly in-depth debate. Limited airtime and an emphasis on entertainment often hinder detailed analysis of themes. Biased or partisan commentary influences public opinion and may promote one-sided narratives. Competence and credibility are not always a given. Continuous evaluation is necessary to critically examine the roles played in the arenas of opinion.

Talk shows become veritable temples of superficial but electrifying discussions. Where else could one hear expertise as sharp as that of comedians turned epidemiologists or politicians showcasing their profound knowledge of climate change? Of course, these are only self-taught insights - undoubtedly tinged with a certain amount of self-promotion. Who needs depth when a storm of online outrage can be provoked in no time? Polarizing staging is often prioritized, aiming less at factual exchange and more at generating drama and provocation. These spectacles, with provocative subjects and heated discussions, may garner attention and boost ratings but often lack the depth and seriousness necessary for meaningful debate.

Opinions are simplified or distorted, and true nuance is lost. At a time when diverse opinions and nuanced discussions are more important than ever, it can be frustrating to see talk shows aim only to stoke emotions rather than create a space for well-founded debates. The underlying principle is as follows: pick a topic as polarizing as possible, preferably with keywords like "scandal," "fear," or "loss of freedom," then garnish it with a touch of outrage. Next, place five guests around a table, ideally from completely opposing camps who not only dislike each other but have also prepared extensively for the show.

Currently, moderators - with very few exceptions - appear as a mix of referees and arsonists, always ready to fan the flames. The result is typically a debate that has little to do with the exchange of opinions and much more with an exchange of blows. Instead of exploring arguments objectively, each viewpoint is compressed into catchy soundbites, simple enough to still work on Twitter or Instagram. Participants deliver nuance only through the volume with which they interrupt one another. Any viewer hoping for genuine, nuanced opinions will be disappointed. The spectacle dominates because ratings must be ensured.

A diverse, high-quality, and balanced media landscape is essential for the proper functioning of a democracy. Media outlets and commentators must provide space for pluralistic discussions. The absence or inadequacy of evaluations leads to an amplification of misinformation, polarization, and manipulation. Evaluations should contribute to creating transparency, establishing quality standards, and strengthening the credibility of the media. In an era of misinformation and growing political polarization, this is more important than ever.

This includes, above all, how information is presented. It is always crucial to determine whether commentators' claims are based on evidence. Additionally, it is important to observe which perspectives are highlighted and which are overlooked. Understanding political biases is critical for a critical analysis of media content. Competence, impartiality, communication skills, and empathy are essential to ensuring the quality and impact of serious commentary. Listening to certain remarks, one might sometimes feel that expertise comes directly from the latest trending social media article. Why bother with years of study or in-depth research when a few catchy phrases and a touch of controversy are enough to entertain the audience?

On one hand, there are specific experts, recognized for their professional roles and evaluations. On the other hand, there is a proliferation of pseudo-experts being invited. This could stem from the fact that some media hosts or contributors have made their way onto the stage based on improvised skills and a stroke of luck. The public's perception of the media is often shaped by enduring trends and how information is conveyed. In some cases, reality is avoided in favor of a "polite rejection" of information. Conversely, the overwhelming abundance of available information can be so daunting that it diminishes the public's attention span. Yet, the media's mission is to offer a platform for exchanging different viewpoints and arguments on current issues. In doing so, they foster public debate and the confrontation of opinions within society. As the "fourth estate," they play a crucial oversight role. Through investigative journalism and critical reporting, they must expose abuses and monitor political and economic leaders. This function is essential to the workings of a democracy. Within the political system, the media also have a duty to contribute to political education and citizen participation. They are involved in both the necessary stability and the constant change in society. At the same time, the interconnections between the media and politics create a relationship of mutual influence and benefit.

In the 2000s, particularly after the events of September 11, 2001, and the intensification of political polarization, American media faced significant criticism. U.S. news channels often relied on highly emotional journalism to retain their audience. These networks became known for their clearly marked ideological positions, which often encouraged division at the expense of mutual understanding. Moreover, many programs focused more on entertainment and opinion-driven talk shows than on objective reporting. This situation gave rise to the phenomenon of "TV bashing", where the media were accused of promoting polarization rather than contributing to balanced, fact-based information. The consequences of this evolution are visible in the social and political landscape of the United States.

In recent years, however, U.S. networks have taken steps to improve their image and return to more balanced and professional coverage. This includes, in particular, the professionalization of commentators. Many of them possess not only journalistic expertise but also in-depth knowledge in fields such as politics, economics, and international relations, which has enhanced the credibility of these networks. American media have also expanded their range of commentators and experts. This diversification of voices, not only in political terms but also in terms of cultural, ethnic, and gender perspectives, has encouraged more pluralistic discussions. This has allowed many networks to reach a broader audience and be perceived as less partisan. These efforts are beginning to pay off. Criticism of superficiality and bias in reporting has decreased in many cases, and several networks have regained credibility through in-depth reporting and well-trained commentators. This has also led international media and viewers to adopt a more nuanced view of the American media landscape.

However, the temptation to cater to a highly polarized audience remains present. Despite the progress, some networks continue to rely on partisan opinions to target specific demographic groups. The U.S. media landscape remains highly fragmented, and many viewers still get their news from sources that confirm their political beliefs rather than relying on neutral reporting. In German-speaking countries, the media landscape shows a sharp contrast between quality experts and "pseudo-experts." This dualism is particularly evident in how experts are utilized in different media formats and at different broadcast times. On one side, many qualified specialists possess recognized expertise in specific fields. They stand out for their deep knowledge of their domain, academic qualifications, or significant professional experience. On the other side, a growing number of pseudo-experts appear in numerous programs. They often participate in populist formats where their statements, simplistic and sensationalist, are presented to the audience in a clear but often unconsidered and biased manner. These "experts" use polemical or emotional arguments to grab attention rather than convincing through the depth of their analyses.

The increasing reliance on these pseudo-experts could be linked to the lack of journalistic rigor in some formats. Rather than inviting rigorously vetted specialists, some networks prefer personalities who, while less qualified, align with the program's narrative or offer provocative opinions capable of boosting viewership. This resembles "sensational journalism," focused more on immediate attention than on in-depth analysis. In such settings, true expertise is weakened, and the public receives neither real insight nor reliable information, but rather a superficial discussion designed more to entertain or confirm biases. Consequently, the potential for nuanced debate on complex political and social issues is systematically undermined.

Is it excusable that many talk shows and debate formats are under enormous pressure to achieve high ratings? In this context, pseudo-experts, who often take extreme positions, are seen as useful for stirring lively and controversial discussions, even at the expense of the quality of arguments. This contributes to a distortion of reality, as superficial or incorrect information prevails. Viewers are not adequately informed and may be misled. Moreover, this situation erodes trust in the media and promotes the spread of misinformation. The disparity between qualified experts and pseudo-experts highlights the importance of critically questioning the selection of guests on talk shows. It is the responsibility of the media to ensure balanced and well-informed coverage. Otherwise, the risk is that media-driven misinformation will become the norm, to the detriment of public debate.

Events such as the growing polarization between Republicans and Democrats in the United States, voter divisions, and extreme incidents like the Capitol assault on January 6, 2021, partially illustrate the consequences of a fragmented media landscape. Media credibility has increasingly been called into question. A growing number of people no longer view the press as a neutral entity but as a participant in ideological conflicts. The polarization of media in the U.S. serves as a warning for other regions, underscoring the importance of balanced and responsible reporting to strengthen democratic processes and prevent societal divisions. At the same time, this trend poses a challenge for the media, which must defend against accusations of bias without abandoning their mission of critical reporting.

The devaluation of public broadcasting's mission also stems from the fact that it is not only conspiracy theories and intentional falsehoods that affect information transmission but also the subtle omission of facts. This has occurred repeatedly in Germany and Austria, culminating in media misconduct during the Covid-19 pandemic. Such practices significantly contributed to social insecurity and disorder. In Austria, only one private broadcaster maintained objective coverage. The long-term sociological repercussions were evident. A frequent critique is that public broadcasters disproportionately reflected the positions of governments and established institutions while underrepresenting the critical views of certain scientists or affected groups. Transparency in editorial decisions and their evaluation could help counter allegations of bias. Including a wider range of perspectives, including dissenting ones, would strengthen trust in the media. Additionally, maintaining greater distance from political and economic influences would be essential to preserve media credibility.

The growing digitization of the European media landscape has also brought profound changes. More people consume news and content through social media and digital platforms. This shift has forced traditional media companies to adapt their business models and content to the demands of the digital era. At the same time, international platforms have emerged as new players, competing with European broadcasters for audience attention. The spread of misinformation and "fake news" via social networks and alternative platforms poses a serious threat to public opinion. This presents a significant challenge for the media landscape. During political events such as European Parliament elections or the Brexit debate, the impact of manipulative content on public opinion became apparent.

How people consume media is changing rapidly. For younger generations, social networks and streaming services play a dominant role, while traditional formats like print media and television are losing importance. This transformation raises urgent questions, particularly about funding quality journalism and ensuring a balanced information supply through professional evaluations and expertise. At the European level, various measures and initiatives aim to protect and promote media freedom and diversity. Rather than authoritarian control, private-sector quality monitoring could play a role in ensuring balanced media coverage. The future of the European media landscape will largely depend on the ability of its actors to maintain media independence and diversity while addressing the profound changes brought about by digitization and new platforms. Access to reliable information must be guaranteed while preserving freedom of expression to sustain democratic structures in Europe.

Despite these challenges, Europe - excluding notable exceptions such as Hungary and Bulgaria - performs relatively well compared to other parts of the world. North America also has a strong tradition of press freedom, but growing attacks on journalists and media companies by political actors present significant problems. In Latin America and parts of Asia, press freedom is often threatened by state repression, censorship, or violence against journalists. Countries like China, Russia, and Saudi Arabia exemplify extreme cases where media are tightly controlled by the state, leaving little to no room for independent journalism.

Without free and independent media, there is no critical counterweight to governments and power holders. This accelerates the gradual erosion of democratic structures and the rule of law. When independent media are under pressure, an informational void is created, often filled by propaganda and misinformation. This fuels social polarization and undermines fact-based public debate, which is essential for a functioning democracy. Increasing attacks on journalists foster a climate of fear and intimidation. Media professionals may refrain from critical reporting out of safety concerns, further restricting opinion diversity and enabling authoritarian trends.

If this trend continues, there is a risk of a gradual erosion of democratic values and institutions. In some countries, this could lead to a slide toward authoritarian or hybrid forms of governance. Even in established democracies, the risks of increased polarization and loss of trust in democratic processes remain present. To counter this development, measures to protect press freedom at national and international levels are recommended. It is clear that the media landscape has many interconnected and interdependent weaknesses. On one hand, monopolization often leads to economic constraints, weakening quality journalism. The intertwining of economic and journalistic interests complicates the production of high-level media coverage. Economic pressures drive media companies to produce content that maximizes attention at the expense of quality and depth. The thirst for sensationalism, exemplified by "clickbait" practices and "tabloidization," contributes to a decline in content quality. These mechanisms also exacerbate public distrust of the media, reducing advertising revenues and subscriptions.

This erosion of trust is closely tied to media ownership concentration and commercialization. Public mistrust further fuels the growth of alternative platforms where misinformation and conspiracy theories thrive. These dependencies reinforce monopolization, as major platforms, through their algorithms, dictate which content is visible. Commercialization is incentivized, as content must be optimized for virality on social media. Such practices inevitably come at the expense of journalistic quality.

The spread of misinformation reflects a structural weakness linked to dependency on digital platforms, which often favor controversial content through their algorithms. Misinformation also benefits from the loss of credibility of traditional media and their commercial orientation. Declining quality is also connected to the lack of qualifications among journalists, commentators, and TV hosts. Inexperienced or poorly trained journalists lack the tools to handle complex topics in depth. They focus on catchy themes requiring little expertise or posing less risk.

Journalistic norms and ethics are increasingly neglected in universities and more often taught in practical training, depriving journalists of this essential foundation. Television networks often prioritize hosts with entertainment appeal over subject matter expertise. Moreover, when well-trained journalists leave the poorly compensated field for more lucrative sectors such as public relations or corporate communications, the quality of public media coverage deteriorates further.

Improving training and promoting qualified journalists is a crucial step to counteract the decline in media quality. However, achieving long-term results requires accompanying these educational initiatives with structural reforms in media funding and organization. Journalism schools and universities should establish rigorous quality controls and uniform standards. The shortage of specialized journalists could be temporarily addressed by implementing continuing education courses in fields such as science, economics, politics, and culture. Practical orientation during training also helps apply these skills directly in newsroom settings. Specialized knowledge, journalistic ethics, including principles of objectivity and responsibility to the public, should be priorities in training and regularly updated through evaluation and accreditation programs.

Non-profit foundations could also play an important role. They could fund newsrooms dedicated to investigative reporting and in-depth analysis. Media companies, in turn, could adopt membership models, subscriptions, or crowdfunding to reduce reliance on advertising revenue. These models strengthen the bond between media and their audience, increasing independence while alleviating financial pressures. Reforming the distribution of advertising revenue, including through fair taxation of tech giants like Google and Facebook, which capture a significant share of digital ad revenues, could free up financial resources for traditional media.

Another prerequisite for better journalism lies in stable and equitable working conditions. Precarious employment weakens confidence in the profession and leads to a loss of skilled personnel. Media companies should invest in fair employment contracts to retain journalistic talent. Instead of cutting costs and improvising on training, they should foster cooperation with specialized educational institutions and universities. A continuous training program in new technologies, data journalism, and social media should be developed while maintaining a high standard of traditional writing and analytical skills.

## 33. EUROPEAN POLICY IN A GLOBAL CONTEXT *)

The European Union has evolved over the past decades into one of the central players in international politics. Originally established as an economic union between European countries after World War II, the EU has transformed into a geopolitical actor exerting influence far beyond Europe's borders. This transformation was necessary as global challenges in the 21st century have become increasingly complex and interconnected. Today, Europe finds itself at the heart of major international tensions, the rise of new powers, a shifting security environment, and the need to assert itself in a multipolar world.

European politics has increasingly become globalized in recent years. While Europe was long focused on internal issues such as deepening integration and stabilizing the euro and Schengen areas, foreign policy has now become a decisive field of action. The influence of European countries and the EU as an institution now extends to

*) THE EUROPE-CODE Global Politics and the positioning of Europe
ISBN 978-3-7597-8717-0

numerous areas, including diplomacy, security, human rights, climate change, and economic partnerships. This is due not only to the direct impact of global developments on Europe, but also to the recognition that, in an interconnected world, isolation is not an option. Issues such as climate change, terrorism, migration, and international trade conflicts have global dimensions and thus require global solutions. As a result, Europe has begun to engage more actively in international projects and to develop its own foreign policy strategies.

European foreign policy is increasingly shaped by geopolitical realities and strategic interests. Since the turn of the millennium, the global order has undergone significant changes. The rise of China, now the world's second-largest economy, and its growing influence in the Indo-Pacific region have shifted global power dynamics. At the same time, Russia, particularly since the annexation of Crimea in 2014 and the invasion of Ukraine in 2022, has emerged as a destabilizing force at Europe's borders.

Europe, often positioning itself as a moral and diplomatic leader, must increasingly realize that in today's geopolitical arena, it is no longer just about polite words and eloquent speeches. This metaphor aptly describes Europe's current geopolitical situation and raises the question of whether the continent is truly prepared for the increasingly intense global competition. It is therefore high time for European leaders to acknowledge the reality of their place in the world order and seriously prepare for the competition. This means not just maintaining appearances through diplomatic rhetoric or an elaborate but unrealistic policy, but rather developing a robust, thoughtful strategy that can withstand difficult times. This involves not only improving military and economic resilience but also adopting a clearer stance in international conflicts.

For the EU, these developments represent both a challenge and an opportunity to take several steps forward. On the one hand, Europe is forced to invest more in defense and build closer security cooperation; on the other hand, the changing global order also offers opportunities to form new alliances and assert its position as a mediator and advocate for multilateralism. Relations with the United States, traditionally seen as Europe's most important partner, have also evolved in recent years. While NATO remains essential for European security, the "America First" doctrine under the Trump administration prompted the EU to rethink its dependence on the United States. Europe is now seeking strategic autonomy, with France and Germany at the forefront of developing a common

European defense policy.

Beyond security issues, international trade is a key area of European foreign policy. The EU is the largest internal market in the world and one of the largest exporters of goods and services. Free trade agreements with third countries are an important tool for placing European products on global markets while setting standards for fair trade, workers' rights, and environmental protection. In light of the growing importance of the Indo-Pacific region, which is increasingly viewed as the global economic center, the EU has expanded its economic relations. Free trade agreements with Japan, South Korea, and Vietnam, as well as negotiations with countries like Australia and India, demonstrate Europe's determination to make its presence known in Asia. The region is not only seen as a growing market but also as a strategic partner to balance the rising influence of China. This could be an invitation for self-reflection and renewal. Europe may be encouraged to leverage its strengths, apply historical lessons, and work with confidence and determination to remain an influential force in a complex and multipolar world order. At the same time, a new approach to global cooperation could be outlined, one that goes beyond traditional power structures and focuses on values and innovation.

The EU's foreign policy is increasingly shaped by geopolitical realities and strategic interests. Since the early 2000s, the global order has undergone profound changes. China's rise as the world's second-largest economy and its growing influence in the Indo-Pacific region have shifted the balance of power. Simultaneously, Russia has emerged as a destabilizing force on Europe's borders, particularly following its annexation of Crimea in 2014 and its invasion of Ukraine in 2022.

Europe, often positioning itself as a moral and diplomatic leader, is coming to realize that in today's geopolitical arena, eloquent speeches alone are not enough. The current situation raises the question of whether the continent is truly prepared to face an increasingly fierce global competition. It is imperative for European leaders to acknowledge their actual place in the world order and to prepare seriously for this competition. This requires not only enhancing military and economic resilience but also adopting clearer stances in international conflicts. The changes in the global order offer Europe a dual opportunity: to strengthen its defense capabilities and establish strategic partnerships. While transatlantic relations with the United States remain crucial for European security, recent political divergences, particularly during Donald Trump's presidency, have prompted Europe to reconsider its reliance on the U.S. France and Germany are leading the push for a common European defense policy.

Economically, international trade remains a key tool for the EU, which boasts the world's largest single market. Free trade agreements with Asian countries such as Japan, South Korea, and Vietnam, as well as ongoing negotiations with Australia and India, underscore Europe's commitment to strengthening its presence in the Indo-Pacific region, regarded as the new economic center of gravity. These partnerships also aim to counterbalance China's growing influence.

Migration remains one of the most complex challenges for the EU, both internally and externally. Migratory pressures from the Middle East, Africa, and Asia require coordinated and global responses. Tackling the root causes of migration, such as through development cooperation and diplomatic initiatives, is a priority. At the same time, Europe is working to enhance its capacity to manage migration flows and equitably distribute asylum seekers among member states. Security is another area where the EU has intensified its efforts.

Yet Germany has enough other issues to deal with on the organizational and economic stage alone. There is the lack of innovation in industry in recent decades, the excessive bureaucracy, weakly rated CEOs with individual deficits in the managerial and socio-political spectrum and many other triggers for the unfortunate situation in the economy. The political and economic potential of a country depends on the ability of the population and its leadership to deal with the available resources and challenges. Technology, innovation and human capital play the central role. The qualifications of the population, in particular the education system and investment in human capital, are crucial for the long-term development of a country. A well-educated population can better exploit a country's potential. Weak institutions or internal conflicts can severely impair a country's development potential. How well the available potential and challenges are dealt with determines success in global affairs. Countries must be able to use their natural and human resources efficiently in order to ensure long-term development. No country can exist in isolation. It is not the mere existence of institutions or geographical borders that is decisive, but how a society manages its resources, capabilities and challenges.

The cost-benefit equation between the US and Europe seems to be shifting with the election of D. Trump and the authoritarian lurch towards protectionism. As a former bastion of democracy disappears into the waves of unpredictability and the bridges of transatlantic cooperation have collapsed, Europe is forced to develop more independent strategies to protect its own interests and advance its role in the world. Europe is increasingly keen to be less dependent on the US, be it on security issues, energy supplies or technology. Only such independence will strengthen Europe's negotiating position and give it the freedom to make independent decisions that serve the interests of the European people.

If a democracy no longer leaves room for dissent, criticism and freedom of expression, it moves dangerously close to the limits of authoritarianism or even autocracy. A democracy thrives on the diversity of opinions, openness to criticism and the opportunity for participation and control. If this basis is stifled by suppressing dissent and placing power in the hands of a single person or a small, insular group, the system loses its democratic character. With the change in the tone of US policy as a separatist power, new demands of the world community are coming to light in the background. The interactive nervous system of international politics is becoming sensitized.

A power-hungry leader without deeper education or ethical responsibility can be particularly dangerous, as they may develop authoritarian tendencies and care less about the values and mechanisms of democracy. Such individuals often tend to centralize power and resist any checks and balances that might limit their power. History and the present show how often a lack of education and a fixation on the abuse of power can lead to the dissolution of democratic norms and the rise of autocracy. When democratic institutions such as courts, parliaments and free media lose influence or are controlled, a nomenclature of autocracy emerges. In this scenario, the political system effectively becomes a dictatorship, even if it may still have outwardly democratic features. The nomenclature of authoritarian rule, i.e. the language and structure that characterizes such a system of power, leads to the transformation of public life and thinking in society. When opposition and critical voices are deliberately eliminated or defamed, society gradually loses its ability to question the power of the rulers. Such developments can also occur in modern democracies if the public is not vigilant and not prepared to defend its rights and freedoms.

The ever-changing uncertainties have already sparked a significant movement in Europe toward strategic autonomy. Europe cannot rely on the permanent stability of transatlantic relations and must therefore take greater responsibility for its own security and economic independence. A confident Europe must position itself to act without unconditional loyalty to the United States, using this time-tested bridge only when truly necessary. NATO, a key component of the transatlantic security structure, provides Europe with protection and a counterbalance in an unstable world. Abandoning this cooperation would be risky and could leave Europe more vulnerable, particularly as it lacks a robust and independent European defense structure. Europe may also need to learn to act selectively and manage its relations with the United States in a more nuanced way, moving beyond simplistic categories like "close partners" or "distant foes." In any case, the EU must present a united front in strategic thinking and action.

Europe's strategic redefinition requires a deliberate realignment of its alliances. Europe is in a phase where it must clarify its position in a changing global landscape. Diplomatic overtures, maintaining respectful dialogue between partners, remain crucial for preserving existing frameworks. The idea of strategic autonomy, increasingly debated within the EU, shows that Europe is striving for greater sovereignty to make independent decisions in defense, technology, and trade. Europe must also invest more in regional partnerships, particularly with African and Asian states, to strengthen its global position. This redefinition also presents an opportunity for Europe and the United States to cooperate as equals, with clearer role delineation and an independent European contribution to global stability and security. These new alliances, though constructed carefully and strategically, are built with the hope of solid support, without animosity toward traditional partners.

NATO remains a cornerstone of transatlantic security. However, Europe must adopt a more selective approach in its relations with the United States, moving away from binary notions of "close allies" or "distant enemies." The EU is not a casual house-share where disagreements are followed by reconciliations over coffee. Nor is it a temporary adventure, marked by uncertainty about whether the partner to the left or right is applauding or plotting the next twist. The day often ends with consensus on the need for consensus, followed by a gathering in the canteen, with the hope that strategic unity will finally be achieved at the next meeting.

To remain strong and credible in the long term, the EU must develop a culture of decisive action that goes beyond symbolism. This means acknowledging and productively utilizing differing opinions without diluting the goal of strategic autonomy and capability in endless consensus discussions. A pragmatic and action-oriented structure is crucial, not only for fostering internal cohesion but also for addressing external challenges effectively. It is imperative that EU members understand that strategic unity, not endless negotiations, is the way forward. The EU should focus less on traditions of goodwill and instead confront real geopolitical demands with clear decisions, without resorting to "canteen diplomacy" at every conflict.

Geopolitical tensions, from Russia to the Middle East, represent a growing threat. Europe must enhance its defense capabilities to build its own security architecture. NATO remains a key pillar, but Europe is also exploring ways to expand its military capacities through initiatives such as the European Defense Union. Europe's economy must become more resilient to global crises and dependencies. The war in Ukraine highlighted Europe's reliance on Russian gas. Diversifying energy sources and supply chains, especially for critical raw materials and technologies, is essential for economic stability and independence. Dependence on U.S. technology giants and Chinese manufacturing capacities poses a risk. Europe is increasingly investing in its own technologies, such as semiconductor production, AI, and cybersecurity, to reduce reliance on external actors and secure its digital infrastructure. The energy transition is central to Europe's goals, aiming to eliminate dependence on fossil fuels and achieve climate neutrality. This energy independence would not only protect the environment but also strengthen Europe's geopolitical standing.

Given the growing tensions among major powers, the EU must diversify its trade relations to explore new markets and partnerships. Cooperation with regions like Southeast Asia, Africa, and Latin America is becoming increasingly important to reduce dependence on traditional partners. In a world where authoritarian states are expanding their influence, promoting democratic values is a vital strategic mission for Europe. This would contribute to a more stable and predictable international order. Relations with the United States remain important, but Europe must increasingly act confidently and independently. Its modus operandi must adapt to global realities to ensure sustainable stability and security.

Europe must transition from being a mere partner of the United States to becoming an autonomous actor that defines and defends its own interests. This includes the ability to make strategic decisions independently and, if necessary, diverge from the positions of other major powers. Over the past decades, Europe has often focused on reacting to crises rather than addressing them proactively. A proactive approach requires a long-term vision, incorporating economic and security objectives to address emerging risks. Resilience becomes a key factor in this new strategy. This includes resistance to economic shocks, geopolitical tensions, cyber threats, and environmental crises. A more resilient Europe would be less dependent on external influences and capable of developing its own crisis strategies.

While NATO remains a crucial factor for cooperation, Europe needs its own security architecture based on flexible and adaptable defense capabilities. The European Defense Union could gain strength through joint armament projects and improved cross-border collaboration. Building and protecting strategic infrastructures, from energy to digital technology, must become a priority. Europe's technological independence can be bolstered through investments in homegrown technologies and the promotion of European innovation hubs. Securing access to critical raw materials and supply chains is central to these efforts. Adopting a multipolar perspective means no longer relying solely on traditional partners. Europe must boldly engage with emerging nations and regions like Asia, Africa, and Latin

America. This would reduce dependence on a few dominant trading partners while opening access to new markets and resources. However, it also involves using sanctions and leverage when its values are undermined, even if this entails short-term economic losses.

The rapid expansion of renewable energies and the transition to a green economy are imperative not only for climate protection but also for geopolitical reasons. Independence from fossil fuels and self-sufficiency in energy production will help position Europe as a secure and sovereign economic area. This strategic shift would increase Europe's influence and enable it to defend its interests independently and sustainably. While these changes might be costly, they are unavoidable if Europe is to solidify its desired role in the global order.

Europe sees itself as an actor that does not merely react but actively seeks to shape the world order. The coming decades will be crucial for determining whether the EU can establish itself as a leading global player. The increasing importance of European incentives in geopolitical and economic contexts is reflected in Europe's active role in various regions of the world, including the Indo-Pacific. An example is the EU Indo-Pacific Strategy, aimed at deepening relations with countries in this region to ensure not only security and stability but also access to vital trade routes and resources. By participating in discussions and initiatives in the region, Europe signals its readiness to take responsibility for global challenges while safeguarding its own interests.

Given the current political and economic tensions in the Indo-Pacific, Europe's influence is becoming increasingly relevant. Europe has recognized that its interests extend beyond its own continent to the stability and security of global markets and international relations. European policy in this context encompasses strategies to promote diplomatic, economic, and security interests. These include trade agreements, humanitarian aid, development cooperation, and the exchange of technology and expertise. These approaches are significant not only for the stability of the regions concerned but also for Europe's economy and geopolitical security.

A global alliance between Canada, Europe, Australia, conservative Asian middle powers, and some participants from the Global South or BRICS nations could become a strong force capable of economically and militarily countering major powers such as China, Russia, and, in extreme cases, the United States if it veers toward political instability.

Global trade and security aspirations could be effectively governed by such alliances. It raises the question of why these nations hesitate to forge effective partnerships. Emerging perspectives should not be dismissed as mere wishful thinking. The dynamism of the economy, along with politics, continually draws new lines and creates networks that should be utilized. Markets should swiftly unite under forward-thinking strategies, as adversaries will work to prevent such alliances from forming. Europe's proposals, in particular, should be so compelling that potential partners recognize the value of such alliances with little resistance.

Considering a potential military cooperation between European states and selected BRICS countries opens up interesting prospects. Here are some key aspects that could make such collaboration pragmatic and attractive without aiming for full military integration: The BRICS nations have varied geopolitical goals and security priorities. For example, India, in its ongoing tensions with China, seeks strategic partnerships that support its security interests. Cooperation with Western states could offer India an advantage, creating a political counterweight to China.

Countries like Brazil, India, and South Africa economically benefit from trade with Western nations and could face setbacks if partnerships with the West were jeopardized by military alignments with rival powers. These nations might, therefore, seek a strategic balance that aligns economic and security interests.Military cooperation need not entail full integration. Joint military exercises or the implementation of compatible communication systems could offer nations like India and South Africa valuable operational experience and logistical benefits without committing to complete military unification. Initiatives could include targeted cybersecurity programs or joint counter-terrorism efforts, particularly beneficial for countries with internal security concerns.

Emerging economic and technological hubs such as Vietnam, Indonesia, Malaysia, and Nigeria could show interest in Western alliances and engage in strategic partnerships in areas like industrial production, digitalization, and cybersecurity. These partnerships would provide these nations with economic and technological advantages, contributing to a multipolar world order free from the dominance of authoritarian powers.

Integrating science and business into political decision-making would fuel such innovative solutions. A move toward implementing new climate protection industries and a global security shield against aggressive powers could serve as the perfect response to Sino-American rivalry while countering dominant autocracies. European institutions must avoid overly restrictive regulations that hinder timely responses to geopolitical changes. As the Global South evolves dynamically, European institutions must not lack agility.

A surprising combination of military collaboration, an integrated market, and a clear political alliance agenda could significantly reshape the global order. Regular military exchanges could enhance interoperability across distant regions. Joint intelligence operations and frequent briefings would enable early threat detection and preemptive measures. Mechanisms for crisis management and conflict prevention could defuse tensions and find diplomatic solutions before conflicts escalate.

In parallel with military efforts, the alliance could create a robust interconnected market that facilitates the free flow of goods, services, and capital. Harmonizing standards and regulations would reduce trade barriers, boost innovation, and spur the development of new technologies. Economically interconnected countries often have stronger incentives for peace and cooperation. This approach is far preferable to saying, "We have no idea what we're doing."

Such an alliance would create an extraordinary geopolitical constellation, akin to a "Champions League" of international politics. It could function as a network of like-minded states that are not only economically and politically significant but also share common interests in global issues such as security, trade, climate change, and human rights. This strategic alliance could safeguard a rules-based order against cyber threats, expand trade agreements, and collaborate on joint technological advancements. It has the potential to reshape the geopolitical landscape significantly and serve as a counterbalance to other major blocs or the dominance of individual superpowers.

A coalition bolstered by the Global South would be remarkable because it would bring together actors with diverse cultural backgrounds and political systems, yet capable of finding consensus on strategic issues. The resulting optimum-minimum configurations could form a global alliance that leverages the unique strengths and interests of its members. Such unconventional partnerships could be supported by the security backing of Canada, Japan, Europe, or Australia, with mutual investments laying the groundwork for forward-looking projects. A quiet breeze of cooperation could swiftly escalate into a powerful storm.

These configurations would unite states that complement each other in values, geopolitical goals, and economic capacities. Through careful selection and alignment, synergies could emerge that exceed the individual capabilities of any single member. This strategic alliance could create a particularly stable and influential platform, capable of addressing global challenges coherently and in a coordinated manner. Such an alliance would benefit not only Europe but also the Pacific and South American regions. Its strategic orientation could grant it extraordinary effectiveness, establishing it as a reliable and independent actor on the international stage. This would position the alliance not just as a counterbalance to established power blocs but as a source of innovative solutions to complex global problems, reshaping the geopolitical dynamics in a novel way.

Europe, with its long history of immense progress and painful experiences, has cultivated a form of tempered wisdom. It should be capable of learning from past mistakes and contributing to solving global problems. With its wealth of expertise in science, technology, diplomacy, and governance, Europe can quickly overcome existing deficits if determination and willpower are present. The call to bolster confidence and maintain a resilient mindset is a plea for

Europe not to be discouraged by global challenges or internal crises. A strong sense of community and long-term perspectives are crucial to remain capable of action under pressure.

The Western world is gradually losing its former dominance as other actors, particularly the two great powers, aggressively expand and consolidate their influence. Europe is thus challenged to navigate a multipolar world and find its place within it. The proposal to establish a worldwide alliance, free from traditional power structures or hegemonic interests, highlights an innovative and cooperative vision. This alliance could be founded on shared values such as sustainability, justice, and respect for diversity. It would focus on transnational challenges like climate change, global health, social inequality, technological standards, and peacekeeping. It would move beyond mere power politics, bringing together global actors willing to collaborate as equals. With its tradition of diplomacy, diversity, and commitment to multilateral solutions, Europe could become the catalyst for a new global model.

Canada, Europe, and Australia share democratic values, high living standards, and similar understandings of human rights and the rule of law. They frequently collaborate on security issues and find themselves both competing and cooperating economically with major powers like the United States and China. Countries like Japan, South Korea, and some ASEAN states such as Singapore might seek economic and security protection in the alliance while reducing their strategic dependencies on the U.S. or China. Integrating countries from the Global South and even some BRICS members could be symbolically significant and contribute to geopolitical balance in political and economic terms.

The members would pursue economic integration to stabilize global trade and establish reliable partnerships. This might manifest in agreements emphasizing standards like sustainable development and climate goals. An alliance spanning all these regions could play a central role in combating climate change. It could focus collectively on green technologies, clean energy, and climate-friendly development models that also provide economic benefits. Such alliances would offer mutual advantages: Europe could export new technologies and expertise, while partner countries modernize their energy infrastructure and achieve greater independence.

The backing of established economic nations could act as a catalyst, offering the Global South the opportunity to shape its own development while benefiting from the experience and resources of more stable countries. If such alliances were designed with foresight and genuine commitment to shared values and interests, they could drive transformative global changes. This might even disrupt the current geopolitical power distribution and create new multipolar structures that fundamentally influence the global economy and international politics.

Charismatic leadership on all sides could articulate a clear and inspiring vision for the alliance, motivating countries to engage in shared efforts. Involving science, business, and civil society in political decision-making processes would fuel innovative solutions. Such an alliance could respond to Sino-American rivalry, counter authoritarian regimes, promote climate protection industries, and act as a global security shield against aggressive powers. The European Union's often cumbersome bureaucracy prevents it from responding promptly to geopolitical shifts. By contrast, the Global South tends to be more dynamic and flexible—a quality often missing in European institutions.

The concept of resilience through interconnectivity suggests that strong networks and tight links between states and regions help mitigate crises and respond flexibly to change. New alliances formed by Europe could foster reciprocal partnerships that are economically, ecologically, and politically sustainable. These interconnections enable better resource management, diversified supply chains for raw materials and energy, and mutual knowledge exchange, enhancing innovation and adaptability.

Faced with growing threats from cyberattacks, disinformation, and global instability, members of such an alliance could deepen cooperation on security issues and establish technology standards for artificial intelligence and cybersecurity. This alliance could help create a more balanced multipolar world order by positioning itself as an alternative to other major alliances and powers such as the U.S. and China. Reducing trade and security dependencies and minimizing geopolitical pressures historically dominated by superpowers would be a core objective. To overcome these challenges, the alliance would need mechanisms for balancing interests and building trust. Flexibility and a clear orientation toward shared values and goals would be crucial.

A novel strategic alliance could become a milestone for a sustainable and equitable world order. This coalition would have the potential not only to reduce individual burdens but also to create synergies through integrated political cycles, conserving resources and accelerating technological progress. By building shared security structures, establishing technological sovereignty, and promoting global cooperation in space exploration, the alliance could tackle the challenges of the 21st century. Such collaborations could foster a sustainable, secure, and innovative world, reducing geopolitical tensions, conserving resources, and making progress accessible to all. Through closed political cycles, circular systems, and international project linkage, a sustainable and equitable model can be created. This is not only a technical or economic necessity but also a moral obligation to leave future generations a livable world. Such an alliance holds the potential to bridge the gap between ideals and pragmatic action, shaping a new reality that benefits all involved. A closed political cycle in a global alliance means that national and regional strategies are closely interconnected to minimize overlaps and achieve maximum efficiency. Instead of countries individually addressing challenges like the energy transition or technological transformation, the alliance would define joint projects and standards to share burdens and distribute risks. By aligning strategies and unifying technology policies, redundant investments and inefficiencies can be avoided.

In light of increasing geopolitical tensions, technological dependencies, and growing challenges in space, international actors must collaborate closely to ensure long-term security and progress. A strategic alliance based on shared security structures, technological development, and space research could form the foundation for a stable and innovative world order. Climate change, cyberattacks, terrorism, and geopolitical conflicts require coordinated defense strategies. National security approaches are insufficient. Joint structures, through cooperation in prevention, can avert escalations and offer rapid response mechanisms during crises, such as natural disasters, pandemics, or military conflicts. A new security alliance could include global partner states. Defense and security projects could be funded through multilateral funds to distribute the burden more equitably.

Given the ongoing dependence on technologies from China or the United States, building an independent technological base is crucial. Semiconductor production, artificial intelligence, green energy, and quantum technology should be the focus of joint development. Space offers potential for scientific discoveries, economic expansion, and Earth's security. To avoid militarization and resource wastage in space, strong alliance coordination is essential. Investments in global energy systems, such as hydrogen economies or cross-border power grids, could be collectively funded and utilized by multiple countries. Nations with technological strengths can share knowledge and innovations in exchange for access to other resources. Research collaborations between universities and alliance companies can accelerate developments in key areas like green hydrogen, storage technologies, or $CO_2$ capture. Joint research centers could explore strategic areas, such as battery technology or hydrogen use. Knowledge and technology transfer to Global South partners can accelerate global development and reduce dependencies. Many of these countries possess immense raw material reserves and could serve as suppliers of critical materials while developing sustainable extraction strategies. Global educational initiatives that highlight the connection between individual actions and global impacts are promising for the future.

The withdrawal of a global power creates a power vacuum that other actors seek to fill. This often leads to geopolitical competition and can cause conflicts and uncertainties in regions previously stable or under the strong influence of the departing power. Examples include the rise of new regional powers attempting to exert influence in areas once dominated by the vacated superpower. In response to the departure of a dominant power, new alliances or economic partnerships naturally emerge. Countries that previously relied on the superpower's support seek new partners and secure their political and economic futures. At the same time, new counterbalances may arise as states seize the opportunity to establish a multipolar world order.

When a global power that once upheld certain norms scales back its international role, ideological and political shifts threaten global institutions. This could result in fundamental values like democracy, human rights, and free trade being less consistently upheld and defended. Retreating into self-interest inevitably has economic consequences. Especially if the power held a dominant position in financial markets or technologies, its withdrawal causes economic uncertainty. Exchange rate fluctuations, investment insecurities, and trade shifts could lead to global recessions or restructuring.

Who could deny the countries cited above the right to play a similarly influential role on the world stage as China, Russia, or the United States? Who lacks the imagination or courage to consider such a possibility? There is growing resistance to autocratic governments, manifesting in various forms, including elections and public pressure.

This resistance can raise the cost of human rights violations and force autocratic regimes to rethink their strategies. Despite setbacks, there are signs that the fight for democracy is at a turning point. Autocrats are not infallible, and their mistakes offer opportunities for democratic forces. However, this requires overcoming traditional mindsets and embracing new risks. Others are not secondary players or mere appendages in the dramas of international politics, as Putin, Trump, or Xi might prefer to think. Active participation in societal, economic, and scientific endeavors is essential for everyone. For countries with the largest political criminal cartels, an intelligent democratic process might be their only salvation. In the race for prominence in global significance, everything is open in terms of the interconnectedness of politics, economics, and even science. All major powers competing for development show the same deficiencies.

The desperate war posturing of Vladimir Putin and the deceptive smile of Xi Jinping are hardly guarantees of predictable future developments. It cannot be concealed that North Korea's military support for Putin in Ukraine relies on Chinese materials. How many eyes does the free world need to avoid blindness on all sides? It was already insensitive when Putin not only reinstated Stalin's old anthem but also adopted Stalin's methods of repression and internal murder. He embodies not just the image of a wannabe tsar but also that of a committed Marxist who believes truth is solely human-made. And how long has the Chinese leader been leading international politics and economics by the nose? Xi has positioned China as a global player pursuing not just economic interests but also ideological influence. The Chinese government has established itself as a counterweight to Western dominance, promoting a model of state control over the economy and society.

Effective protection of Europe primarily involves ensuring the continent's security and stability against various threats. NATO's defense alliance remains a cornerstone of Europe's military protection. The European Union has strengthened its defense cooperation through the Common Security and Defense Policy (CSDP). Initiatives such as the Permanent Structured Cooperation (PESCO) promote military collaboration among member states. With the rise in cyberattacks on state institutions, infrastructure, and businesses, Europe is investing more in cybersecurity measures.

Since Russia represents an authoritarian, nationalist governance model that contrasts sharply with the EU's liberal and democratic values, sudden Russian hegemony would lead to ideological confrontation. The influence of authoritarian ideologies would quickly spread in countries vulnerable to populist and authoritarian tendencies. To protect against this, Europe must pursue a multidimensional strategy that includes strengthening its democratic institutions, countering disinformation and populist narratives, and enhancing international cooperation. This is not just about opposing Russia militarily or economically but also about increasing the resilience of European societies and political systems. Only through close cooperation within Europe and with international partners can Europe's liberal and democratic values be upheld in an increasingly authoritarian world order.

A secure and humanitarian approach to migration is also a key pillar of the European security process. By enhancing surveillance and cooperation with third countries, irregular migration should be controlled, and legal migration pathways strengthened. The EU's single market protects the continent through economic stability and promotes prosperity for both itself and its partners. Trade agreements with third countries provide Europe with consolidated strength in the face of global economic crises. Climate change poses one of the greatest threats to the Global South and to Europe's long-term security, as it exacerbates economic and social instability.

In addition to directly combating terrorism, preventing radicalization within Europe is a crucial protective measure. This includes educational initiatives and actions against social exclusion. Through joint information platforms and the exchange of data on criminals and terrorist cells, Europe enhances its internal security. In a worst-case scenario of an international crisis, Europe would need to develop a multifaceted and coordinated strategy across multiple levels. NATO would have to expand its presence and collaboration to ensure deterrence and defense readiness—but is it capable of doing so? Simultaneously, economic, social, and ecological challenges would need to be addressed. Domestically, a strong civil society, the defense of democratic institutions, and the promotion of shared values could counteract populist or authoritarian tendencies. In such a scenario, Europe would face a critical test where solidarity and cooperation would need to be the central responses to global threats.

A new global alliance could serve as a catalyst for the development of new industries in the area of climate protection. Through joint efforts, technologies could be developed that offer both economic and ecological benefits. Ordoliberal structures could act as stabilizing factors in this dynamic, seeking to mitigate geopolitical tensions. The potential of European incentives should not be underestimated. These can serve as vital tools to exert influence, reduce tensions, and foster cooperation. Europe has the opportunity to act as a mediator and support constructive solutions in crises. This role is also critical regarding climate change, the fight against poverty, and the promotion of human rights - issues of growing global significance.

The European Union is striving to connect and integrate the diverse digital, physical, and economic infrastructures of European countries. Well-developed interconnectivity is crucial for economic and political cooperation within Europe as well as for the continent's global competitiveness. This includes physical interconnectivity, such as integrated transport systems and advanced energy infrastructure. For a long time, the EU has been working on economic and political interconnectivity, starting with the idea of a common internal market through the harmonization of regulations and European investment policies. Expanding interconnectivity in quantum computing, artificial intelligence, and cloud computing now contributes to Europe's digital and economic autonomy and strengthens the continent's capacity for innovation.

Europe's interconnectivity is essential for the continent's economic, digital, and social integration. It enhances competitiveness, builds on innovative strength, and ensures the free exchange of data, goods, and services. By developing its own satellite system, the EU is reducing its dependence on third countries in the field of satellite communications. This bolsters Europe's digital sovereignty and makes it less vulnerable to external influences or disruptions. The system is also intended to improve border and critical area surveillance and provide faster and more effective crisis responses.

Europe's overall economic performance must be urgently optimized, while its military capacity for self-preservation needs to be expanded. The most effective way to achieve efficiency on all fronts is by concretely realizing innovative alliances. This core message of a new era emphasizes establishing new strategic alliances without fearing the departure from a well-meaning but paternalistic guardianship. Europe stands strongest on its own feet, forming alliances with the Free World of its own choosing. The stars of great opportunities shine across continents for all participating regions.

Rational European politics thus aim to achieve the EU's shared goals and values through evidence-based, strategically oriented, and consensus-driven decision-making processes using various governance instruments. These must always consider the complexity of Europe's multi-level system and the diversity of national interests. Rational policies will always prioritize the common good, stability, and progress while maintaining a balance between security, freedom, and prosperity. Should there no longer be a single European internal market, as some right-wing populists advocate, international trade would also cease. Isolationism would quickly lead to widespread loss of prosperity.

The European idea, based on the principles of peace, freedom, and democracy, currently faces significant challenges. The war in Ukraine, handling of refugees, erosion of democratic principles in some EU states, and a latent identity crisis are putting the foundations of the European Union under great strain. At the same time, this is a great opportunity for an effective reset of the European framework. The war in Ukraine has highlighted the importance of a unified foreign policy to respond to external threats. Concurrently, the economic repercussions of the conflict, such as rising energy prices and inflation, have raised concerns in many EU countries. These circumstances contribute to unease, which extremist fringes are eager to exploit.

The question of whether Europe is undermined by defamation of its own culture touches on deep issues of self-perception and cultural change. This debate is waged by various political camps and intellectual movements, either defending traditional European values or focusing on structural issues. Europe finds itself in a phase of self-reflection, driven by global political and cultural developments in recent decades. This self-criticism is sometimes perceived as self-denial or defamation of one's own culture. History shows that Europe has a turbulent past, marked by great achievements in science, art, and philosophy, as well as dark chapters in colonialism, imperialism, wars, and genocides. Recent decades have seen an intensified engagement with these darker chapters, leading to a critical reassessment of its cultural heritage. While this critique is necessary to acknowledge past injustices, some argue that it must not drown in excessive rejection of its own culture.

A crucial aspect of this debate is cultural change, exacerbated by globalization and migration. The increasing cultural pluralism in Europe is often seen as a threat to traditional European identity. Critics fear that this pluralism could dilute European values. The integration of migrants and managing cultural diversity have become central topics of European politics. Advocates argue, however, that

Europe has always been a continent of change and cultural diversity and that multiculturalism enriches societies, making them more resilient and dynamic. A significant portion of Europe's intellectual elite appears to believe that self-criticism is a sign of cultural maturity. The resulting values form part of Europe's new heritage, rooted in lessons learned from its history. Self-criticism, in this perspective, does not mean defaming one's own culture but learning from mistakes and continuously improving. A strong Europe is one that confronts past challenges and embraces change without denying the achievements and positive aspects of its culture.

Europe is less at risk of resorting to nationalism as long as it avoids promoting hegemonic ideas of the old continent. This is one of the most significant cultural changes in Europe's self-image. This vision is based on overcoming the mistakes and ideologies of the past, particularly hegemonic ambitions that have often shaped Europe's history. The idea that Europe might "perish through the defamation of its own culture" stems from the notion of an impending decline of Western civilization, a recurring theme in many political and intellectual discourses. The myth of decline has a long tradition in Europe, dating back to ancient civilizations. Fears of cultural and political downfall have been repeatedly invoked, whether through external invasions, internal moral decay, or cultural erosion. In modern times, this has been amplified by globalization and the weakening of traditional institutions.

The opacity often associated with a Freemason metaphor could reflect the EU's bureaucracy and decision-making processes, which are frequently perceived as opaque and inaccessible to the general public. In many EU member states, Brussels is often portrayed as a "distant power" making decisions that affect people's lives without their involvement or understanding. Significant collective capacity must be invested in the European community. Visionary political capacity involves forging new alliances, both within the EU and globally. To address the great challenges of our time, Europe needs strong partnerships with other countries and regions. Political leaders who understand how to build international relations and strategic alliances lay the foundation for a more resilient Europe. Visionary political capacity is also about pursuing groundbreaking goals even when politically inconvenient. European integration must transcend short-term political cycles and focus on Europe's long-term development and stability.

Decision-making processes must be transparent if they are to achieve high levels of acceptance. Conspiracy theories often claim that decisions are made behind the scenes that run counter to the public interest. When goals and activities remain hidden and escape public scrutiny, there is a suspicion that the exercise of power lacks ethical justification. Europe is exposed to the distortion of ethical principles that prioritize singular national interests over those of the European Union.

In some EU states, democratic principles are being undermined. Populist movements and authoritarian tendencies are questioning the rule of law and judicial independence. This development not only endangers the stability of the affected countries but also impacts the EU as a whole, undermining trust in shared values and the Union's integrity. Despite these countercurrents, the European construct is not necessarily at a breaking point. There are opportunities to strengthen the foundations of the European Union. Nevertheless, the European idea faces a crucial crossroads.

The success of the EU depends on how its institutions respond to the current crises. A strong, united Europe is essential to meet the challenges of the 21st century. Reconnecting with the shared values and fundamental principles upon which the EU is based could be the key to convincing the European public and initiating a new era of cooperation. In this time of uncertainty, it is crucial to understand and promote the European idea not just as a concept, but as a living reality. European identity is not a static concept; it is subject to constant change and discourse. It develops through the interaction and exchange between the peoples and cultures of Europe. It is the result of historical experiences, cultural diversity, and shared values. In light of the current turbulence, it remains important to continue the dialogue on European identity and find new ways of unity.

The symbolic and political main axis of European interconnectivity is represented by the Weimar Triangle, around which the other major regions revolve. This axis has the potential to act as a catalyst for action in politics, economy, security, and culture. Germany often serves as a hub between the North-South and East-West axes. France shares a vision with Germany for a strongly integrated Europe and secures European foreign policy, defense, and economy through cooperative projects. Poland plays an important role in promoting Eastern European interests and sees itself as a bridge between Western and Eastern Europe, particularly with countries in Central and Eastern Europe such as the Baltic States, the Czech Republic, Slovakia, and Hungary. The Benelux countries, Ireland, and the

Scandinavian countries have historically been at the heart of European integration and contribute organizationally to Europe's networking. Belgium, as the seat of key European institutions - the European Commission, the European Parliament, and NATO - forms the symbolic center of Europe. The Southern European countries of Italy, Spain, Portugal, Greece, and, in the future, the Balkan states, are strategically and historically important partners within Europe, both politically and economically, towards the other direction. The interconnectivity between the Weimar Triangle and Southern Southeastern Europe is crucial for the stability and cohesion of the EU. The interconnectivity of Europe's major regions around the axis of the Weimar Triangle with the Western, Southern, and Northern European regions is the engine of Europe's connectivity. This interconnectivity extends across several dimensions and is crucial for the coherence of the European project.

Given its capabilities, the European Union has much to do. One cannot simply sit back and be swept along by the waves. This responsibility cannot be taken away from the EU. While it is still a precautionary policy for its own security, it can quickly turn into a bitter and more costly reactive security policy. Meanwhile, hostile states are already using terrorist gangs that wreak havoc within the individual entities of Europe, but also globally.

Later reactions to security crises are often much more expensive because they occur under time pressure and in an unstable environment. The principle of coordinated action and aligning joint efforts with common views is crucial for strengthening the EU as a global actor. It allows the Union to respond more coherently and effectively to international challenges and represent its interests on the world stage. All involved actors must agree on the key issues, challenges, and goals. This requires intense exchange and open communication. The actions and decisions of the involved parties will be coordinated to complement each other and create synergies, rather than conflicting or competing with one another.

Europe must stop hiding behind moral appeals and symbolic gestures and begin to use its economic and political power more deliberately. Sanctions must come faster and more forcefully, economic dependencies systematically reduced, and its strengths proactively showcased. Moreover, a new understanding of geopolitical realities is needed. The assumption that authoritarian rulers can be convinced through good arguments and appeals to reason is a dangerous illusion. They respect power, not morality. Europe must learn to represent its interests clearly and without hesitation, even if it means taking short-term risks or making uncomfortable decisions. One example could be a military presence in geopolitically sensitive regions or the expansion of strategic partnerships with countries willing to oppose authoritarian forces.

Finally, the behavior of European leaders must also change. It takes not only smart teams but also strong personalities who can act on equal terms with the power players of the world. A chancellor who stumbles at international summits, whether metaphorically or literally, sends a signal of insecurity. The behavior of German leaders on the international stage has often given the impression of trying to hide behind the facade of a moderate, almost innocent actor. The political response to international challenges, such as the energy crisis, the refugee issue, or geopolitical tensions with China, repeatedly showed a tendency toward a so-called crisis management approach rather than proactively steering events. In doing so, German leadership often seemed more concerned with maintaining its political image than with actively solving the problems.

Political leadership means responsibility - not only for decisions made but also for those that are delayed or avoided. Particularly in crises like the Ukraine war, it becomes clear that hesitation or deliberate delay often has fatal consequences. These are decisions with immediate consequences, sometimes in the form of lives that could have been saved or conflicts that could have been defused through bold action. While Russia's attacks continue, certain political actors often engage in lengthy discussions about the provision of weapons, aid, or sanctions. Each delay means not only another day of suffering but also the possibility that the aggression will expand and solidify. The limited approach shown is not just a political failure but a moral wrongdoing. Hesitation is not a sign of careful consideration or caution; it is a deliberate manipulation. The actors avoid taking clear positions to protect themselves or to shift responsibility away from themselves.

The question is: How will Europe, and especially Germany, stand in this environment? The answer lies not in diplomacy but in complementing it with decisive action and a clear strategy. Diplomacy cannot be meant as softening and endless talking, where in the end, nothing of an identity remains. But perhaps it is precisely the fine art of strategic patience that is being perfected—waiting long enough for problems to resolve themselves, preferably without disturbing the cocktail parties at summit conferences. What would the extermination of a people with the means of murder, the targeted bombing of kindergartens, schools, hospitals, and essential infrastructure be regarded as? This attitude is not only shortsighted but deeply immoral, as it risks the lives of innocent people. Every day of a worldwide stalemate in international politics damages the social fabric.

The fundamental realities must be addressed. One must not hide behind slogans of supposed prudence out of fear of public opinion in the camps of Putin supporters, the AfD, BSW, or the german Left. A free society must be clear about what is worth defending. Ultimately, it is about more than just a false peace; it is about living in freedom. The freedom we cherish seems to be under attack from many sides. It is not only being undermined by external actors such as authoritarian governments but also by internal forces that act with hatred against everything that opposes open and pluralistic discourse. In this context, such ideologies are not just opinions at the edges of the political spectrum; they are potentially dangerous threats to the principles of democracy and human rights.

Society must confront extreme ideologies, as they can lead to intolerance, discrimination, and violence. Protecting democracy and human rights requires active engagement against such movements. It is the responsibility of civil society to promote education, enlightenment, and dialogue to defend the values of tolerance, respect, and diversity. Furthermore, institutions and political actors must ensure that laws and regulations exist to counter extremist views and foster an inclusive, democratic community. Democracy does not work automatically; it is an ongoing process that requires commitment, vigilance, and foresight. The dangers posed by extreme political movements are not merely theoretical. There are enough historical examples that should teach us what happens when the incursions and influence of radical ideologies are ignored.

## 34. INTERCONNECTIVITY OF POLICY MANAGEMENT

The axiom "The management of politics must be worthwhile" implies that political action and governance should be designed so that the results benefit not only politicians but, above all, citizens and society as a whole. For political management to be worthwhile, certain principles and objectives must be pursued, delivering both short-term successes and long-term benefits. The ideas of international politics thrive when the will and the necessary collective intelligence are present to be efficiently utilized. Emotions must be adapted to the framework of rational political management.

Emotions like fear, hope, or outrage can drive political processes, mobilize people, and create public attention. While they often serve as catalysts for change, they must be channeled to avoid destructive impulses such as populism or overreactions. Political management requires decisions based on facts, strategic analysis, and clear goals. Emotions should not dominate these processes but must be incorporated into a system that ensures rational action. Politics can address emotional concerns but must do so in a way that encourages constructive solutions.

Effective political management requires efficient and transparent organization. Resources must be used optimally to achieve the best possible results, whether financial or human. Political decisions should align with clearly defined objectives and measure their success against tangible outcomes. This is why much emphasis is placed on being "evidence-based." Evidence-based policymaking means that decisions rely on scientific data and analyses to develop informed and forward-looking strategies. Foresight entails not only responding to current crises but also anticipating and preparing for future scenarios.

Political decisions should not aim solely for short-term successes but also seek to create lasting positive impacts on society and the economy. Political programs must be consistent and mutually reinforcing to create synergies. A results-oriented approach requires monitoring the effectiveness of decisions through concrete outcomes. This means setting measurable goals in advance to focus on actual effects rather than mere resource allocation. To make political management effective and gain public support, it is crucial to ensure transparency and understanding of political decision-making processes. An open information policy requires political decision-makers to proactively and clearly communicate upcoming decisions, their rationale, and their implications. Weak communicators often argue against transparency, claiming instead that sowing confusion is more effective. They believe trust is overrated and that what ultimately matters is mobilizing voters on election day, while misunderstandings add an element of suspense.

Worthwhile political management requires actors to take responsibility for their decisions and their impacts. This also means acknowledging mistakes and being willing to learn from them. Mismanagement combined with corruption damages the reputation of politics and undermines trust in institutions, yet it remains a global issue. Ethical conduct and adherence to integrity standards are essential prerequisites for political management to be seen as worthwhile.

This brings us back to the crucial issue of evaluation. Political programs and projects need continuous monitoring to detect deviations early and take corrective actions. This ensures ongoing adjustment and optimization of measures. Regular reports and reviews make progress transparent and assessable. This helps avoid unnecessary expenditures and ensures that policy stays on track or makes timely adjustments. Evaluations play a vital role in identifying mistakes, establishing accountability, and initiating improvements.

They provide an opportunity to learn from past decisions and optimize the overall decision-making process. Although evaluations often reveal criticism and uncomfortable truths, they are an essential tool for promoting transparency, efficiency, and long-term success.

Global transformation is underway - socially, politically, and economically. Climate change, technological disruptions, and geopolitical shifts are just some of the challenges requiring profound changes. However, transformation can only succeed by accepting the underlying truths, which requires transparency and accurate evaluation. Transparency is the cornerstone of building trust in transformative processes. Without clear information about the necessity and goals of changes, skepticism or even rejection arises. Openness allows understanding of the context of measures and aligns decisions accordingly. Only complete and unbiased information enables precise evaluation of developments. Political or ideological distortions lead to mismanagement. Science and evidence must take precedence. Evaluation results must be comprehensible and accessible to all to foster acceptance and trust. Many truths are uncomfortable, whether it is the necessary shift away from fossil fuels or social upheavals caused by automation. The willingness to recognize such truths is often low, as they generate uncertainty and fear of loss. Transparency alone is not enough. Communication must emphasize the added value of changes while presenting concrete solutions.

Facts are immutable and objective, at least in their ideal form. However, the way people perceive, interpret, and communicate them is rarely free from bias. Prejudices, deliberate or unconscious manipulations, and the suppression of inconvenient truths mean that even an apparently honest approach to facts can be distorted. It is therefore essential to identify prejudices as disruptors of fact-based decision-making and to study them systematically.

Statistics can be misused through "cherry-picking" or selective presentation. Facts can be intentionally embedded in narratives that alter their meaning. Even research is not always free from bias, such as ideological influences or economic interests. Without malicious intent, human perception still filters, interprets, or suppresses certain facts. Prejudices are a central driver in this process. They often suppress uncomfortable truths and prioritize alternative explanations. People tend to ignore or distort information that contradicts their worldview. Facts can be selectively perceived to reinforce existing beliefs. Group pressure can also distort facts to ensure conformity. These mechanisms are not only individual but also systemic. They influence political decision-making processes, public opinion, and media reporting.

The danger of merely approaching the truth arises when uncomfortable aspects are ignored. This often leads to issues like climate change or social inequality being glossed over. An uncritical attitude reinforces misconceptions. Societies must be willing to acknowledge their own blind spots and ideological biases. Open debates that include diverse perspectives prevent one-sided interpretations. The path to truth is uncomfortable, but it begins with the courage to recognize and overcome one's own prejudices. Facts, by definition, are incorruptible, they describe what is. However, their presentation and interpretation are strongly influenced by context, perspectives, interests, and technology. AI plays a crucial role in this dynamic. It has the potential to profoundly change the quality of information processing while also creating new risks. AI systems learn from data provided by humans, which often reflects existing biases, inequalities, or gaps. Decisions about data weighting and prioritization, whether conscious or unconscious, can distort facts. AI can embed facts into specific contexts that shape understanding, allowing narratives to be purposefully crafted.

One example is the risk of "confirmation bias". When AI models are programmed to serve specific interests or ideologies, they amplify existing echo chambers. A particular risk lies in the perception of AI as neutral, a supposedly objective purveyor of facts. In truth, its neutrality heavily depends on how it is programmed and trained. This illusion of objectivity can lead to distorted information being accepted as truth without scrutiny. AI technologies enable the creation of convincingly realistic but false content, undermining trust in authentic information. AI-based algorithms analyze user behavior and disseminate misleading content tailored to individual biases. Subtly worded texts generated by language models can convey a specific reality, even if incomplete or manipulative.

If the international community and individual states fail to adequately address current geopolitical threats, the consequences could be severe. The dynamics of global power relations, economic dependencies, and technological advances demand active engagement, as threats are becoming increasingly complex and interconnected. The consequences of inaction in addressing these threats would be manifold. Without efforts in conflict resolution and prevention, regional disputes could quickly escalate into broader military confrontations between states. A lack of mechanisms to address such issues leaves nations vulnerable to great power conflicts, leading to global security crises with extensive humanitarian, economic, and political ramifications. Without targeted efforts toward disarmament and the establishment of trust mechanisms, a new arms race among major powers—especially in nuclear, cyber, and other advanced military technologies—becomes unavoidable. This would not only endanger international security but also consume immense economic resources that are desperately needed in other critical areas like health, education, and the environment.

If governments fail to implement effective cybersecurity measures, critical infrastructures - ranging from energy and water supplies to financial systems - will be increasingly at risk. Cyberattacks by hacker groups and state actors could destabilize nations, paralyze economic systems, or foment political unrest. This threat becomes even more acute with the continued digitization of the global economy. Inaction on climate change would exacerbate environmental disasters, with more frequent and intense natural catastrophes such as droughts, floods, storms, and rising sea levels. These would force millions of people to flee, triggering global migration crises. Scarcity of resources, especially water and food, would deepen conflicts within global societies. Similarly, without determined action against global terrorism and extremist networks, destructive forces would gain ground, particularly in unstable or failed states where such groups can freely expand their activities.

Without active international cooperation to tackle global threats, institutions like the World Trade Organization or NATO could become ineffective. Withdrawal from multilateral processes and institutions would erode the international community's ability to respond effectively to challenges. This would inevitably lead to a "every man for himself" approach, where national interests outweigh international collaboration. The repercussions of unresolved global crises—whether driven by climate change, economic instability, or political tensions—would spiral out of control.

Unemployment, economic inequality, and lack of prospects create fertile ground for populism, extremism, and authoritarian movements. This could destabilize democracies worldwide and lead to a rise in authoritarian regimes and domestic repression. Geopolitical instability and unresolved conflicts disrupt free trade and global supply chains. A lack of international collaboration to resolve crises could promote trade wars, sanctions, and economic blockades, hindering global growth. Developing and emerging countries, which are heavily reliant on international trade and investment, would be particularly vulnerable. Regional conflicts, extreme weather events, and state collapses could force millions to flee, increasing global migration flows and posing immense challenges for both origin and host countries. Without international coordination and humanitarian support, refugee crises could cause humanitarian catastrophes and amplify political instability in host nations.

Understanding the political and economic frameworks that influence goal attainment is as important as effectively communicating these goals. The tensions between globalization forces and nationalist politics in various parts of the world challenge political actors to steer their international engagements with flexibility. Globalization has changed the parameters of political action without inherently weakening individual units. Instead, it has shifted incentives toward certain economic policy options. The heightened global competition for mobile resources increases the appeal of market-liberal reforms, while interventionist policies become costlier. While this may limit governments' autonomy at the smallest-unit level, it does not necessarily weaken their ability to ensure growth and prosperity.

Resistance to globalization comes from various political quarters but is particularly pronounced on the political right. Influenced by these opposing forces, states face the challenge of flexibly adapting their policies. Political figures such as Donald Trump, Marine Le Pen, Viktor Orbán, Germany's Alternative for Germany party, or the so-called Islamic State criticize globalization and resonate with parts of the population. The goal is to harness globalization's potential for innovation and growth through targeted liberalization while mitigating any adverse effects of structural change.

New forms of international governance are emerging. Politics must navigate international engagements flexibly, leveraging globalization's opportunities while addressing nationalist counter-movements. This requires a complex interplay of various actors and governance forms at municipal, local, and international levels. Their interconnectedness must be considered. Pragmatism and risk-taking in implementing foreign policy goals are two central principles shaping actions in international politics. Both concepts reflect how countries pursue their foreign policy objectives and act in the international arena. Pragmatism and risk-taking are not necessarily contradictory. In many cases, governments act both pragmatically and boldly. A pragmatic decision-maker may take calculated risks if deemed necessary to achieve long-term foreign policy goals.

Conversely, a risk-tolerant actor may pragmatically adapt their strategy when circumstances change.

Even when dangers appear to have passed - they never truly do - the opportunities must not be overlooked. Issues are never purely matters of the past. They leave traces that often only become visible years later. An example is the Cold War, whose fault lines are resurfacing decades after its official conclusion. Similarly, economic crises may pass, but their structural causes often persist, creating new risks. In truth, the cycle of challenges never ends. History repeatedly demonstrates that threats considered relegated to the past re-emerge in new forms, whether geopolitical tensions, economic crises, technological upheavals, or societal and ecological issues. Retreating into passivity leads inevitably to paralysis—a fatal stance in a globalized, dynamic world.

This underscores the need to place the best minds in key observation and decision-making positions. Those at the helm must be able to think beyond the immediate horizon. The task is to identify risks before they become acute and seize opportunities before they slip away. This requires that excellence, not mediocrity or mere loyalty, is the top priority in appointing critical positions. A culture that fosters the best minds and grants them the necessary freedoms is essential for sustained effectiveness. It is not the times themselves that are destructive, but the outputs of human and political actions.

In international politics, listening, weighing opinions, understanding contexts, and considering diverse perspectives are undeniably indispensable. These processes enable decision-makers to grasp complex interrelations, respect cultural sensitivities, and minimize potential risks. However, this process also entails a responsibility that is often underestimated: the duty to transform insights into decisive, concerted actions. Excessive dwelling in evaluation mode can lead to paralysis. While thorough examination is vital before acting, if the analysis of data and opinions becomes an end in itself, the critical step of decision-making is neglected. Analyses alone do not save lives, secure borders, or resolve conflicts. Clever management acrobatics require a sensitive understanding of the dynamics at play, as well as the ability to respond flexibly and creatively to diverse situations. This inevitably involves employing consensus-building, mediation procedures, or intercultural communication strategies.

Navigating various interests, actors, and perspectives is a delicate art. A skilled player understands the priorities of all stakeholders and plans ahead. Not every opinion carries equal weight. The key lies in listening without losing focus and elevating the perspectives that contribute to a strategic solution. Acting too early or too late can have fatal consequences. A trained ear for signals and developments will favor proactive action, ensuring the right move is made at the right moment. In rare cases, waiting is part of the strategy, but only when it is well-reasoned and carefully managed. Stagnation, disguised as a "review process," ultimately poses the greatest danger of all.

## 35. INTERCONNECTIVITY OF DEMOCRACY

Traditional political parties are losing significance in many countries, while new political movements are emerging. Changed forms of communication, the growing complexity of political challenges, globalization, transnational interdependencies, and the overcoming of nationalist tendencies are the determining factors of the future. Normative cornerstones for future parliamentary movements in place of parties include human rights, subsidiarity, alliance commitments, democracy, freedom, and security. If such principles are established as a basis for new parliamentary movements, it could be seen as an attempt to reshape and modernize current political structures. While nationalist currents often dominated in the past, there is now a focus on global challenges. Climate change and environmental protection cannot be addressed without international cooperation. Economic interdependencies transcend national borders.

Migration movements highlight the necessity of transnational solutions. These ideas emphasize that subsidiarity alone is insufficient to create a well-functioning political and social system. It must be complemented by a structured framework that regulates and coordinates the connections between different levels—local, regional, national, and international. A future parliamentary movement should strive for a deeper and more inclusive democracy, potentially more direct and participatory than today's models. Digital participation platforms will need to address future challenges. Future conferences, transparency in decision-making regarding new fields of evidence-based evaluations and assessments should ensure that political interest movements adapt to circumstances to remain relevant. A transformation of the party system would offer opportunities for a reorientation of politics beyond narrowly defined national interests. At the same time, it presents established democratic structures with the task of evolving and finding new forms of representation. This is also the only real way to protect against extremism on both the left and right fringes.

These new parliamentary movements should take on their international responsibility through alliance commitments. This involves a commitment to multilateral institutions such as the reform-needed United Nations or NATO, which are based on collective defense, cooperation, and global peace. These alliances are crucial for addressing global challenges such as climate change, international security, or humanitarian crises. This is not merely about individual freedom rights, but also about economic freedom and the self-determination of citizens.

It is the primary obligation in the interconnectivity of humanity's civilizational thought to place the dignity of the individual at the center of events. Democracy, in this mission, is not an ideology but rather an instrument for problem-solving in global conflicts. If it adheres to the rules of rationality, it operates amidst power struggles with far more insight than autocracies.

In the tension between collective interests and the responsibility to protect the dignity of the individual, doing so is not only a moral imperative but also an essential basis for social peace and stability. Democracy enables, through open debates and pluralism, more sustainable conflict resolution since it creates space for diverse perspectives and interests. The rules of rationality in democratic processes foster insight and understanding by grounding decisions in facts, logic, and debate. The democratic structure aims to develop solutions that benefit the majority while simultaneously protecting minority rights, an indispensable factor in a global context increasingly characterized by the mixing of different cultures and interests. In autocratic systems, the value of the individual and rationality are often supplanted by strategies for maintaining and expanding power. Thus, the civilizational progress of humanity will largely depend on how consistently democracies worldwide center the principles of rationality and human dignity in their interactions.

The courage to change plays a crucial role in preserving and renewing democracy in its original sense. Many of the current challenges facing democracies have been exacerbated by global developments, technological upheavals, and social divisions. Addressing these challenges requires not only political will but also the readiness to rethink and adapt existing subsystems and sub-structures of democracy. Thus, a renewal must take into account the functionality and adaptability of institutions, administrations, media, and civil society organizations.

Many political institutions still remain in rigid structures that hinder dialogue between citizens and decision-makers. Modernizing these institutions could make them more accessible, transparent, and responsive. A renewed democracy must consider these tensions and develop mechanisms to find global solutions that can be implemented at the local level. Democracy is now facing a series of crises that have become a permanent phenomenon. These ongoing difficulties test the resilience and adaptability of democratic systems. To remain resilient, democracies must demonstrate their capacity for renewal.

In a high-quality democracy, it is not compromise that is upheld, but consensus. In some pluralistic democracies, compromise is a preferred method for reconciling divergent interests, opinions, and needs. Each party makes concessions to reach an agreement. However, compromise is a kind of middle ground in which none of the involved parties achieves their full objectives. This often leads to a feeling that compromises are merely temporary solutions that do not fully resolve existing conflicts but only mitigate them. In a democratic reality characterized by a wide variety of interests, compromises can lead to fragmentation or even dissatisfaction because no one is completely satisfied.

In contrast, consensus relies on a deeper and more comprehensive form of agreement. It means finding a solution or decision that is accepted by all parties as fair, just, and in the best interest of the entire society. This involves not only that each party makes concessions but also that a common foundation is established that transcends mere balancing of interests. Consensus is primarily pursued as an ideal since it represents a deeper form of political agreement. It assumes that the goal is not only to manage conflicts but to develop a shared vision that emphasizes unity and the common good of society. Consensus processes require an intensive and constructive dialogue in which not only interests but also values and norms come into play. In this way, a solution is created that truly convinces all relevant actors rather than being merely accepted. A consensus is more stable in the long term than a compromise, as it is based on broader societal agreement and is not shaped by the necessity of short-term political deals.

Consensus-building in an organizational context is generally seen as positive and productive, whereas compromises in politics are often interpreted as weakening or a renunciation of clear principles. In management, consensus is a valuable strategy aimed at considering the interests of all stakeholders. Consensus serves as a way to minimize conflicts and foster collective commitment to a common goal. In businesses, consensus is viewed as desirable because it ensures that all decision-makers and stakeholders are aligned. This strengthens the team and typically leads to more sustainable and stable outcomes, finding solutions that are supported by a broad range of actors. When a management team makes decisions based on consensus, it means that the likelihood of resistance and blockages decreases, as the involved parties have jointly supported the decision-making process. This is especially important in complex organizations where many diverse interests from technical developers, marketing personnel, sales, and export specialists must be harmonized. The ability to make viable decisions through consensus is considered a central leadership approach in various organizational contexts, whether in business, project management, or even diplomacy.

In politics, compromise has a negative connotation, as it is interpreted as a sign of weakness or lack of principles. Particularly in polarized societies, political leaders are expected to represent clear and firm positions. A compromise is therefore seen as a giving up of beliefs to achieve short-term successes. Politicians who frequently compromise risk losing their credibility or the support of their electorate. Compromises in politics are sometimes referred to as "soft compromises" when they are perceived as solutions that truly satisfy no one and do not resolve the deepest issues. They are criticized as half-heartedness or a departure from strong convictions. This leads to the feeling that politics is ineffective, as decisions are diluted by too many compromises.

A consensus-based management style promotes a positive working environment where all participants feel heard. This can enhance productivity and employee engagement. In this case, consensus is considered a means to satisfy all stakeholders, which in turn supports the overall goal. In politics, however, compromise is seen as a necessity to keep government processes running. However, it is often regarded as undesirable because it rarely provides the ideal solution. It symbolizes a retreat from clear ideals and firm beliefs, which is critical to assess especially in times of political polarization.

In international politics, there is an alternative approach. Several states or regions can form pragmatic alliances and utilize more flexible cooperation forms tailored to specific issues. "Coalitions of the willing" bypass the dilemma that all states must agree to a compromise. They allow for progress in specific areas. For example, the G20, as a group of major economic powers, collaborates in many areas such as financial regulation and combating global economic instability. Although it does not represent a consensus of all nations, it can make significant progress by focusing on specific shared interests. Flexible mechanisms, such as the principle of "differentiated responsibilities," applied in climate change agreements, allow states to undertake different commitments based on their capacities and national circumstances. This prevents rigid compromises from leading to dissatisfaction and allows for differentiated solutions. Through measures like transparency initiatives, arms control agreements, or trust agreements, states can work towards a consensus situation in the long term. As trust in the seriousness and predictability of negotiating partners increases, so does the willingness to find innovative solutions.

Targeted measures against specific companies that impair the interests of NATO or EU states through harmful behavior would be a more effective and balanced strategy than general punitive tariffs. The advantage of such precise competition policy is that it directly targets the issue while causing less harm to broader economic relations. These sanctions could include access bans to markets or trade restrictions on specific products. The allied states could exclude certain companies from public tenders and government contracts for violating security interests. Allied states could scrutinize more closely when companies from third countries seek stakes in strategically important areas such as infrastructure, technology, and energy. A precise mechanism for investment screenings could prevent companies with ties to third states imposing punitive tariffs from acquiring critical market positions. This control could also extend to mergers where sensitive technologies are involved. Instead of general punitive tariffs, specific import restrictions or regulatory requirements could be introduced for certain industries, such as high technology, telecommunications, or energy. This would specifically target companies that violate the alliance's competition rules or security standards without restricting overall trade.

The alliance could strategically invest in research and development to create independent technological capacities in areas dominated by problematic third-state companies. These strategic investments could help make the alliance partners less dependent on companies that present potential security risks, such as in telecommunications or critical infrastructures. This coordinated approach would increase pressure on the affected companies while promoting compliance with international norms. These targeted measures against specific companies would be less economically damaging to the overall economy and politically easier to implement.

The interconnectivity of democracy refers to the mutual relationship between democratic systems as well as the interlinkages and mutual influences between democracies worldwide. In a globalized world, democracies are not isolated; rather, they are embedded in a network of political, economic, and social relationships that significantly influence their functioning and development. Democratic systems influence each other through the exchange of ideas, institutions, and practices.

Concepts such as the separation of powers, human rights, and the rule of law, which have been developed within a democracy, inspire other democracies. The so-called "democratic diffusion effect" describes how democratic reforms can spread from one country to another, often triggered by revolutionary upheavals, political reform movements, or technological innovations. Now, democracies face global challenges that do not allow for purely national solutions, such as climate change, international security threats, or migration. These problems require close cooperation among democratic states, where shared values like transparency, accountability, and inclusion play a central role. This means that democracies must not only be stable and functional internally but also take international responsibility to address global issues.

A state is not a nation, and a nation is not yet a state; a state is not yet a country. The political significance lies in countries and their populations. It depends on their capacities to deal with the potentials and contents. The ability of political leadership to develop long-term strategies that create prosperity, justice, and stability is crucial everywhere. Short-sighted or even destructive policies will ultimately harm the potentials of a country. Key is the ability of democratic leadership to develop long-term strategies. The ability to establish international relations and participate in global processes is now more important than ever to secure one's interests and assert oneself in an increasingly interconnected system.

In the fast-paced and conflict-laden international politics, a sense of duty, sincerity, decency, and responsibility are not only idealistic concepts but necessary cornerstones for peace and cooperation. Ultimately, they are crucial for addressing global challenges from climate change and global injustice to conflicts and security threats. A sense of duty in the international context requires transparency and sincerity in communication with other states. This includes openly committing to international obligations and avoiding deception that could undermine trust in multilateral relationships. Sincerity allows governments to clearly define their responsibilities and justify their positions and actions. It encourages a willingness to take responsibility for misconduct or misunderstandings and to find solutions through dialogue. Responsibility requires that states be honest about their capabilities, intentions, and actions. Irresponsibility often manifests itself in deception, such as failing to disclose nuclear programs or misrepresenting military actions.

Strengthening reliability and credibility is critical for governments to act effectively in international politics. Through the consistent implementation of strategies focused on transparency, consistency, and multilateral cooperation, states can assume new positions in an increasingly complex global environment. A state known for its credibility can more easily assert its political and economic interests. Countries that are known for environmentally friendly practices will advocate for climate protection measures more effectively on the international stage. Countries considered reliable can often negotiate better conditions in international trade negotiations because they are viewed as predictable partners.

The interconnectivity of a sense of duty, sincerity, decency, and responsibility in international politics forms the ethical foundation for global politics. Responsible and sincere actors promote stability and the global common good, while decent and responsible actions help to avoid conflicts and mobilize trust in international institutions. The absence of any of these values leads to distrust, instability, and conflicts, such as through secret agreements, non-compliance with contracts, or the disregard of international norms.

## 36. INTERCONNECTIVITY OF THE POSITIVE AND NEGATIVE

The interconnectedness of positive and negative forces in politics and society has left deep marks throughout history. These two forces are not mere opposites but exist in a dynamic balance: when one prevails, the equilibrium is disrupted, and societies can drift into extreme states. While positive developments bring hope, progress, and constructive change, the dominance of negativity often results in terror, oppression, and profound societal depression. The historical record demonstrates that sustained negativity leads not only to crises but also leaves lasting scars on a nation's collective psyche and social cohesion.

Take, for example, the French Revolution. What began as a surge of enthusiasm for equality and liberty descended into the Reign of Terror under Robespierre. As fear of betrayal and abuse of power grew, a policy of purges and persecution emerged. The guillotine became a symbol of terror, and society experienced profound disillusionment as friendships and neighborhoods were shrouded in suspicion, eroding communal trust. This trauma cast a shadow over Europe, which only regained stability years later.

Similarly, during the Stalinist "Great Purge" of the 1930s, the persecution of perceived enemies of the state reached its zenith. Millions were imprisoned, executed, or exiled to gulags. The omnipresent uncertainty and climate of fear led to a paralyzing collective despair, leaving society closed-off and distrustful. The outcome was a populace weakened in survival and morally exhausted, a condition that persisted for decades after the terror subsided. Does the nation still suffer from this trauma today?

In contemporary Russia, under a renewed wave of authoritarian rule, the legacy of the gulag system remains palpable. The fear of persecution and repression has resurfaced, further undermining trust in social and political institutions. The horrors of the gulag, which affected millions of families and left deep scars on the collective memory, continue to resonate in Russia. Generations of grandparents and parents passed down silent lessons: don't speak too loudly, trust sparingly, and, when in doubt, remain invisible. Yet in recent years, particularly with the emergence of a new generation, this silence seems to be breaking. Young people delving into their nation's past are drawing strength and determination from the knowledge and suffering of their ancestors. Civil society initiatives and cultural projects are daring to ask questions, break the silence, and lay the groundwork for potential change. However, these tender shoots of renewal have been trampled again. Old wounds, never fully healed, have been reopened. As political institutions stifle public discourse and erode trust, perhaps a quiet, clandestine resistance is forming. Small movements may emerge that defy resignation, embodying the face of a new, young generation no longer willing to hide from its history.

The impacts of the gulag experience remain present in Russian society today. The collective trauma, passed down through generations, continues to influence social dynamics and individual behavior. Yet society is also developing strategies for resilience and potential healing. Confronting its history will be critical for Russia's ability to learn from these dark chapters and create a hopeful future. How societal and political conditions evolve will determine whether Russia can free itself from the dystopian legacy of the gulags.

Young Russians are acutely aware of the dangers that remembering the past still entails today. They perceive the parallels between past and present, which weigh heavily on them. Yet within this awareness lies a potential determination—not merely to live through history but to understand and carry forward its lessons. May they have the chance to achieve inner liberation and share it with the world, as the Ukrainian society has done, albeit through immense suffering. The act of engaging with the past must be bold and emotionally charged. They will see the ruins of the gulags, the devastation of their neighboring Ukraine, and install plaques to commemorate those who can no longer shed tears. This process demands strength but also holds hope. It is a call for justice and truth, a message that they will not sink into the darkness of oblivion.

Though not yet tangible, there lies a great opportunity in this for a different kind of European project based on solidarity, justice, and mutual understanding. Cultural initiatives can foster dialogue among future generations. These platforms offer space for critical engagement with the past and may enable participants to learn from historical mistakes. The young generation, through social media, has new tools to connect and make their voices heard globally. This digital networking can serve as a catalyst for change, allowing local concerns to resonate across Europe.

While political tensions between Russia and Europe remain high, there is still potential for a different future centered on historical reckoning. A rebuilt and revitalized Ukraine could play a central mediating role. It might become a bridge for new identities on both sides, acknowledging the past while forging a future of European cooperation that takes these experiences seriously and integrates them into the collective memory.

We are all aware of the challenges and risks involved. Those directly affected know they are up against powerful structures and that many of their voices may initially go unheard. The pursuit of truth, reckoning, and justice must be stronger than the chains of fear. Within a new generation lies the potential for transformation—using the suffering of the past to shape a future where these horrors are not repeated. This quiet revolution of hearts is not yet loud enough to shake entrenched regimes. But it is loud enough to touch souls and remind people of our shared humanity. If we listen and incorporate this voice into our vision of Europe, it may ultimately bring about a change that begins to heal the deepest wounds.

Visions of a Europe built on human values and mutual exchange are always inspiring, offering unexpected perspectives for the continent's future. The European Union is already based on a strong foundation of values that transcend mere politics. Courage and hope are cornerstones of any political society, everywhere in the world. Courage enables societies to face challenges and embrace change. Hope provides the confidence and motivation necessary to work toward a better future. Due to its geopolitical position and history, Ukraine could act as a bridge between East and West. The country's experiences in its fight for democracy and freedom could provide valuable lessons for Europe as a whole. A successful rebuilding of Ukraine could serve as an inspiring example of resilience and European solidarity.

While this vision is undoubtedly optimistic, it outlines a potential path toward a values-based Europe. The challenge will be to translate these ideals into concrete policies and actions. This requires not only political will but also the active engagement of European citizens. The EU's foundational principles, such as freedom, democracy, and the rule of law, already provide a solid basis for this vision. By further developing and deepening these values, paired with courage and hope, Europe may indeed find a path to greater unity and resilience.

Overcoming collective traumas often requires profound societal changes that go beyond individual healing processes. In many cases, the roots of such traumas lie in historical events and shared experiences that shape a country over generations. It is feared that the war in Ukraine will continue to have psychological repercussions beneath the surface of affected societies for a long time. Historical traumas often persist across generations, transmitted through memories, narratives, and cultural codes. The war in Ukraine is leaving scars in affected communities, resulting from loss, violence, and displacement. The psychological burden caused by the war can also affect the social stability of impacted countries. When a significant portion of the population lives with untreated trauma, it can significantly impair societal functionality, trust in institutions, and overall quality of life.

At this juncture, the European Union faces a monumental task in both physical and intercultural reconstruction. Through a wide range of measures, the EU has the opportunity to ensure that societies in Europe heal not only physically but also emotionally and socially, creating a foundation for peaceful and stable coexistence. Reconstruction should not merely replace old infrastructure but also integrate modern, environmentally friendly technologies. The EU must adopt an approach that centers on the needs and experiences of the affected country while opening long-term perspectives for a stable and prosperous future. By successfully addressing these challenges, the EU can not only contribute to Ukraine's recovery but also redefine its own roles. A focus on specific industries, sustainable energy sources, and eco-friendly construction methods could boost the entire European economy and enhance security, while reducing dependence on fossil fuels and protecting the environment. Political leadership will play a critical role in promoting reconciliation and societal healing. Without targeted, long-term support, countries risk that trauma will persist in the form of political radicalization, distrust, or social conflicts.

However, an open debate about these issues can help address old wounds and raise awareness about the need for change. Strengthening democratic institutions is crucial, as they provide a platform for incorporating diverse perspectives into societal discourse and fostering participatory processes. Education and public awareness are also essential for breaking patterns of silence and repression. At the same time, it is important to recognize the risks of authoritarian tendencies or corruption that may arise during reconstruction periods. Often, feelings of insecurity or threat lead to repressive measures and a return to old, often traumatic behavior patterns. The challenge lies in finding a balance between protecting society and preserving individual freedoms.

For russian society, this means that the path to an open and resilient future requires an honest and critical examination of its own history. Only then can an inclusive and just social climate be created, capable of addressing present and future challenges. Looking back at the past can not only aid healing but also serve as a foundation for a new understanding of identity and community. However, the conflict could also exacerbate existing tensions between different population groups or create new ones.

Despite gloomy forecasts, the unpredictability of historical developments lies ahead of us. History has often shown that unexpected turns are possible. After World War II, former enemies like Germany and France managed to become close partners. A similar process could be possible between Ukraine and Russia in the long term. Times of crisis can also foster greater cohesion and societal renewal. Ukraine could emerge stronger and more united from the conflict. The broad international support rooted in European solidarity for Ukraine could accelerate its integration into European and global structures, further expediting reconstruction and healing. In contrast to its struggles, Ukraine could experience a flourishing of culture, identity, and economy that resonates far beyond its borders.

While the psychological aftermath of the war will undoubtedly pose significant challenges, the way Ukraine and the international community handle the consequences of the conflict will be decisive for its long-term impact. It will be crucial to focus not only on physical reconstruction but also on social healing. Promoting social cohesion and providing international support can help mitigate negative effects and even foster positive developments. Ultimately, history shows that societies possess a remarkable ability to regenerate and renew. With the right support, Ukraine could emerge from this crisis as a resilient and perhaps even more innovative society.

For millions of Ukrainians, the war has become an experience that has irrevocably changed their lives. These individual stories will ultimately play a key role in determining the future resilience and social cohesion of Ukrainian society. Collective trauma can lead to mistrust and even societal division, especially when different groups hold divergent perspectives on the causes and consequences of the war. At the same time, collective trauma can foster new cohesion, renewed solidarity, and connectedness, traits that Ukrainians have often demonstrated. A long-term reconstruction process must therefore aim to overcome these societal divides and promote social cohesion. Ukraine faces comprehensive reconstruction that must not only rebuild infrastructure but also reestablish the societal fabric. Such challenges can drive innovation and progress, including new concepts for sustainable urban development and digitalization. Crises have historically acted as catalysts for innovation, whether technological, social, or cultural.

Beyond physical destruction, the war has shed new light on Ukrainian culture and identity. In the face of crisis, art, music, literature, and collective memory could experience a renaissance with far-reaching effects. Artists and intellectuals are shaping new symbols of Ukrainian resistance, contributing to a shared identity that will provide a crucial foundation for the country's reconstruction.

The positive potential inherent in Ukraine's recovery and resilience within a strengthened Europe offers the chance to revive long-held but recently overshadowed visions in Western Europe. The challenges arising from the war in Ukraine could prompt the EU to redefine its core values and vision. The war could serve as a wake-up call to focus on shared challenges such as security, climate change, and social justice. The processes initiated by supporting Ukraine and upholding shared values could deepen integration in the West and revive European unity. Many of these visions—such as a common foreign and defense policy, closer economic cooperation, and a deeper appreciation of diversity—have often faded from focus in recent decades. However, given the current geopolitical situation, they are regaining significance. A resilient Europe acting in unity during crises could not only provide sustainable support to Ukraine but also unleash other dynamics. These opportunities must not be squandered. The necessity of rebuilding Ukraine could inspire Europe to develop and share innovative, future-oriented concepts that benefit all countries and strengthen resilience against future crises.

A renaissance of a united and progressive Europe would rejuvenate not only economic ties but also cultural and social connections, fostering resilience and unity. Ukraine's resistance against an aggressive neighbor and its efforts to defend European values could enrich the sense of shared identity. This points to a Europe that emerges from the experience of resistance as more united and self-assured, confidently asserting its place in the world. The persistence of negativity pushes a society into depression. Prolonged challenges such as political instability, economic crises, or social conflicts act like chronic stressors on a society. In the absence of positive turning points, a sense of endless stagnation develops, leading to hopelessness. Similar to individual burnout, a prolonged burdensome situation results in societal exhaustion. People lose faith in improvement, withdraw emotionally, and this leads to paralysis in public life.

Studies show that people in repressive states suffer disproportionately from mental illnesses such as anxiety disorders. Historically, such states have often developed surveillance and propaganda systems that, by fostering constant distrust, undermine the psychological well-being of the population. When political discourse focuses solely on threats and enemies, negative rhetoric dominates. This climate of fear and hostility forms the basis for political factions to face each other irreconcilably, eliminating the possibility of rational, constructive exchange.

This is particularly evident in highly polarized political systems, such as in the United States. Hostility between political camps has created a situation where cooperation seems almost impossible, and the population increasingly succumbs to hopelessness and resignation. The divide between factions leads to a growing perception of opponents as adversaries rather than fellow citizens. This distrust deepens social tensions and hinders constructive, factual discussions on political and social issues. Instead, supporters often resort to emotional and aggressive rhetoric, further fueling conflicts and normalizing extreme positions.

Europe, as a unique entity, must be cautious of this trend. The risk also exists in Europe that political factions may drift apart, reducing the ability to collaborate. With targeted preventive measures, a respectful discussion culture, and strengthened trust in democratic structures, Europe can counter societal resignation and division, developing a model of political and social resilience. The European Union must remain vigilant against the dangers of political polarization within and take proactive measures to cultivate a healthy, inclusive, and cooperative political culture. The ability to collaborate, the pursuit of consensus, and the awareness of shared values are critical to advancing the European project. By learning from the experiences of other regions, Europe can build a culture of dialogue and cooperation that endures even in challenging times. Media focusing on crises and conflicts also contribute to the dominance of negativity. When public debate is primarily centered on problems and challenges, it reinforces the notion that everything is bad and will remain so.

When political leadership emphasizes threats and crises, constructive initiatives quickly lose priority. The Covid-19 pandemic worldwide increased negativity in political communication, as governments focused on crisis management and positive future visions took a back seat. This often leads to a form of general crisis fatigue, emotionally draining the population and reducing their willingness to engage in political processes. In a collectively depressed society, people often retreat to private spaces and avoid public life. This isolation reduces interactions and relationships, which should ideally foster optimism and cohesion. A lack of cohesion and rising mistrust often result in social tensions and conflicts. Such fragmentations weaken society by undermining solidarity.

The dominance of negativity often makes it easier for authoritarian forces to gain power. When people feel worn out and directionless, authoritarian regimes appear to offer stability and security. Historically, dictatorships have often established themselves after crises and prolonged societal uncertainty by presenting authoritarian solutions to social problems. Examples include the rise to power of Franco in Spain or Mussolini in Italy. Post-totalitarian phases then give rise to long-term psychosocial problems within the population. Political psychology confirms that societies that have lived under repressive conditions for extended periods often suffer from a lack of social cohesion even after regime changes.

This was evident, for example, in post-communist Russia and other former Eastern Bloc countries, where the collective sadness and disillusionment accumulated over the years led to a passive and often apathetic attitude towards political processes. In repressive systems, people often learn to develop mistrust of others, including their neighbors and fellow citizens. This mistrust often persists even when the authoritarian regime falls. The lack of trust among members of a society makes it difficult to build stable communities and social cohesion. After a regime change, the population can be disappointed to find that the hoped-for changes in terms of freedom, justice and social conditions do not materialize immediately. This disappointment then leads to a kind of political apathy in which people lose faith in political institutions and the democratic process.

To avoid the destructive effects of a dominance of the negative, a society needs positive visions that unite and motivate the population. Societies that focus on innovation and positive goals are usually more resilient to crises and authoritarian endeavors. Positive developments not only create prosperity, but also social cohesion and trust. The post-war period in Germany shows how the focus on reconstruction and reparation revitalizes a society. The balance of positive and negative discourse leads a society to resilience, overcoming the challenges of the time with a certain stability.

Creating mechanisms for dealing with the past, such as truth commissions or memorial projects, also restores the public trust that forms the basis for cohesion. By actively involving citizens in the political process, for example through local initiatives and participatory decision-making, the feeling of powerlessness can be overcome in the long term. Community projects and initiatives can bring people from different walks of life together and gradually restore trust in the social fabric.

History shows that the encroachment of negativity, whether through a reign of terror, repression or polarizing discourse, not only brings short-term horror, but also wears down the collective psyche of a society in the long term. Chronic negativity destroys trust and creates sadness and resignation, which permanently weakens a society. It is important to strike a balance between positive and negative forces. Only through a mixture of realistic threat analysis and constructive visions of the future can a society remain stable and healthy.

## 37. INTERCONNECTIVITY OF TENSION AND RELAXATION

It has an impact on various aspects of inter-state relations, conflicts, and diplomacy. Throughout history, tensions have initially arisen from territorial disputes, then from economic competition, and today, from ideological differences. These tensions lead to conflicts that manifest in military confrontations. It is only through the desire for peace or stability that diplomatic efforts are engaged to defuse these tensions. Negotiations, mediation, and international agreements are implemented to mitigate mutual points of conflict and establish stable relations. Successful diplomacy can be seen as a form of peace in international politics, while failed negotiations further increase tensions.

The security dilemma describes the state of perception and evaluation of measures aimed at increasing security. It highlights the difficulty of finding a balance between security, meaning tension, and international stability, meaning peace. In regions of intense conflict, special measures are sometimes necessary to establish a state of peace and reduce tensions. Such missions encompass military security as well as social and economic programs to create a lasting climate of peace. The security dilemma easily arises in an anarchic international system where states must act within a conglomerate of self-help, since there is no overarching authority. They strive to increase their own security, which is perceived by others as a potential threat. Thus, forums for communication and dialogue are necessary to enable coexistence. In a globalized environment, individual entities are economically and politically interconnected in such a way that their interdependence can both reduce tensions and create them through competition for resources or influence. Understanding this relationship is fundamental to the formulation of foreign policy.

The security dilemma illustrates the complexity of international relations and the difficulty of finding a balance between national security and international stability. Unilateral measures to increase one's own security can be counterproductive. This underscores the importance of skillful diplomacy, trust-building, and international cooperation to maintain peace. Open communication channels are essential to clarify misunderstandings and respond to emerging concerns. Diplomatic negotiations can help resolve conflicts before they escalate.

The modern interconnectedness of collaborations refers to the increasing interconnection and cooperation among individuals, teams, and organizations. At a time when technologies such as the Internet, cloud computing, artificial intelligence, and social media are ubiquitous, the way people cooperate and communicate is profoundly altered. Through technical interconnectivity, individuals from different countries and time zones can work together, allowing for a more diverse perspective in projects and increasing creative potential. AI-based tools optimize work processes, automate repetitive tasks, and thereby enhance the efficiency of cooperation. Digitization has significantly accelerated the flow of information among foreign policy actors. This enables a more flexible and rapid response to global events such as natural disasters or international conflicts.

Modern collaborators in interconnectedness can work independently of time and location, providing them with greater freedom and flexibility. However, they must ensure that they communicate and collaborate in a secure manner that complies with data protection standards, while safeguarding sensitive information. The more actors involved in global foreign policy, the more difficult it becomes to find consensus and make decisions. Divergent interests and priorities can hinder cooperation and lead to deadlocks. Indeed, in global teams, misunderstandings and communication barriers can easily arise. The increase in connections also heightens the risk of cyberattacks and data theft.

It is therefore clear that intensive dialogue on strategic issues is best conducted at a personalized level to achieve valid and intelligent outcomes. This must take place at international conferences. These not only play a role in deepening understanding but also in establishing the trust relations crucial for cooperation on complex global issues. Such an approach promotes creativity and innovation when different countries confront their opinions and experiences. This thinking underscores the importance of individualized and direct dialogue, particularly in strategic and complex thematic areas. International conferences provide the platform where these bespoke discussions and decisions occur, allowing policymakers to exchange directly and immediately with experts. Only through personal interaction can the nuances and detailed requirements of strategic issues be truly grasped and effectively addressed. Conferences offer the atmospheric space in which global perspectives can be gathered and reasonably harmonized.

Those who operate solely with superficial arguments and apparent aspects will only yield illusory results. This assertion applies well to the dynamics of international politics, where the quality of arguments, the depth of analyses, and the honesty of intentions play a central role. If international political actors settle for superficial or manipulated arguments, such as through propaganda, one-sided narratives, or incomplete data, their decisions often lead to misleading outcomes— the "illusory results." These outcomes may suggest short-term successes that, in the long run, are unsustainable or may even have destructive consequences.

Thus, entities that base their environmental policies on cosmetic measures and apparent successes, like greenwashing, risk aggravating the real ecological challenges. The results may look good on paper but solve no sustainable problems. In peace negotiations where symbolic compromises are sought rather than genuine conflict resolution, unstable agreements form. These may be presented as successes but collapse quickly, as the underlying issues remain unresolved. Governments that present themselves as peace-makers or guardians of human rights using superficial arguments, while their actual actions prove contrary, tarnish their international standing. An example is the discord between foreign political rhetoric and genuine economic or military interests.

Military alliances like NATO demonstrate how collective security strategies can be modeled through interconnected impulses. Countries collaborate, sharing military resources, intelligence information, and thus coordinating their strategic decisions. Through free-trade agreements, investment partnerships, and global supply chains, individual entities become more efficient but also increasingly interdependent. Consequently, one of the additional roles of foreign policy actors is to avoid trade disputes and regulate global markets.

The culture of direct dialogue helps build trust, identify common interests, and find intelligent consensus. New approaches are discussed and redefined through project-focused coalitions. Personalized dialogue at the highest level of international conferences will continue to be the central element of international cooperation. Simultaneously, it is necessary to constantly adapt these formats to changing circumstances to address complex global challenges. Personal conversations among international actors often lead to solutions more quickly than formal negotiations, as they provide the opportunity to convey emotions and nuances that are lost in written documents. During crises, such as those that occur during geopolitical tensions or military conflicts, direct dialogue helps prevent escalation. Quick decisions are made that challenge trust and mutual understanding. Long-term relationships among heads of state increase the likelihood that they collaborate during difficult times, as personal ties often transcend political differences.

Conferences not only offer a platform for the exchange of ideas but also for expanding networks and alliances that are crucial for future negotiations and cooperation. By involving numerous states in decision-making processes, the legitimacy of decisions is strengthened, especially when some national interests initially contradict global challenges. Conferences act as catalysts for new ideas, bringing together not only experts but also key decision-makers from various fields. The increasing difficulties within the UN Security Council and other international bodies underscore the need to reform decision-making processes to respond more effectively and swiftly to global challenges. The growing skepticism toward multilateral institutions necessitates a critical reevaluation of their functions and a dialogue on possible reforms. The formation of project-based coalitions allows for targeted responses to specific challenges without relying on the approval of all stakeholders. In this context, the discussion around the strategic autonomy of the EU is particularly relevant. It aims to ensure that Europe can independently respond to global challenges. With all the security repercussions, particularly due to the conflict in Ukraine, it is crucial for the EU to consolidate and develop its security and defense policy.

## 38. DANGERS FOR INTERCONNECTED FOREIGN POLICY

From the perspective of philosophy and physics, one might ask: Is reality at all dependent on functionality, such as that of foreign policy or international relations? One could argue that reality exists as a potential for functionality, similar to a structure without movement or a system that remains in a sort of idle mode. According to Aristotle, something can exist without actively functioning or appearing. Thus, potential itself is already a form of reality, even without active action or utility. In quantum mechanics, one could understand reality as a cloud of probabilities that only manifests in a "functional" manner when it is observed or measured. In international politics, there are parallels to the concepts of potentiality and probabilities, which are reflected in the contours of states, alliances, and their conflicts. The dynamics are constantly marked by uncertainty; nonetheless, reality is shaped by the interactions of the actors and their perspectives.

The alarm points of interconnectivity are precisely the critical moments that illustrate how closely countries and systems are interconnected. When these connections encounter tensions or become unstable, the fragility of the international order is revealed, often exposing the limits of its functionality. At these junctures lies the challenge of managing crises and maintaining stability, even though reality is often more complex than the functional rules and institutions that attempt to order it. Alarm points arise when these connections reach a certain threshold and lead to conflicts or upheavals.

Water, energy, and other resources are often limited and concentrated in specific geographic regions. Countries reliant on these resources increasingly find themselves in conflict with those that possess or control them. The pursuit of technological dominance, such as in the field of semiconductors or artificial intelligence, is also an alarm point for global tensions, as demonstrated in the conflicts between the U.S. and China. International institutions should actually function to respond to global challenges. However, reality shows that in times of crises, national interests often take precedence, and the functionality of international cooperation is restricted. At these points, the fragility of international collaboration becomes evident. Sanctions, economic wars, and military conflicts put the system under pressure and jeopardize its ability to remain stable.

With the deceptive psychology of the famous Trojan horse and the intrusion via opinion manipulation, digital fake news, and attempts to bribe entire populations - similar to how Trumpism operated during the U.S. election campaign - the Russian dictatorship is crafting a compendium of threats and violent scenarios of unprecedented magnitude. Internally, it is aided by direct and indirect collaborators from both the left and right extremist ranks, who seek to dazzle the public with efficient modern technologies. The triumph of dictatorial forces would incur immeasurable collateral damage to global society. Does society not sense the avalanche rolling down, or will it know how to defend itself? Why does the collective memory of history completely fail? A logical insight from history should be that in circumstances of which we may yet be unaware, it could very well happen that the world inadvertently slides into times of global slavery. Intentional developments on one side easily shift to the other side and slip there. Let us take the double standards in international politics as a warning sign. What constitutes political progress in the Global South or the Arab world? Will they be able to extricate themselves from global dilemmas?

Should the world accept or even yield to the influence of dictatorial states or authoritarian leadership, it could have profound and far-reaching consequences for global order and the lived reality in many countries. Such a shift would undermine existing values and principles in numerous areas. If the world succumbs to authoritarian leadership, a significant decline in democratic principles, such as free elections, independent judiciary, and press freedom, is likely to ensue. Human rights could be systematically violated, as authoritarian governments often exhibit little tolerance for dissenting opinions and restrict freedom of expression. This could lead to a wave of oppression where dissenters and activists are pursued, imprisoned, or even eliminated.

The success of authoritarian states could result in a rise in the prestige of authoritarian forms of government globally, promoted as seemingly effective alternatives to democracy. States may begin to increasingly curtail fundamental rights and monitor societies to maximize control over their citizens. In such a scenario, even democracies might start adopting authoritarian practices to remain competitive internationally and maintain internal peace. Authoritarian states typically have an ambivalent relationship with international organizations, which are founded on principles such as human rights and peace. A world dominated by authoritarian states could lead to a disintegration of these institutions or significantly limit their influence. International law could be undermined, preventing countries from imposing sanctions for human rights violations or unlawful warfare.

If authoritarian practices go unchecked and technologies for surveillance and control, such as facial recognition, online tracking, and big data analysis, are expanded globally, these tools would enable governments to exert widespread control over the population and significantly restrict personal freedoms. States could surveil citizens, control movements, and stifle potential dissent at its inception, severely hampering free development and open exchange of ideas. A world yielding to authoritarian influences would likely be marked by a new global arms race and geopolitical tensions. Authoritarian states tend to assert power claims aggressively and resolve conflicts through threats or even violence. The risk of international conflicts, military interventions, and so-called proxy wars would disproportionately increase, threatening regional and global stability. In an authoritarian-driven world order, economic isolationism could increase, and free trade could be restricted. This would long-term hinder innovations and economic growth, leading to a global economic crisis. A world under dictatorial influence would heavily control education and science to enforce certain ideologies and suppress critical thinking. The result would be a generation of citizens with less access to independent information, rendering them less capable of making independent and critical decisions. An authoritarian world could also jeopardize climate protection, as cooperation and transparency in combating global warming might be suppressed or ignored. The global climate goals would become difficult to achieve, resulting in massive environmental damage and social upheaval. Authoritarian regimes often exhibit high levels of corruption and social inequality, as resources and political power are concentrated in the hands of a few. If authoritarian systems gain influence worldwide, it would mean a global entrenchment of social inequalities. Access to education, healthcare, and opportunities could be severely restricted in these systems, reducing social and economic mobility.

In this context, Europe faces a significant credibility problem if it continues to not speak and act with a unified voice. Consider only the absurdity of current German politics, which expresses disappointment with its German president of the European Commission for thinking in European rather than national terms. To maintain Europe's credibility, it is essential to foster a European identity that transcends national borders. Education and joint projects should contribute to creating a sense of belonging. The EU must make its decision-making processes more transparent and effective to gain the trust of citizens internally and credibility in its own capabilities externally. Only through a common approach can counterproductive national interests be pushed into the background, and a unified voice be achieved.

One can see how the interconnectivity of foreign policy is accompanied by artificial contradictions, massive geopolitical dynamics, and simultaneous technological advancements. Its effectiveness is constantly threatened by numerous dangers. The geopolitical rivalries among major nations have intensified in recent years and pose a serious risk to international cooperation. They have led to a decline in multilateral engagement and promoted nationalist and isolationist trends in various countries. In the South China Sea, China and other states compete for strategic resources and maritime rights. Meanwhile, the situation in Ukraine demonstrates how geopolitical ambitions can lead to aggressive actions that jeopardize stability in Europe and the world. These examples illustrate that geopolitical rivalries foster a mindset that prioritizes national interests over global challenges. The consequences are wars, trade conflicts, and an increasing inability to find joint solutions for global problems due to the decline of international agreements. The rise of populist and nationalist movements in many countries has reduced the willingness for international cooperation. If states are not transparent in their actions or do not adhere to international agreements, it becomes difficult to follow an interconnected foreign policy. Trust is a fundamental prerequisite for cooperation, and its absence leads to the erosion of multilateral institutions.

The metaphors "wild west of cowboy mentality" and "blind, furious eastern imperialism" represent two extremes that are considered dangers to a values-based, free world. The "wild west" symbolizes a form of isolationist politics, where national self-interests are prioritized over international cooperation, a mindset often associated with ruthless, profit-oriented actions and a lack of concern for global consequences. Conversely, "eastern imperialism" refers to expansive power-seeking and the readiness to pursue geopolitical goals without regard for the sovereignty and human rights of other states. Both extremes can threaten the values and stability of Europe, as they stand in opposition to principles such as peaceful cooperation, respect for sovereignty, and the promotion of universal human rights.

The notion that U.S. presidential cowboyism, a kind of political wild-west-show, is merely a transient spectacle is hopeful. Thankfully, not everyone is ready to heed the call of the lonely cowboy. Thus, in the center of the world, there is hope for reason, for moderation, and less for the rattling of spurs. On the other hand, the eastern ungovernability seeks to seize power through violent outbursts. Preventing this will come at a corresponding cost so that the beams of the world system do not collapse. For Europe, this means not resting on its laurels but rather taking responsibility and actively countering these developments. The challenge lies in finding a balance between economic and military independence and global responsibility.

The metaphors of the "Wild West cowboy mentality" and "reckless Eastern imperialism" represent two extremes that are perceived as threats to a values-based, free world. The "Wild West" symbolizes a form of isolationist politics where national self-interest takes precedence over international collaboration—a mentality often associated with ruthless, profit-driven actions and a disregard for global consequences. Conversely, "Eastern imperialism" highlights an expansionist power agenda and a willingness to pursue geopolitical goals at the expense of the sovereignty and human rights of other nations. Both extremes threaten Europe's values and stability by opposing principles like peaceful cooperation, respect for sovereignty, and the promotion of universal human rights.

The hope that the U.S. presidential "cowboyism" is merely a transient spectacle offers a glimmer of optimism. Thankfully, not everyone is willing to follow the lone cowboy's call. Hence, the global center hopes for reason, restraint, and less spur-rattling. On the other hand, Eastern recklessness seeks to seize power through violent outbursts. Countering this will require a price to be paid to prevent the collapse of the world order's framework. For Europe, this means not resting in complacency but taking responsibility and actively countering these developments. The challenge lies in balancing economic and military autonomy with global responsibility.

A confident, unified European foreign policy is crucial in today's world to assert Europe's values and interests against autocratic tendencies and geopolitical rivals. This policy must combine determination and diplomacy while maintaining the capacity for swift and coherent response - a challenging endeavor for a union of 27 nations with diverse priorities and traditions. Particularly problematic are separatist dissenters who, driven by national or regional interests, undermine collective European action. Their agendas, often prioritizing national identity and sovereignty over European unity, complicate the urgently needed solidarity. These forces tend to act against common European decisions at critical moments, sometimes placing parochial interests above the collective good. Europe must remain vigilant and counter these separatist trends by fostering internal cohesion and clearly communicating the benefits and protections offered by a united Europe. Only a strengthened, unified Europe can project the authority and stability necessary to emerge as a significant and credible actor on the global stage.

Europe faces substantial challenges in its defensive propaganda efforts, as disinformation campaigns and targeted propaganda increasingly threaten stability and trust in democratic institutions. Countries like Russia and China, along with domestic actors, exploit modern media to sow doubts, undermine trust in the EU, and exacerbate national divisions. These actors often leverage fears and social tensions to stoke conflict and impede the Union's unified stance.

To build an effective defense against propaganda, Europe requires widespread media literacy within its population. In parallel, European institutions must prioritize digital literacy and proactively showcase their achievements, values, and policies. Transparent communication strategies and better coordination among EU countries are essential to responding quickly and cohesively to misinformation. A European platform that both educates and provides real-time information on current issues could play a central role. Moreover, protecting digital infrastructures and social media is critical. EU-wide standards and closer cooperation with major technology firms could help detect and counter disinformation campaigns early. Collaboration with international partners facing similar challenges is equally vital to building an effective and resilient propaganda defense.

While the world in the 20th century feared Nazi Germany, it now feels threatened by three powers ruled by Putin, Xi, and Trump. But fleeing in fear is not the correct response. Retreat would not only endanger freedoms but also weaken global achievements built over decades. These threats demand courage, steadfast principles, and a resolute defense of democracy and international law. The global community must work together in a changing world to preserve and actively protect values like freedom, the rule of law, and human rights. History has often shown that appeasement and hesitation cause more harm than firm, united stances. Now, as the world faces multiple influential powers challenging democratic ideals, it is more important than ever for the world's democracies to unite rather than succumb to resignation. The courage to act decisively may be the strongest response to today's uncertainties.

The prospect of Xi Jinping, Vladimir Putin, and Donald Trump dividing global dominance remains a grim thought experiment. Such an arrangement could radically reshape the global political and social landscape. The world would fragment into spheres of influence, with each region governed according to the interests of its respective ruler. Xi Jinping seeks to expand control over Asia, the Pacific, and Africa through strategic investments. Russia's military prowess and geopolitical ambitions underscore Putin's influence over Europe, Central Asia, and the Middle East. Developments in the U.S., especially the potential erosion of the rule of law and the rise of individuals with questionable legal standing to high offices, pose a crisis not only for the U.S. but also for global order and the trust of international partners. In such a scenario, Europe and other democratic actors' positioning will be critical to maintaining stability and principles without succumbing to political naivety. If the U.S. falters as a moral leader and defender of democracy, its international credibility will erode. Europe must evaluate whether an unreserved transatlantic alliance remains viable in this context. A weakened or unpredictable U.S. could embolden geopolitical adversaries like Russia and China. Europe must prepare for this while avoiding a dangerous power vacuum.

The possible devaluation of the rule of law in the U.S. puts Europe in a precarious position, balancing loyalty and principles. The key lies in an independent, strategic stance that enables pragmatic cooperation with the U.S. without compromising democratic values. Europe can assert its role as a global stabilizer, forging new partnerships to compensate for a potential intensification of U.S. partnership losses. How to escape the inferno of dictatorial powers? Exiting such a predicament requires decisive actions from individuals, communities, and international actors. Resilience, education, international support, and faith in the power of freedom and justice are foundational to overcoming such systems. Dictatorships rely on control, propaganda, and suppression. The first step toward liberation is recognizing these mechanisms and presenting alternatives. The next step is to use technology to expose disinformation and ensure access to trustworthy information.

Civil society is the backbone of any movement against authoritarian regimes. Democratic movements and institutions need financial and technical support to drive change. Economic dependency and social dissatisfaction within dictatorships are vulnerabilities that can be exploited. Breaking free from authoritarian rule is a collective process requiring unity, patience, and international support. Historical examples like post-apartheid South Africa or the fall of the Berlin Wall show that change is possible when people unite in the pursuit of freedom and justice. As Nelson Mandela said, "It always seems impossible until it's done."

This complex reflection has far-reaching implications for international relations, the global order, and individual freedom. Even within a division of power, tensions among the actors could arise. Conversely, the global loss of freedom and a new type of cold war could drive worldwide movements for democracy and liberty. This would be a positive counterforce. Europe, still the world's second-largest economy and largest exporter of goods and services, plays a vital role. It contributes significantly to global trade and innovation in areas like renewable energy, engineering, and pharmaceuticals. The European Green Deal exemplifies how the EU seeks to align economic growth with environmental goals. With its scientific and economic assets, Europe could forge a new international alliance to occupy a strong global position. Europe's history, scientific expertise, and economic interconnectedness provide a solid foundation for this. Renowned institutions like CERN and the European Space Agency serve as platforms for international collaboration. Joint technology development in renewable energy, artificial intelligence, and biotechnology could foster robust partnerships with countries in Africa, Asia, and South America.

This alliance should attract global talent and integrate it into scientific networks. Strategic trade alliances with emerging markets in Africa and Southeast Asia could diversify trade routes. By leveraging its scientific expertise and economic significance, Europe can create an influential international coalition that is both forward-looking and powerful. If Europe strategically deploys its scientific and trade resources, it could shape global power dynamics while fostering a multipolar world order.

The challenge is whether a geographically dispersed alliance can succeed. The path forward requires enhanced collaboration, political engagement, and economic reforms on an international scale. Only through concerted efforts can the euro serve as the foundation for broader alliances and new market cooperation. This could counter the unpredictability of inward-looking U.S. policies and the authoritarian ambitions of Russia and China with a fourth force in a multipolar world order. In an era where geopolitical tensions and protectionism strain global markets, a new strategic alliance, leveraging trade power and the euro, could provide stability and promote novel cooperation models. Integrating economic powers like the EU, Canada, Japan, South Korea, and Australia, complemented by emerging markets from Asia, Africa, and South America, could create a trade and innovation platform capable of challenging dollar- and yuan-dominated systems.

Such an alliance would focus on joint investments in key areas like green energy, artificial intelligence, digital infrastructure, and health research. These investments strengthen technological sovereignty and sustainable development. The thematic emphasis lies in fostering a global free trade system based on fair and sustainable principles, as well as joint projects in renewable energy and decentralized innovation hubs for science and technology. A coordinated security strategy that builds on partnerships while addressing regional security concerns would promote stability and strategic balance.

The geopolitical complexities can be untangled if the Global South and democratic nations of the free world are willing to think beyond national interests and embrace new paths of cooperation. Political progress demands innovative approaches and a rethinking of existing structures. The key lies in strengthening collaboration, dialogue, and the pursuit of common solutions.

In this dynamic world, the interconnectedness of intelligence and research hubs drives progress and diversification. As Europe positions the euro as a leading currency and integrates it with emerging digital technologies, it has the opportunity to redefine the global financial system and encourage equitable international relationships. This would support sustainable market cooperation while maintaining a balance between risk and reward, ensuring transformative power is applied justly and effectively.

For Europe, much will depend on how partnerships with the Global South develop. The term "Global South" describes a socioeconomic and political category. It refers to countries and regions historically shaped by colonialism, economic dependencies, and unequal power structures. This includes many states in Africa, Latin America, Asia, and Oceania, which are often equated with developing or emerging countries. However, the distinction is fluid and not always clear-cut. The Global South encompasses many countries that were under colonial rule. This past has created economic and political structures that continue to perpetuate inequalities even after formal independence. Economic relations with the Global North have often been characterized by raw material exports and dependence on global markets.

There are countries in the Global South marked by high poverty rates, low incomes, and a weak industrial base. At the same time, there is a growing middle class and dynamic economic centers in some regions, such as India, Brazil, or South Africa. The Global South is experiencing significant population growth, which brings both opportunities and challenges such as unemployment and the need for infrastructure. These countries are often more affected by the consequences of climate change, even though they have historically contributed only minimally to global emissions.

Europe faces the challenge of making its relationships with the Global South more equitable and sustainable. This requires a comprehensive understanding of global power dynamics and a departure from paternalistic or purely interest-driven approaches. Europe should reduce subsidies that disadvantage products from the Global South. Investments in sustainable supply chains can help improve labor and environmental standards. Access to innovative technologies, particularly in agriculture or the energy sector, could strengthen the economic independence of many countries.

Development cooperation should not rely on pre-made models but should respect local needs and priorities. Transparent and well-monitored financial aid can strengthen infrastructure, education, and healthcare systems. Europe should provide financial and technological resources to assist the Global South in adapting to climate change and transitioning to renewable energy. Ambitious climate policy in Europe is essential to minimize the impacts of climate change on the South.

By supporting economic development and stability, the root causes of migration can be mitigated. Legal and regulated migration pathways can benefit both the Global South and Europe. What cooperations and strategic alliances arise from this? The realignment of European policy towards the Global South opens up numerous possibilities for collaborations and strategic alliances. These partnerships can be shaped in areas such as trade, climate policy, security, and development. The focus is on equal collaboration that respects the interests and priorities of both sides. Trade agreements with countries in the Global South, such as the Economic Partnership

Agreements (EPAs) between the EU and African states, could be revised to eliminate asymmetric advantages. Europe can support regional groupings like the African Continental Free Trade Area (AfCFTA) to strengthen trade within the Global South and thereby create stronger regional markets in the long term. The EU can promote infrastructure projects such as roads, power grids, or digital networks in collaboration with the African Union (AU). Joint initiatives in renewable energy can create sustainable jobs and reduce dependence on fossil fuels. Strategies to promote local industries in the Global South can help countries process their raw materials locally and benefit from higher added value. Collaborations with countries like India, Brazil, or Indonesia can strengthen Europe's economic resilience and promote South-South trade.

Europe could increase its contribution to existing funds such as the Green Climate Fund (GCF) and additionally establish its own regional funds to promote adaptation to climate change. Collaborations to provide technologies like wind and solar installations or climate-friendly agriculture create win-win situations. Countries with rainforest areas such as Brazil, Indonesia, or the Democratic Republic of Congo could work together with the EU to develop protection strategies for these ecosystems. European states could create incentives through transparent carbon markets to finance carbon sequestration projects in the Global South. Research initiatives in areas such as medicine, agricultural science, or sustainable energy can strengthen technology transfer. Joint projects for early warning and combating pandemics can mitigate global health crises.

What can be done to stabilize fragile states? European and southern states can cooperate intensively in combating human trafficking, drug trade, and terrorism. Any new strategic alliances can promote legal migration, addressing both labor shortages in Europe and development goals in the South. Return programs for migrants can be linked with development projects in their countries of origin to create local prospects. In issues such as climate policy, digitalization, or financial market regulation, Europe and the Global South could team up to balance the influence of individual great powers. Through closer cooperation with non-aligned or Southern-oriented states, Europe could form new strategic alliances that promote global peace. Partnerships with oil and gas-producing countries in the Global South could facilitate the transition to renewable energy and reduce dependencies.

European teamwork would pool resources to achieve common development goals with partner countries. They could increasingly focus on projects in the Global South. Cooperation with the African Union could be intensified through investments in education, digitalization, and healthcare systems. A European alternative to China's "Belt and Road" initiative could promote infrastructure projects in the Global South that are more aligned with sustainability and local needs.

One benefit of these new alliances is the strengthening of the influence of all participants in a multipolar world. New capacities and structures emerge by supporting projects that are ecologically and socially compatible. This brings about a stronger inclusion in global decision-making processes. The inner core of currently strong countries within the alliance could increasingly provide technologies and infrastructure to bridge the digital divide, but always under the premise of avoiding any debt traps. This requires clear communication of goals and methods to address any skepticism. Conflicts of interest can be avoided by declaring clear priorities in joint strategies. The behavior of the alliance necessarily builds on coherent action. Through a values-based policy that includes the Global South as an equal partner, global challenges could be addressed more effectively. Such an alliance would not only have the chance to strengthen its own position in a multipolar world but also to make a significant contribution to global sustainability, security, and justice.

## 39. CONCLUSIONS FROM INTERCONNECTIVITY

Strategies like "nudging" - an immediate nudge towards something new - could encourage governments worldwide to favor resource-efficient and fair practices. The philosophy of utilitarianism might inspire companies to take actions that create the greatest benefit for the majority of people. Competing policies or companies should operate more like networks, sharing knowledge, resources, and responsibilities. Philosophical approaches to ethics and justice argue that knowledge must be regarded as a global common good. This could support the introduction of "Open Science" initiatives on a global level. Research on social identity shows that people are more engaged when they feel part of a community. Campaigns should aim to promote a sense of global togetherness. Governments could deliberately foster stories and narratives that create a feeling of global belonging.

Decaying thought networks in global politics refer to outdated or ineffective mindsets and structures that have become entrenched in the fabric of international relations and political strategies. These concepts hinder progress and are the reason why significant challenges are not adequately addressed. Traditional power dynamics, which often no longer correspond to current global realities, biases and misunderstandings between different cultures that complicate dialogue and collaboration, and military approaches that do not address today's challenges or global health crises, call for overcoming through innovative approaches and a willingness to question existing paradigms.

Is it all negative? Not necessarily. There are plenty of initiatives advocating for a holistic view of global challenges and encouraging interdisciplinary solutions. Cluster formations and large regional structures contribute to creating a more stable international framework. Promising political formats bring fresh perspectives and innovative solutions into politics. Advances in technology and communication promote collaboration and open new avenues for the exchange of ideas.

One frequently criticized aspect is the tendency towards short-term thinking in politics. Electoral tactical considerations and the pressure to deliver quick results hinder long-term important decisions. One way to renew the decaying thought networks would be to rely on evidence-based decision-making. This means making political decisions based on scientific findings and empirical data. Incorporating reflective and weighing elements into the political process could lead to improved decision quality. Structured exchanges of ideas and rational arguments allow for more thorough consideration of complex issues. Greater transparency in political decision-making processes and serious accountability of decision-makers would enhance the quality of decisions.

Implementing such improvements is often hindered by conflicts of interest and established power structures. Various motivated actors in global politics pursue different goals, which impedes the development of coherent strategies. Renewing the thought networks in global politics requires a multidimensional approach. It is about combining decision-making with deliberative processes while considering the complexity of global challenges. Interconnectivity emphasizes that by taking into account the interplay of different areas, the best solutions can be found.

It would be pivotal to highlight the mutual understanding between politics and research from a holistic perspective. Educational institutions, research organizations, and political decision-makers need to work beyond their traditional boundaries. Interdisciplinary teams bring together diverse perspectives, including socio-political and natural sciences as well as philosophical and cultural factors.

Education needs new standards overall. With the help of technological possibilities, systemic thinking can take into account the interconnections and interdependencies of various elements. They stimulate cognitive feedback loops and cascading effects, thereby generating an understanding of emerging properties arising from the interplay of parts. Isolated, one-dimensional solutions should be disregarded. Educational systems must be designed not only to impart knowledge but also to promote critical thinking, problem-solving skills, and the ability to collaborate. Redesigning education in the field of international relations requires a holistic approach that integrates theory, practice, and ethical considerations. By considering these points, a future generation of professionals and leaders can emerge, equipped to tackle the challenges of an increasingly complex and interconnected world.

The interconnective thought approach is particularly helpful when key factors and leverage points within the system are precisely identified, but also when unintended consequences of incorrect interventions are anticipated. Overall, humanity could be better prepared for the challenges of the future. A society oriented towards systemic thinking will be better able to respond to changes and crises. Resilient communities can adapt and recover more quickly because they understand the dynamics within their systems.

Interconnectivity encompasses a wide range of factors that go far beyond purely technical aspects. It connects socio-political, natural scientific, philosophical, and cultural dimensions into a complex whole. The call for a holistic worldview that integrates various aspects of reality ultimately hinges on the individual's ability to find a connection to transcendence, as demanded by the great philosophers of antiquity. Transcendence is understood as a kind of broader reality that goes beyond the physical world and undoubtedly includes metaphysical dimensions. This demand ultimately leads to the question of the individual's capacity to connect with what lies beyond immediate experience.

This idea is based on the premise that humans can establish a connection to a deeper level of reality to develop a more comprehensive, holistic perspective. The statement implies the possibility of achieving a holistic worldview, not just from material capabilities, but also from an intuitive openness. This suggests that a deeper, holistic insight can only be achieved when one is able to connect with what goes beyond the purely material or empirical. It would also be an invitation to consider the individual in terms of mind and feelings in their entirety. The decoupling of interconnectivity, whether among people, cultures, or between humans and nature, carries the risk of losing our footing. The foundation of self-understanding is lost when we remain isolated in our own thought circles and avoid engaging with other perspectives and realities.

Interconnectivity is the foundation for thinking and understanding our world, as our consciousness, identity, and knowledge are inextricably linked to the interplay of political, cultural, economic, and above all, philosophical networks. When these connections are weakened, we risk retreating into a one-dimensional way of thinking that not only overlooks the complexity of reality but also brings about a form of self-alienation. People lose their connection to reality and enter a false world. An inflated self-image leads to arrogance and a lack of empathy. Fundamental human values and ethical principles fall out of focus. People increasingly feel alienated from the world and from each other. The loss of connections and grounding leads to a sense of meaninglessness. A lack of reference to reality increases the risk of misjudgments and poor decisions.

The grounding of humanity means retaining an understanding of our position within the fabric of life, a kind of anchoring in the natural and the supernatural, which is strengthened through interconnectivity. Without this anchoring, we could find ourselves in a crisis of thought that leaves us disoriented and susceptible to extreme positions and simplifications. Superficial, isolated perspectives do not do justice to the complexity of reality. We should always be on our way to what is determinative. The development of a multifaceted integrated perspective depends on our willingness to engage in exchanges with others and thus continually expand and question our own thinking. What is "determinative", could be understood as the fundamental, essential or even the true nature of our being. It is a kind of fundamental truth or a meaningful goal that provides orientation. This path requires vigilance, reflection, and the willingness to leave entrenched paths to align thinking and action with what is determinative. Thus, the path itself becomes a symbol of a life open to transformation and devoted to a deep anchoring in the essential.

The pace of interconnective shifts will be decisive for both upheavals and desired stabilizations. It will constantly fluctuate in the tension between the best-case and worst-case scenarios. What is dangerous about interconnectivity, and what are its opportunities? Interconnectivity is a double-edged sword: on the one hand, it offers opportunities for rapid progress, global cooperation, and collective resilience. On the other hand, it can trigger dynamics that give rise to unexpected risks and instabilities. The growing connectivity and interdependence between systems, actors, and regions harbor both great potential and serious dangers, especially because the speed and reach of interconnective changes are often difficult to control and foresee.

International challenges are complex and require a networked way of thinking, as promoted by systemic approaches in management. Leaders should be trained to recognize and manage interactions between politics, economy, and science. The principles of agile management, such as flexibility, iterative planning, and quick feedback, can be applied to international institutions to respond swiftly to dynamic problems. Companies should be encouraged through tax incentives and standards to implement measures that generate the greatest benefit for society: businesses should disclose how their actions positively impact society. Utilitarianism demands that the focus is not only on shareholder value but also on stakeholder value, which encompasses society, the environment, and future generations. Companies could orient themselves towards principles such as the common good economy, which measures sustainability and social benefit. Policies could increasingly introduce cooperative mechanisms such as community funds, where countries pool their resources for global crises.

Interconnectivity enables real-time global exchange of knowledge, technologies, and best practices. This can accelerate the development of new technologies, make medical insights available worldwide, and promote joint solutions to crises such as climate change. This transparency and rapid exchange contribute to finding collective responses to global challenges and fostering progress. It enhances the ability to tackle complex, multidimensional problems such as pandemics, migration, and environmental destruction. Ideally, networking promotes collective resilience by making knowledge, resources, and support available in the shortest possible time. Especially in crisis situations, such as natural disasters, the interplay of global actors can provide quicker assistance and solutions.

However, the high speed and depth of interconnectivity also mean that a crisis in one area can quickly jump to other systems, often in unpredictable magnitude. This applies, for example, to financial markets, where a crisis can ripple worldwide within hours, or to pandemic diseases that spread faster through interconnected travel routes. Supply chains are becoming longer and more complex, so that a single bottleneck or disruption can jeopardize the entire system. This dependence increases vulnerability to external shocks and fluctuations, whether from political instability, natural disasters, or economic downturns.

The more complex the interconnective systems are, the more difficult they are to oversee and manage. Many global networks operate through a multitude of decentralized actors who act independently, making the governance and predictability of such systems challenging. This creates uncertainty, as even small misjudgments can have significant consequences when they spread uncontrollably in global interconnectedness. Ideally, interconnectivity enables a forward-looking, united, and cooperative global community that promotes collective resilience and prosperity through knowledge and exchange. Whether the positive or negative effects of interconnectivity prevail depends heavily on how networks and systems are designed. The ability to cope with crises, adapt, and ensure fairness is crucial for maintaining the balance between progress and stability. Continuous weighing and adjusting are therefore essential to harness the opportunities of interconnectivity while minimizing risks.

A paradigm shift in thinking and action is required to better understand and manage these systems. We must accept that complete control is an illusion. Instead, it is about shaping and influencing systems to be robust and adaptable. What governance leaders must learn in their rethinking are emergence and dynamics. The former means managing the individual parts correctly, from which new properties arise at the system level. The latter symbolizes the fact that complex systems can constantly change, leading to high variability in system behavior. Including the many perspectives, properly understood, will help to manage situations better. It falls under the umbrella of adaptive management of collective intelligence, which transcends itself if it is to reflect quality and effectiveness. The key lies in finding the right balance between diversity and capability to act, as well as implementing suitable methods and structures. If this succeeds, international politics can indeed rise above itself and better tackle complex challenges.

What's going on when admirers of dictators suddenly turn up everywhere, vie for the highest offices and mix everything up? It is strange enough. Perplexity arises in the world of democracies in the face of the protagonists and wheel robbers of audacious stupidity. It is spreading rapidly in the sea of the public sphere and everyone is amazed to find it there. What can change offer? When it is so difficult to find majorities, you have to be particularly clever in planning, structuring and communicating. Careless underestimation and a lack of knowledge are poison in interconnectivity. What does political knowledge mean in this context? The stakes are not low. At stake is the very existence of civilizations.

The increasing presence of admirers of authoritarian systems and political actors willing to challenge fundamental democratic principles is indeed alarming. Their ability to attract attention and create chaos poses significant challenges to democracies. These developments cannot simply be dismissed as temporary aberrations. Rather, they raise fundamental questions about how democratic societies can show resilience and stay the course in the midst of turbulence. The appeal of autocratic ideas and charismatic but divisive figures often feeds on insecurity, frustration and the desire for simple solutions to complex problems. These tendencies are reinforced by the acceleration of digital communication, which fuels polarization and disinformation. In a sea of headlines and opinions, the audacity of stupidity often seems easier and more accessible than the complexity of reason.

The inclusion of multiple perspectives, properly understood, will help to manage situations better. It falls under the catchphrase of adaptive management of collective intelligence that goes beyond itself to reflect quality and effectiveness. The key is to find the right balance between diversity and the ability to act and to implement suitable methods and structures. If this succeeds, international politics can truly rise above itself and better manage complex challenges. Creating scope for positive action is a matter for political intelligence. Political insight means going beyond mere reaction and understanding the structures that shape our societies. A sound knowledge of history, political processes and the mechanisms of power is essential to resist authoritarian temptations. Education that promotes critical thinking is a key tool to counter the spread of misinformation.

We have now seen several times how things could sometimes be done differently. Next, the power of decision is needed in the collective, in society and above all in the personal. Their summation brings the breakthrough. However, if the weighting is not right, the balance no longer works. The scales fall. Every decision, like every conflict, has its starting point and strives towards a goal from the outset and, if it is misdirected, also seeks an exit from the mess. The question of who or what is the current situation is also the question of the right time, which must not be omitted, and we will participate in determining whether reason, freedom or the counterpart who wants to avoid this will gain the upper hand in the current spectrum of history. Will it be acceptable or scary or even cruel?

Perplexity and amazement in the face of the current chaos are understandable, but must not lead to resignation. Rather, democratic societies must find the courage to defend their values with conviction and reinvent themselves. This requires not only resistance to destructive forces, but also the creation of new approaches that are inclusive, transparent and sustainable. The future of democracy depends on our ability to move from helplessness to an active design mode.

## ABOUT THE AUTHOR

J-G Matuszek

Universities Innsbruck, Perugia, Salzburg.
Language sciences. Graduate interpreter, Master's degree.
Political sciences, Empirical system sciences, International relations,
Communication sciences, Philosophy, Doctorate.
Postgraduate studies at various institutes: Marketing, Advertising-PR-
CI, Management-Controlling, Innovation and Development
Management. Licensed business-consultant.

Career: High-school teacher, translator and interpreter, journalism.
Manager at multinational corporations.
Management contracting in medium-sized companies.
Consulting and coaching in marketing, international management,
and HR. Board member and director in several companies in
Germany, Switzerland. Management in the field of certification of
companies and organizations. Board member of the Foundation
"Globility-Circle", Switzerland.

Guest lecturer at various universities and business schools. Author.
Parallel-career as athlete, Austrian Taekwondo Federation President,
High-tech collaborations for performance diagnostics/optimization
in business and sports.

## BOOKS OF THE AUTHOR

| | |
|---|---|
| NEW VALUE ECONOMY - Manager quo vadis? | ISBN 9783981263206 |
| MANAGEMENT DER NACHHALTIGKEIT | ISBN 9783658022891 |
| SPORT FÜR MANAGER | ISBN 9783658036379 |
| MANAGEMENT DER POLITIK - EUROPA | ISBN 9783990108529 |
| EUROPÄISCH DENKEN | ISBN 9783738625592 |
| EUROPÄISCH HANDELN | ISBN 9783750414501 |
| MANAGEMENT VERSUS SPIRITUALITÄT? | ISBN 9783854314501 |
| RUF NACH DEM SINN | ISBN 9783748144199 |
| MUT ZUM SINN | ISBN 9783750418943 |
| KICKOFF ZUM SINN | ISBN 9783752690200 |
| MANAGEMENT SET-UP | ISBN 9783751941884 |
| DER MANAGER *Roman* | ISBN 9783752648911 |
| REFLEXIONEN  Lyrik | ISBN 9783752603866 |
| DIE TAEKWONDO MATRIX | ISBN 9783754352571 |
| **THE TAEKWONDO MATRIX** | **ISBN 9783754395394** |
| **TAEKWONDO MATRIX - SPORT EFFIZIENZ** | **ISBN**9783758307423 |
| EVALUIEREN | ISBN 9783756228805 |
| PSYCHE DER WELTGESCHICHTE | ISBN 9783757810108 |
| POLITIK @ GLOBALE WELT . INTL | ISBN 9783758307942 |
| **POLITICS @ GLOBAL – WORLD . INTL** | **ISBN 9783759706041** |
| **THE EUROPE CODE** | ISBN 9783759787170 |
| DER EUROPA CODE | ISBN 9783759708182 |

© 2024 J-G Matuszek
Publisher: BoD · Books on Demand GmbH, In de Tarpen 42,
22848 Norderstedt
Print: Libri Plureos GmbH, Friedensallee 273,
22763 Hamburg
ISBN: 978-3-7597-9348-5